Build a Virtual Network and Practice

Linux Network Services Administration

Build a Virtual Network and Practice

Linux Network Services Administration

Tashi Wangchuk

Linux Network Services Administration
Build a Virtual Network and Practice

All rights reserved ©2018
No part of this publication may be reproduced, stored in a retrieval system or transmitted in any form or by any means without the prior permission in writing from the author or publisher.

Limits of Liability
The publisher and the author make no representation or warranties with respect to the accuracy or the completeness of the contents of this book and specifically disclaim any implied warranties of merchantability or fitness for any purpose. The accuracy and completeness of the information provided or stated herein are not guaranteed or warranted to produce any particular results. Neither the publisher nor the author shall be liable for any loss or damages in any form.

Disclaimer
While every effort has been made to trace the copyright and trademark owners to seek permissions; omissions would be rectified in the future editions if brought to the notice. The contents of this book have been checked for the accuracy and completeness of the information; however, the publisher and the author shall not be held responsible for any errors or damages arising from the use of this book.

Trademarks
All the brand names and product names used in this book are the trademarks, registered trademarks, or trade names of their respective holders. The publisher and author are not associated in any way with the products and vendors mentioned in the book.

❧ ❧ ❧
Dedicated to my students
and
my family
❧ ❧ ❧

Acknowledgement

Firstly I would like to sincerely thank all my past and present students of both Computer Hardware and Networking as well as Computer System and Network of Jigme Namgyel Engineering College (Royal University of Bhutan). It was with you all that I have learned so much and I am writing now.

I don't want to forget my colleagues for being one of the encouraging factors to go on with the idea of coming up with this book and of course my small family for bearing with my share of problems and hassles too.

My immense gratitude goes out to Kezang Wangmo for being very supportive in my endeavor of writing and also for designing this Book's cover in a very special way, the way I liked and wished for.

Finally to all the students who have bought a copy of this book and I look forward to getting valuable feedback and suggestions for improving the future editions.

Contents

Linux Network Services Administration

Build a Virtual Network and Practice

Part A 1

Install and Configure GNS3. 3
Emulation and Simulation 4
Configuring GNS3 14
Adding IOS Image for the Router 18
Adding IOS for the EtherSwitch Router. 28
Further Reading. 35

Install and Configure VirtualBox. 37
Download and Install VirtualBox. 38
Virtual Machine Settings 46
   General Settings 46
   System Settings. 48
   Display Settings 49
   Storage Settings 49
   Network Settings 50
Installing Operating System on the VM 50
Further Reading. 56

Creating Adaptors and Cloning VMs. 59
Host-Only Networking 60
Creating VirtualBox Host-Only Ethernet Adaptors 61
Removing VirtualBox Host-Only Ethernet Adaptors 65
Virtual Machine (VM) States 67
Saving and Discarding VM's State 68
Cloning VMs. 69
Further Reading. 74

Exporting and Importing Appliances 75
Exporting as Virtual Machine as Appliance 76
Importing Virtual Machines as Appliance. 81
Removing Virtual Machines. 85
Further Reading. 87

Integrating VMs with GNS3 89
Adding VMs. 90
Browsing End Devices 95

Contents

Further Reading 95

Creating a GNS3 Network Topology 97
Creating and Saving Projects 98
Configuring the Windows 7 (End device) 103
Creating Links Between the Devices 104
Status of the Devices and Nodes 106
Verifying the Network Adaptors 107
Starting the Devices 109
Further Reading 112

Configure and Test Network 113
Network Scenario 114
Accessing and Configuring Router 115
    Configuring Router's Interface 0/0 117
    Configuring Router's Interface 0/1 118
    Configuring DHCP Service 118
    Configuring NAT 118
Testing the Network 119
Further Reading 119

Part B 121

Network Interface Configuration 123
Static vs Dynamic IP Addresses 124
Methods of Configuring IP Addresses 124
    Using the Network Interface File 125
    Network Setting via GUI 128
    The NetworkManager Text User Interface 130
Further Reading 134

Introduction to Firewall 137
Your Default Firewall 138
Disabling iptables 138
Enabling Firewalld 139
Firewalld Zone Management 139
    Listing Zones 140
    Zones 140
    Description 140
    Default Zone 141
    Active Zones 141
    Setting a Default Zone 141
    Changing the Interface's Zone 141
    Viewing the Zone's Configuration 142
    Interface's Associated Zones 144

Contents

    Creating New Zones. 144
    Adding an Interface to a Zone 144
    Listing the Assigned Interfaces 145
    Removing Interface from the Zone. 145
Service Management 145
    Getting the Services 145
    Adding the Service 146
    Surviving the Next Reload or Reboot 147
    Removing the Services 148
    Adding and Removing Multiple Services at Once 148
Port Management. 148
    Opening Ports for the Zones. 149
    Denying Ports for the Zones. 149
    Listing the Opened Ports 149
    Masquerading. 150
    Port Forwarding 150
Rich Rules 151
    Rich Rules Command 151
    Adding a Rich Rule 152
    NAT using Rich Rule 153
    Port Forwarding using Rich Rule 153
    Listing Rich Rules 153
    Removing Rich Rules 153
Further Reading. 153

Virtual Network Lab. 155

Requirements and Presumptions 156
Creating Envisioned Virtual Network 159
Adaptor Assignment in VirtualBox. 164
IP Addressing. 165
Configure the Router's Interfaces 165
Configure NAT on Router 166
Further Reading. 166

Setting Up a DHCP Server. 169

Static and Dynamic Hosts 170
Network Scenario. 170
Configuring the DHCP Server Details. 171
Installing DHCP Package. 178
Configure DHCP Server 178
    Parameter Configuration 179
    IP Subnet Declaration 179
    Assign Static IP Address to Host. 180
Start and Enable DHCP Service. 181
Setup Client System 181

xi

Contents

Further Reading 183

Setting Up an FTP Server 185
Network Scenario. 186
Configuring the FTP Server Details 187
Installing vsftpd (FTP) Package 193
    Files Installed with vsftpd 193
    Configuration Options for vsftpd 193
Configure FTP Server 195
Start and Enable the vsftpd Service 196
Adjusting the Firewall 196
SELinux 196
Managing FTP Server with Filezilla 197
Accessing from the Clients 204
Further Reading 204

Setting Up a Mail Server 205
Network Scenario 206
Configuring the Mail Server Details 207
Adding Hosts Entry 213
Disable SELinux 213
Firewall Adjustment 214
Installing Postfix 214
Configuring Postfix 214
Start and Enable Postfix 215
Dovecot Installation 215
Configuring Dovecot 215
Start and Enable Dovecot 216
Installing SquirrelMail 216
Configuring SquirrelMail 218
Creation of vhost for squirrelmail 230
Start and Enable Apache 230
Creating Mail User Accounts 230
Accessing the Webmail 231
Further Reading 232

Setting Up a Web Server 233
Network Scenario 234
Configuring the Web Server Details 235
Install Apache Web Server Package 242
Configuring the Web Server 242

Contents

Start and Enable Apache. 243
Installing MariaDB 244
Start and Enable MariaDB. 244
Securing MySQL/MariaDB server 244
Creating Database for the Web Server 246
Install and Configure PHP. 247
Firewall Adjustment. 247
Testing the Web Server. 248
Further Reading. 249

Setting Up a DNS Server 251

Network Scenario. 252
Configuring the DNS Server Details 253
Install BIND DNS Server Package. 260
Configuring BIND. 260
    Creating Forward Zone file. 262
    Zone File Parameter Values. 262
    Creating Reverse Zone file 263
Starting and Enabling the named Service 264
Firewall Adjustment. 264
Testing the Functionality of DNS Server 265
Further Reading. 267

Setting Up a YUM Repository 269

Network Scenario. 270
Configuring the YUM Server Details 271
Apache Installation. 277
Remote Sync (rsync) Installation 277
Configure the YUM Repo Server 277
Downloading the CentOS 7 ISO 277
Configuring Cron Job 278
Configure the Yum Client 279
    Creating a Repo File. 280
Testing the YUM Server. 280
Further Reading. 280

Troubleshooting SELinux 283

Network Scenario. 284
SELinux Configuration File 285
Modes of SELinux 286
Viewing Context and Labels. 286
Guided Exercises and Examples 287

Contents

Changing the Contexts.. 290
Restoring the Contexts... 291
SELinux Log Files.. 292
Troubleshooting SELinux for the Mail Server............................ 294
Further Reading.. 297

Part A

Chapter 1
Install and Configure GNS3

The best way to practice and learn Network Services Administration without having to buy any hardware is by building a Virtual Lab. An open source software, GNS3 can be used for building a Virtual Lab which we can download and use for free. Today, GNS3 is used by thousands of network engineers worldwide to emulate, configure, test and troubleshoot networks. It allows running a small topology consisting of a few devices on your laptop or desktop. In this chapter, we will learn to install and configure the GNS3, and also add the IOS images.

Emulation and Simulation

The GNS3 emulates the hardware of a device and run the actual images on the virtual device. We can use the IOS of a real, physical Cisco router and run that on a virtual, emulated Cisco router in GNS3 and simulate the features and functionality of a device such as a router.

Downloading GNS3

The GNS3 software can be obtained from the official website of the GNS3. However, before we get to download, we have to signup if we don't have an account or login if we already have an account created. Follow the link https://www.gns3.com/ and download the software appropriate for your Operating System.

> *At the time of this writing, GNS3 Version 2.1.5 (for Windows) was released, however, it appeared to be behaving in an unexplainable way and instead Version 2.0.0a3 is used in this book. You can continue to use the latest GNS3 Version or the one used in this book as most of the basic features and functionalities remain similar.*

The following screen would be shown for downloading in the GNS3 official download page. The download is available for Mac and Linux as well but in this book, the platform used is Windows. However, you can choose to use either Linux, Mac or Windows, depending on the convenience.

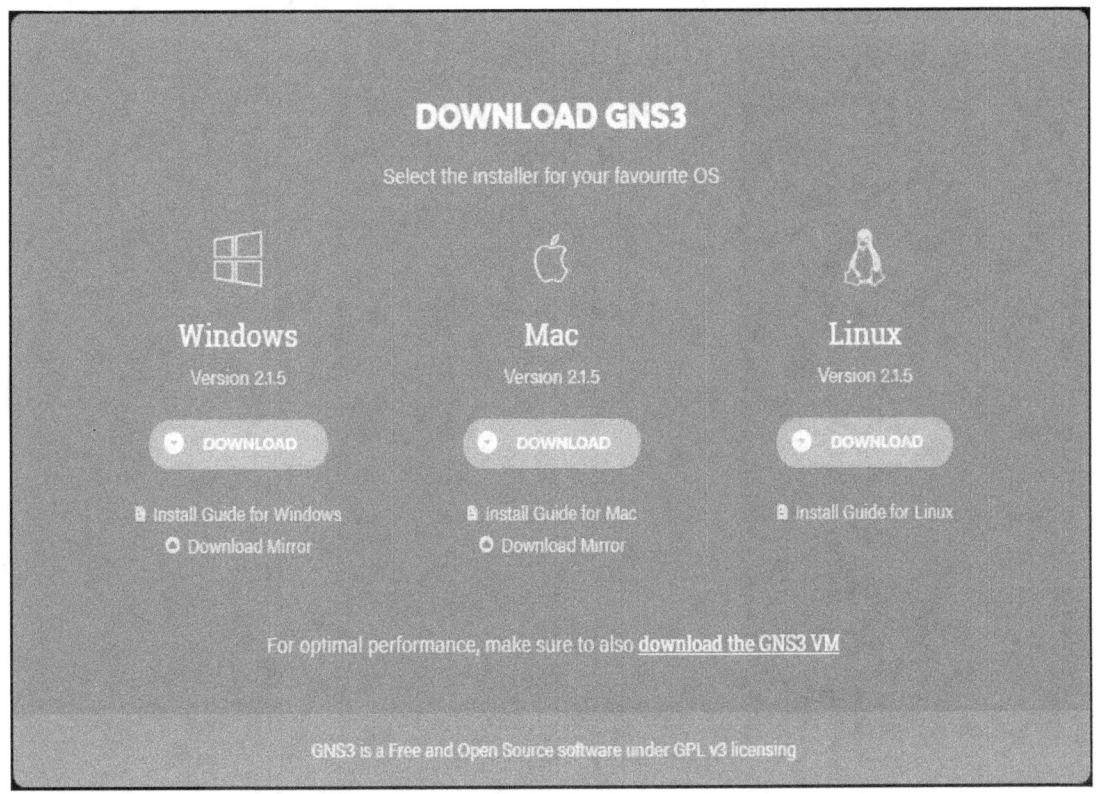

Figure 1.1: GNS3 Download Options

Installing the GNS3

After the download is complete, run the software as administrator and then the GNS3 setup will begin. Click the "Next" button.

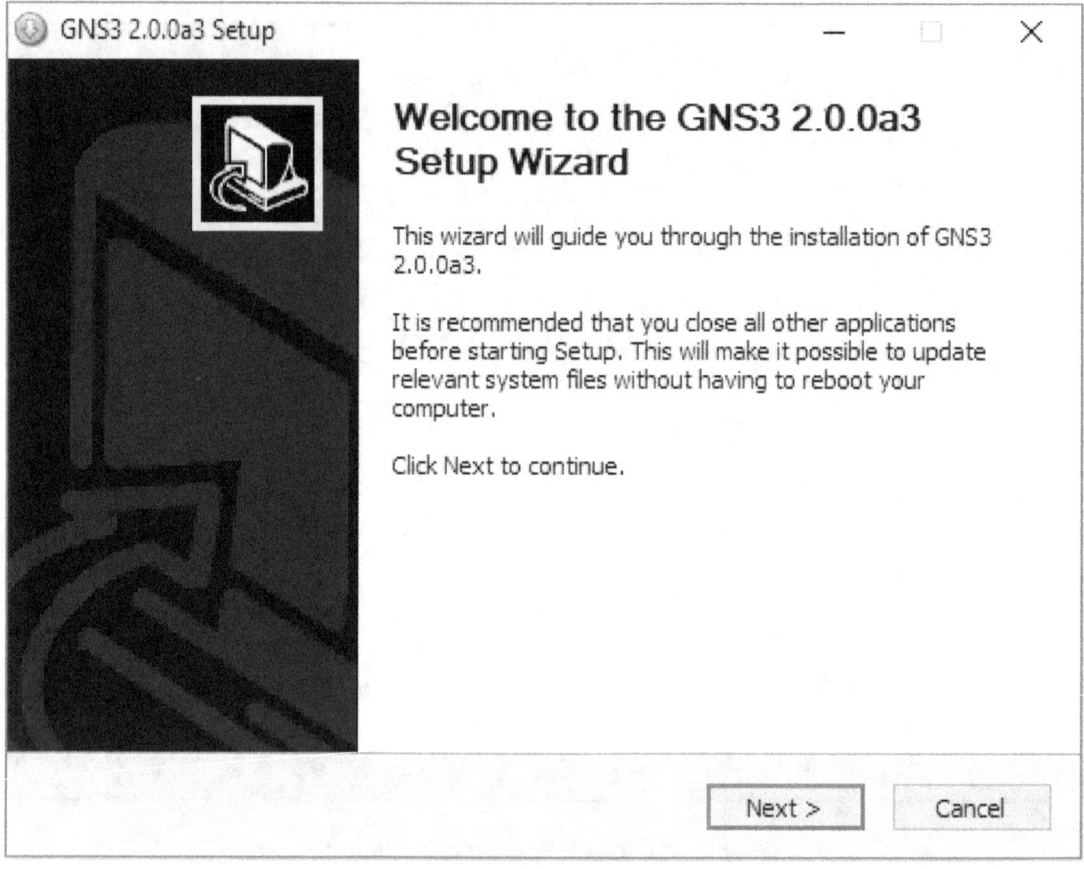

Figure 1.2: GNS3 Setup Welcome Screen

In the next screen, choose "I Agree" for the License agreement to proceed with the installation.

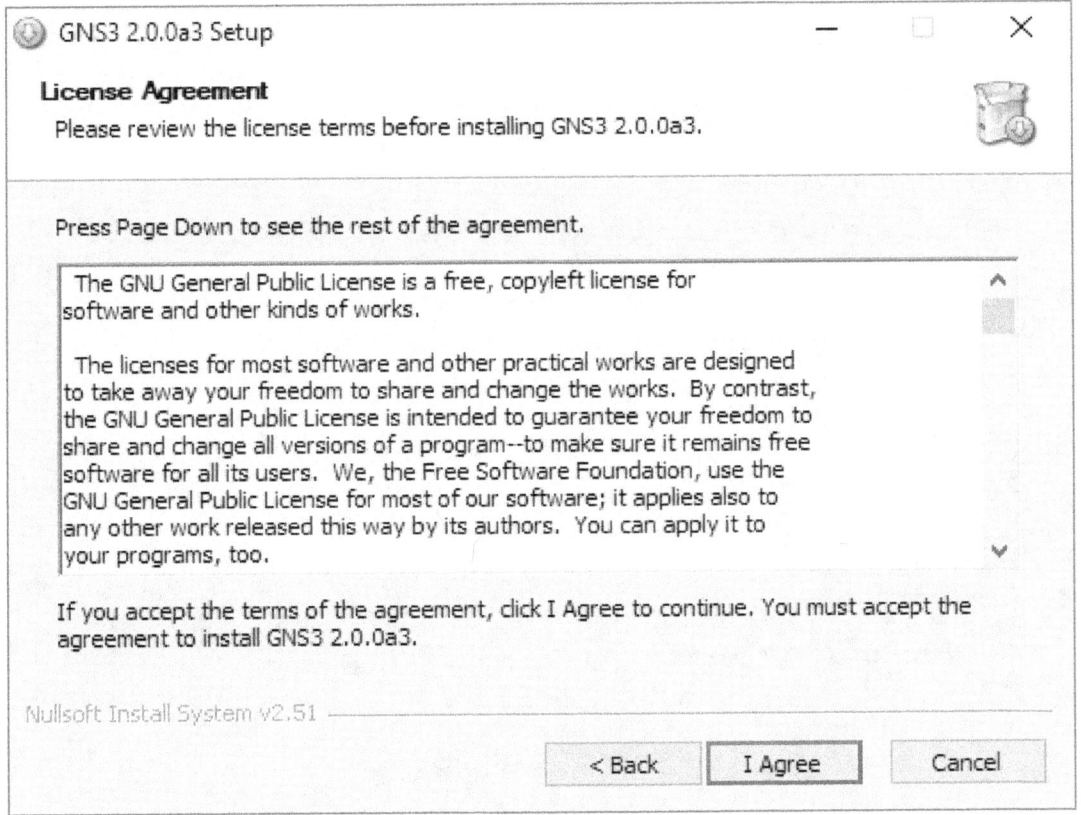

Figure 1.3: License Agreement Screen

Allow GNS3 to create a "Start Menu" folder with the default name GNS3 by clicking the "Next" button.

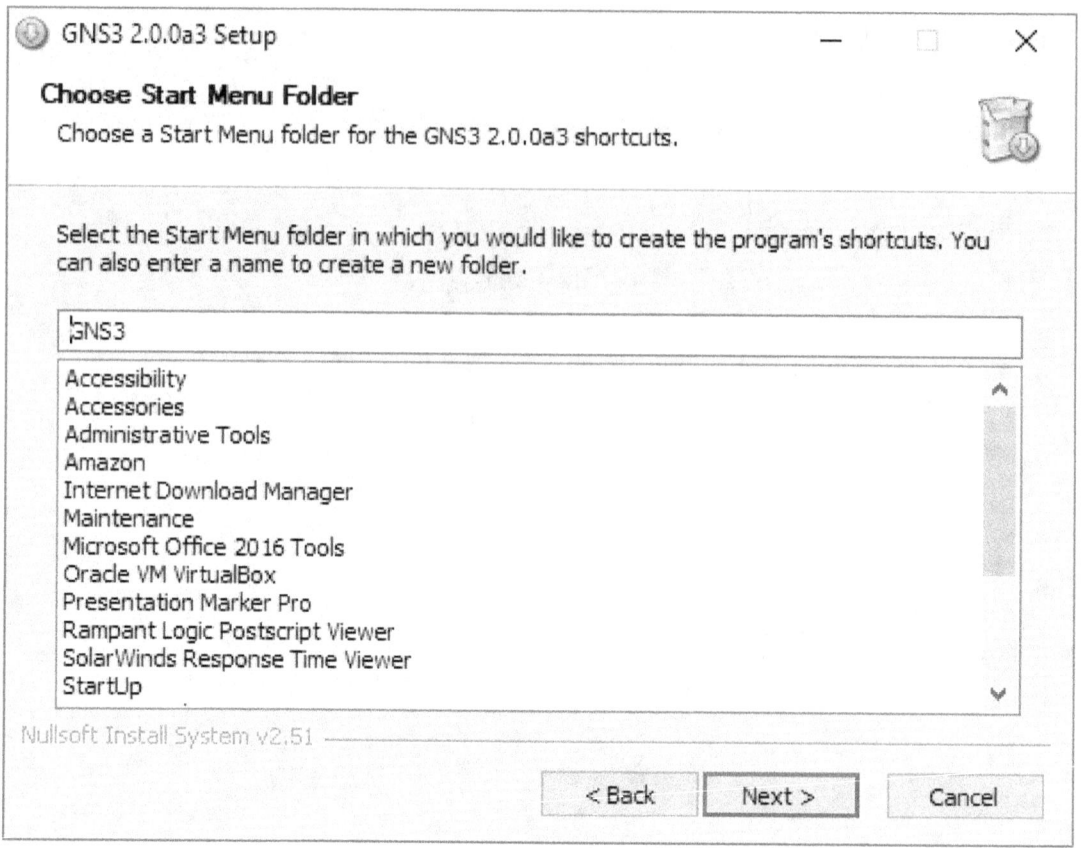

Figure 1.4: Startup Menu Folder Selection

The GNS3 software depends on several other programs to function. These dependencies along with GNS3 are all chosen by default for installation, if not choose all and click the "Next" button to continue.

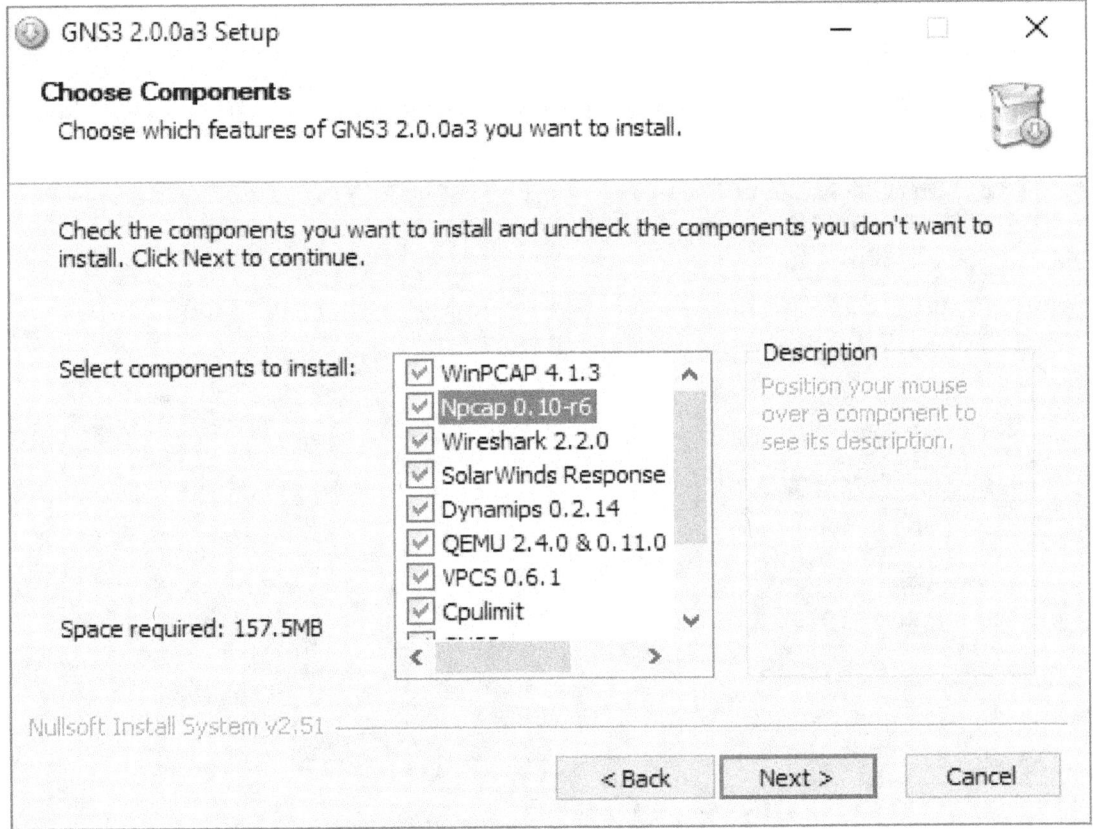

Figure 1.5: GNS3 Component selection for installation

A default location is chosen for GNS3. Click the "Install" button to accept the default location and to begin the actual installation of files.

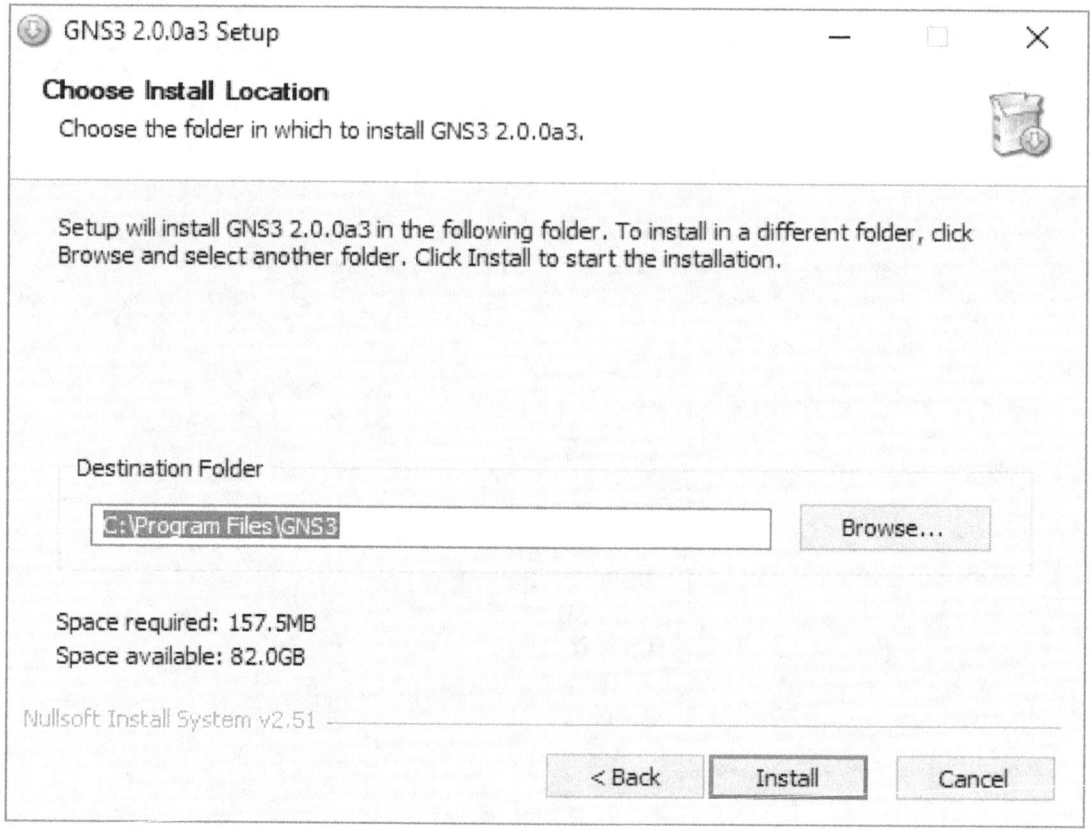

Figure 1.6: Choosing the installation location

Click "Next" to proceed with the installation and then the installation would be complete.

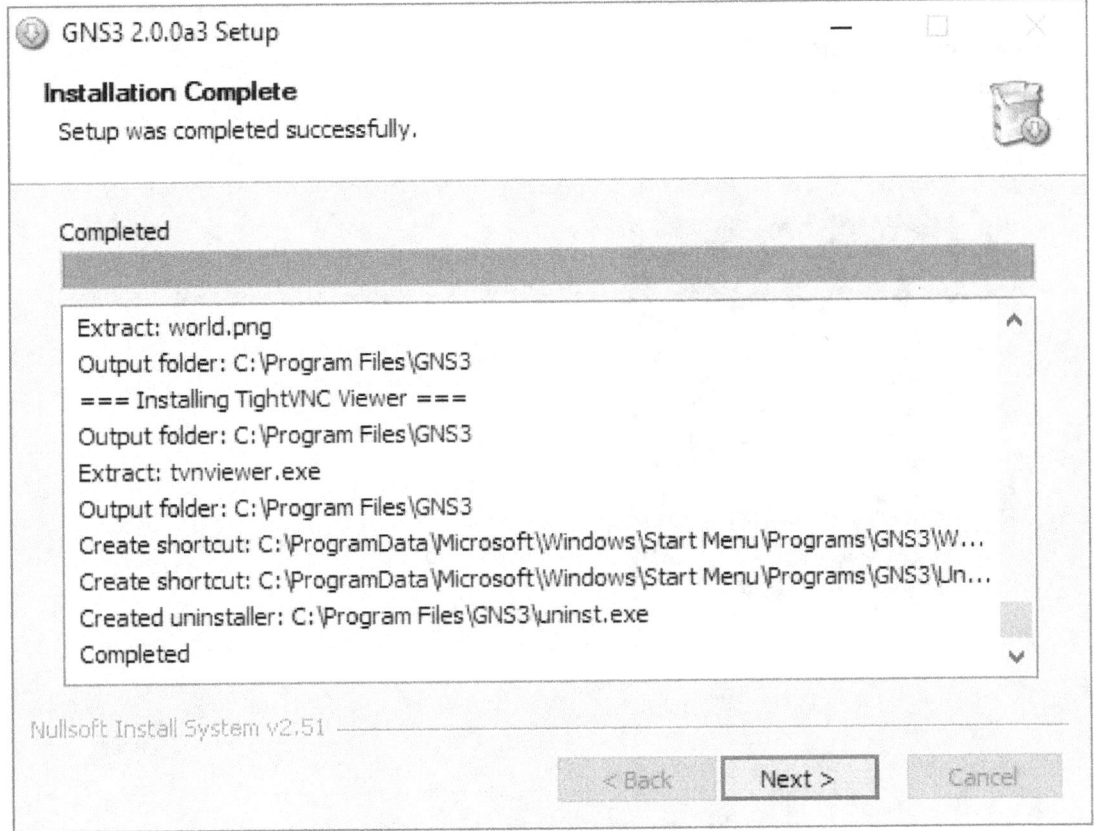

Figure 1.7: Installation Complete Screen

Choose "No" and then click "Next".

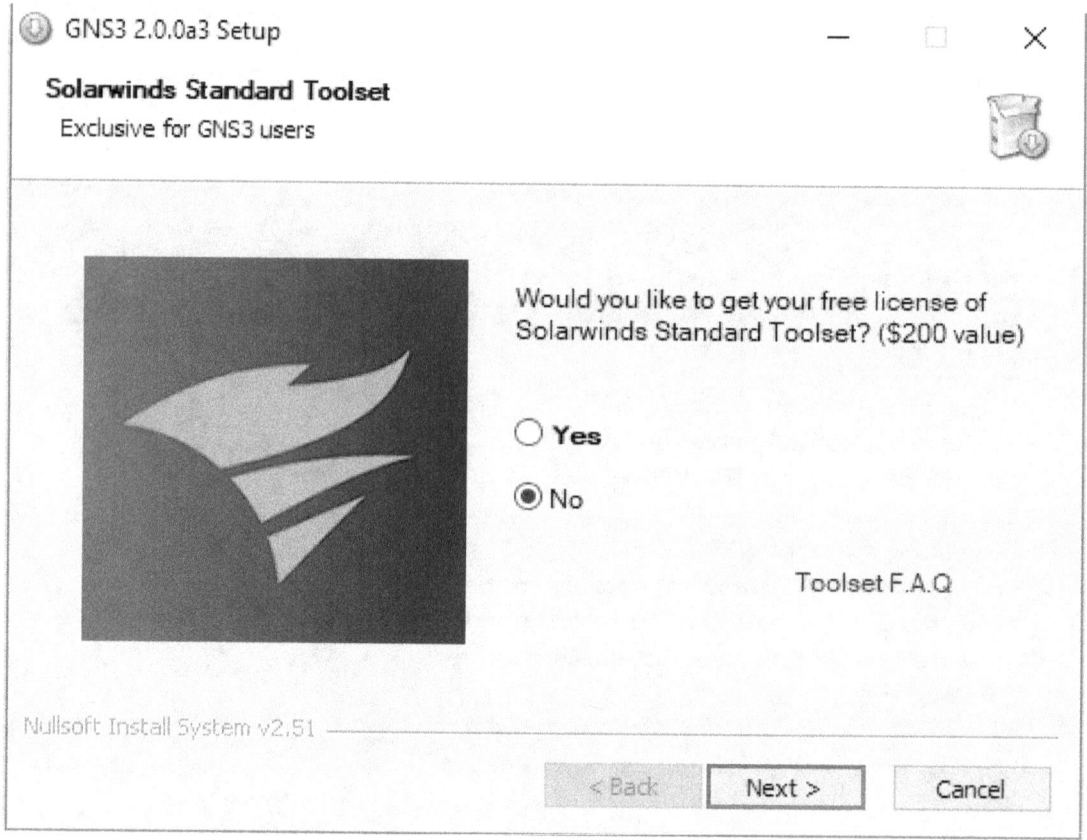

Figure 1.8: Solarwinds Standard Toolset Option

Click "Finish" and complete the GNS3 installation.

Figure 1.9: GNS3 setup Complete Screen

Configuring GNS3

Immediately after the installation is complete, you will be shown the following screen. Choose "Run only legacy IOS on my computer" and then click "Next".

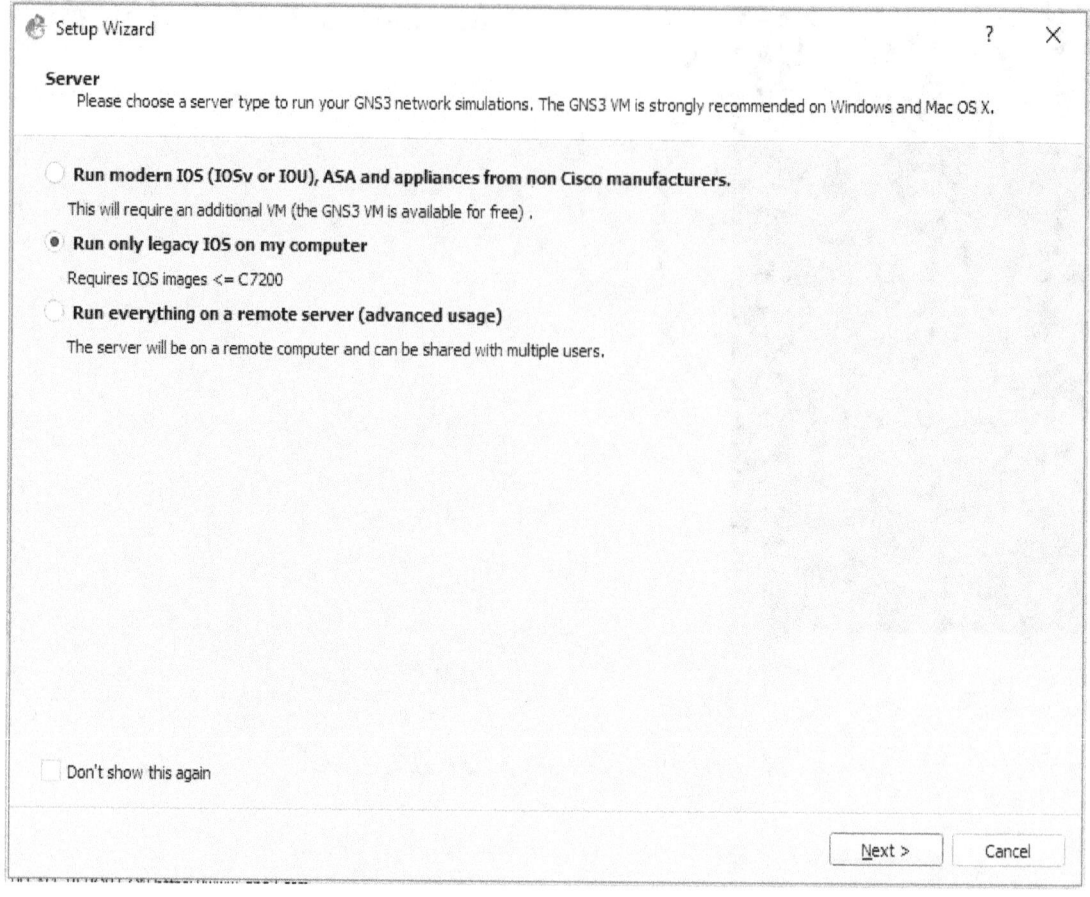

Figure 1.10: Choosing GNS3 Server Type

In the options shown, keep the "Server path" and "Port" to defaults, set the "Host binding" to 127.0.0.1 in case if it is set to something different. Click "Next" and proceed with the configuration.

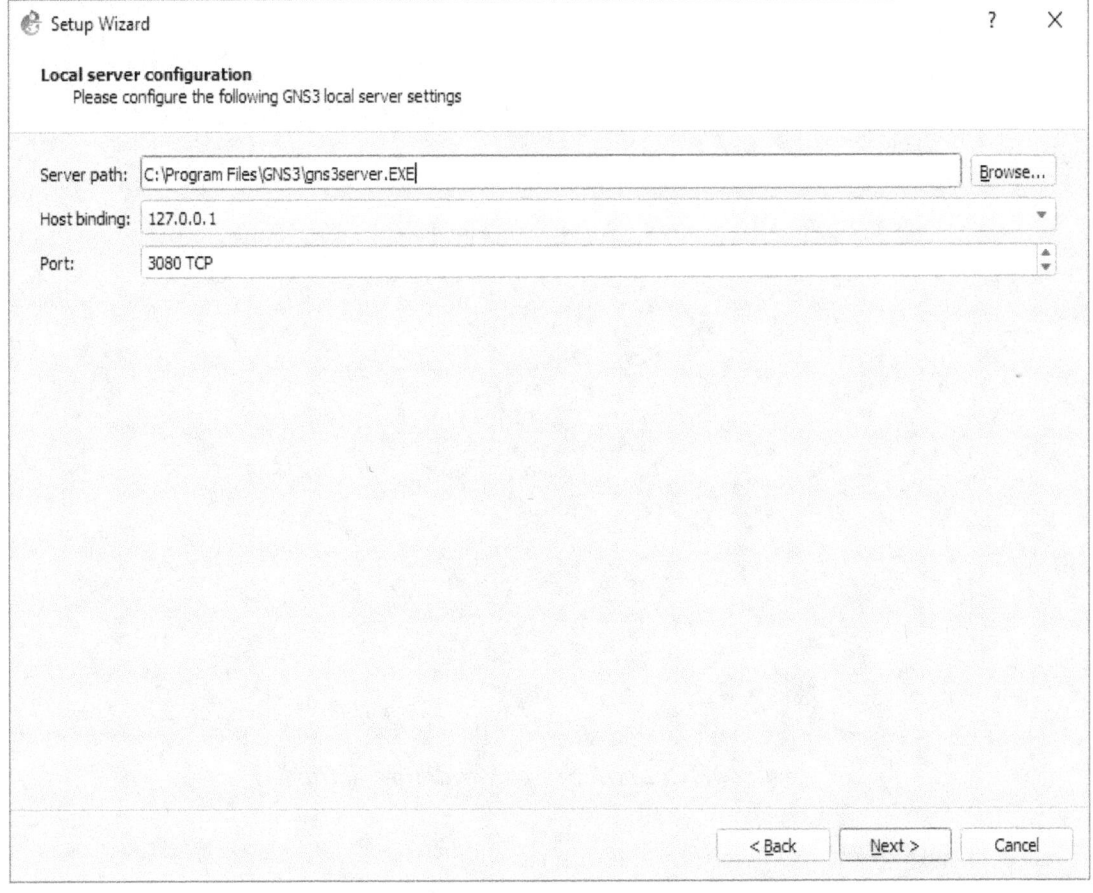

Figure 1.11: Local GNS3 Server setting

Upon the successful configuration validation and connection to the server, click "Next".

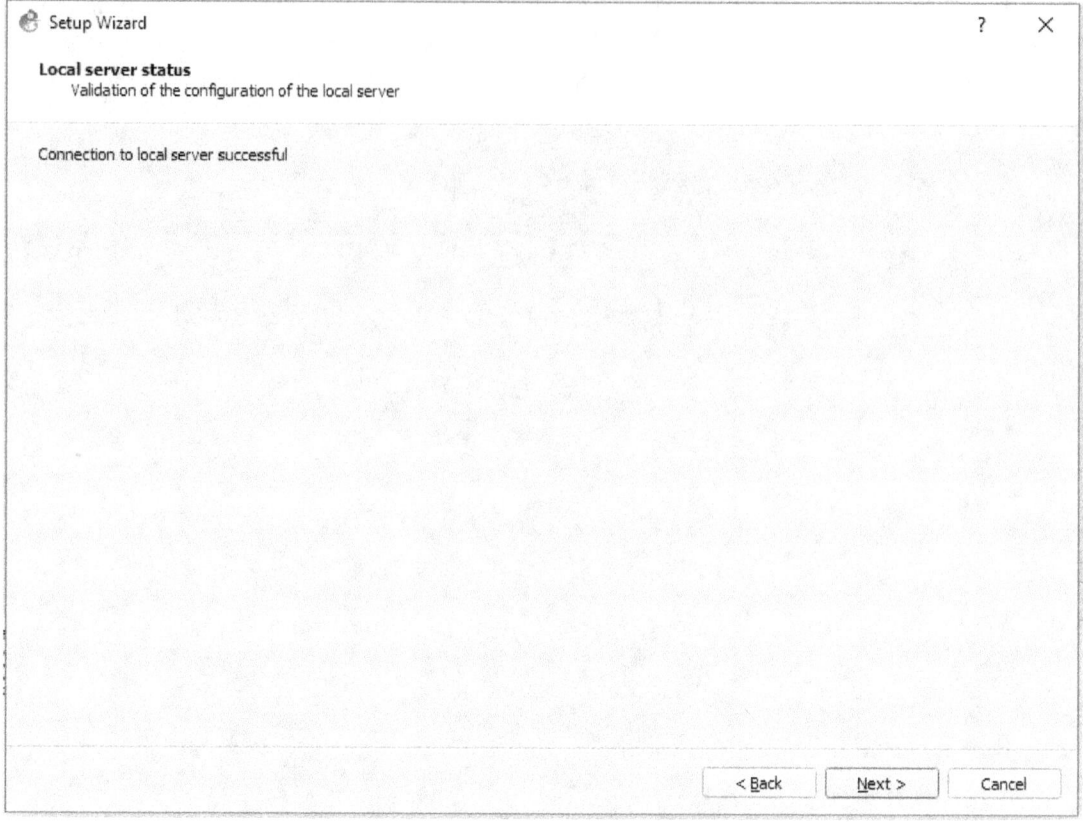

Figure 1.12: Local Server Validation Status

On the summary screen of the configuration, click "Finish".

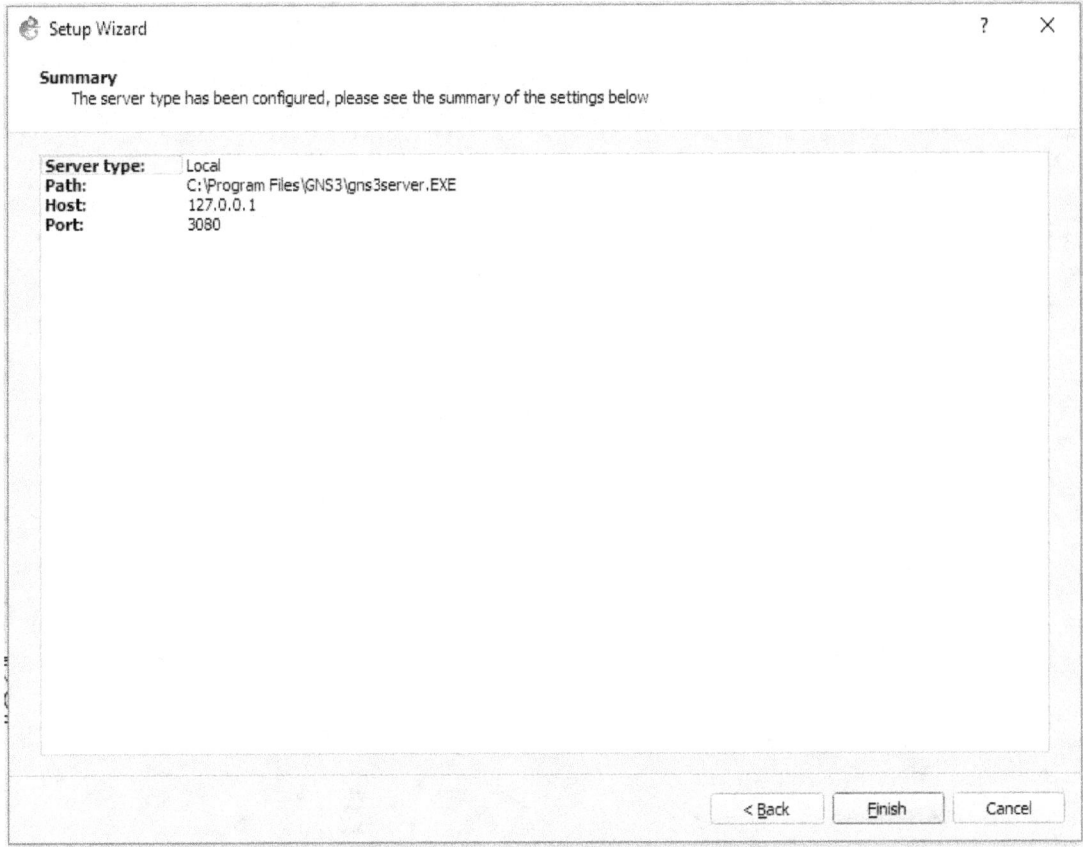

Figure 1.13: Local Server Configuration Summary

Adding IOS Image for the Router

The following template takes us through the adding of router's IOS to be used with the GNS3. Choose "Add an IOS router using a real IOS image (supported by Dynamips)" and click "OK" to continue.

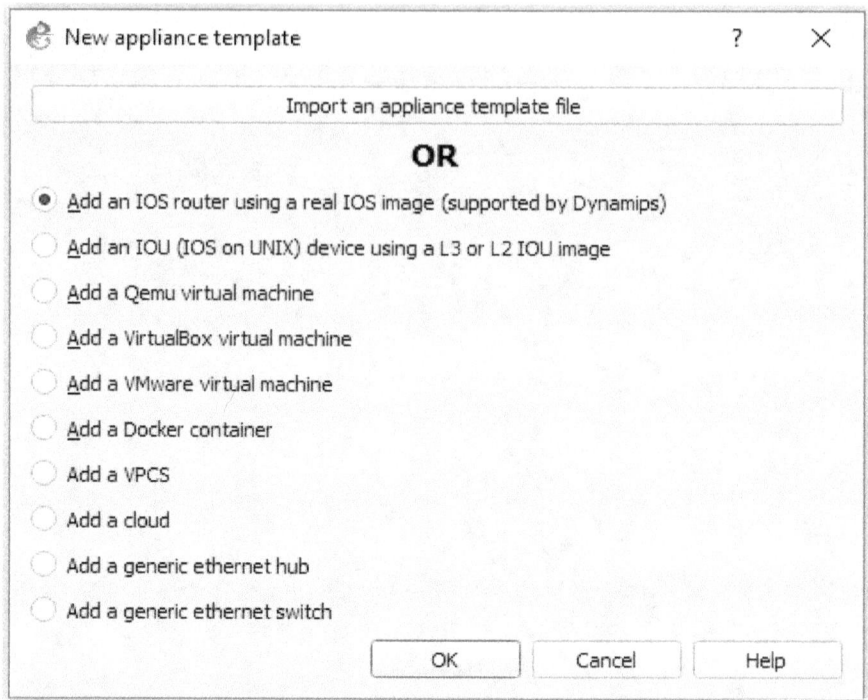

Figure 1.14: IOS Importing Options

In this step, we have to browse to a location where your router's IOS is stored and select the IOS image to be used.

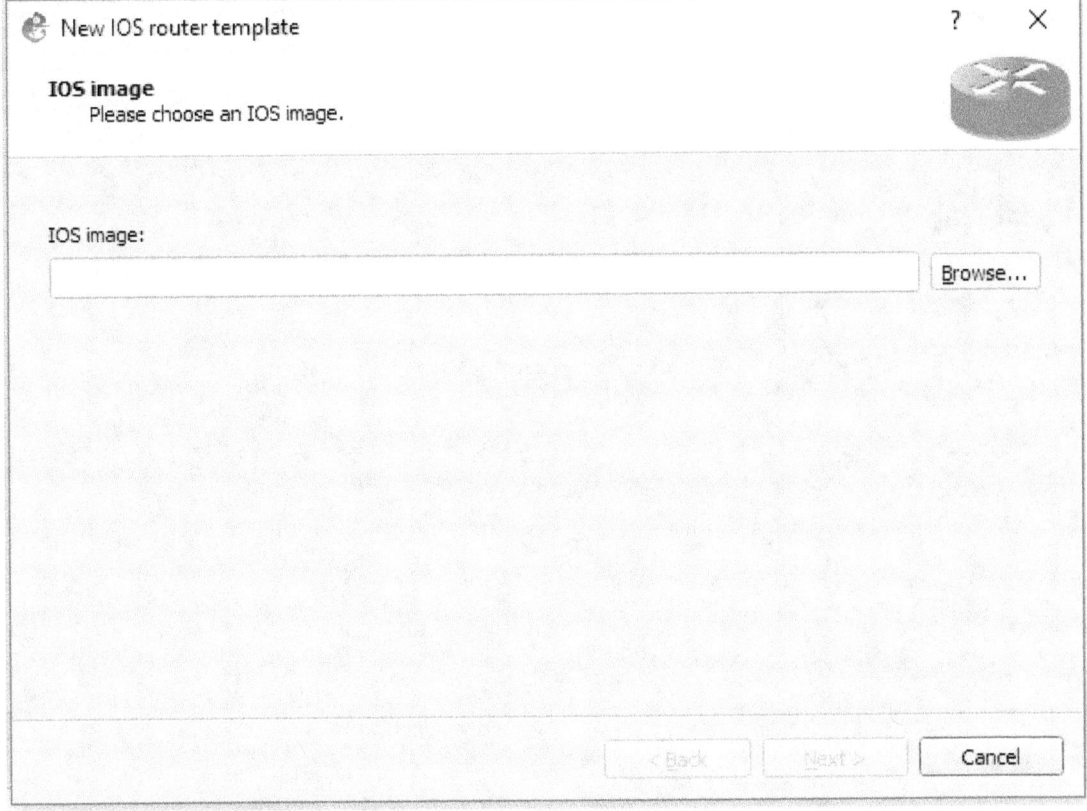

Figure 1.15: Browsing to the IOS Image location

Once the IOS is chosen and loaded, click "Yes" button to start decompressing the IOS image.

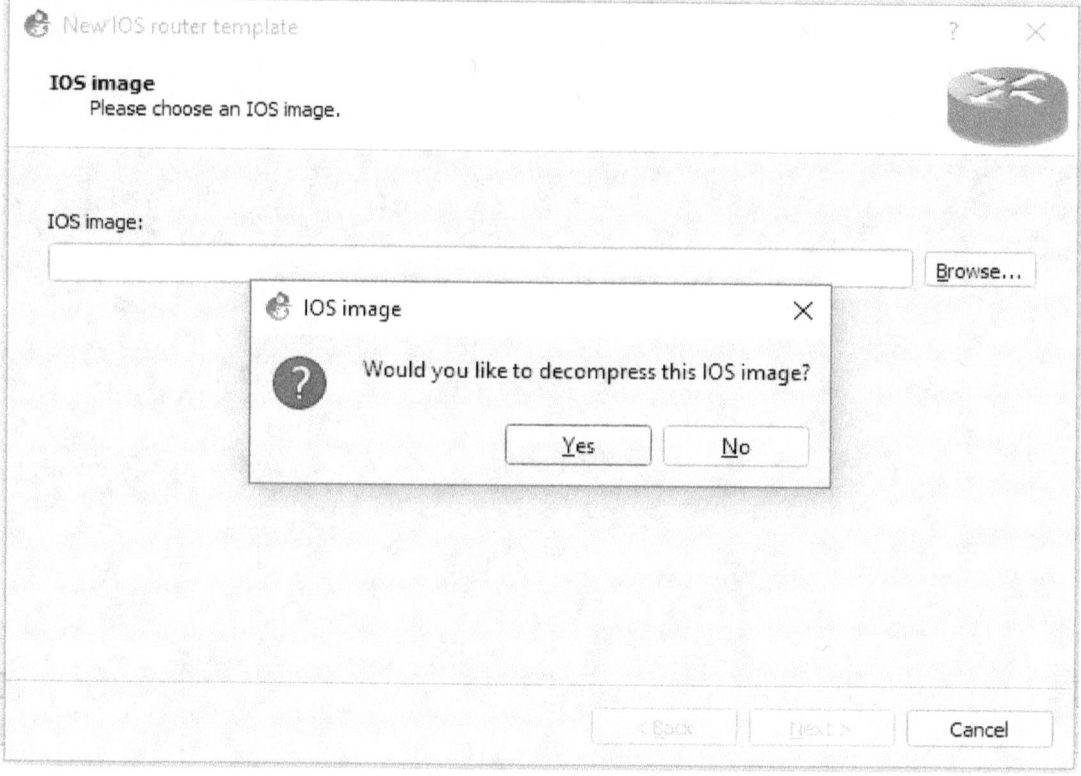

Figure 1.16: Decompressing the loaded IOS image

Once the image decompression is completed, click "Next" to continue.

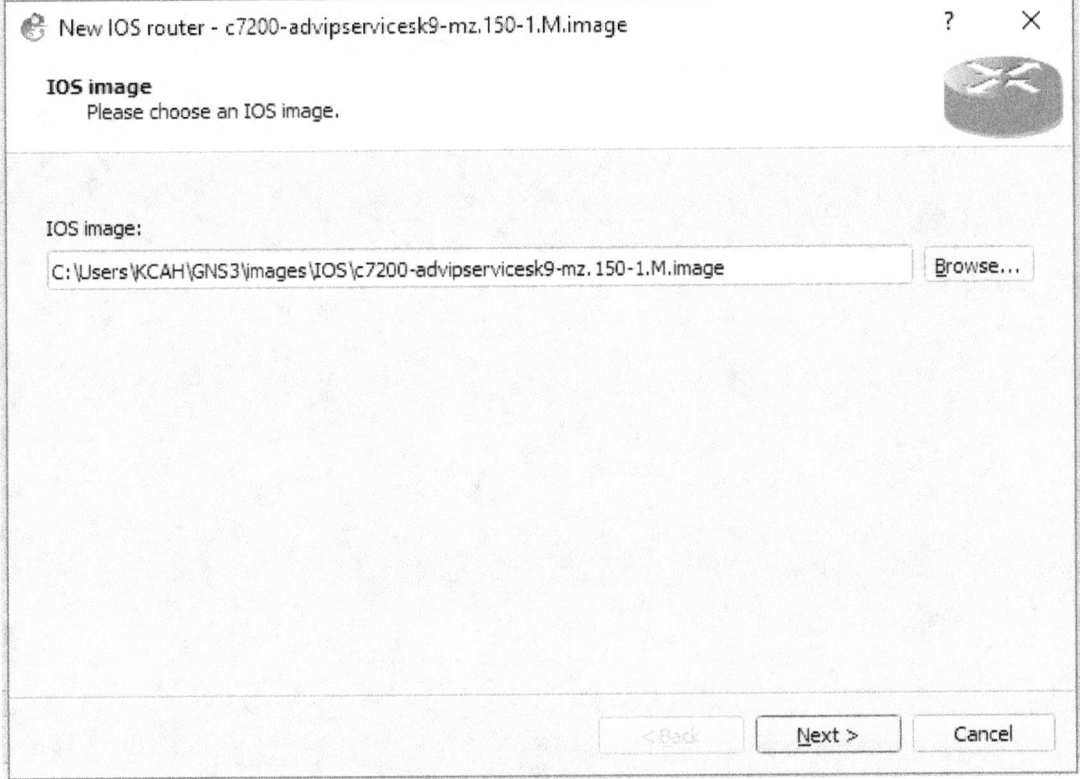

Figure 1.17: Path to the loaded IOS image

In the "Name" and "Platform" options, leave to the defaults and continue by clicking "Next" button.

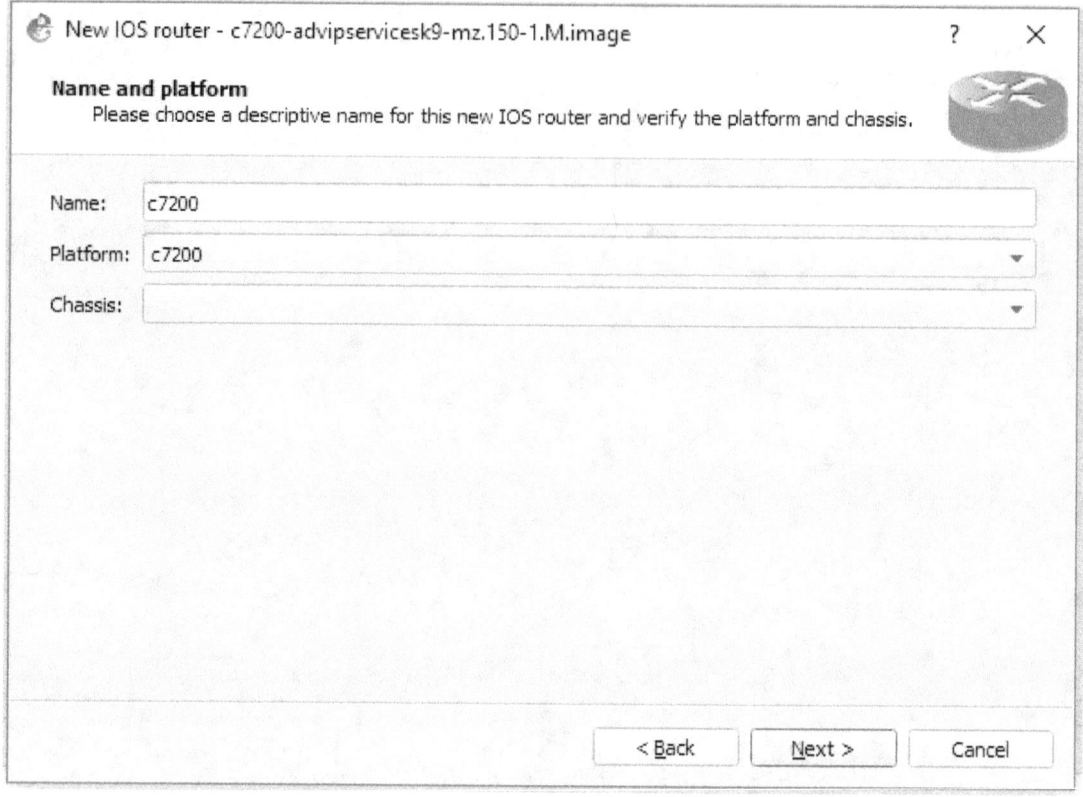

Figure 1.18: IOS router name and platform details

In this step, you have to allocate the amount of RAM size for the IOS and it is recommended to keep it to the default or allocate a bit higher. Allocating too much or too less would cause issues in the router startup. Assign the required amount of RAM as per the requirement and then click "Next" button.

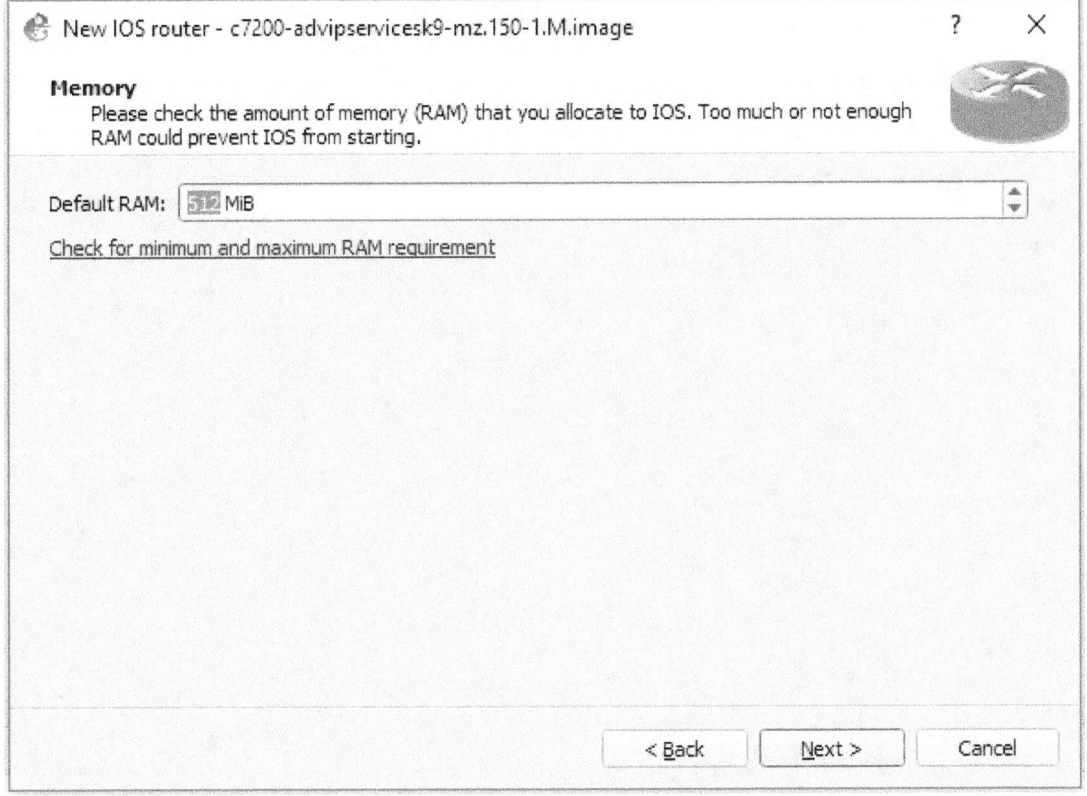

Figure 1.19: Memory allocation for the IOS

Virtualize Network Test-Labs

Here, we can specify the type and the number of interfaces to be created whenever new router instances are initiated. In the following, two fast ethernet interfaces (C7200-IO-2FE) are specified to be created for a router in every instance. Once it is specified correctly as per the need, click "Next" to proceed.

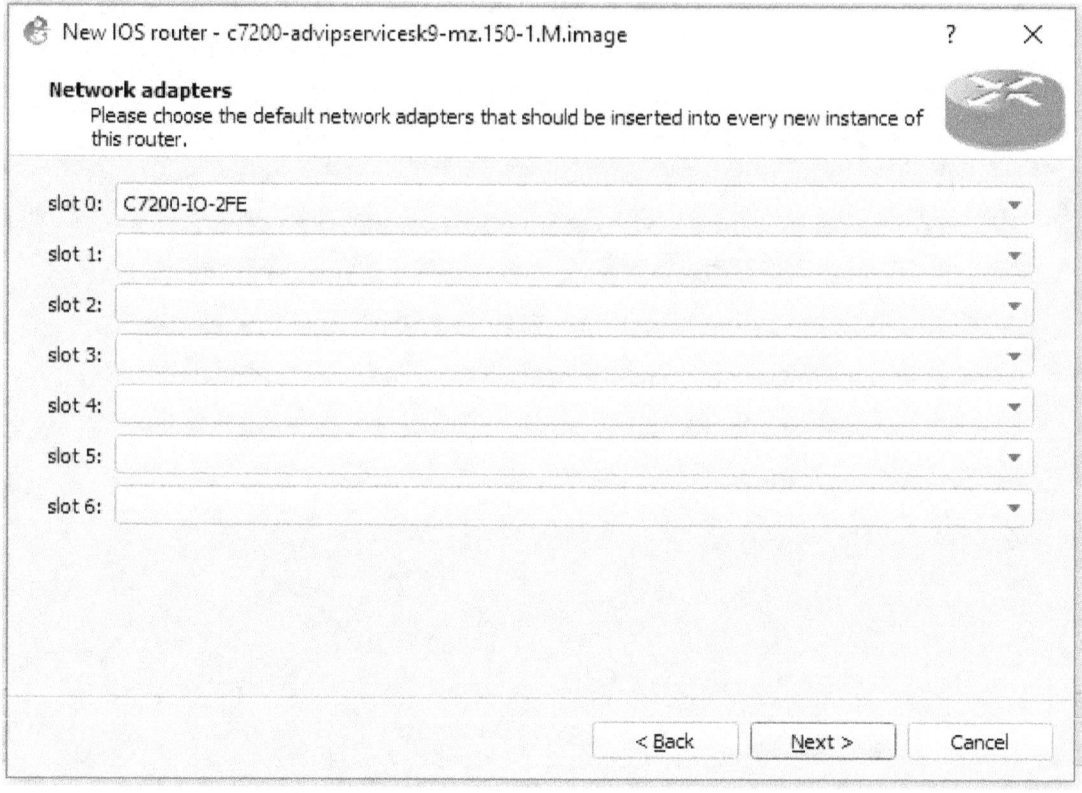

Figure 1.20: Default Network Adaptor specification

The Idle-PC value helps in reducing the percentage of CPU usage whenever we have to run multiple instances of routers at the same time. So, click on the "Idle-PC finder" button and wait for the system to find the suitable value for the IOS image. Once the Idle-PC value if found, accept the value by clicking "OK" and then click "Finish".

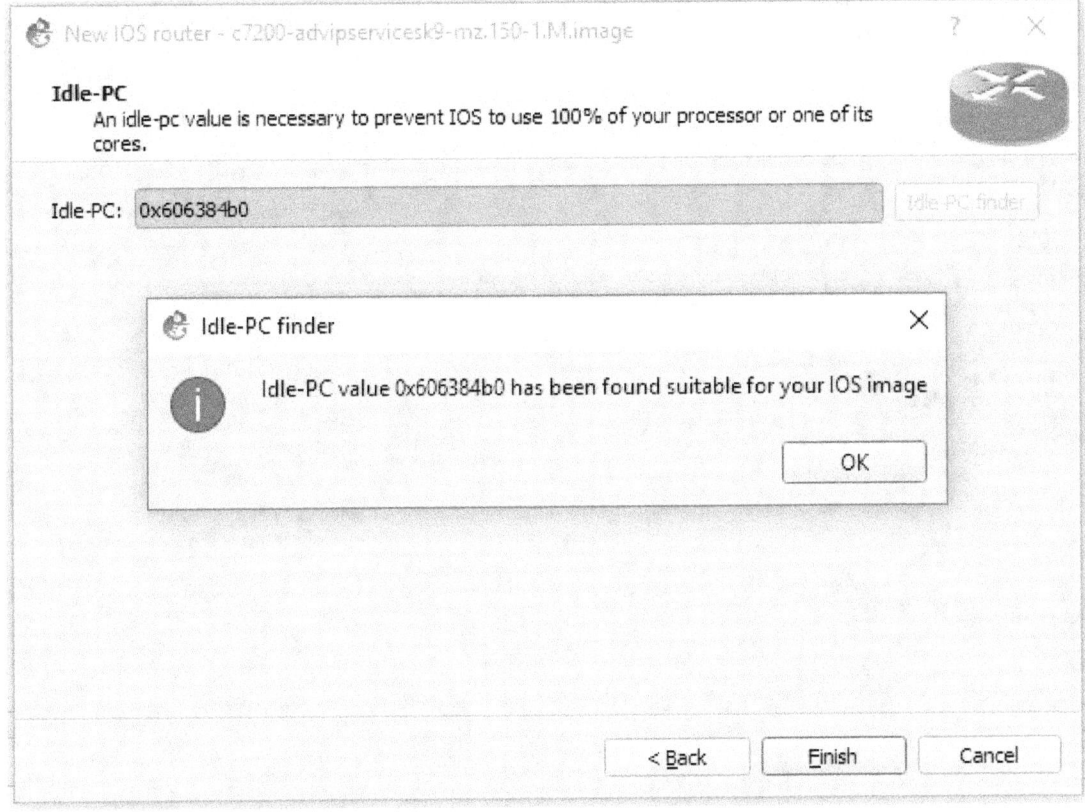

Figure 1.21: Finding Idle-PC Value for the IOS

When the process is complete, your IOS must be listed in the IOS routers list. Further, to accept the changes to take effect, click "Apply" and then "OK".

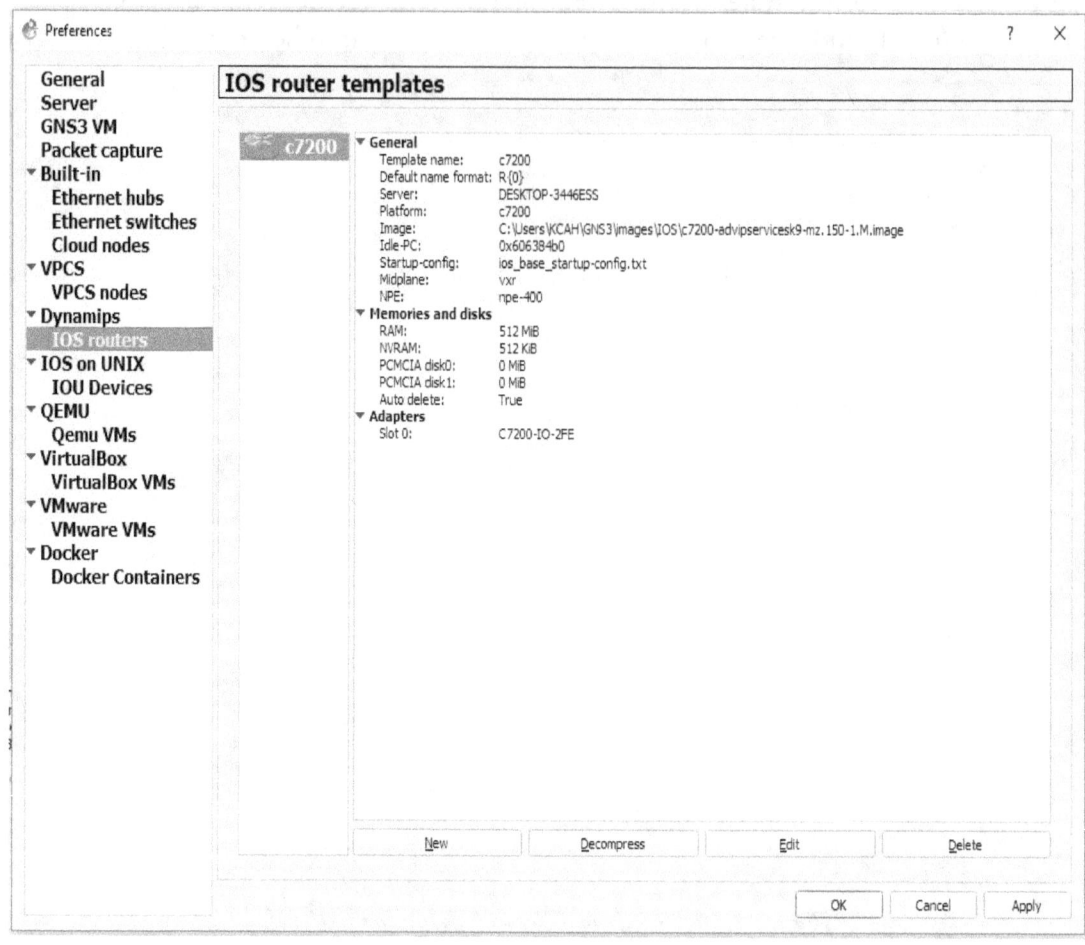

Figure 1.22: Imported Router IOS List

When the IOS adding is completed, GNS3 takes directly to the creation of the project. It shows a dialog box where we can specify the name of the project and the default location of the project to be saved is shown. At this point, click the "Cancel" and abort the project creation step.

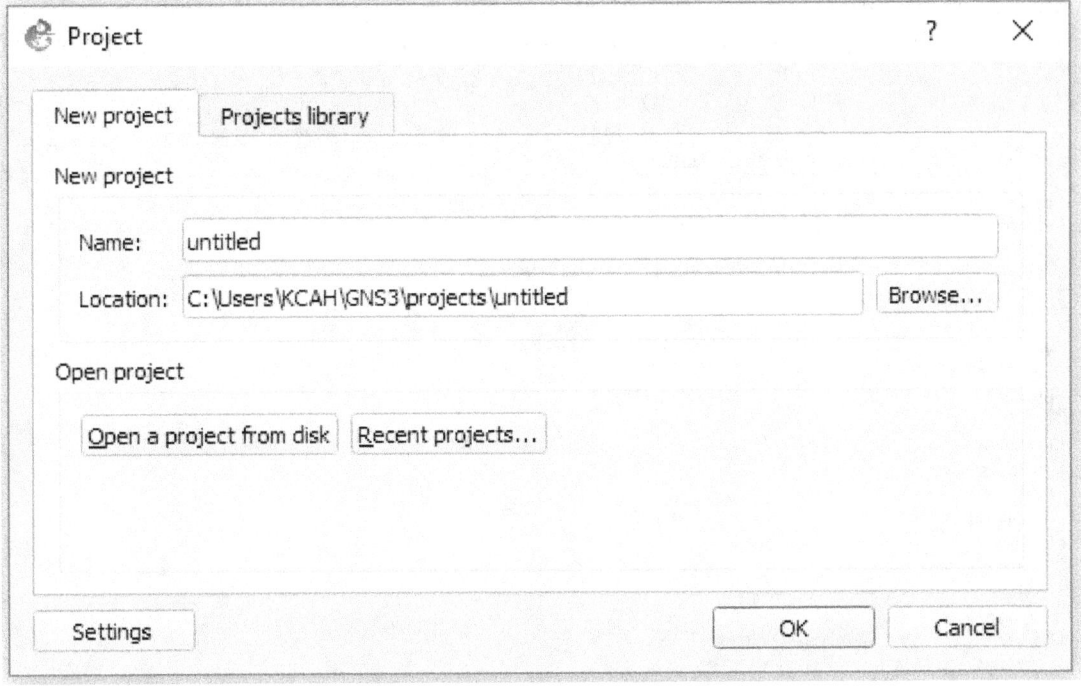

Figure 1.23: New project dialog box

Adding IOS for the EtherSwitch Router

In the previous step, you have added an IOS image to be used as the router. Now, in the following steps, we will try to add an IOS image of a router to be used as an EtherSwitch Router. After the launching of the GNS3 application, go to Edit --> Preferences --> Choose "IOS routers". Here, we get options either to add new, decompress, edit or delete the IOS routers. For now, in order to add new click on the "New" button.

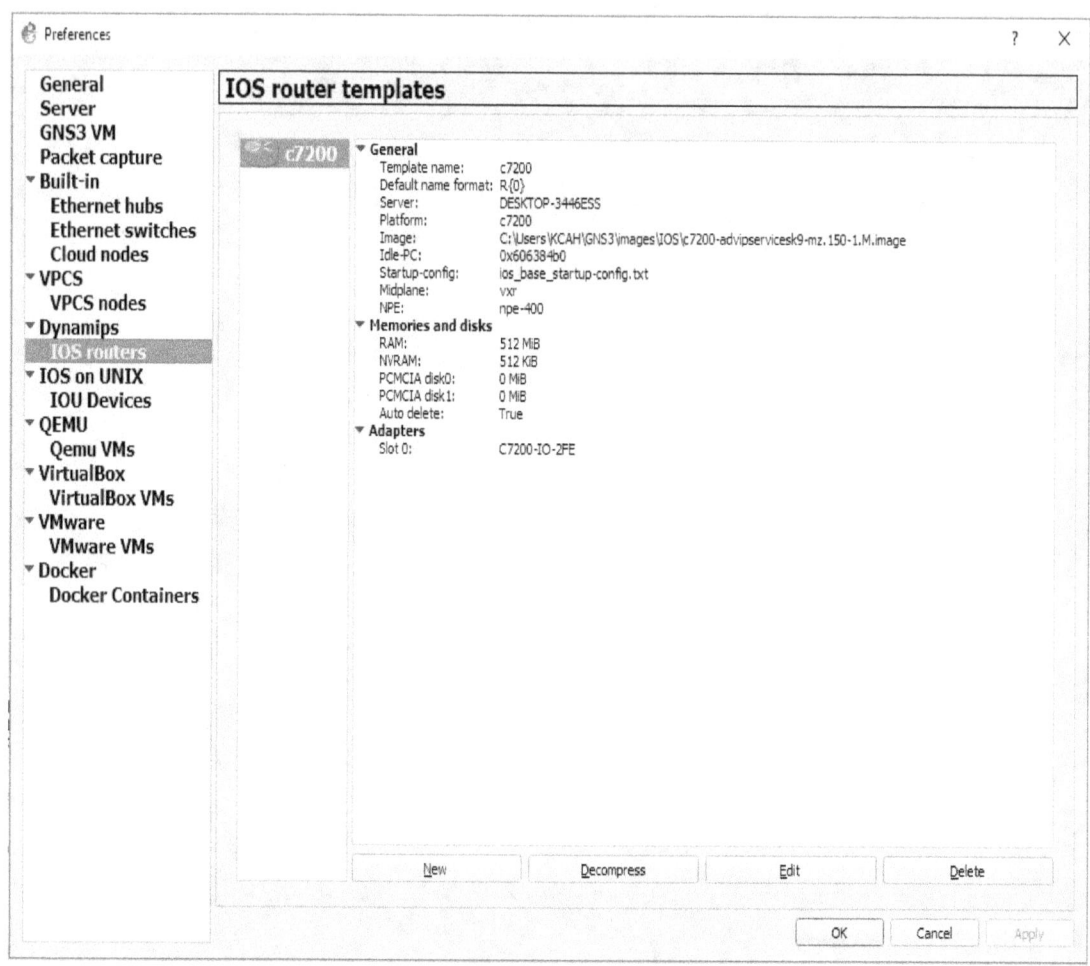

Figure 1.24: Adding more IOS Images

Choose "New Image" option, browse to the location where you have stored the IOS of the router, choose to decompress the image and then click "Next" to proceed.

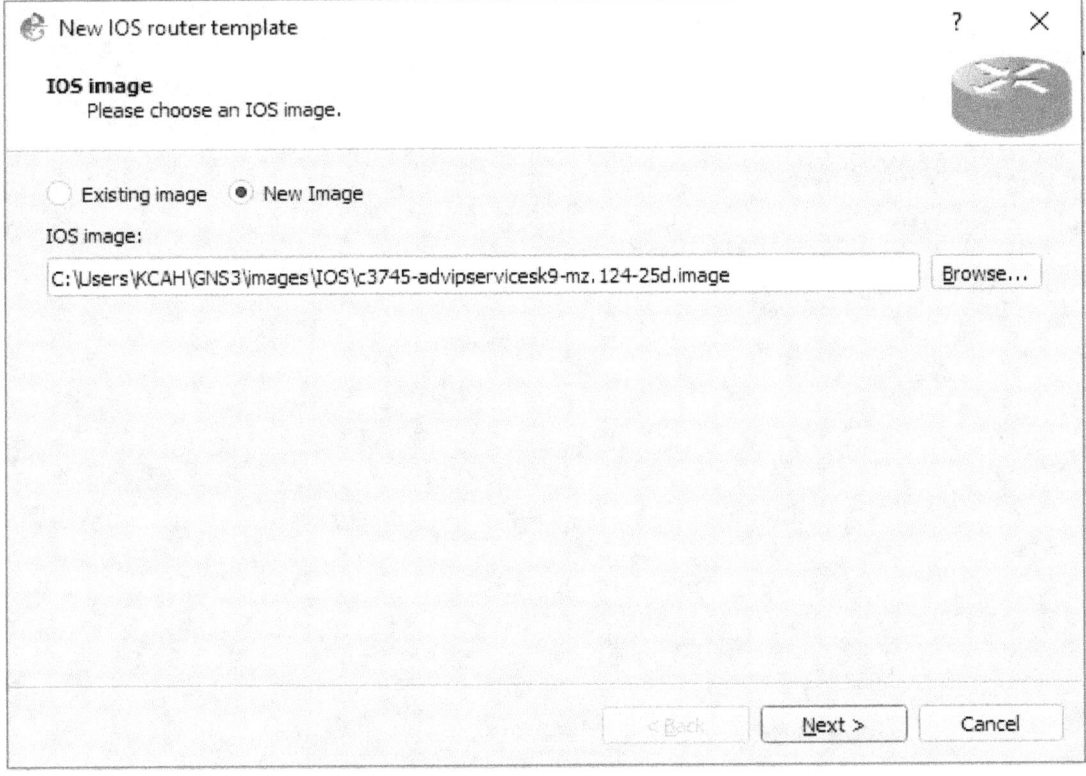

Figure 1.25: Choosing New IOS Image

Here, we have to provide a descriptive name, platform and select "This is an EtherSwitch router" option for our router and then click "Next".

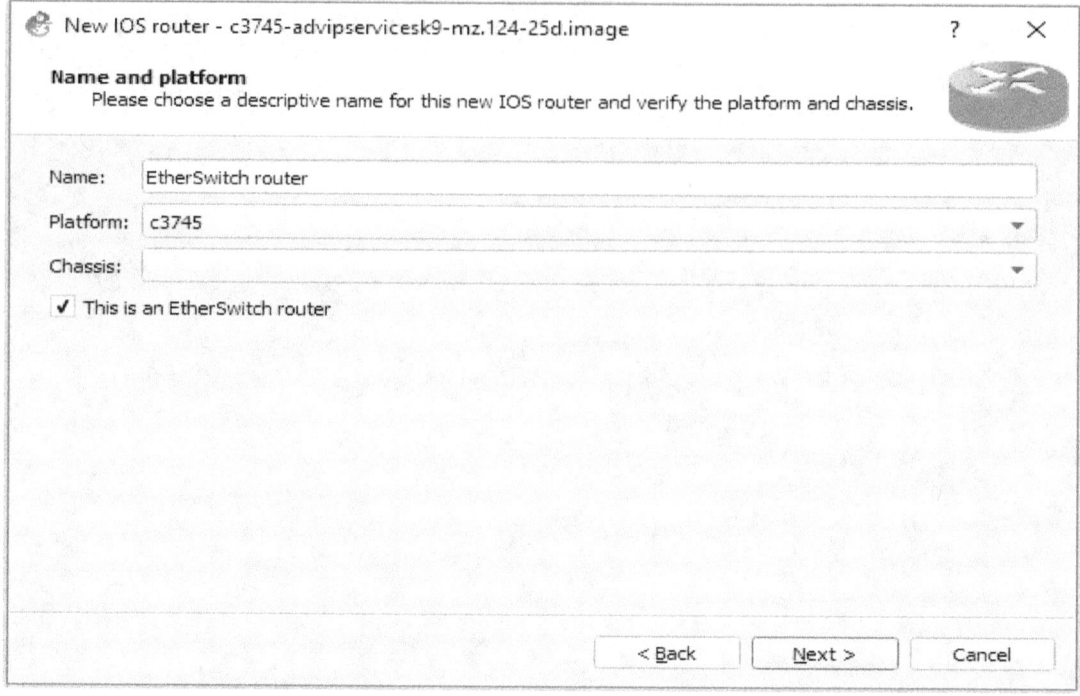

Figure 1.26: Router IOS to EtherSwitch Option

Allocate the required amount of RAM size for the IOS and click "Next" to continue.

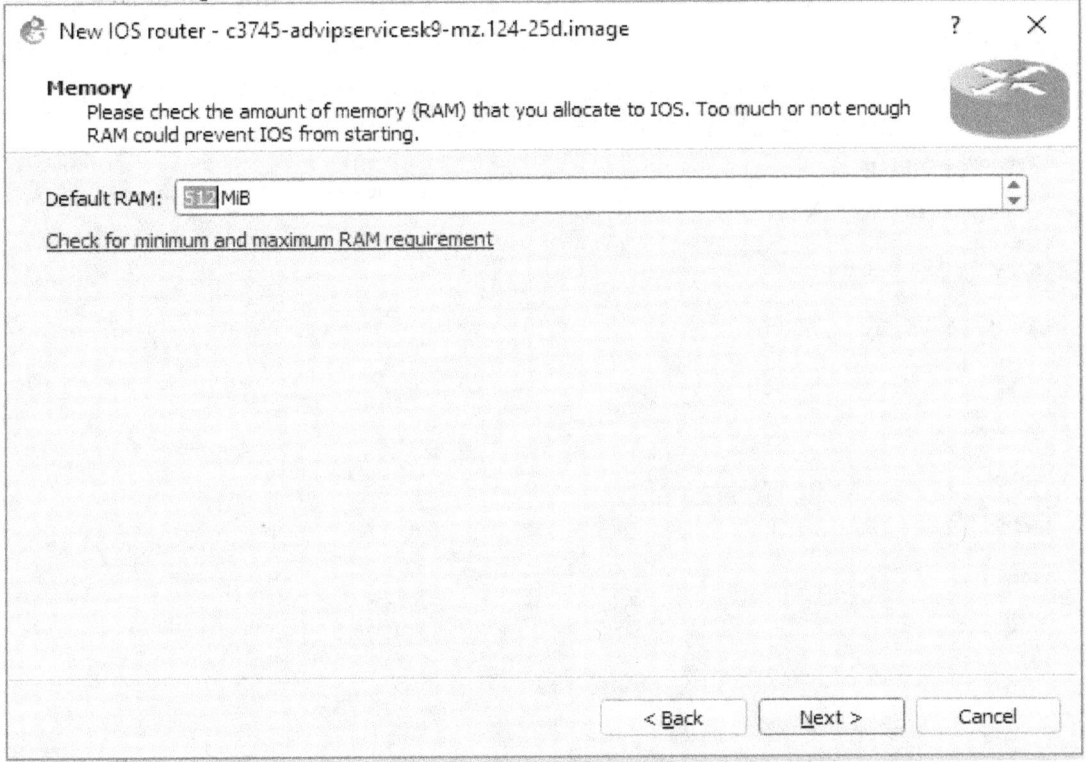

Figure 1.27: Memory allocation for the EtherSwitch Router

In this step, don't forget to add a module with 16 interfaces, since our intention is to use it as a switch. So, selecting NM-16ESW is recommended in this step and continue by clicking "Next".

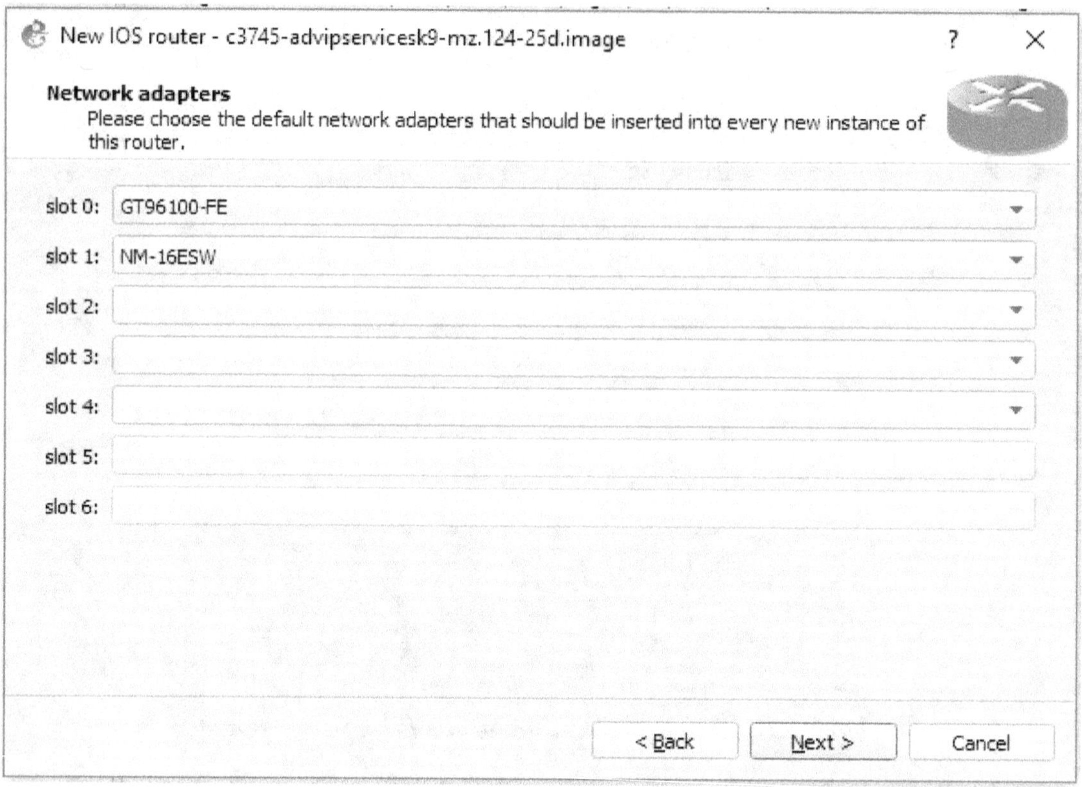

Figure 1.28: Specifying Default Ethernet Adaptors

Click "Next" to proceed with the setting.

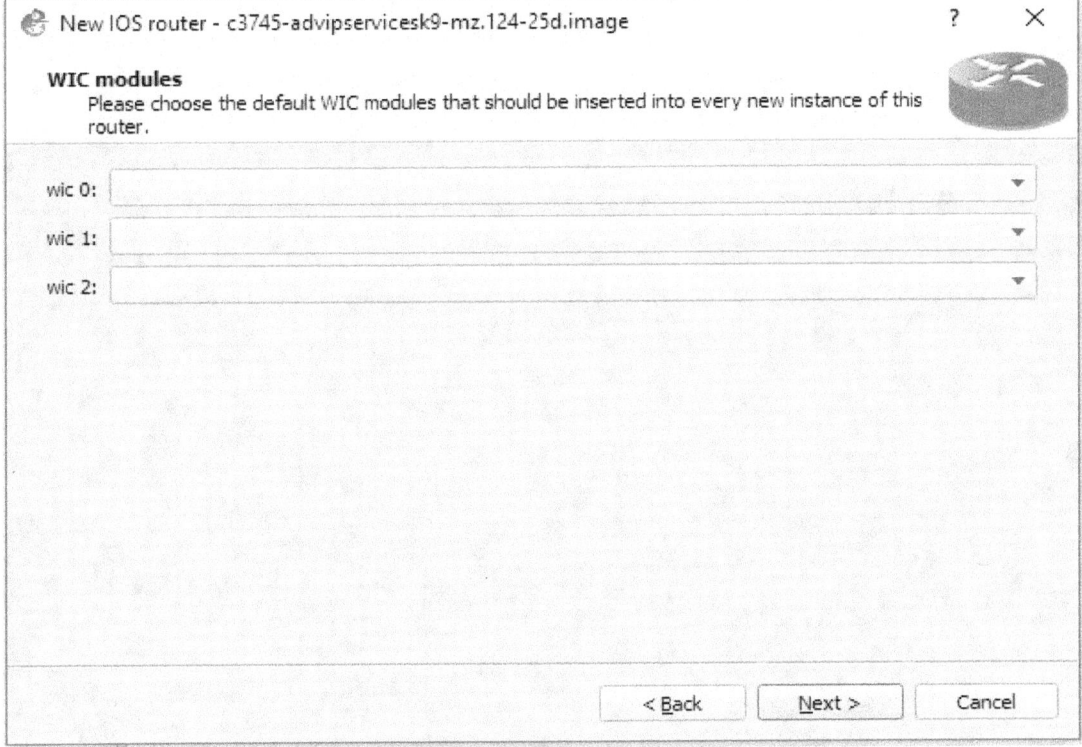

Figure 1.29: Specifying WIC module options

Look for the Idle-PC value and click "Finish". Even if the Idle-PC value is not found by the system, you can continue by clicking "Finish".

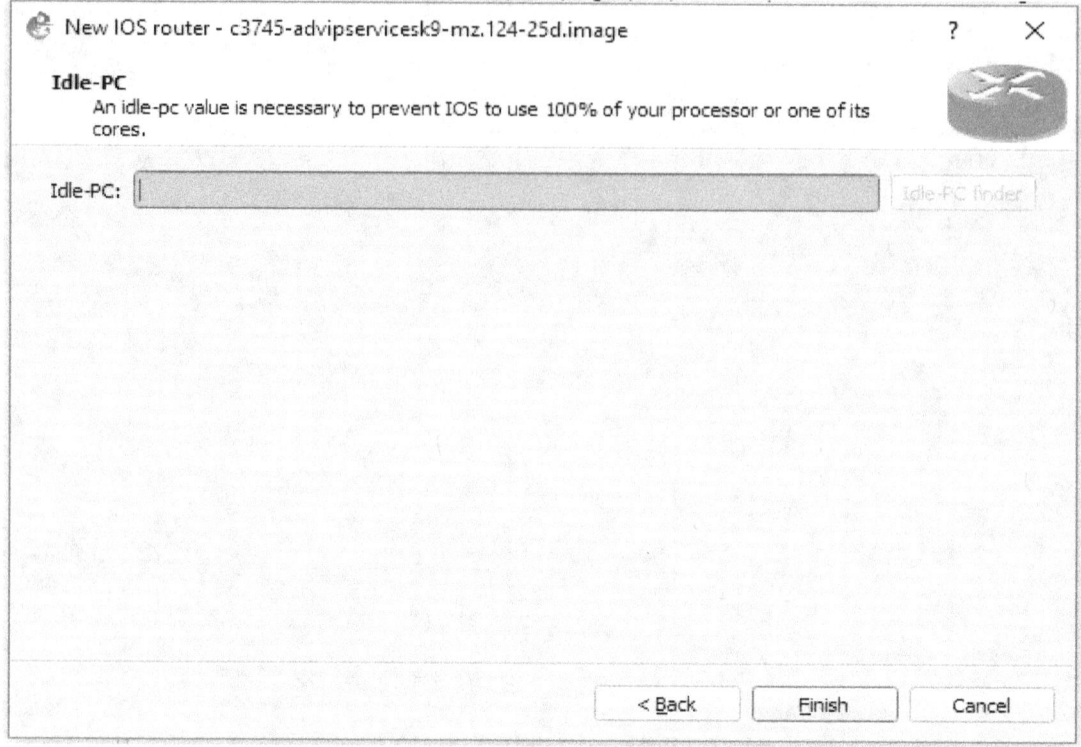

Figure 1.30: Idle-PC Value for EtherSwitch Router

Once the setting is complete, we have to accept by clicking "Apply" and then "OK".

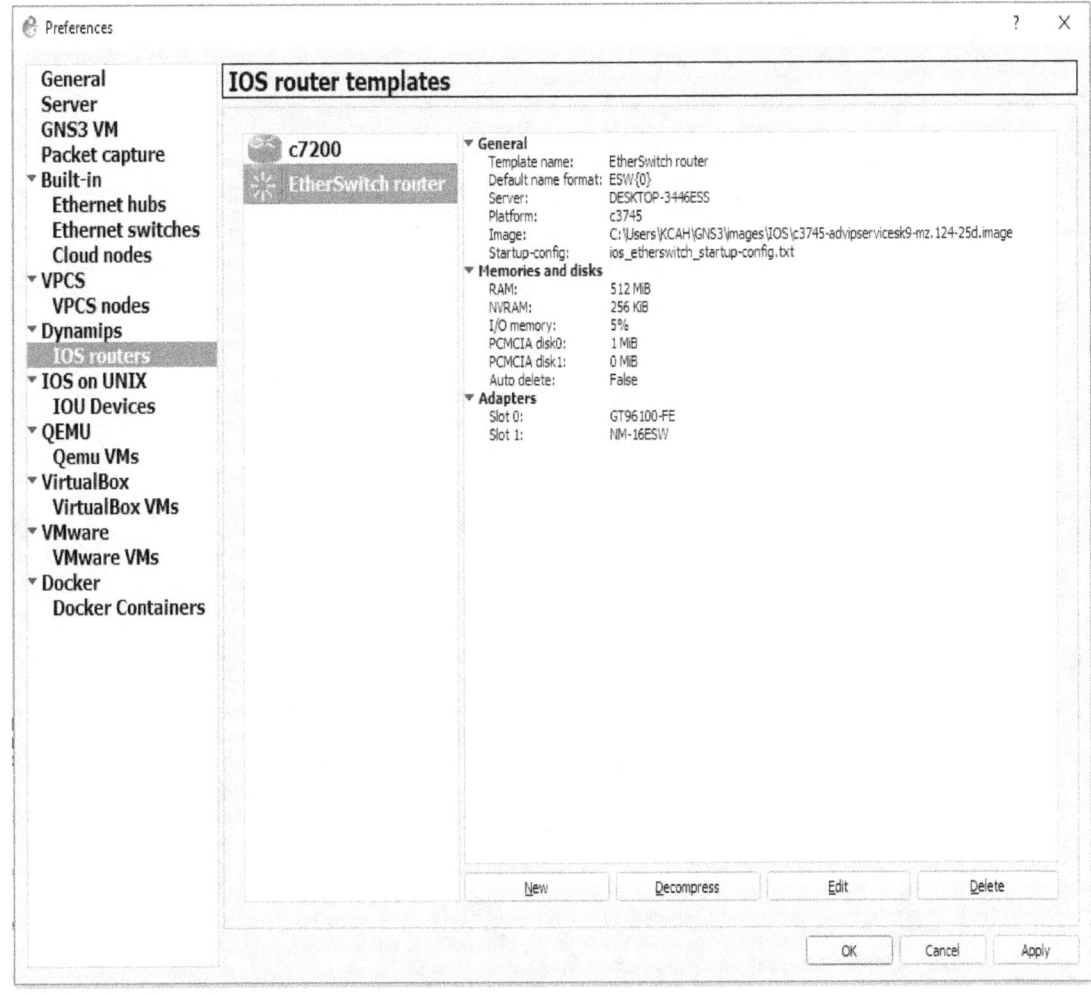

Figure 1.31: Imported IOS Image List

This completes the adding of IOS images to be used while working with GNS3. In case, a number of IOS images are required, the same procedure can be followed and added. Here, c7200 will be used as a router while EtherSwitch router is going to be used as a switch.

Further Reading

Cisco IOS images for Dynamips. (n.d.). Retrieved April 06, 2018, from https://docs.gns3.com/1-kBrTplBltp9P3P-AigoMzlDO-ISyL1h3bYpOl5Q8mQ/

GNS3 Labs | CCNP | CCNA Labs. (n.d.). Retrieved April 05, 2018, from http://commonerrors.blogspot.com/2012/12/gns3-installation-and-configuration-on.html

GNS3 Labs | CCNP | CCNA Labs. (n.d.). Retrieved April 05, 2018, from http://commonerrors.blogspot.

com/2014/10/add-router-ios-in-gns3-10-beta2.html

How to Add Router IOS Image in GNS3. (2016, July 16). Retrieved April 06, 2018, from https://protechgurus.com/how-to-add-router-ios-image-in-gns3/

Introduction. (n.d.). Retrieved April 05, 2018, from https://docs.gns3.com/1PvtRW5eAb8RJZ11maEYD9_aLY8kkdhgaMB0wPCz8a38/index.html

Chapter 2
Install and Configure VirtualBox

The Oracle VM VirtualBox Manager is an open source virtualization software developed by the Oracle. It allows running a wide range of guest operating systems including Windows, MAC, Solaris, and Linux. In this chapter, we will install the Oracle VM VirtualBox Manager and also learn to install CentOS 7 as the Guest Operating System.

Download and Install VirtualBox

The VirtualBox is available for download for Linux, Windows and Mac. At the time of writing this book, the latest version available for the Windows platform was 5.2.8. To download the latest version of the VirtualBox for the appropriate platform follow the URL https://www.virtualbox.org/wiki/Downloads which is the official download link.

When the download is complete, you can install it on the host which could be running any operating system.

Creating Virtual Machine in the VirtualBox

Once the installation of the VirtualBox is completed, launch the Oracle VM VirtualBox Manager and click on the "New" to create a new Virtual Machine. Here we will create a Virtual Machine for installing the CentOS 7 Operating System.

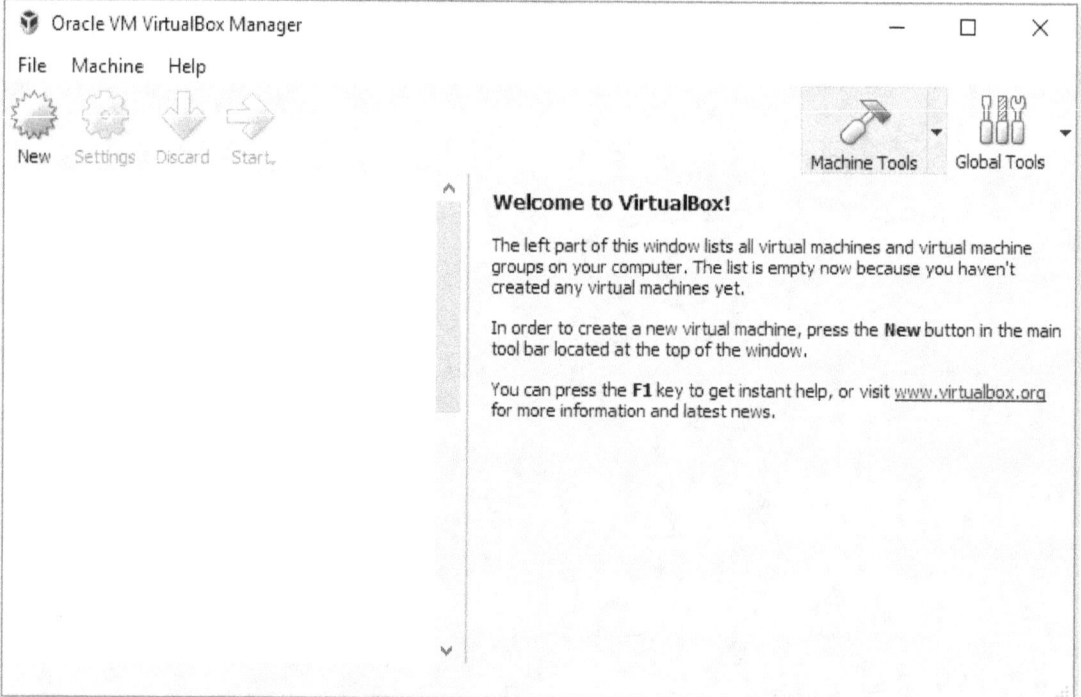

Figure 2.1: Oracle VM VirtualBox Manager's interface

In the following, we have to specify the name of the Virtual Machine, type of the Operating System and the version. As we are intending to install CentOS 7, the type is going to be Linux and then the version as Red Hat (64-bit), since CentOS is a Red Hat family. Click "Next" to continue.

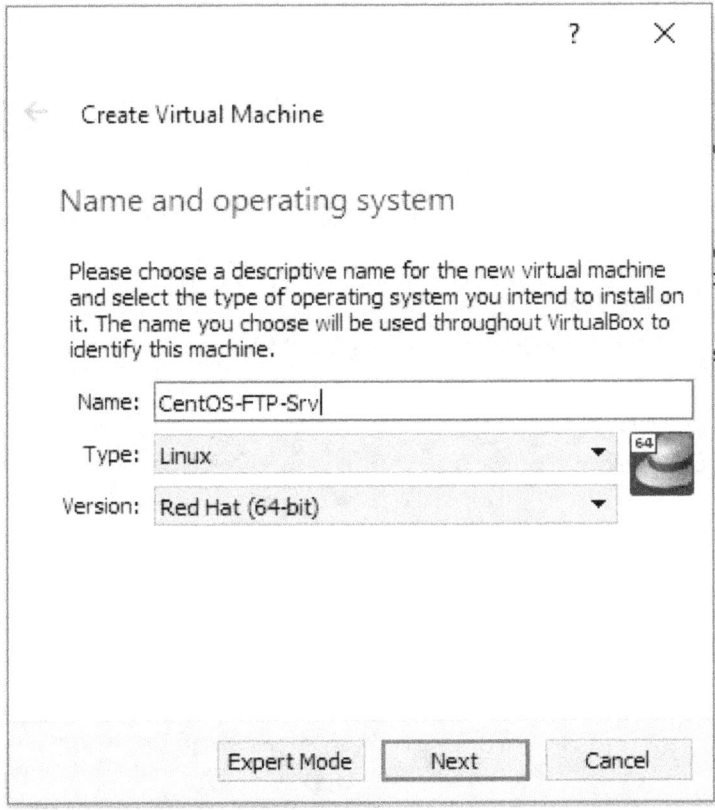

Figure 2.2: Assigning name and type of OS

In the following, VirtualBox automatically assigns memory size to the virtual Machine but if there is more memory to be spared, you can increase as per the need and availability. However, assigning lower than the recommended would pose issues. Click "Next" to continue.

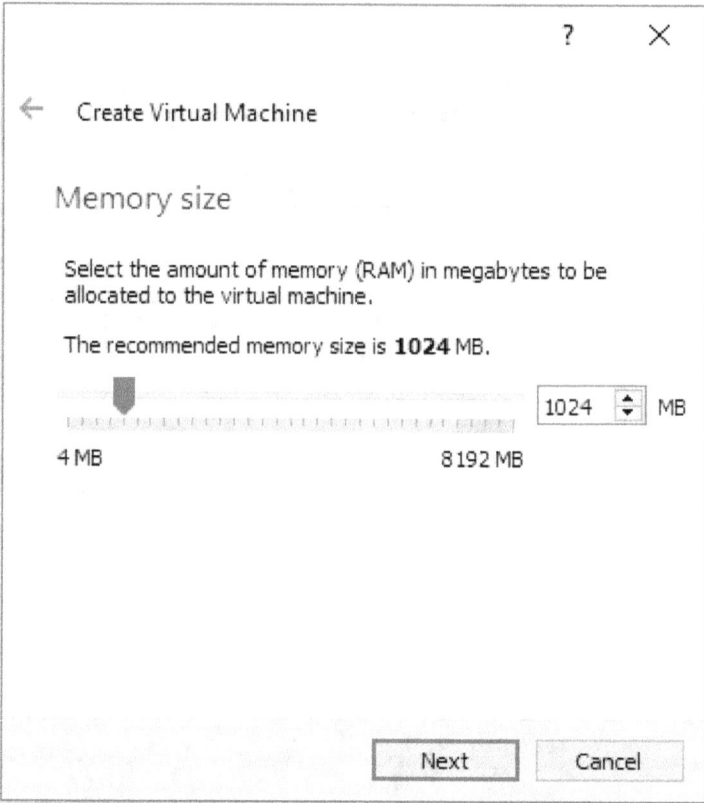

Figure 2.3: Allocating memory size for the VM

In this screen, if we already have a pre-configured Virtual Hard Disk (VHD) file, select the "Use an existing virtual hard disk file" and select the VHD that you want to use. If you want to create a new virtual hard disk, select "Create a virtual hard disk now" and click the "Create" button.

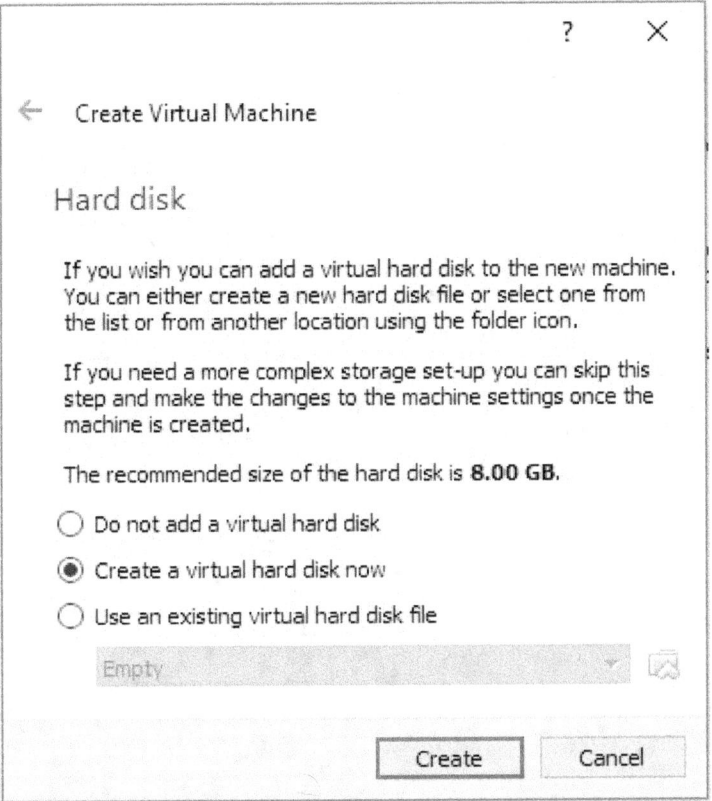

Figure 2.4: Virtual hard disk option

For the Hard disk file type, you can select any of the VHD disk types depending on your choice. By default, the disk type selected is VDI. Let's keep it to "VMDK (Virtual Machine Disk)" and click "Next".

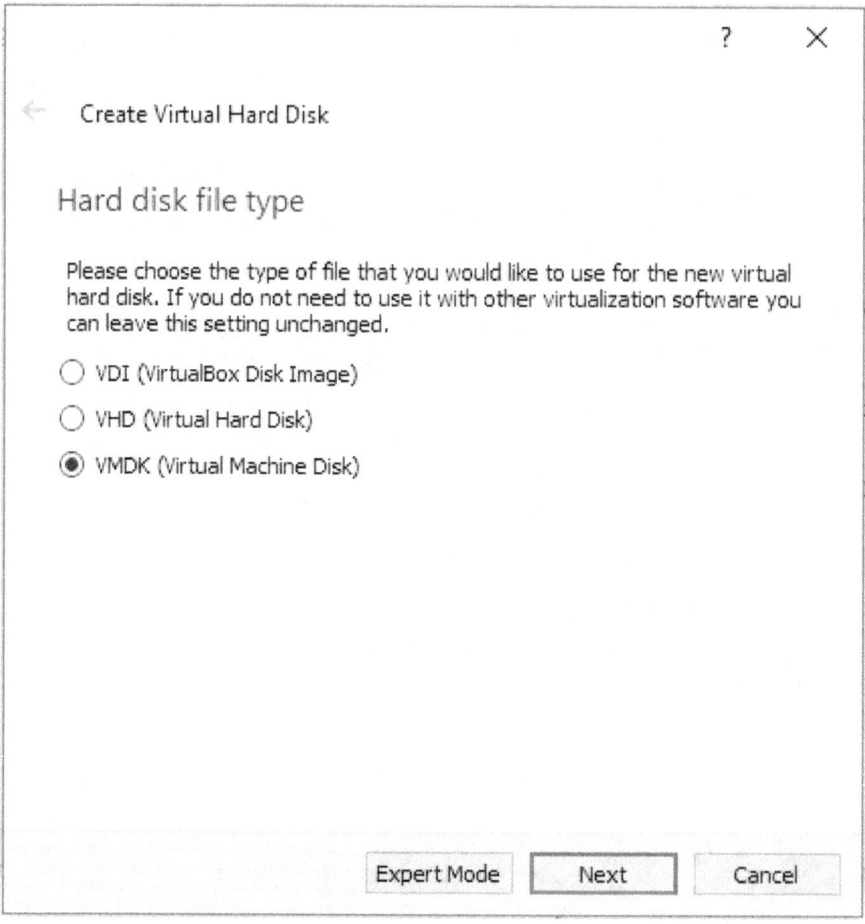

Figure 2.5: Virtual hard disk file type

In the following, choose "Dynamically allocated" and click "Next". If you select dynamically allocated option, VirtualBox will use the disk space from the hard disk only when the virtual machine's data increase. This option is suitable for the disk optimization.

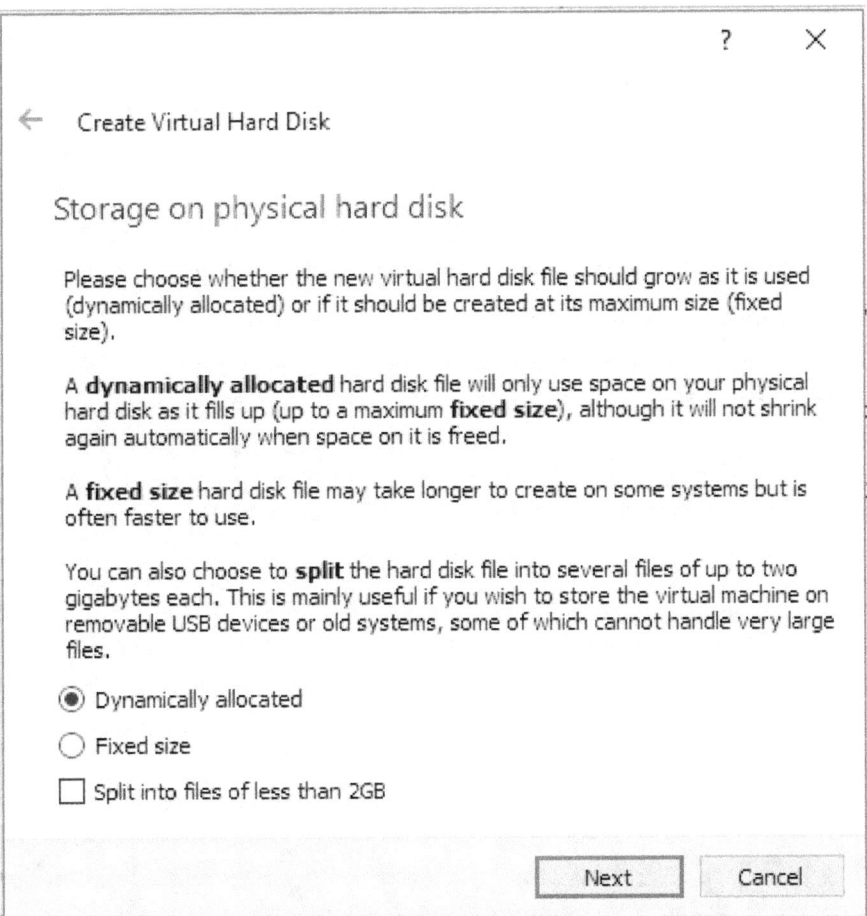

Figure 2.6: Choosing Dynamically allocated storage

Type the disk file name and select the location where you want to save it. Specify the size of the hard disk as well. Else, we can keep it to the defaults and click "Create".

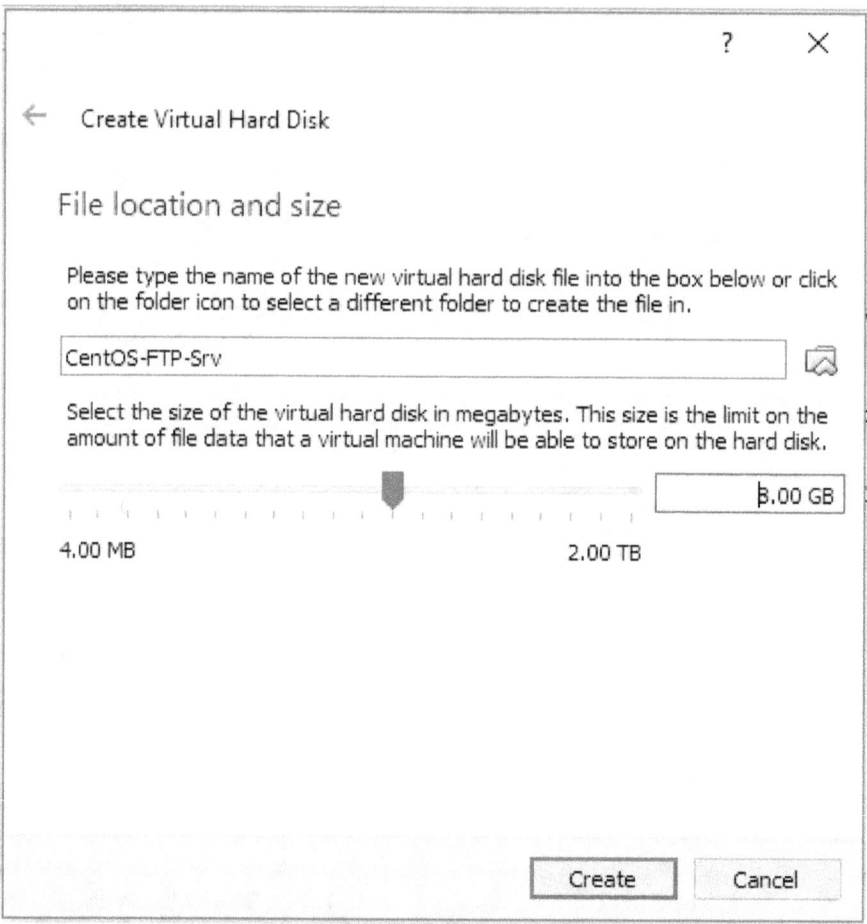

Figure 2.7: Virtual hard disk file location and size

We have completed creating a new virtual machine in VirtualBox for installing CentOS 7. The virtual machine will get listed as shown in the following figure.

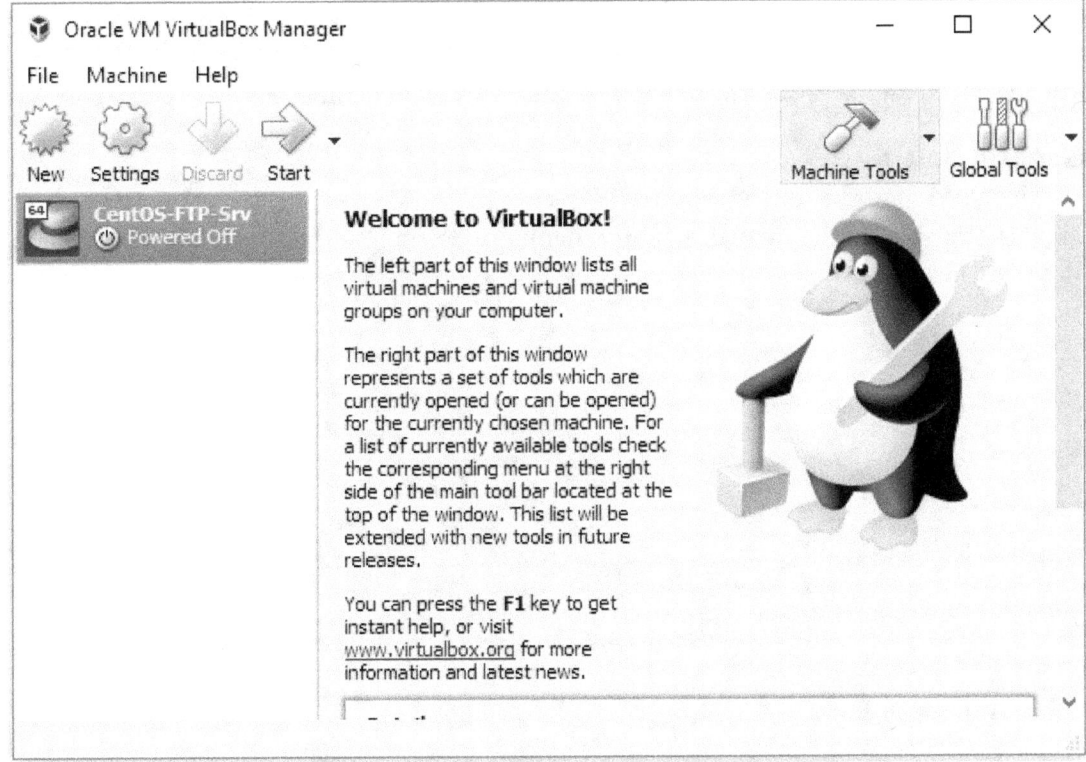

Figure 2.8: Created virtual machine listed

Virtual Machine Settings

In order for the virtual machine to function the way we expect it to, we have to perform some of the required changes in the settings under various sections. So, to change the settings for the particular virtual machine, we can Right-click and choose settings. This will launch the settings screen for the particular virtual machine.

General Settings

The first section of the setting window is "General", which has four tabs. The "Basic" tab allows us to specify the virtual machine name, operating system type, and the version of guest OS.

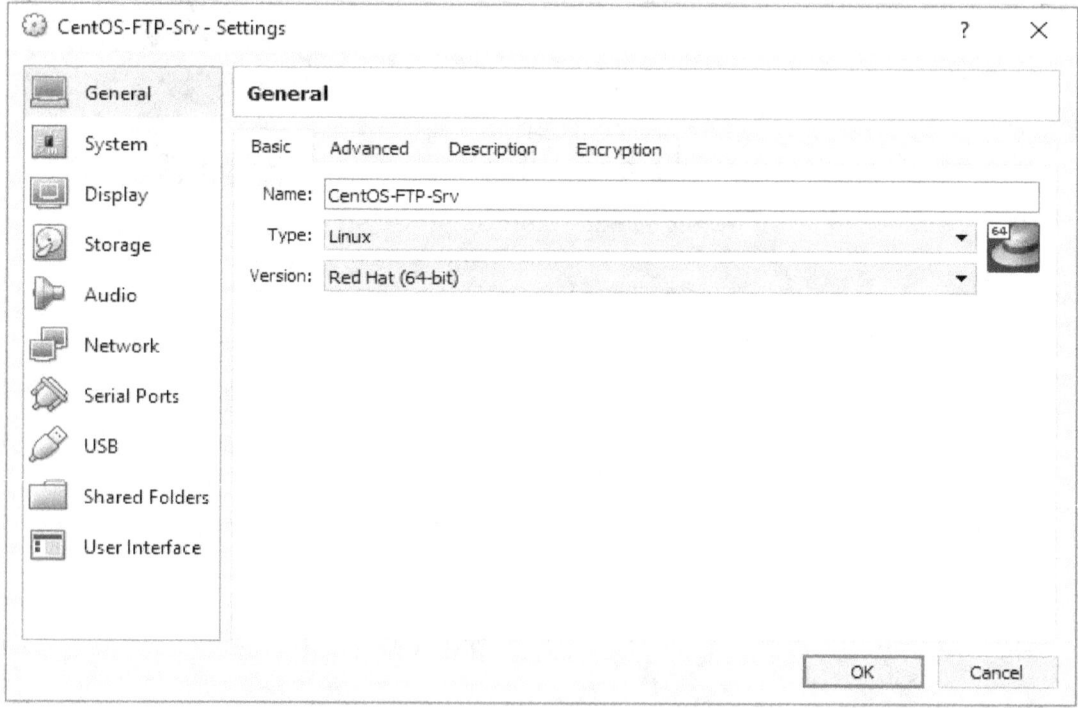

Figure 2.9: VM's general settings (Basic)

The "Advanced" tab allows specifying the snapshot folder location and drag-and-drop option between the host and guest machines. So, here the snapshot location is set to default, the "Shared Clipboard" and "Drag'n'Drop" are set to Bidirectional. Click OK to save the changes.

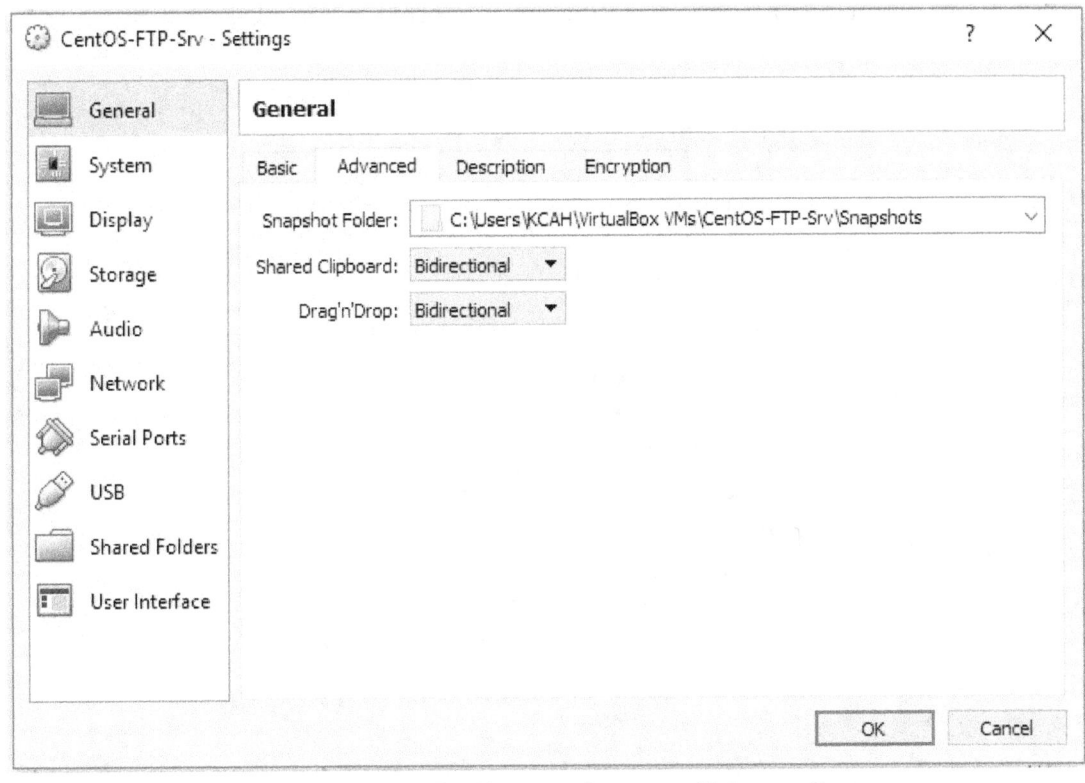

Figure 2.10: VM's general settings (Advanced)

System Settings

The "System" section of the setting has three tabs. In the "Motherboard" tab, we can adjust the allocated size of the memory and the order of bootable media to install the guest operating system. So, it becomes important for us to select and set the boot order based on our requirement. Here, the "Optical" is selected and is taken to the first.

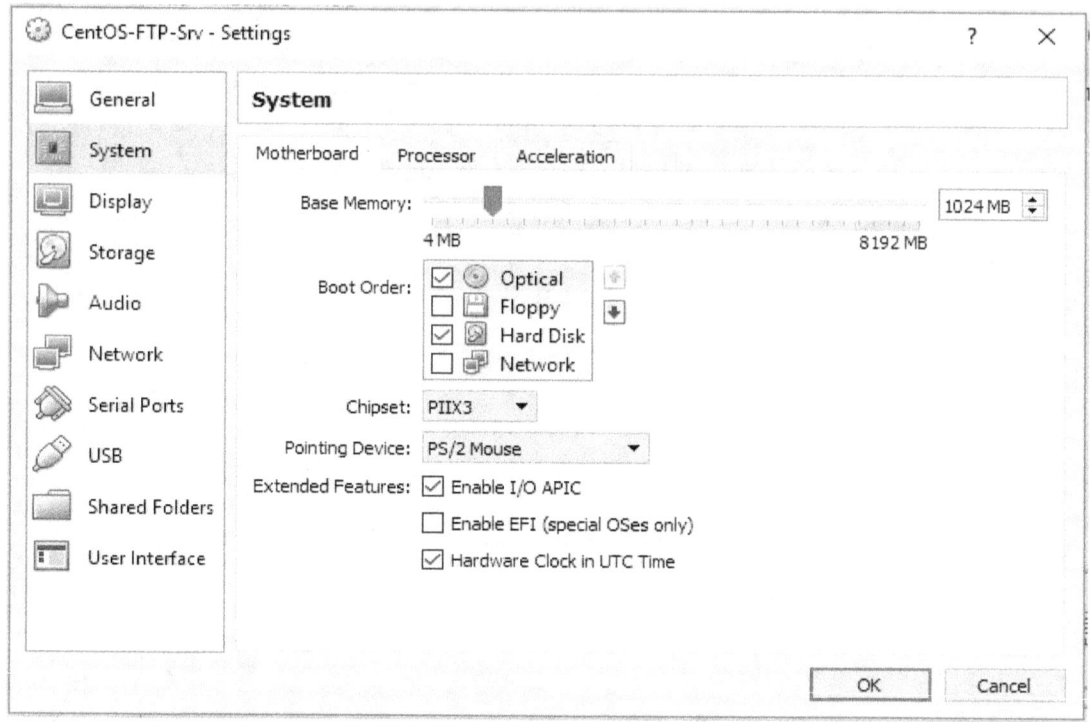

Figure 2.11: VM's system settings

In the Processor and Acceleration tabs, leave the settings to the default at this time. We will make changes to those settings whenever required.

Display Settings

In the "Display" section, we can leave the settings of all the tabs to the defaults for the time being.

Storage Settings

Under the "Storage" section, we can customize the settings related to the storage devices such as HDD, VHD, and CD/DVD. More importantly, since we are going to install the CentOS 7 as the Guest Operating System, we have to browse to a location where we have stored the ISO file of the CentOS 7.

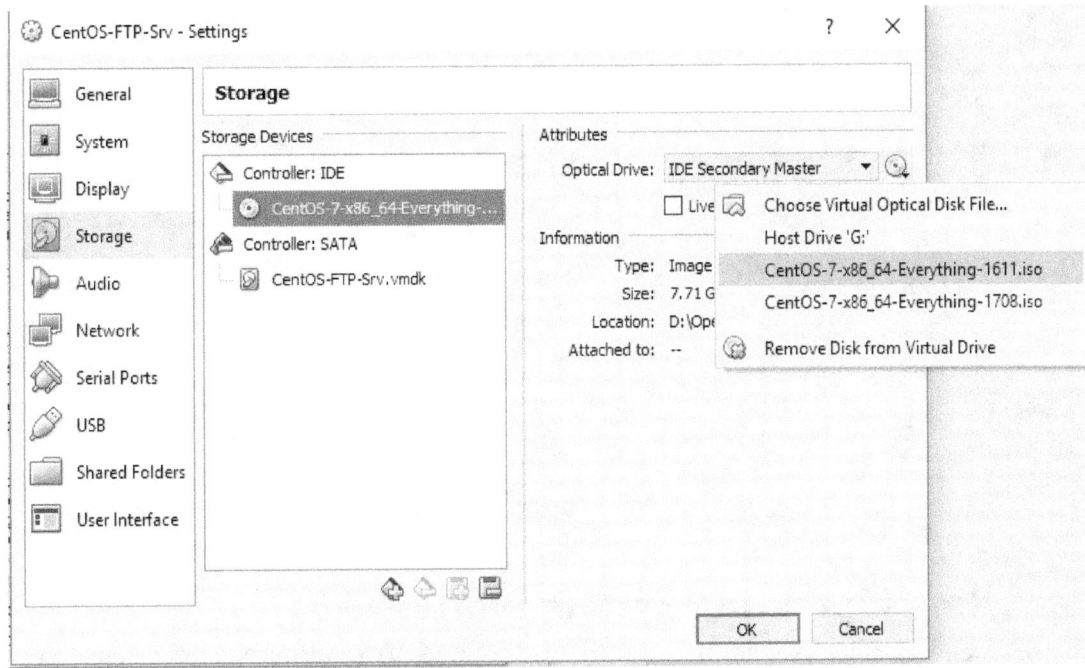

Figure 2.12: VM's storage settings

Network Settings

This section allows attaching the virtual machine to the desired network. Choose the network type that fulfills your requirement. As of now, we will leave it to the defaults and click "OK".

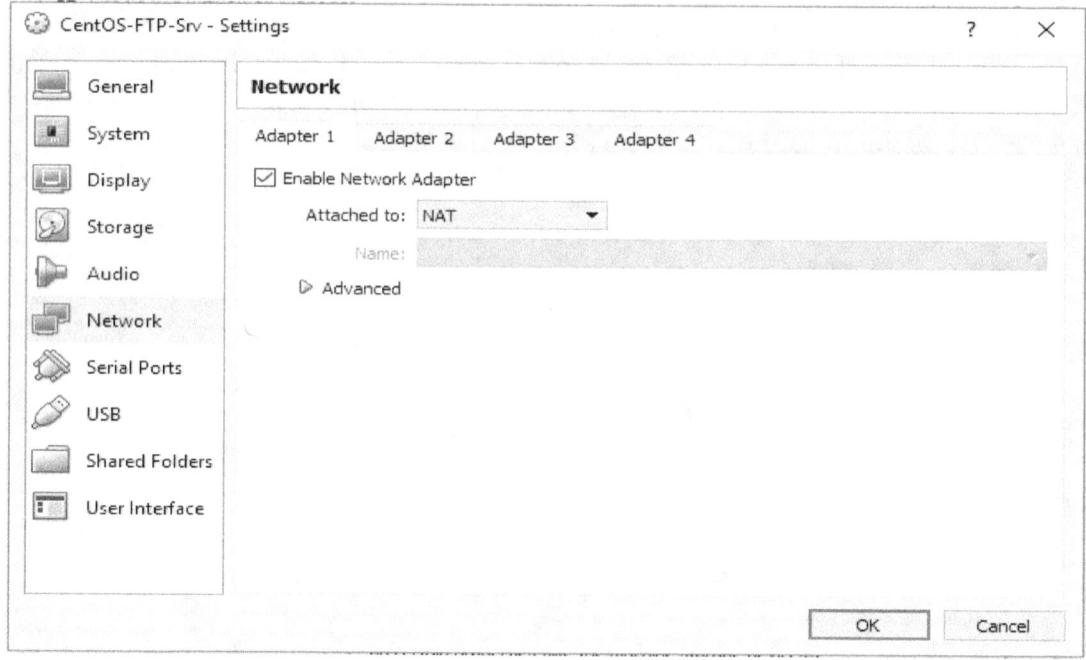

Figure 2.13: VM's network settings

Installing Operating System on the VM

In the previous steps, we have installed Oracle VM VirtualBox Manager, created a Virtual Machine and the configuration settings for the Virtual Machine was completed.

In this section, we will try to install the CentOS 7 as the operating system on the Virtual Machine (CentOS-FTP-Srv). Installing the CentOS 7 on the Virtual Machine is almost similar to installing on a host machine. Follow the steps indicated below to install on the Virtual Machine:

Before we start, we need to have in place, the installation media (DVD or ISO) of the guest operating system which we are intending to install. In our case, we need to have CentOS 7 DVD or the ISO file.

If you have more than one virtual machine, make sure that you select the particular virtual machine and click the "Start" button.

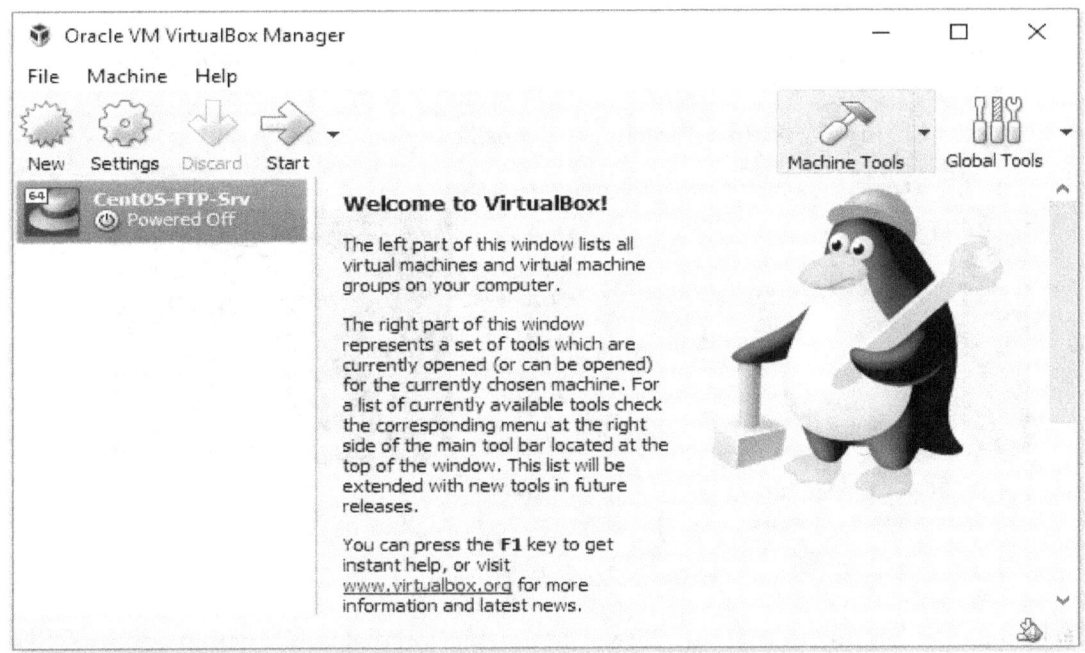

Figure 2.14: Selecting a VM to start

To use an ISO image file for CentOS 7 as an installation media, click "Devices", choose "Optical Drives" and then "Choose disk image" option. Browse and select the desired ISO image of CentOS 7 that you want to use as an installation source. This step is required only if you have not done the image selection in the previous steps.

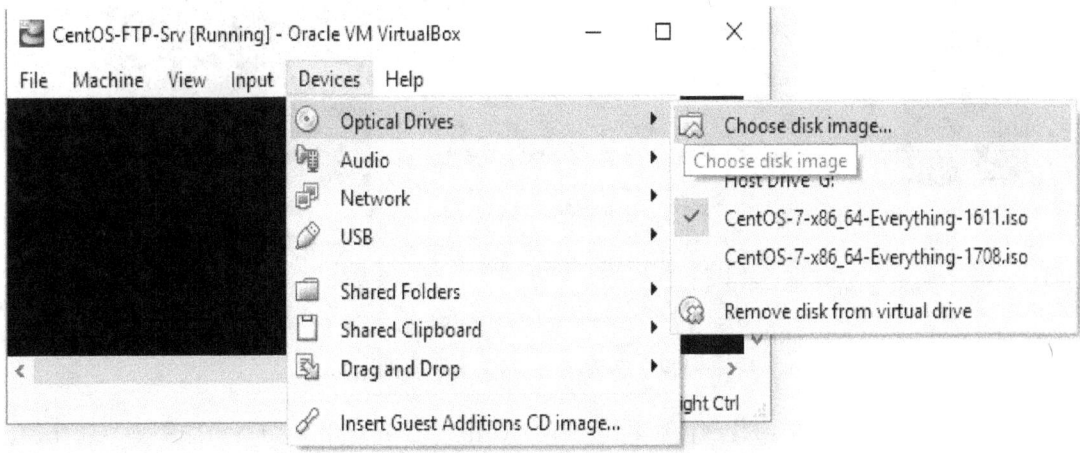

Figure 2.15: Selecting an ISO file for installation

You may consider resetting the virtual machine to restart it if the booting failed message appears. To reset the virtual machine, go to "Machines" and then click the "Reset".

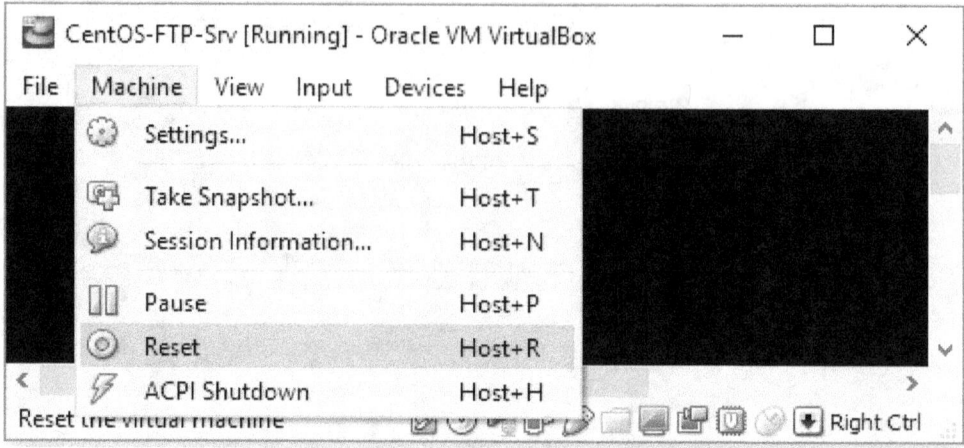

Figure 2.16: Resetting VM

Once the reset command is given, the reset confirmation dialog box would appear. Click "Reset" to confirm the reset action and then proceed with the installation.

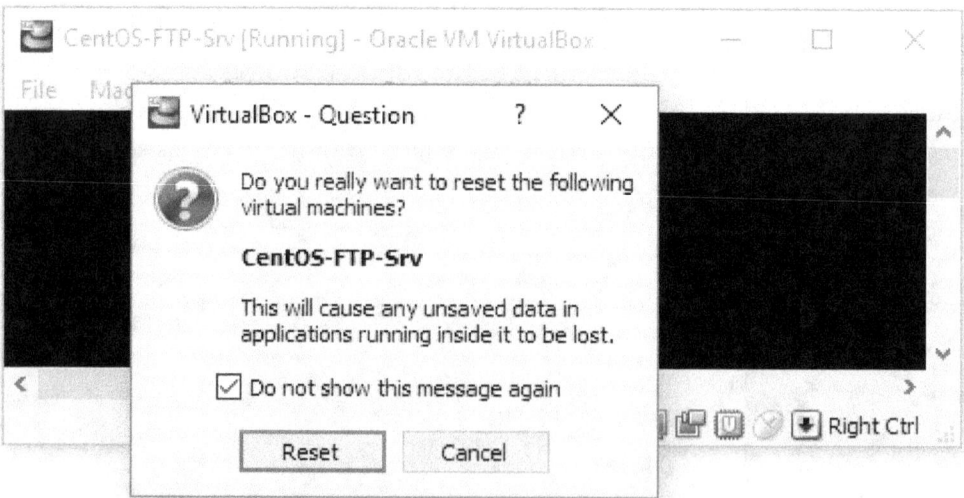

Figure 2.17: Resetting confirmation

From this point onwards, the procedure is similar to installing CentOS 7 as a host Operating System on a real hardware. For this virtual machine, the CentOS 7 minimal install is only required to be carried out.

If you require the virtual machine to fit the whole display screen use Ctrl (right) + F key combination, or if you want the virtual machine to be viewed in a scaled mode use Right Ctrl + C key combination. Also, in case if your mouse cursor gets caught up inside the Virtual Machine's window, use Ctrl (right) key to let you move and click out of the Virtual Machine's window.

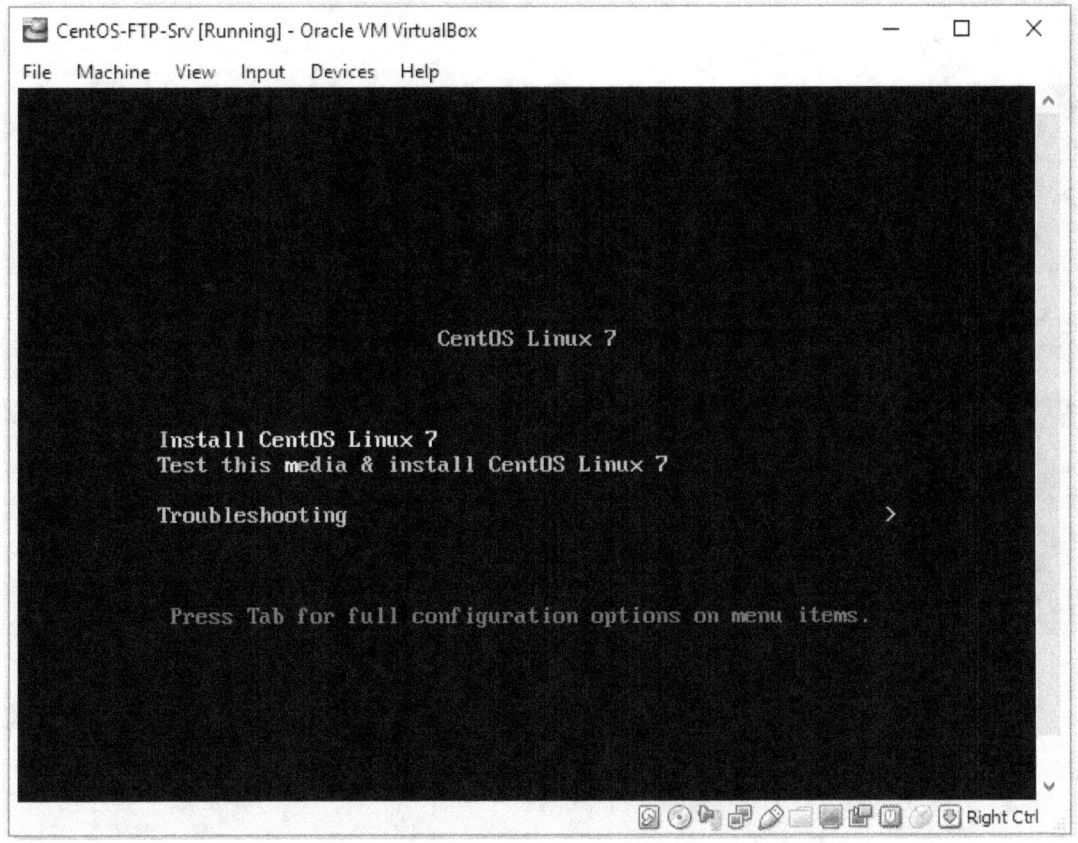

Figure 2.18: Installation process (started)

Once the installation is complete, you can start using the Virtual Machine by clicking "Reboot".

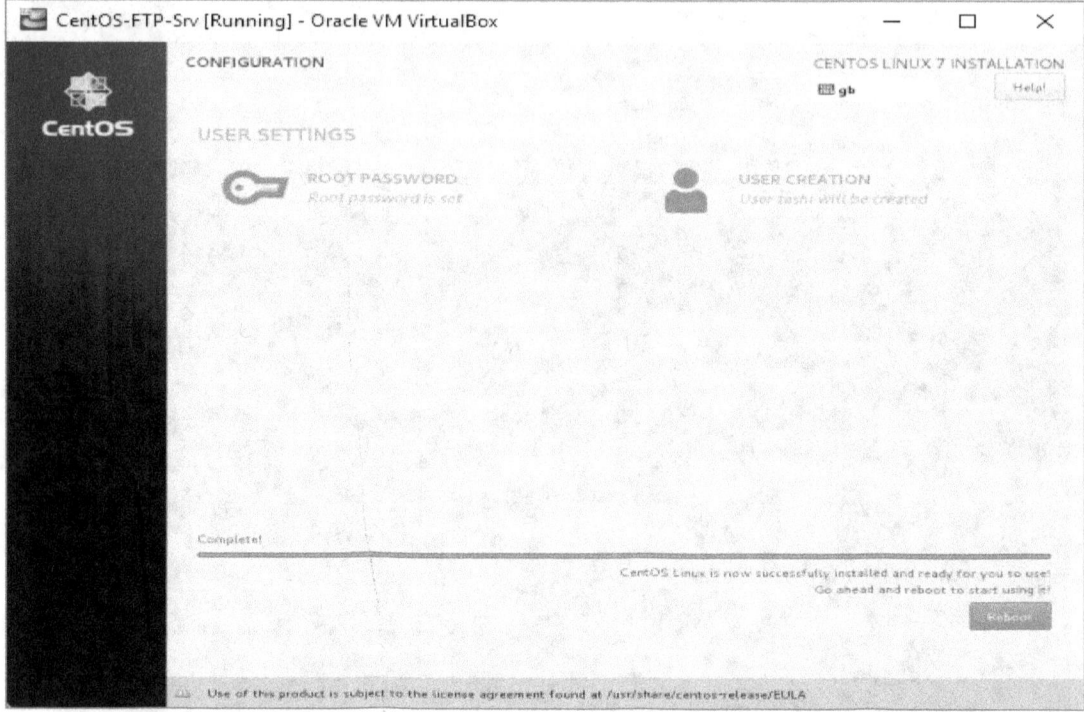

Figure 2.19: Installation process (completed)

The installation process is shown here as fast forward steps. The rest of the steps are skipped assuming that the learner is equipped with the basics of Linux Operating System installation. In case you are a beginner, get a copy of the book Linux System Administration (A Hands-on Guide).

Once the booting completes, the similar login screen would be displayed for the CentOS 7 minimal install.

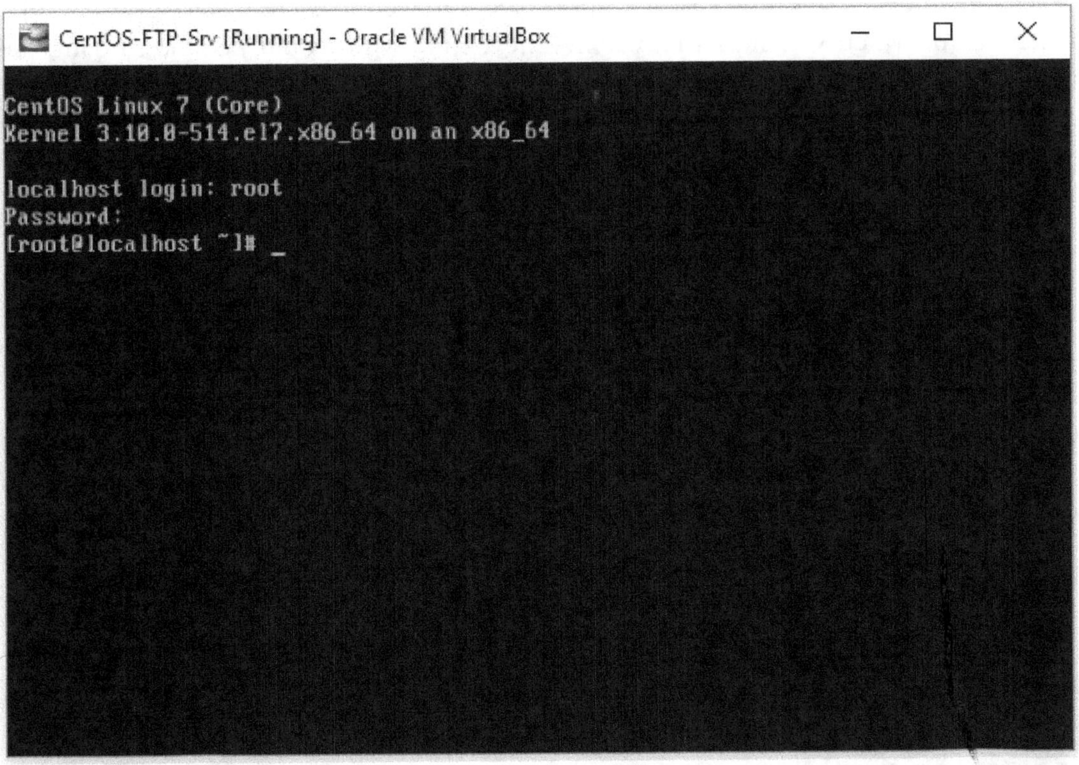

Figure 2.20: Login prompt of the VM

When you are done with the use of the Virtual Machine, you can close the Virtual Machine by choosing one of the options shown when you click to close the Virtual Machine window. Choosing the first option would save the current state of the virtual machine and when you start the machine next time, you would be able to continue from where you left the previous time. If you wanted to shutdown properly, the second option is used, while choosing the third option equates to switching off the system using the power off button on a real system. So, to shut down, choose the second option and click "OK".

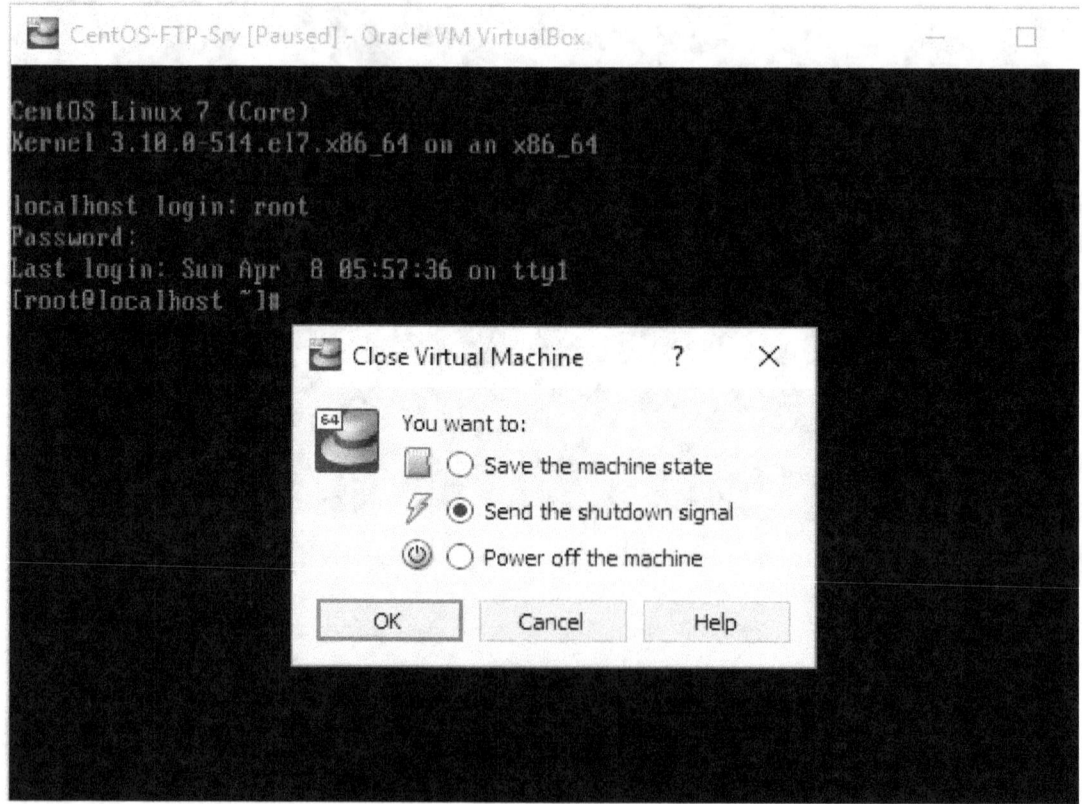

Figure 2.21: Shutting down the Virtual machine

Further Reading

P. (2016, July 27). CCNA. Retrieved from https://protechgurus.com/category/virtualbox/page/2/

Chapter 1. First steps. (n.d.). Retrieved from https://www.virtualbox.org/manual/ch01.html

Configuring virtual machines. (n.d.). Retrieved from https://www.virtualbox.org/manual/ch03.html

Creating a New Virtual Machine in VirtualBox. (n.d.). Retrieved from https://docs.oracle.com/cd/E26217_01/E26796/html/qs-create-vm.html

How to install VirtualBox on Windows 7, 8, and 10? (2018, January 29). Retrieved from https://www.smarthomebeginner.com/install-virtualbox-on-windows/

Installation details. (n.d.). Retrieved from https://www.virtualbox.org/manual/ch02.html

Installing and Configuring CentOS 7 on Virtualbox.

(2017, February 09). Retrieved from http://resources. infosecinstitute.com/installing-configuring-centos-7-virtualbox/#gref

ProTechGurus. (2016, July 28). How To Install Windows 10 on VirtualBox. Retrieved from https://protechgurus.com/install-windows-10-virtualbox/

Stegner, B. (2017, October 18). How to Use VirtualBox: User's Guide. Retrieved from https://www.makeuseof.com/tag/how-to-use-virtualbox/

Chapter 3
Creating Adaptors and Cloning VMs

Virtualize Network Test-Labs

Oracle VM VirtualBox Manager has made working with it very easy. We have to install a particular Guest Operating System on a Virtual Machine in VirtualBox only once; then it allows to clone the virtual machine saving our time and efforts. Also, if multiple VMs are to be used, we can also create virtual adaptors. In this chapter, we will look into creating VirtualBox Host-only Ethernet Adaptors and the clones of a VM.

Host-Only Networking

In Host-Only Adaptor the Host machine and the Guest VMs are on a private network, where the Host can provide DHCP services to the Guest VMs. In order to configure the Host-Only networking, we have to create a required number of VirtualBox Host-only Ethernet Adapter(s). The requirement of the VirtualBox Host-Only Ethernet Adaptors actually depends on the number of the guest VMs to be used for the networking.

By default, one VirtualBox Host-Only Ethernet Adaptor is created when the Oracle VM VirtualBox Manager application is installed. The VirtualBox Host-Only Ethernet Adaptor will be listed under the "Host-only Adaptor" as shown in the following figure.

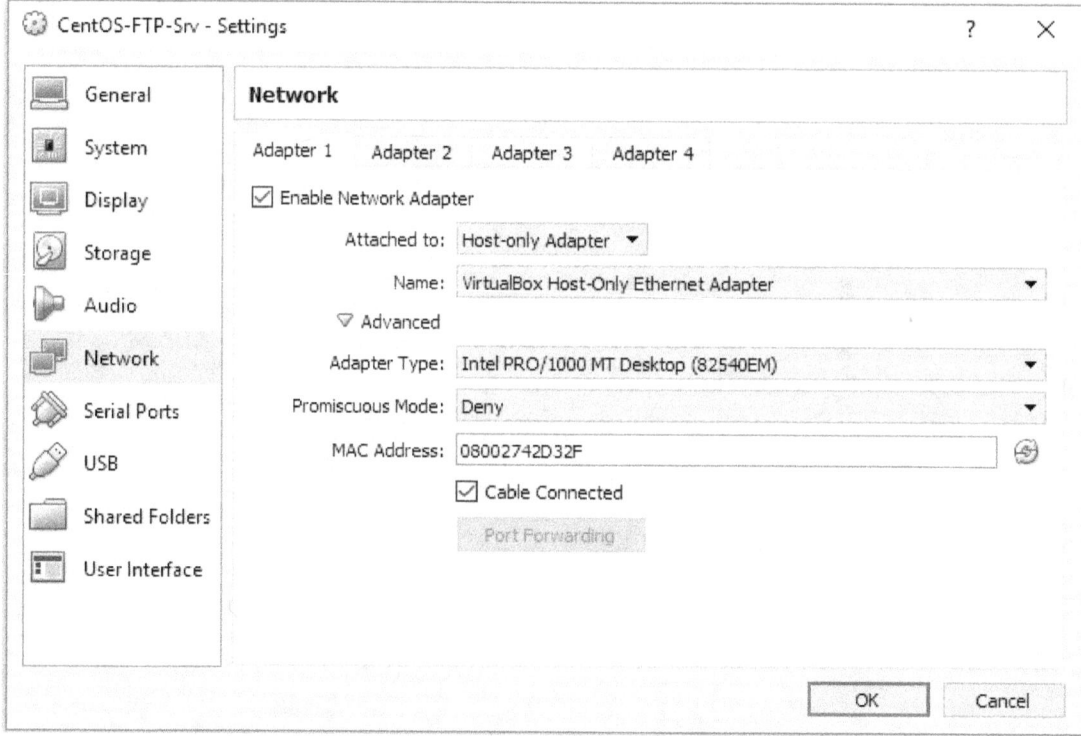

Figure 3.1: Default VirtualBox Host-Only Ethernet Adaptor

If more adaptors are required as per the networking plan, accordingly we have to create the required numbers. Assuming that we require seven VirtualBox Host-Only Ethernet Adaptors excluding the first adaptor, we will go onto the creation of the adaptors.

Creating VirtualBox Host-Only Ethernet Adaptors

To create the VirtualBox Host-Only Ethernet Adaptors, in the VirtualBox Manager Window (Figure 3.2), click on the "Global Tools".

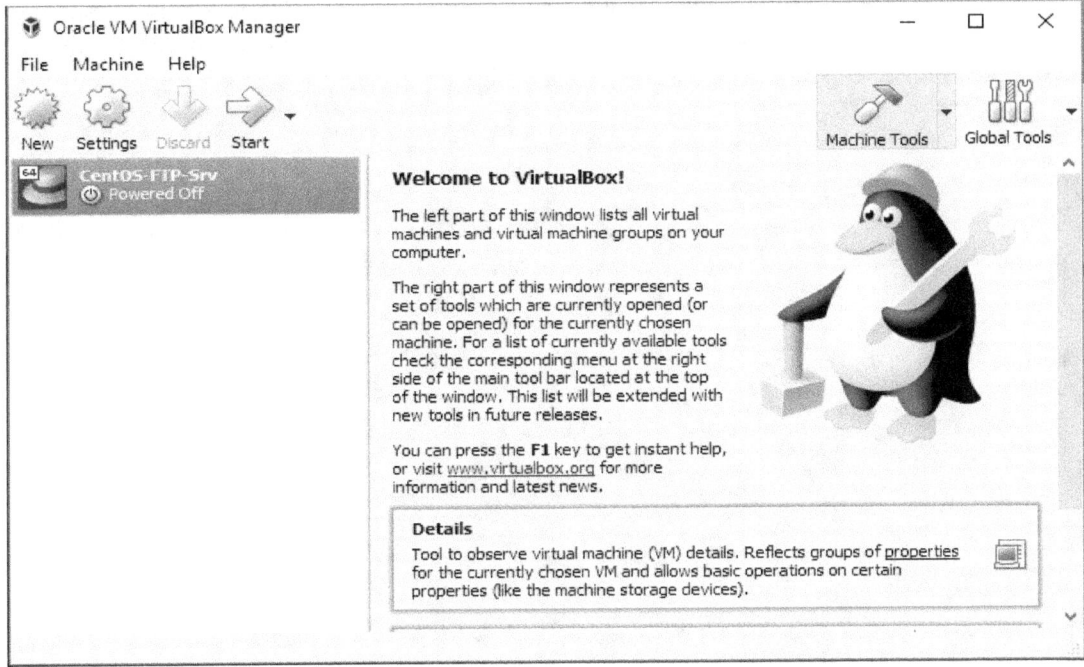

Figure 3.2: Oracle VM VirtualBox Manager window

Virtualize Network Test-Labs

The following screen (Figure 3.3) would be displayed. By default, "Host network Manager" tab would be selected and the "Create", "Remove" and "Properties" buttons would be featured. This would enable us to create new adaptors, remove the existing ones and check their properties accordingly. In Figure 4.3, the first adaptor, VirtualBox Host-Only Adaptor is listed and now we can click the "Create" button to create the second adaptor and add to the list.

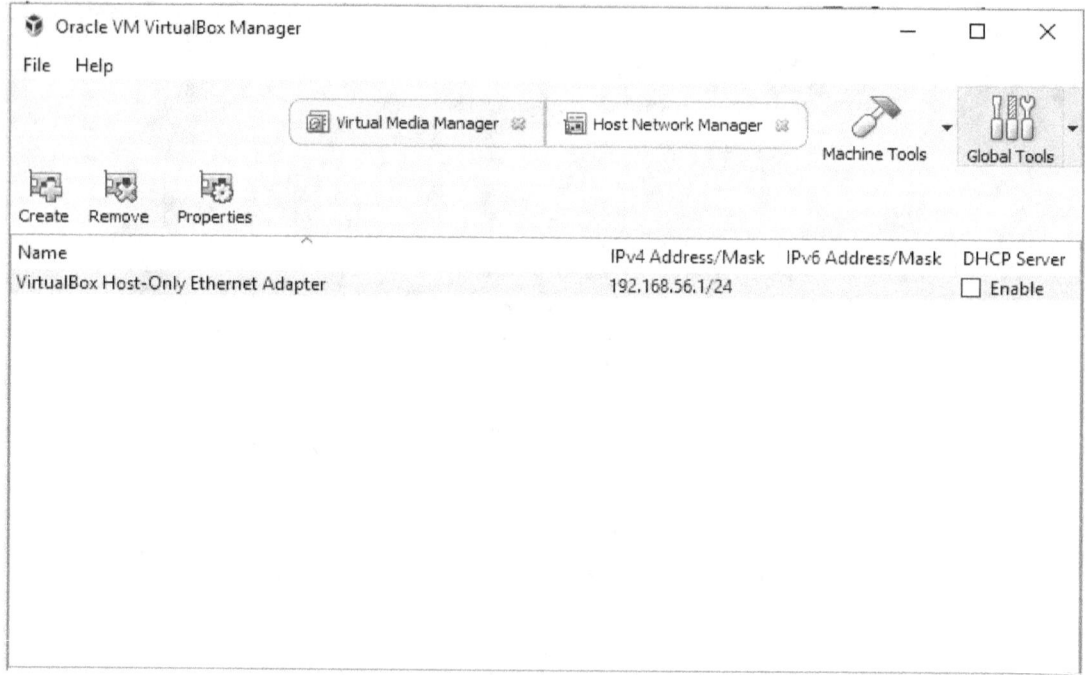

Figure 3.3: Host Network Manager window

After clicking the "Create" button, the second adaptor would be created and added to the list. The second adaptor would be indicated by "VirtualBox Host-Only Ethernet Adaptor #2". The following figure (Figure 3.4) shows two VirtualBox Host-Only Ethernet Adaptors, the first and the second respectively. However, unlike the second adaptor, the first doesn't have any number indication.

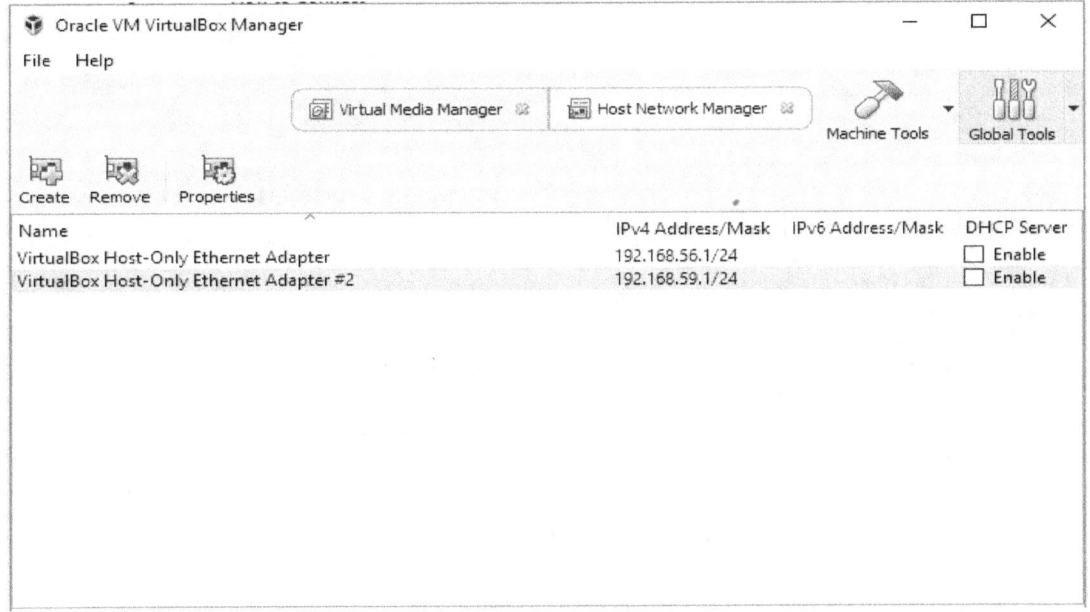

Figure 3.4: VirtualBox Host-Only Ethernet Adaptors

Following the same steps, create the remaining five adaptors by clicking the "Create" button consecutively. Finally, you would be having seven adaptors as shown in the figure below:

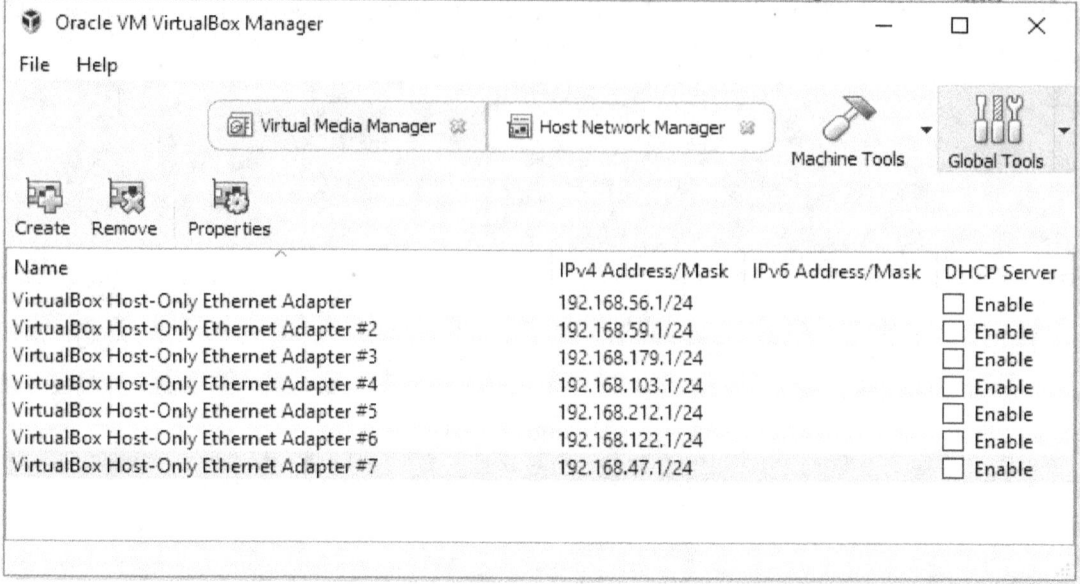

Figure 3.5: All the VirtualBox Host-Only Ethernet Adaptors listed

Removing VirtualBox Host-Only Ethernet Adaptors

In case, we have more than the required number of adaptors, we can delete the excess adaptors by selecting the adaptors and clicking the "Remove" button. Any time creating new adaptors or deleting the extra can be done from this window.

Viewing Properties of the Adaptors

Selecting an adaptor and clicking the "Properties" button gives options either to "Configure Adaptor Automatically" or to "Configure Adaptor manually". Selecting either one requires some network setting details as per the existing network or the planned network. In the following, VirtualBox Host-Only Ethernet Adaptor #7 is chosen and the properties are displayed:

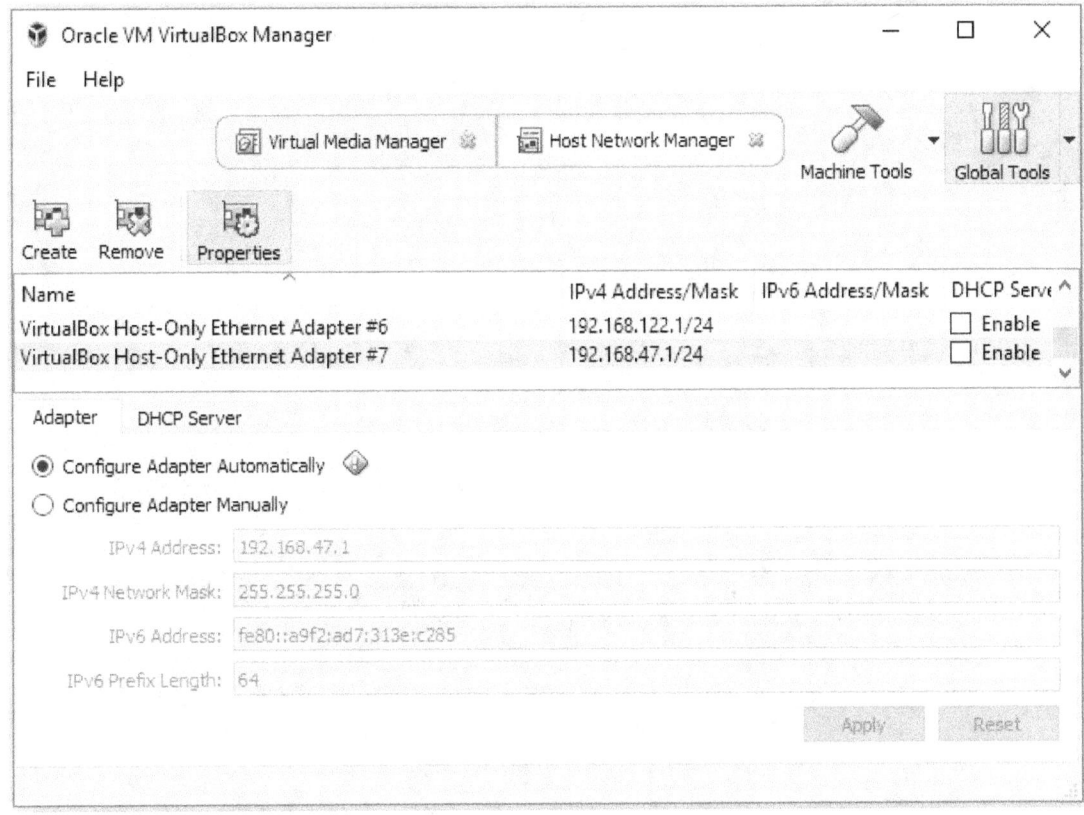

Figure 3.6: Configuring Host-Only Ethernet Adaptor automatically

Choosing "Configure Adaptor Automatically" and enabling DHCP Server would allow the VirtualBox to assign IP addresses and on the other hand, if we wanted to configure adaptor automatically using the DHCP Server other than the in-built VirtualBox's DHCP Server, then it is recommended to choose "Configure Adaptor Automatically" and leave the "Enable Server" option unchecked in the DHCP Server tab as shown below:

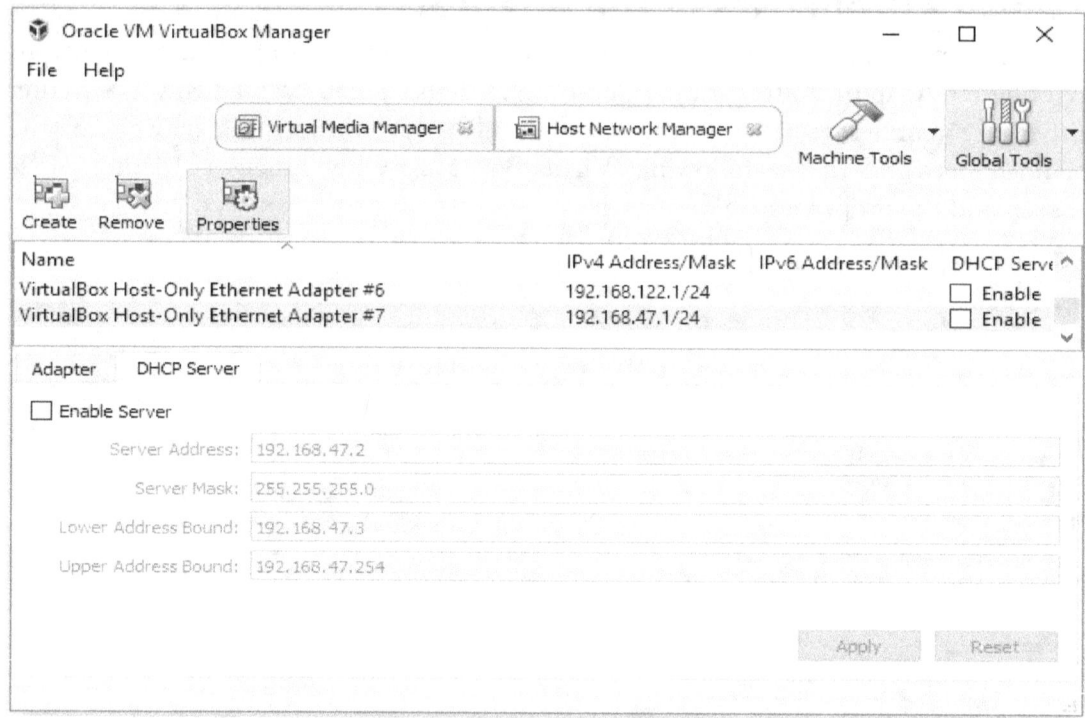

Figure 3.7: Disabling VirtualBox's in-built DHCP Server

The VirtualBox Host-Only Ethernet Adaptors can be set to "Configure Adaptor Automatically" without enabling the VirtualBox's in-built DHCP Server, so that we can use our own DHCP Server to assign the IP addresses without the interference of the VirtualBox's in-built DHCP Server.

Virtual Machine (VM) States

When the attempt is made by the users to close the running Virtual Machine in the VirtualBox by either clicking the close button or by pressing the Host and the Q key combination, the VirtualBox would prompt the user with the options as shown in the following figure (Figure 3.8):

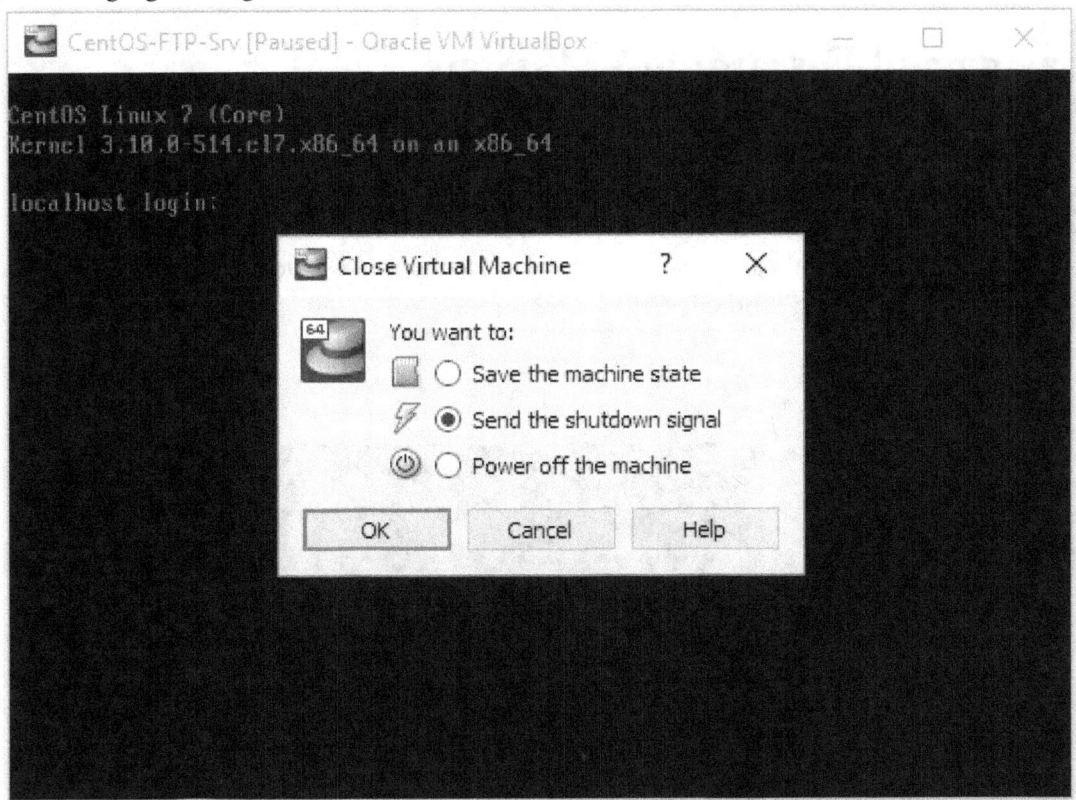

Figure 3.8: Options for closing Virtual Machine

Depending on your need, choose one of these options and choose OK. The description of each of these states are explained below:

- **Save the machine state:** The virtual machine will be stopped from running and VirtualBox completely saves the VM's state to the user's local disk. The virtual machine will resume operation and the programs will be available from the point where you left, when you start it again. The user's computer will resume operation and the programs will still be available.
- **Send the shutdown signal:** This option will send the ACPI shutdown signal to the Virtual Machine, which is similar to pressing the power button on a real computer.
- **Power off the machine:** This option also permits the virtual machine to stop running but it does not save the state of the VM. This option is similar to pulling

the power cord from the real computer hardware which would cause potential loss of information. In the next start, the system will have to go through an extensive inspection of the virtual disks. The same results as powering off the machine will be achieved when pressing the "Discard" button in the main window of VirtualBox.

Saving and Discarding VM's State

While working with the VirtualBox, it pays to save the machine state sometimes and start the VM whenever we need. This saves the time taken for not having to start the VM all over again every time we require to work. So, to save the machine state, choose the VM which you wanted to save its state and click on the close button. Upon clicking the close button, the options as shown in the following figure would be displayed; choose "Save the machine state" and click "OK."

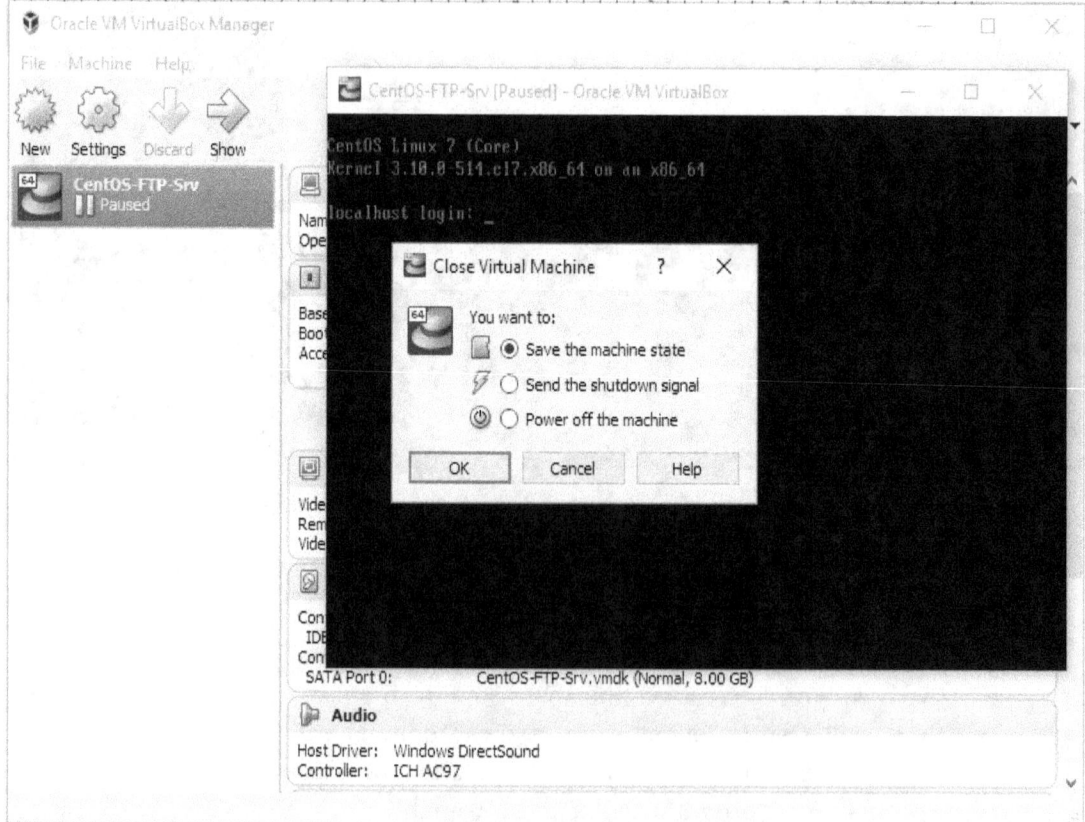

Figure 3.9: Saving the virtual machine state

Once the machine state is saved, the corresponding VM state would appear as saved in the VirtualBox VM list as shown in the following figure (Figure 3.10):

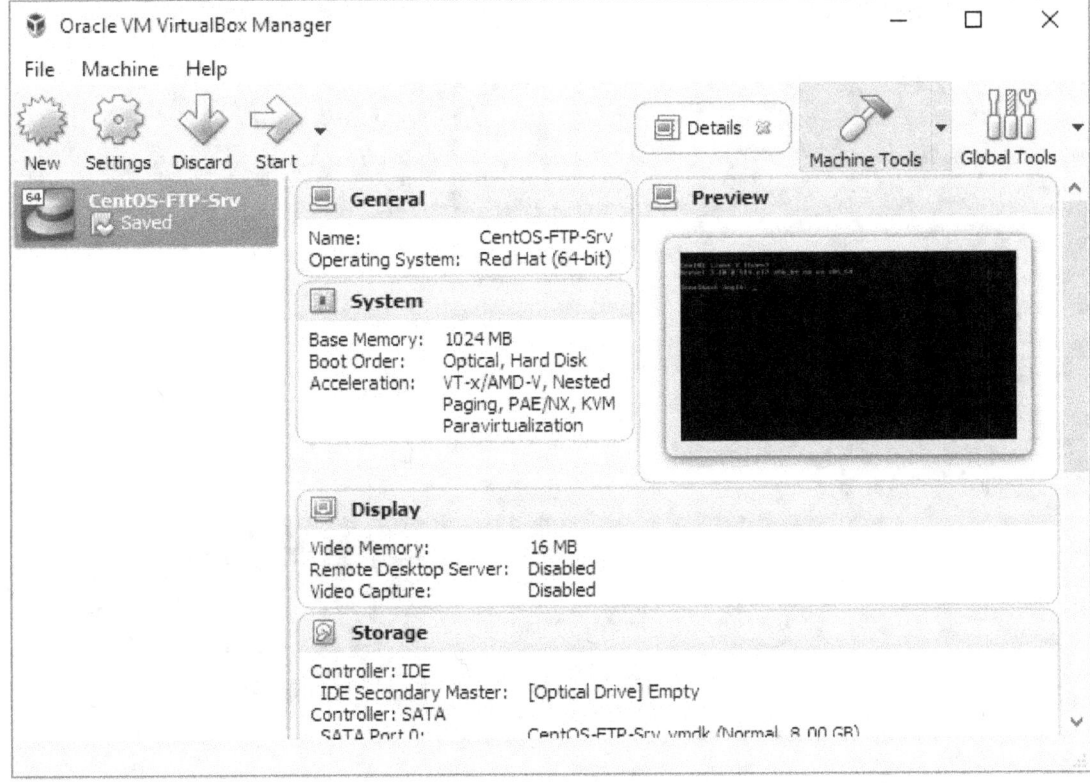

Figure 3.10: Saved machine state

If the machine state had been saved successfully, we will find the "Discard" button enabled in the display menu. So, if you wish to discard the saved machine state, simply clicking the "Discard" button would remove the saved details of the VM and the next time when we require to work with the VM, we won't be able to continue from the point where we left earlier.

Cloning VMs

Cloning a Virtual Machine will result in the creation of an exact copy of the selected virtual machine in the VirtualBox. Cloning saves the time that otherwise would be spent in creating a virtual machine with similar features and settings. Cloning a virtual machine is useful in a number of ways. For example, if you wanted to do some experiments with a virtual machine configuration or want to test the different guest operating systems or want to take the backup a VM, creating a clone of a virtual machine would be a wise decision. In this section, we will learn to make clones of the virtual machines. Assuming that the CentOS on the virtual machine (CentOS-FTP-Srv) is required to be cloned, we will proceed with the cloning of the virtual machine.

Virtualize Network Test-Labs

Launch the Oracle VM VirtualBox Manager and select the desired virtual machine from the list to be cloned, if in case you have multiple virtual machines created. In the figure 3.11, CentOS-FTP-Srv is going to be cloned. Since it is only the virtual machine, by default it gets selected.

> *Before you start to clone, make sure that the selected virtual machine is not in the "Saved" sate. If it is in the saved state, we have to discard the saved state and then only start to clone.*

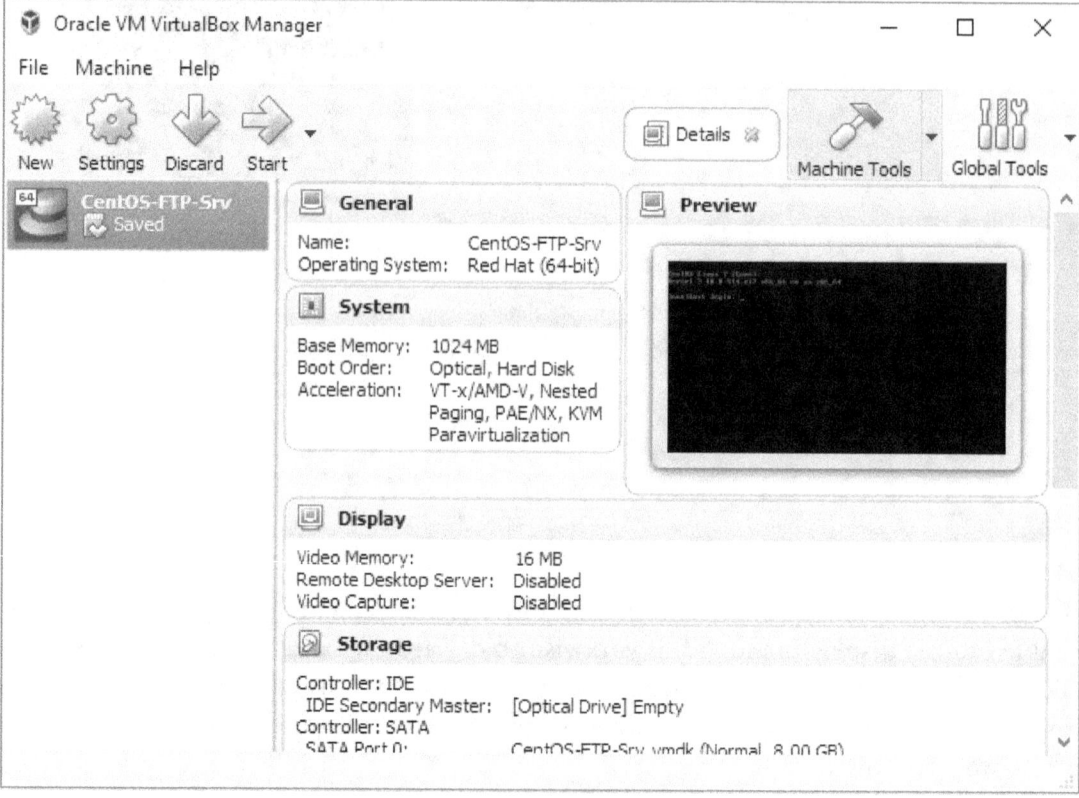

Figure 3.11: Selected Virtual Machine in the list

To create a clone, after selecting, right-click and click Clone in the options provided as shown in the figure 3.12:

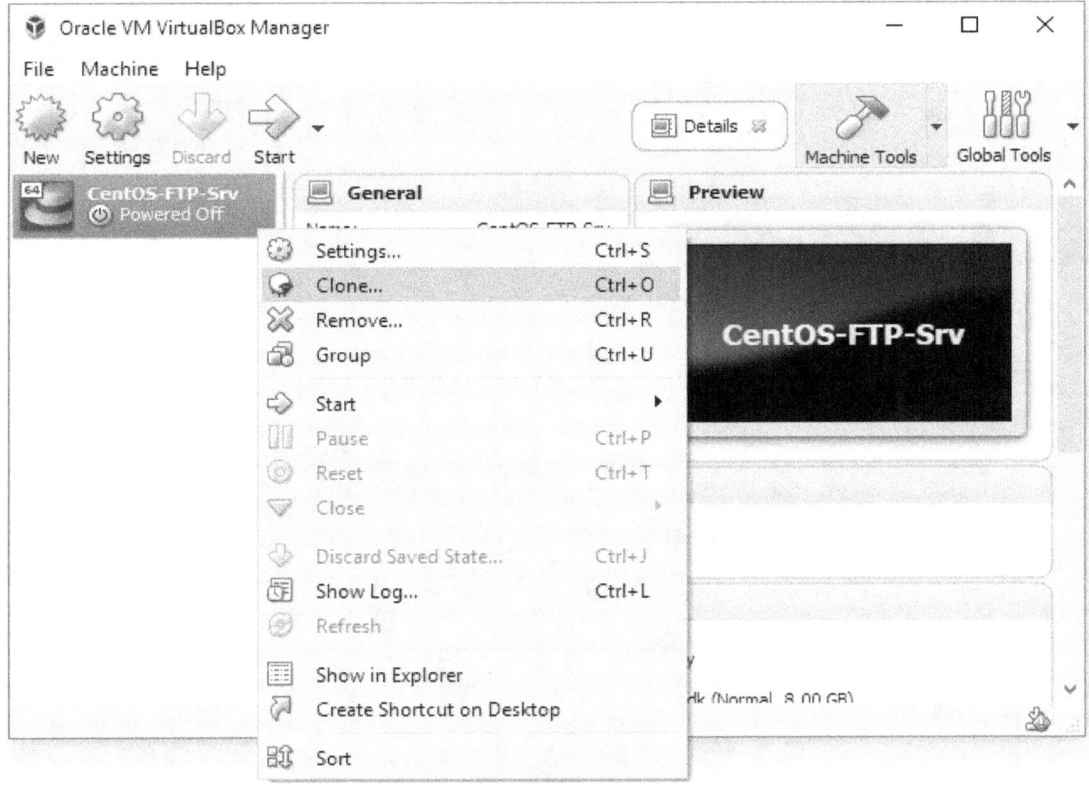

Figure 3.12: Showing the clone option

Virtualize Network Test-Labs

You will be prompted to choose a name for the clone and asked whether you want to reinitialize the MAC of the network card(s) included with the machine. In the virtual machine name field, you can set to something different from the machine (base) where you are cloning from and must choose the "Reinitialize the MAC address of all network cards" option. Here, the name is set to CentOS-DHCP-Srv and the option is chosen to reinitialize the MAC addresses of the network cards as shown in the figure 3.13. Click "Next" to continue.

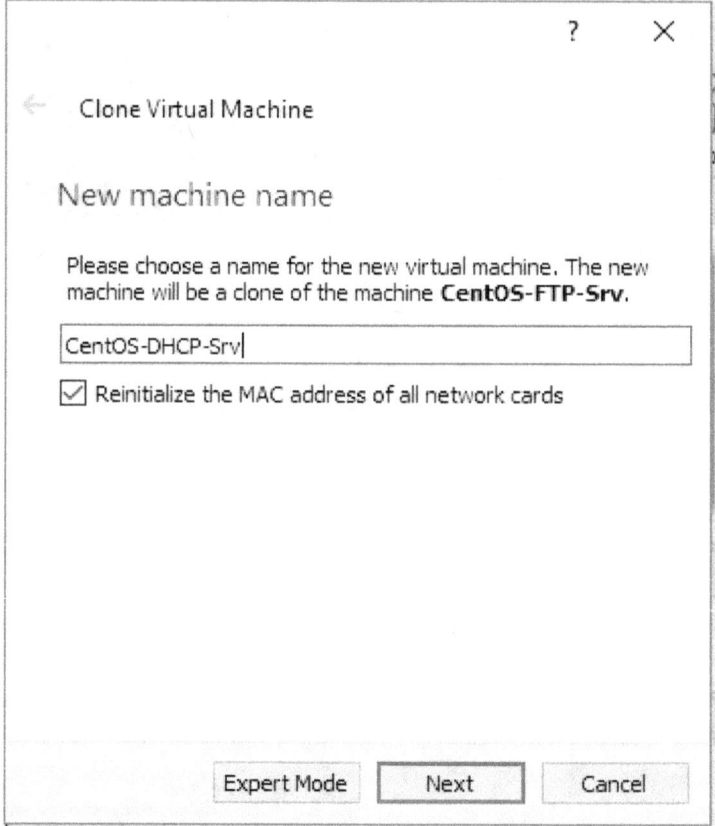

Figure 3.13: Naming the clone and reinitializing network cards

We have the option to either choose the "Full clone" or the "Linked clone". Choosing the "Full clone" would create independent disks for the cloned virtual machine which will enable us to move resources easily around. So, choose the "Full clone" option and click the "Clone" button to proceed.

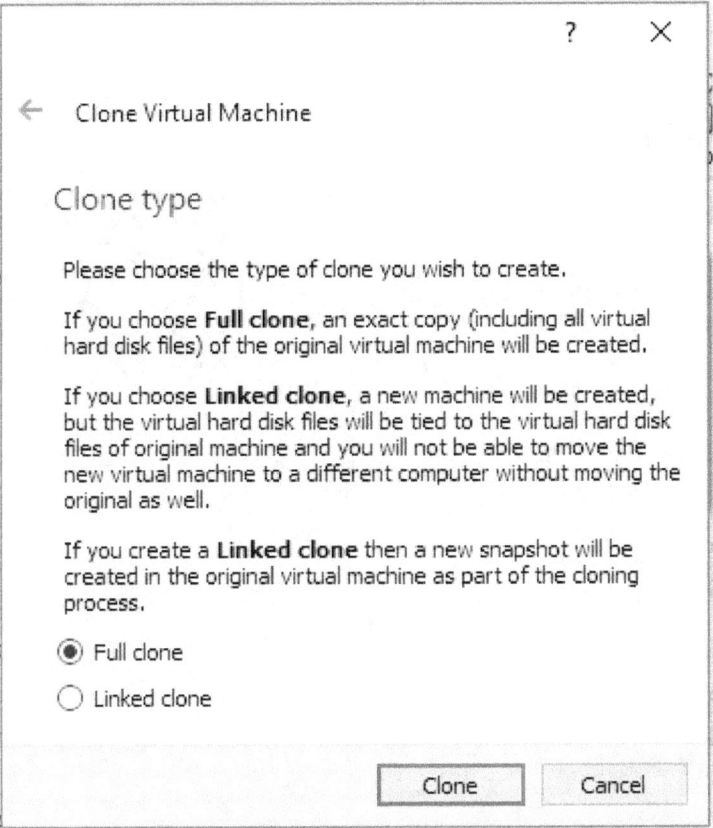

Figure 3.14: Choosing the Clone Type

Upon the completion of the cloning process, the cloned virtual machine will appear in the virtual machine list with the name which we have specified to change.

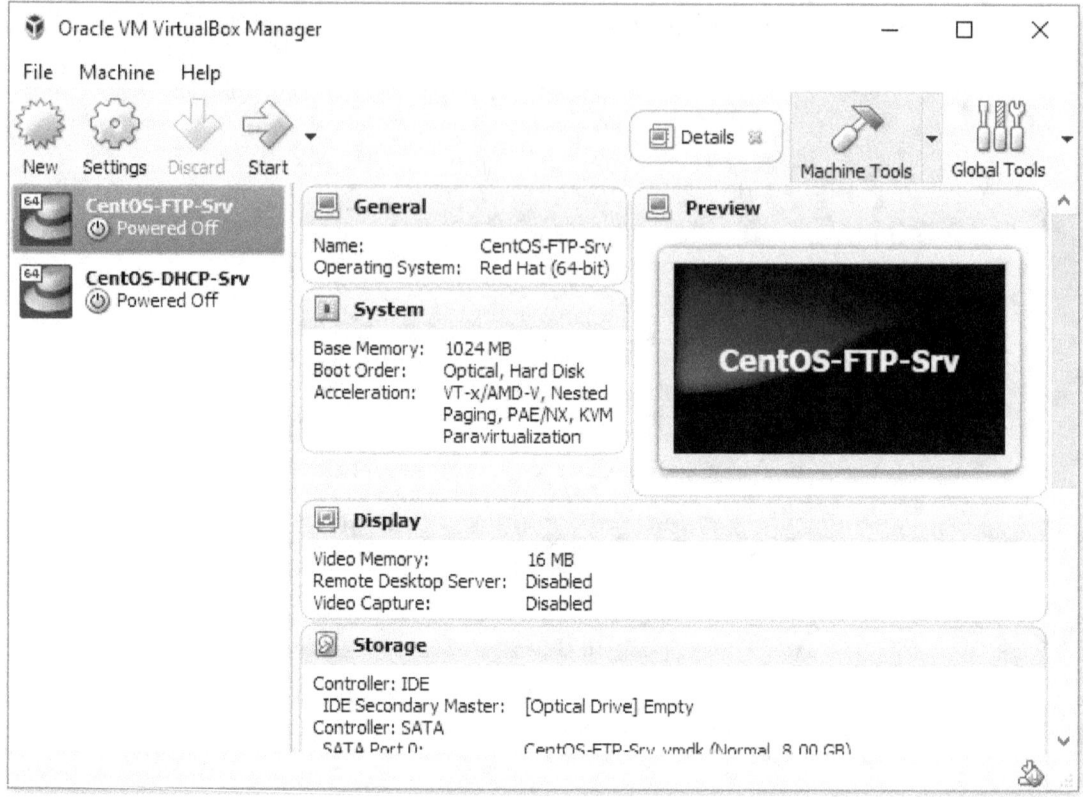

Figure 3.15: Showing the Cloned VM in the list

Further Reading

Canepa, G. (n.d.). Cloning, exporting, importing, and removing virtual machines in VirtualBox. Retrieved from https://www.systemcodegeeks.com/virtualization/virtualbox/cloning-exporting-importing-removing-virtual-machines-virtualbox/

Host-only Networking in VirtualBox. (n.d.). Retrieved from http://condor.depaul.edu/glancast/443class/docs/vbox_host-only_setup.html

Host-only Networking in VirtualBox. (n.d.). Retrieved from http://condor.depaul.edu/glancast/443class/docs/vbox_host-only_setup.html

ProTechGurus. (2016, July 29). How To Clone Virtual Machine in VirtualBox. Retrieved from https://protechgurus.com/clone-virtual-machine-virtualbox/

VirtualBox 5: Saving the State of the Machine - GROK Knowledge Base. (n.d.). Retrieved from https://software.grok.lsu.edu/article.aspx?articleid=13463

Wallen, J. (n.d.). Clone and move virtual machines in VirtualBox. Retrieved from https://www.techrepublic.com/blog/tr-dojo/clone-and-move-virtual-machines-in-virtualbox/

Chapter 4
Exporting and Importing Appliances

In the situations, where you will have to copy the virtual machine files from one system to another system, exporting and importing the virtual machines as a virtual appliance (VA) is a good way. A virtual appliance is a virtual machine file which consists of a pre-configured operating system (OS) environment as a single application. Exporting the virtual machines as appliances is one of the easiest and most reliable ways to move VMs from one host to another host. In this section, we will learn to export the virtual machines as a virtual appliance and import it to another system.

Exporting as Virtual Machine as Appliance

To export the virtual machine as an open virtual appliance (OVA), launch the Oracle VM VirtualBox Manager, go to the "File" menu and then to the "Export Appliance" as in figure 4.1:

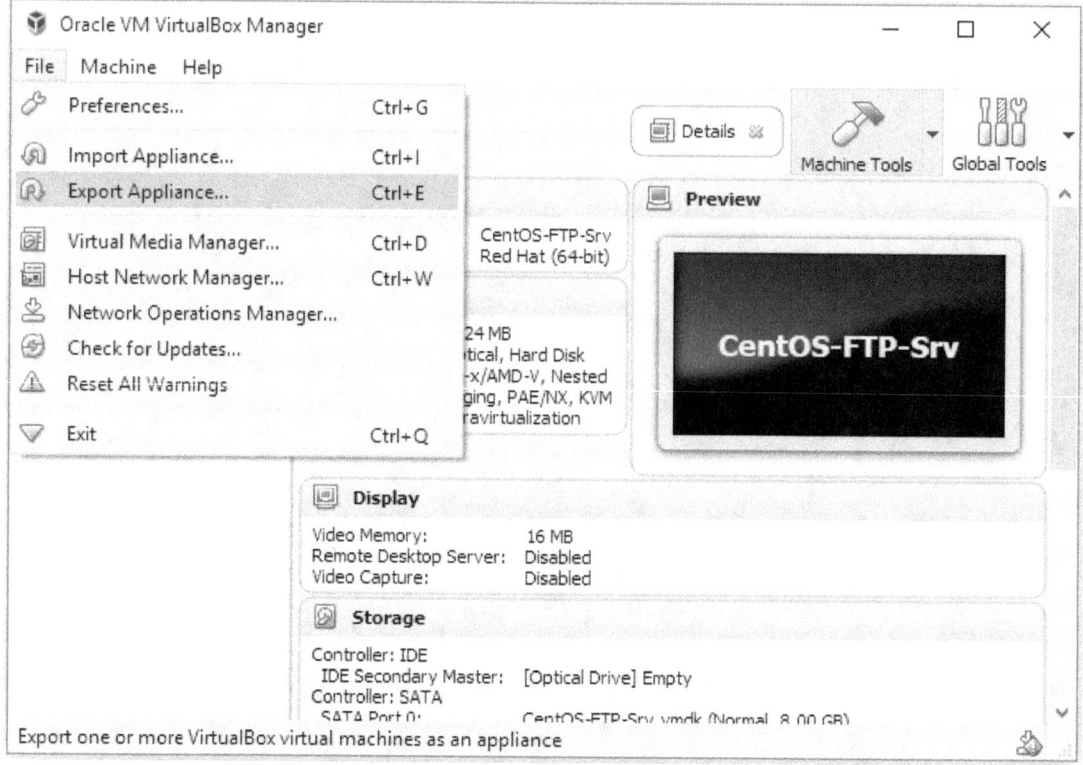

Figure 4.1: Exporting Appliance menu

In order to be able to export as an appliance, your selected virtual machine should not be running. In case if it is running, it must be powered-off. Even if the virtual machine is in the saved state, the exporting will not be allowed unless the saved state is discarded.

In the window presented after choosing "Export Appliance", locate and select the Virtual Machine to be exported and click Next (Figure 4.2).

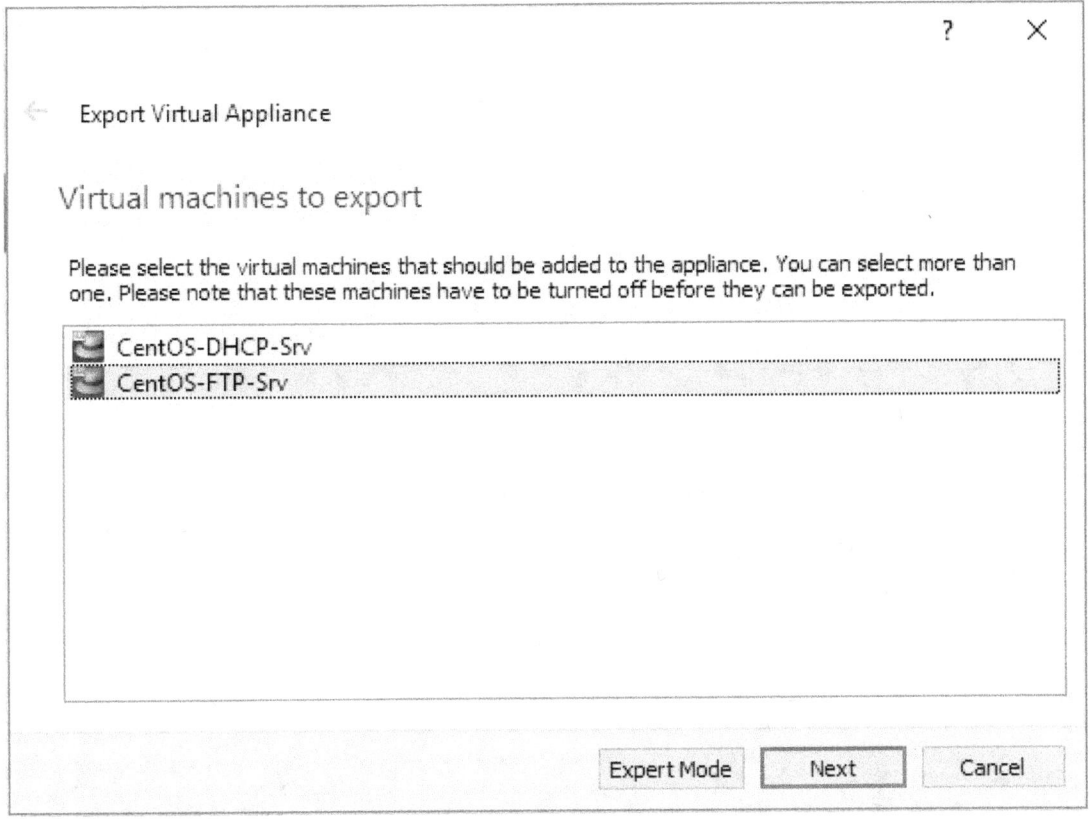

Figure 4.2: Virtual Machine selection for exporting as an appliance

In the next, we are supposed to give a name for the exported appliance file with an extension and browse to the location to save the exported appliance file (Figure 4.3).

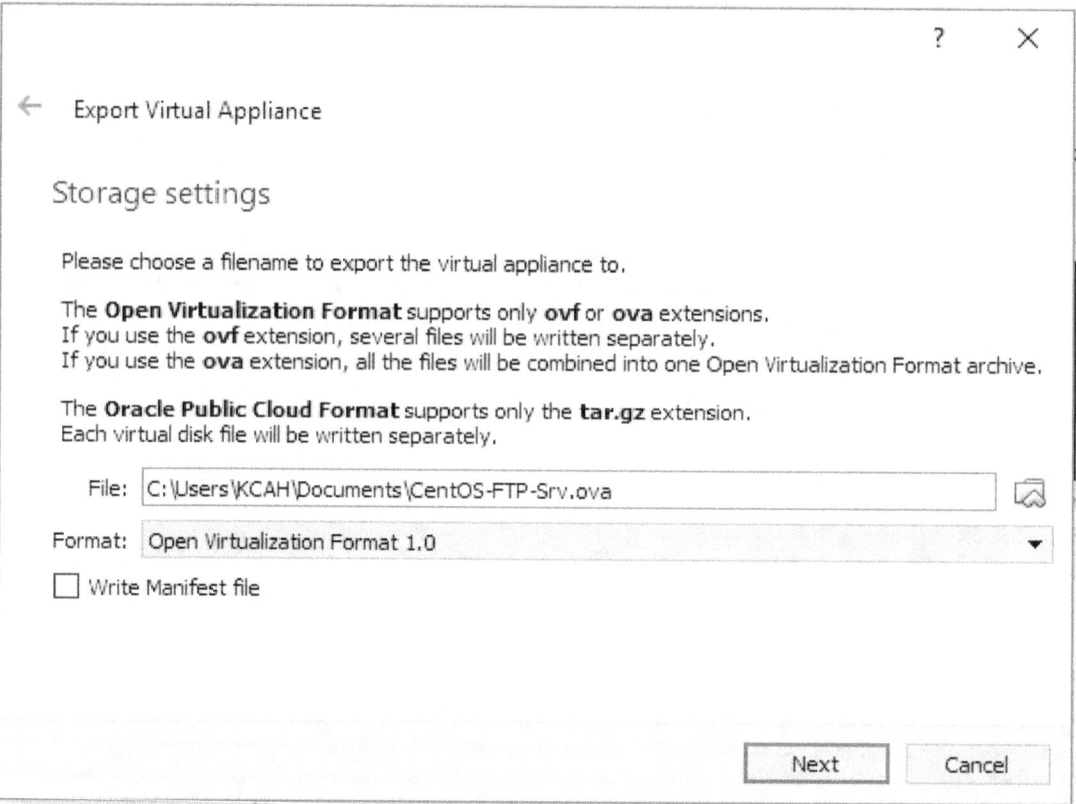

Figure 4.3: Exported Appliance Settings

> *By default, the exported file will be saved with ova extension in the default location. If the extension is ova, the appliance is going to be in a single file whereas if ovf extension is chosen, several files are going to constitute the exported appliance. Just keeping to the defaults should be working fine.*

In the appliance settings, leaving the information, click the "Export" button to start the exporting process.

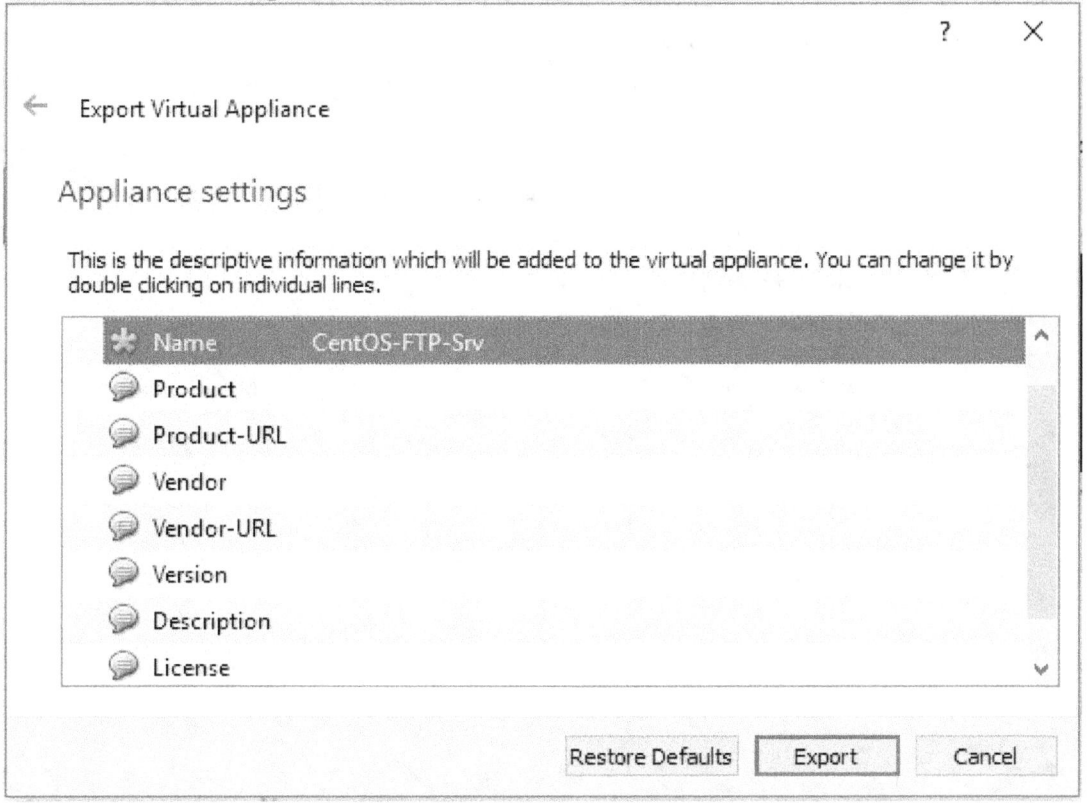

Figure 4.4: Appliance settings

The exporting process would take few minutes to complete and once the process gets completed, the exported appliance with an ova extension is expected to be in the location you have selected for saving. Copying it and saving it to the other safe locations will not have any problem with the exported file.

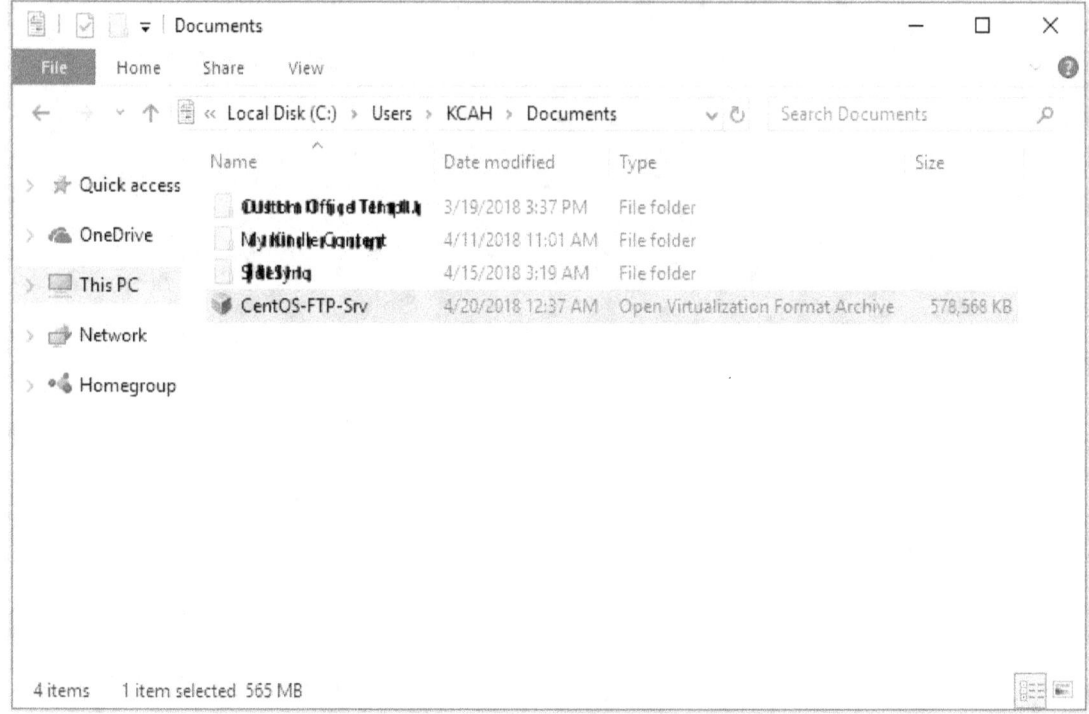

Figure 4.5: Exported Virtual Machine as an appliance

Importing Virtual Machines as Appliance

In the previous part, we have learned how to export a virtual machine as an appliance, in which the exporting process bundled all of the virtual machine resources into a single file with an ova extension. Now, to import the virtual machine, go to "File" menu and then choose "Import Appliance" as in Figure 4.6:

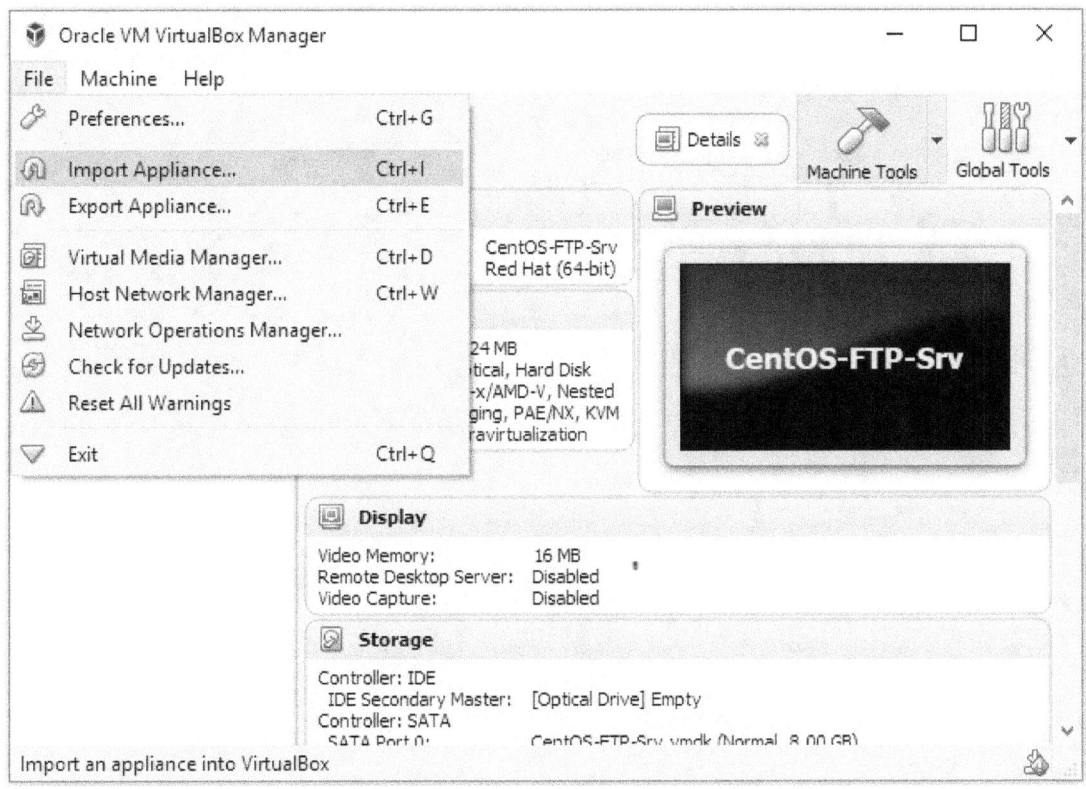

Figure 4.6: Import Appliance option

In the next, you will then be prompted to browse your system to look for the file with an ova extension as shown in Figure 4.7 and then click "Next".

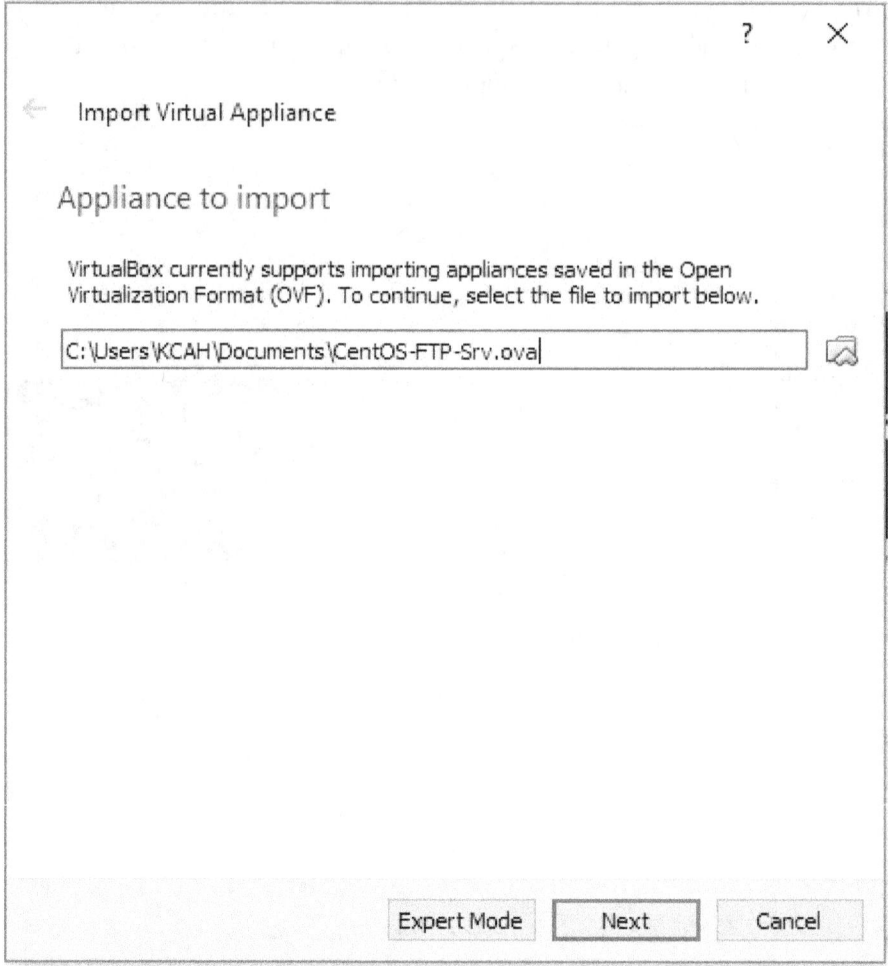

Figure 4.7: Browsing to the file location for importing

In the appliance settings information, the name must not be same as the already existing virtual machine. If the virtual machine with the same name exists, then change the name to something different by double-clicking. In figure 4.8, the name of the virtual machine is changed to CentOS-Web-Srv, leaving the rests of the settings as it is and the "Reinitialize the MAC address of all network cards" option is checked. To proceed, click the "Import" button.

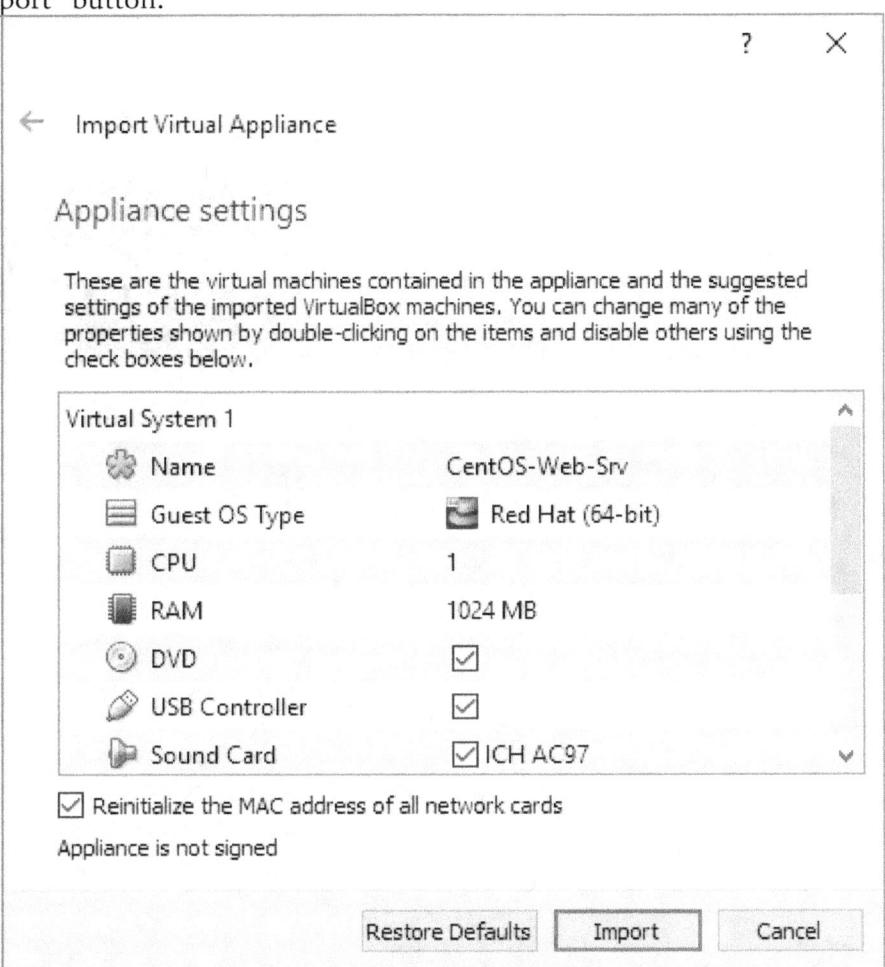

Figure 4.8: Import Appliance settings

During the process of importing, the appliance and storage settings of the virtual machine would be shown as they were set originally when it was first created. You can edit those settings and information by double clicking on the corresponding textbox and enter the desired value.

Importing of the virtual machine would take few minutes to complete and will result in creating a virtual machine with the name specified in the appliance settings. In figure 4.9, CentOS-Web-Srv is the imported appliance from the file.

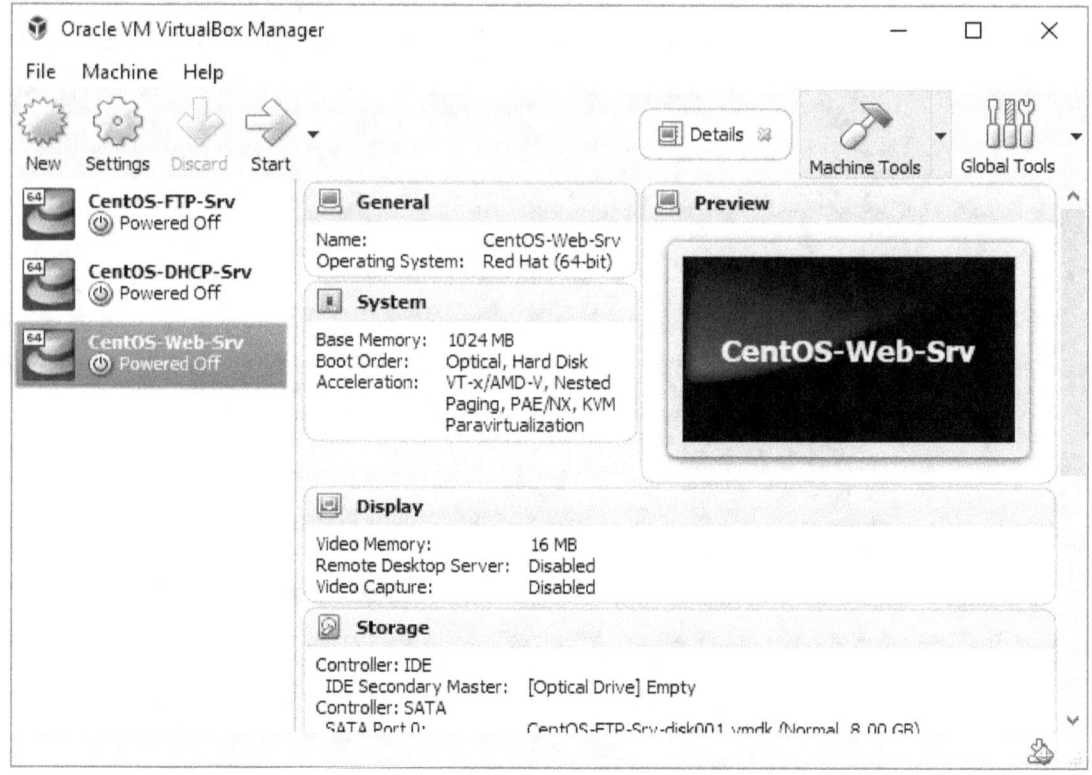

Figure 4.9: List of Virtual Machines

Removing Virtual Machines

It so happens that some of the virtual machines which we have used for testing the configurations can serve no purpose; keeping those virtual machines would just occupy space and the list become long. It is a good idea to delete one or more of such virtual machines which serves no good purpose.

To delete the intended virtual machine from the list, select and right click on the virtual machine in the list as shown in the figure 4.10 and choose "Remove".

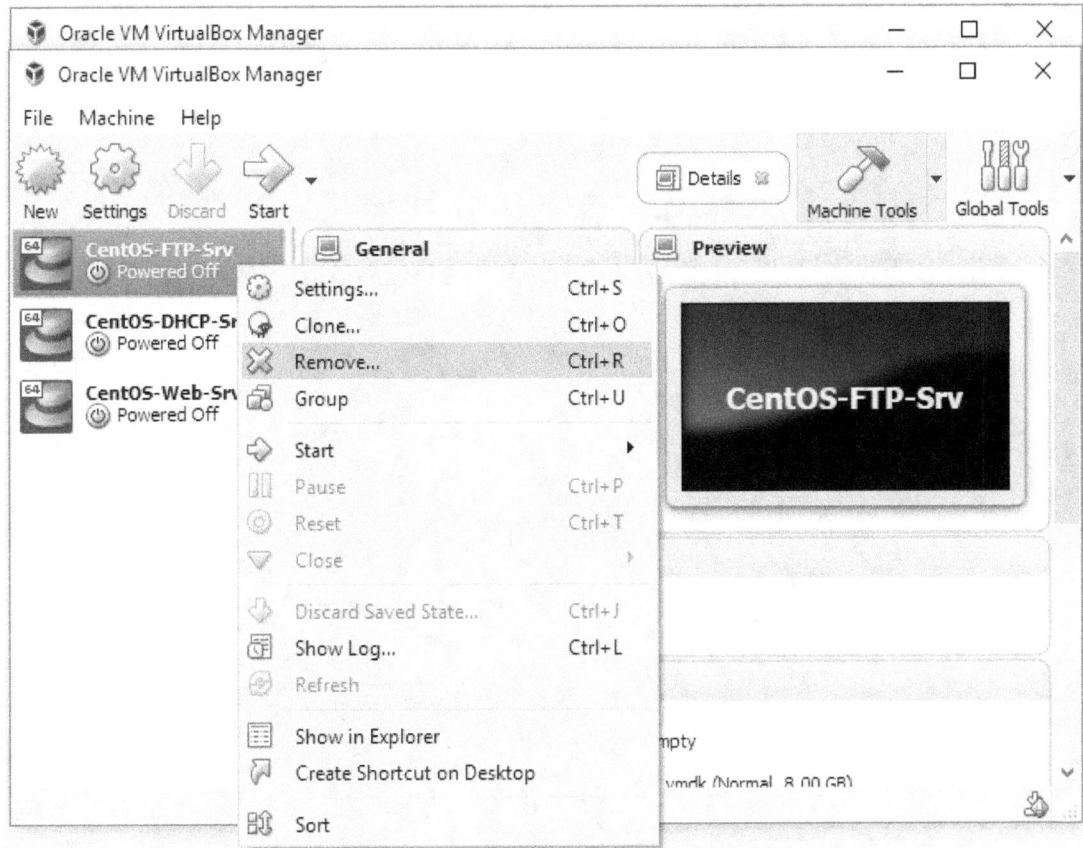

Figure 4.10: Removing Virtual Machine option

We will not be allowed to remove a running virtual machine. For this we have to power off the virtual machine and then only remove it from the list.

In the next screen, we are prompted to choose one of the options. To remove the virtual machine along with its virtual hard disks, click "Delete all files" button as in the figure 4.11.

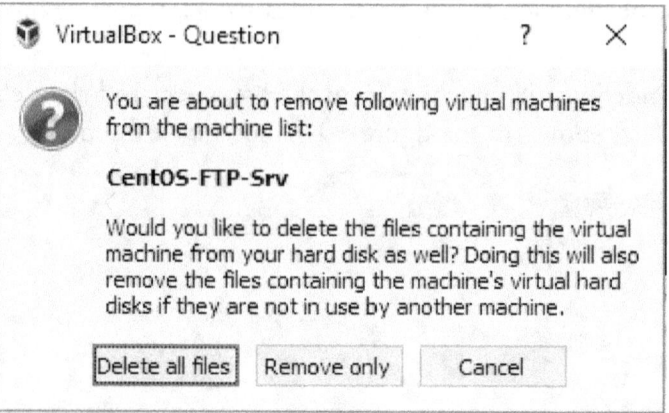

Figure 4.11: Removing virtual machine

Self Activity:

Applying the concept of creating the virtual machines, installing the operating system and cloning; create at least 6 virtual machines with CentOS operating system and then also create one virtual machine for installing Windows (Windows XP, Windows 7, Windows 8 or Windows 10).

In the Figure 4.12, CentOS-DHCP-Srv, CentOS-Web-Srv, CentOS-DNS-Srv, CentOS-Mail-Srv, CentOS-Yum-Srv are clones made from CentOS-FTP-Srv (Base) and Windows 7 a new virtual machine created with Windows 7 as the operating system.

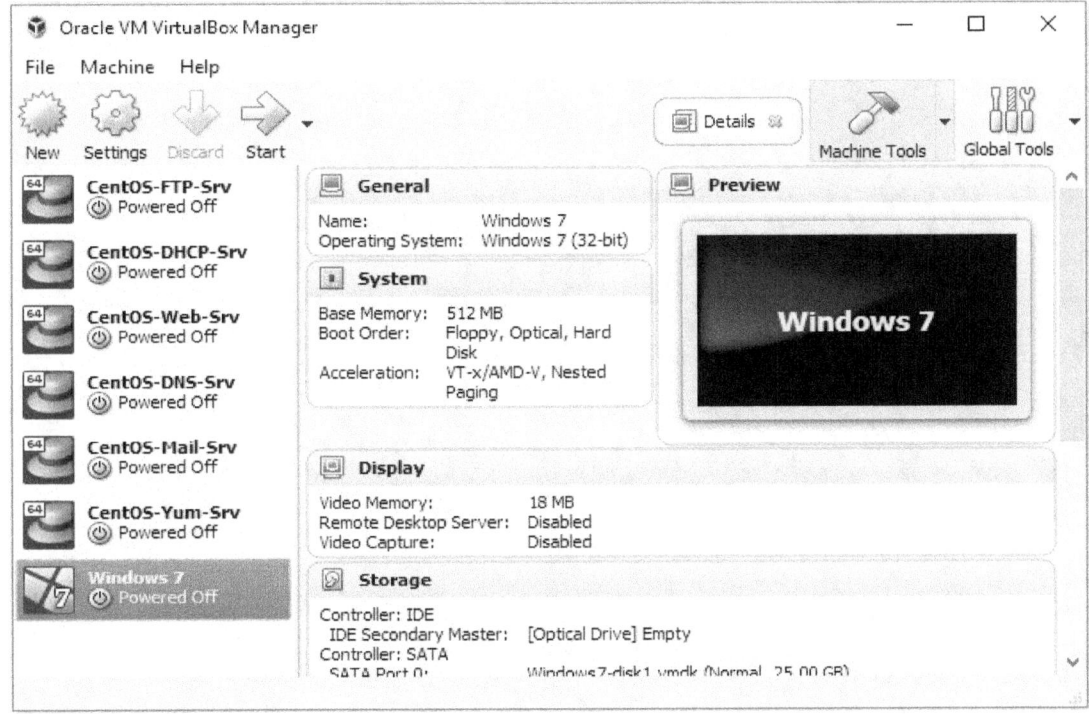

Figure 4.12: Cloned and new Virtual Machines created

Further Reading

4.7.2 Exporting Virtual Machines to Virtual Appliances. (2017, October 03). Retrieved from https://docs.oracle.com/cd/E64076_01/E64081/html/vmcon-repositories-assemblies-export.html

D. (2017, September 13). How to Import/Export OVA Files in VirtualBox. Retrieved from https://www.maketecheasier.com/import-export-ova-files-in-virtualbox/

Stanisic, S. (2017, January 09). Exporting virtual machine as an appliance in the Oracle VirtualBox. Retrieved from https://mivilisnet.wordpress.com/2016/04/04/exporting-virtual-machine-as-an-appliance-in-the-oracle-virtualbox/

VirtualBox 5: Importing and Exporting Virtual Machines - GROK Knowledge Base. (n.d.). Retrieved from https://software.grok.lsu.edu/article.aspx?articleid=13838

Wallen, J. (n.d.). How to import and export VirtualBox appliances from the command line. Retrieved from https://www.techrepublic.com/article/how-to-import-and-export-virtualbox-appliances-from-the-command-line/

Chapter 5
Integrating VMs with GNS3

Virtualize Network Test-Labs

Till this point, we have created virtual machines and the clones of it in the Oracle VM VirtualBox Manager for CentOS and Windows 7. In order for us to be able to use the virtual machines inside the GNS3 virtualized network, we have to link virtual machines existing in the Oracle VM VirtualBox to the GNS3 so that those VMs would be available for use in the GNS3 topologies. In this section we will learn to add the existing VMs to the GNS3.

Adding VMs

Launch the GNS3 application, close the Project dialog box if it appears as shown in figure 5.1.

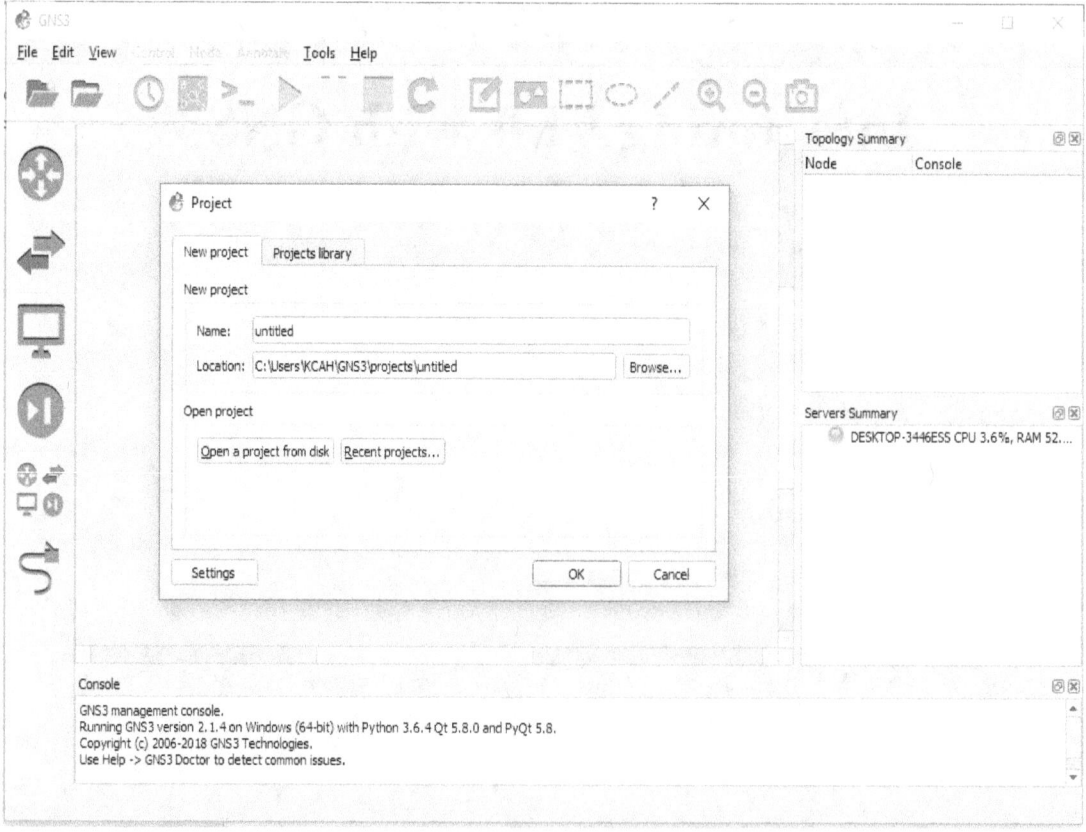

Figure 5.1: Launching the GNS3 application

Then go to the "Edit" menu and then click "Preferences" button. The following screen would be displayed and from the list, select the "VirtualBox VMs" using the mouse and then click "New" button to start adding the VMs to the GNS3.

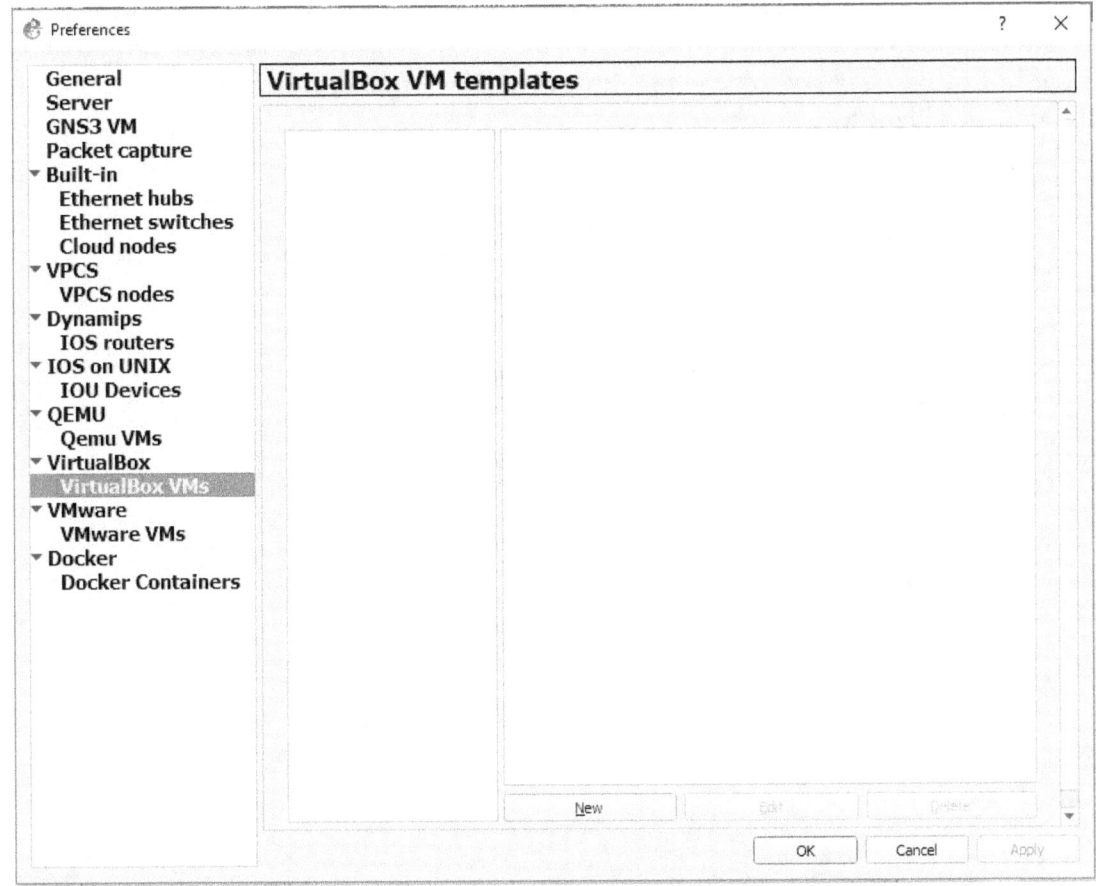

Figure 5.2: VirtualBox VM templates

The GNS3 and the VirtualBox are interconnected, and the GNS3 has the knowledge of where to find VMs. When the "New" button is clicked, GNS3 would take a moment to populate the list of VMs available in the VirtualBox and it will list in the VM list dropdown list. From the populated dropdown list, select whichever VM is desired to be available in the GNS3 network topologies and click "Finish" button. As in figure 6.3, I want CentOS-FTP-Srv to be available in the GNS3 topology, so I choose it from the list and click "Finish".

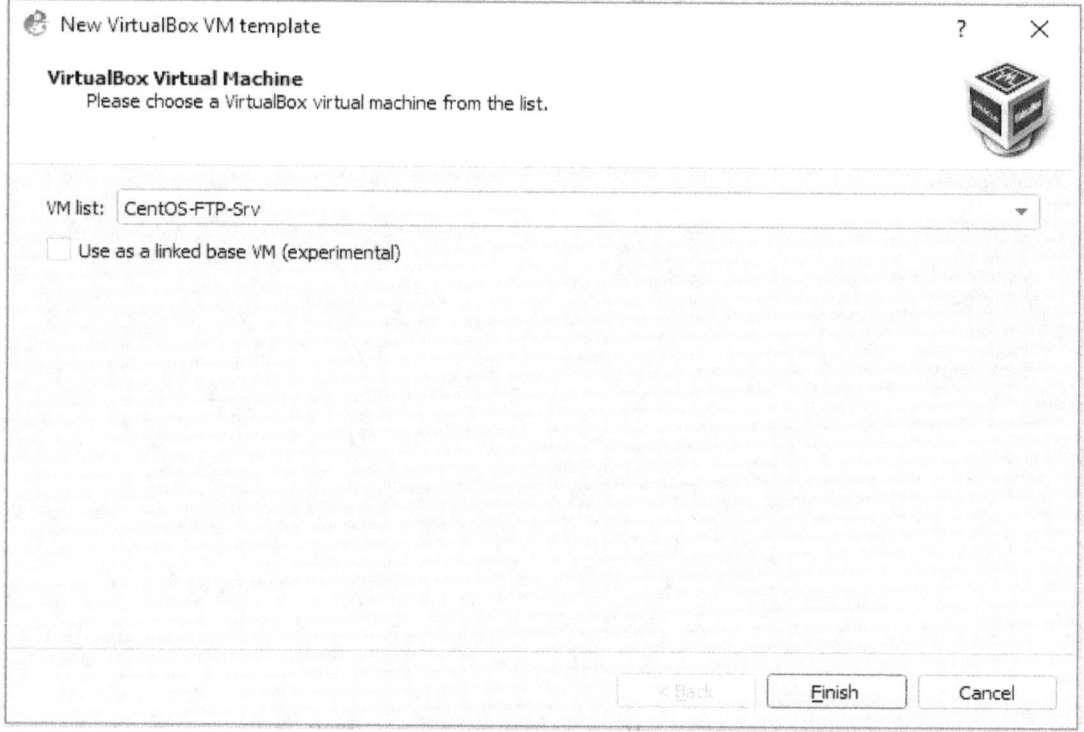

Figure 5.3: Choosing from the populated VM list

Immediately after the "Finish" button is clicked, the VM will be listed in the VirtualBox VM templates list with other details. Click the "Apply" button and if other VMs are desired to be available in the GNS3 topology as well, click the "New" button and follow the same procedure.

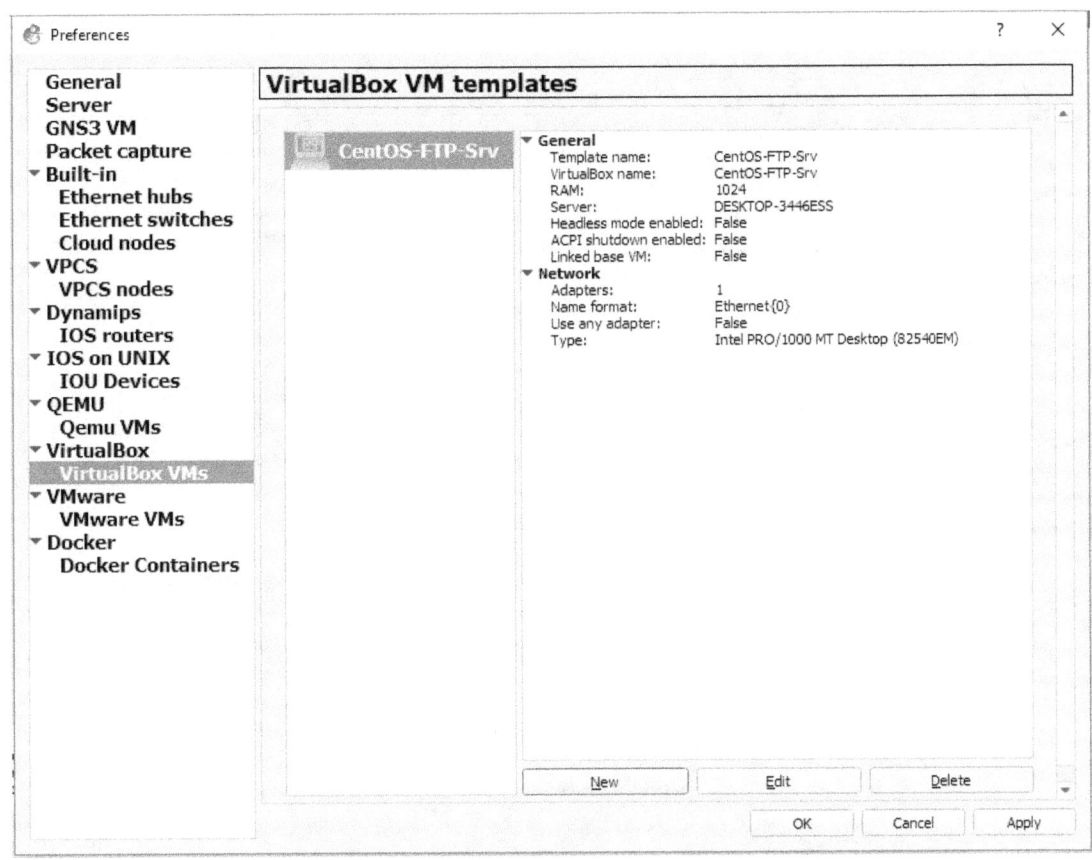

Figure 5.4: Linking the selected VM to GNS3

Finally, when all the VMs are linked and listed, click "OK" to apply the changes. In figure 5.5, all the VMs that I wish to be available for use in the GNS3 topology are listed in the VirtualBox VM template, including the Windows 7 VM. Now click "OK" to apply the changes and the VMs should be available for use.

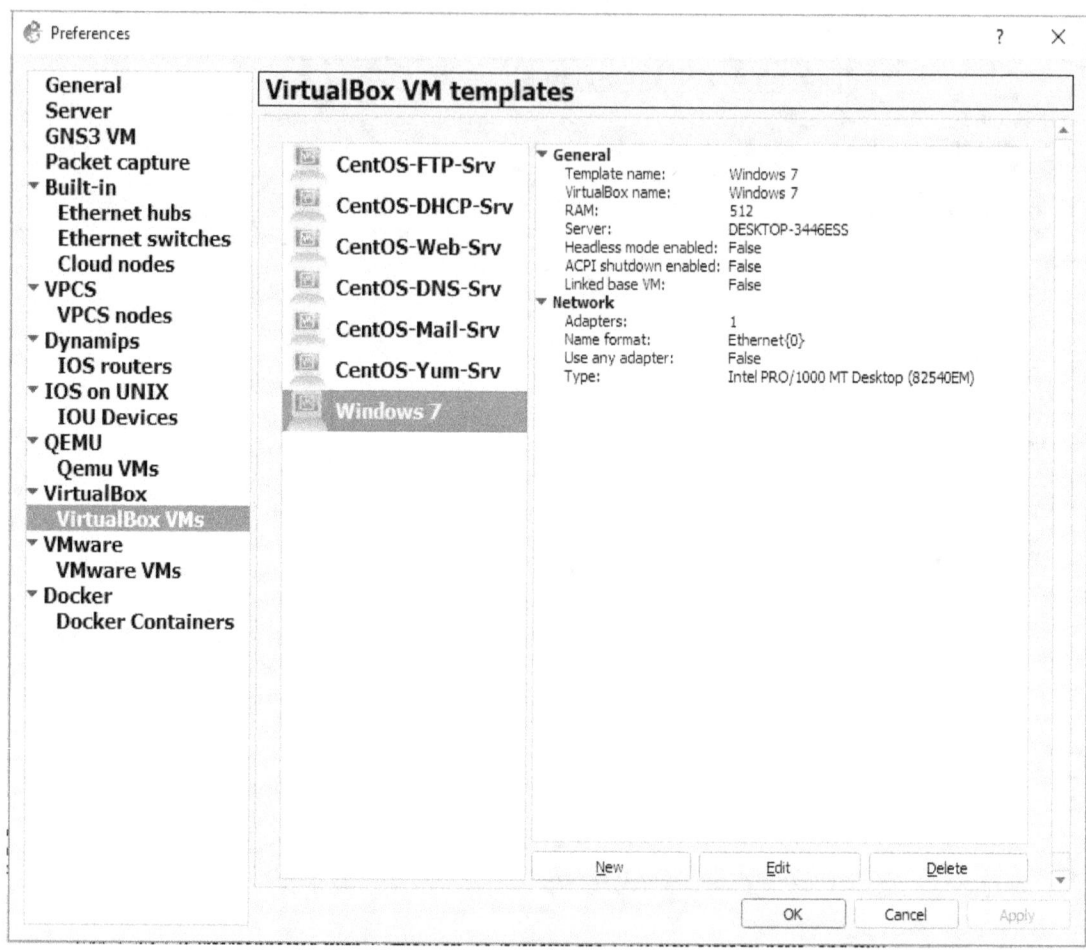

Figure 5.5: All the VMs listed

Browsing End Devices

After that, if we go to "Browse End Devices" (circled) in figure 5.6, then choosing the "Installed category" of the End devices, all the VMs which we have linked would appear in the list. In case, any of the devices are not listed, follow the steps required for adding the VMs and continue.

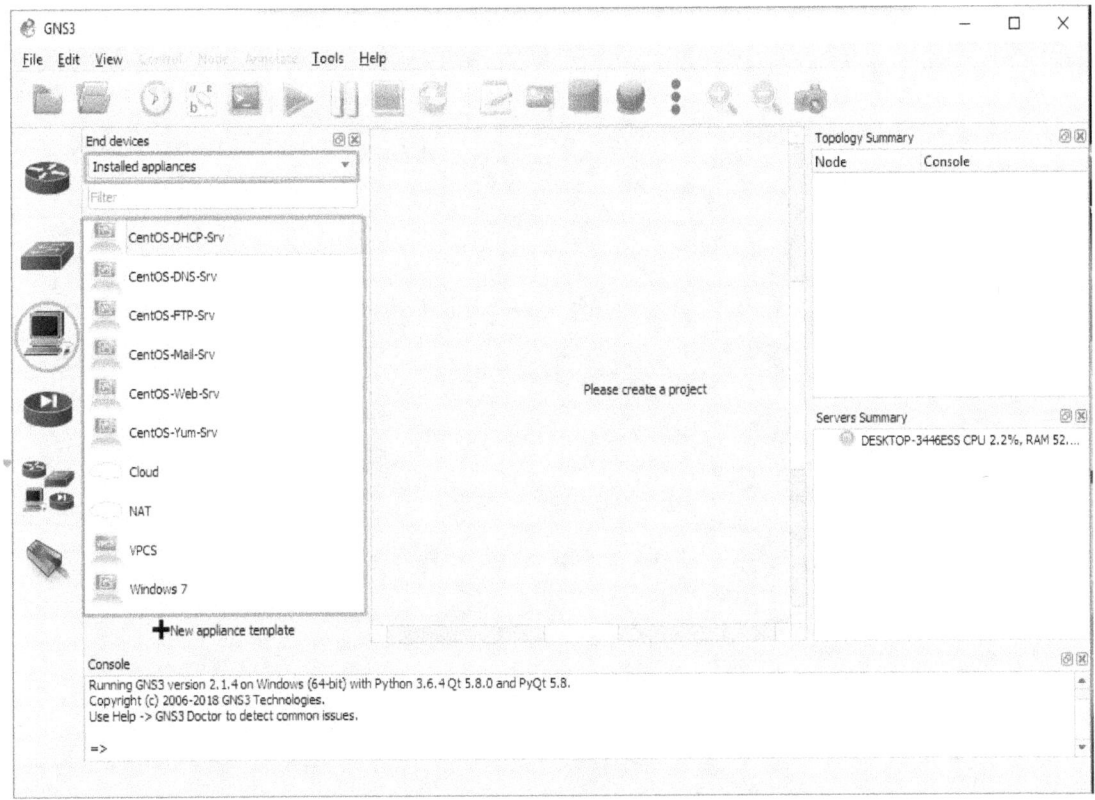

Figure 5.6: Browsing for the End Devices

Further Reading

Import VirtualBox VM template to GNS3. (2016, January 24). Retrieved from http://www.it-tutorials.net/import-virtualbox-vm-template-to-gns3/

Install an appliance from the GNS3 Marketplace. (n.d.). Retrieved from https://docs.gns3.com/1MAdxz0BSEAfGM7tA-w-o3TMmf8XOx7nBf0z6d9nRz_c/

Integrating GNS3 and VirtualBox. (n.d.). Retrieved from https://digi.ninja/blog/gns_vbox_basic_lab.php

Technical Documentation. (n.d.). Retrieved from https://docs.cumulusnetworks.com/display/VX/GNS3 and VirtualBox

Using VirtualBox linked clones in the GNS3 network simulator. (2017, January 03). Retrieved from http://www.brianlinkletter.com/using-virtualbox-linked-clones-in-the-gns3-network-simulator/

Video - How to Connect GNS3 to VirtualBox in Windows 8. (n.d.). Retrieved from https://www.interfacett.com/blogs/how-to-connect-your-gns3-environment-to-a-virtual-box-in-windows-8/

VMs in GNS3: Add VirtualBox servers to your network lab. (2018, March 09). Retrieved from https://www.ictshore.com/gns3/vms-in-gns3-virtualbox/

Chapter 6
Creating a GNS3 Network Topology

Virtualize Network Test-Labs

We have looked into the installation and the configuration of the required applications for building a virtualized network. To continue, it is presumed that all the required applications are installed and configuration is being made accordingly by following the previous chapters. As we go on, you would be getting familiarized with the toolbars and the interface slowly. To begin with, we will create a small network as a test bed for learning purpose.

Creating and Saving Projects

Launch the GNS3 application, click on the New Blank Project button indicated with an arrow in figure 6.1. Give a name of the project and click "OK" button to create a project keeping the location to the default.

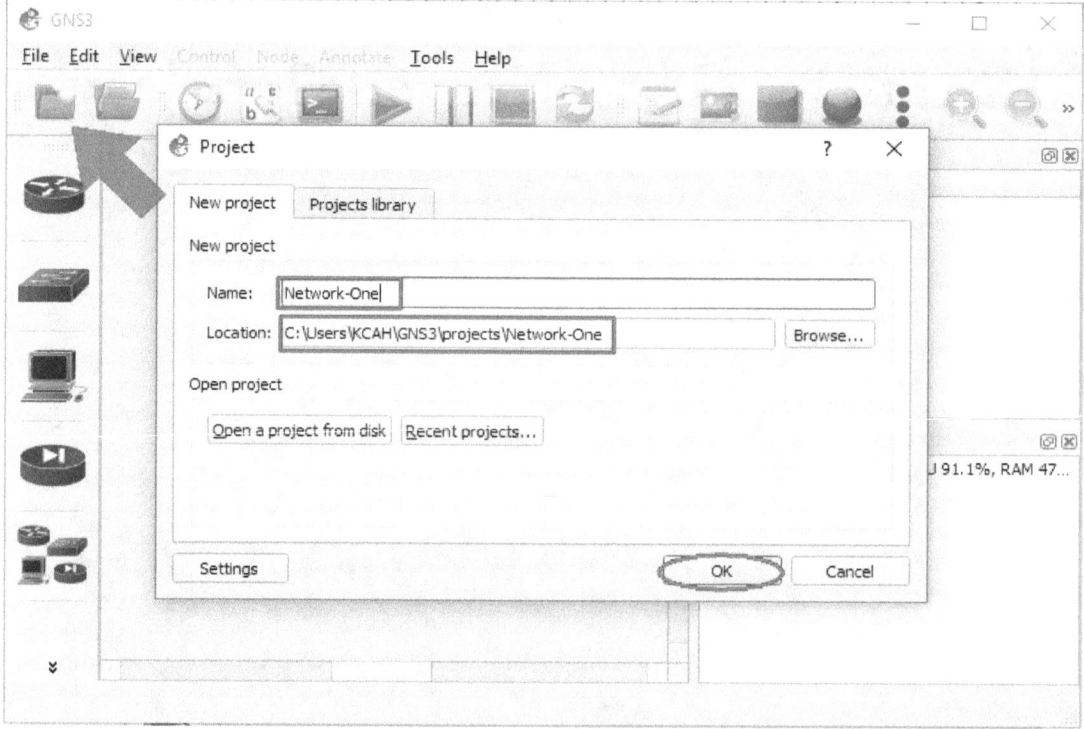

Figure 6.1: Creating a new project

After the project is being created, you would be able to drag and drop the devices to the workspace. First, we will drag and drop a cloud to represent an Internet in our project (Network-One). For this, you can click on the Browse End Devices (1) and the list of end devices would be displayed. Choose the Cloud (2), drag and drop to a location as desired (3) in the workspace. The cloud should appear in the workspace as shown in figure 6.2.

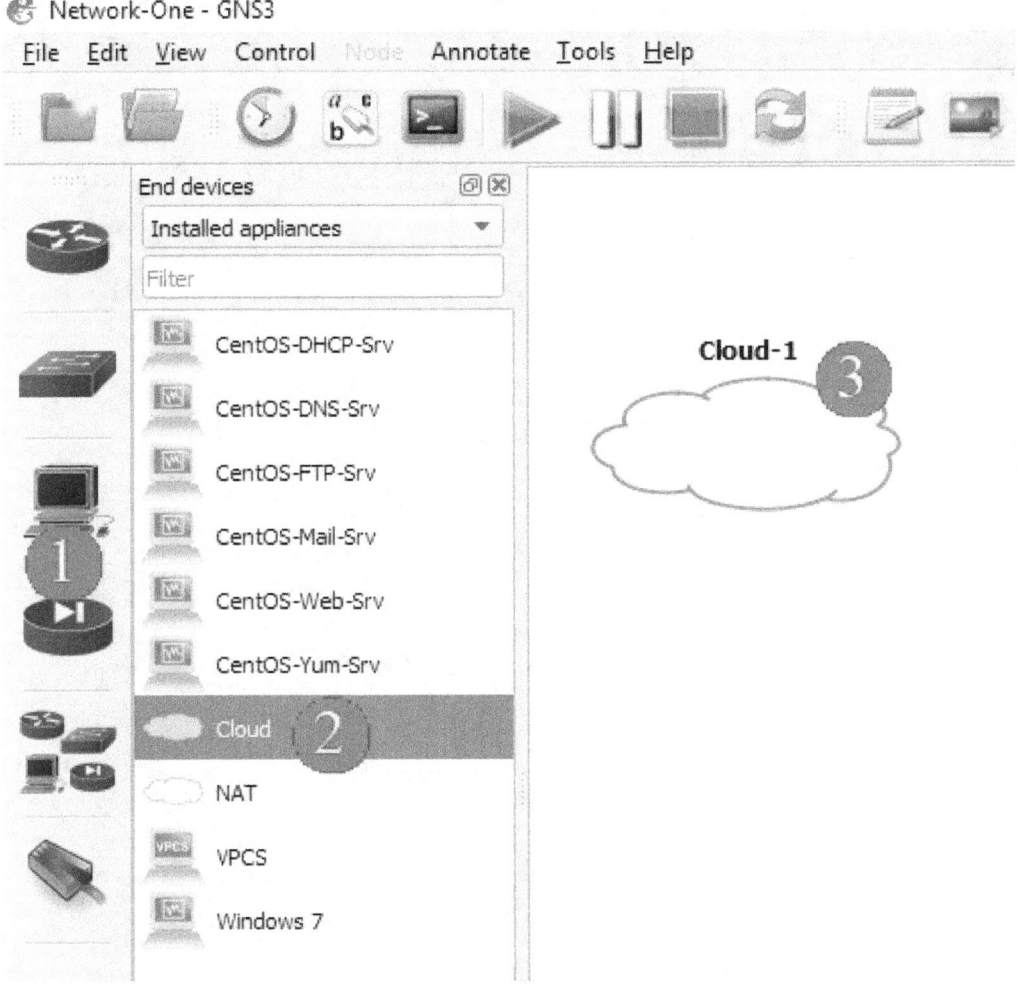

Figure 6.2: Creating a Cloud to represent the Internet

After adding a cloud, we will bring a router to the workspace by clicking on the Browse Routers (1), and then choose the available router (2). Drag and drop the desired router to a location in the workspace as shown in figure 6.3.

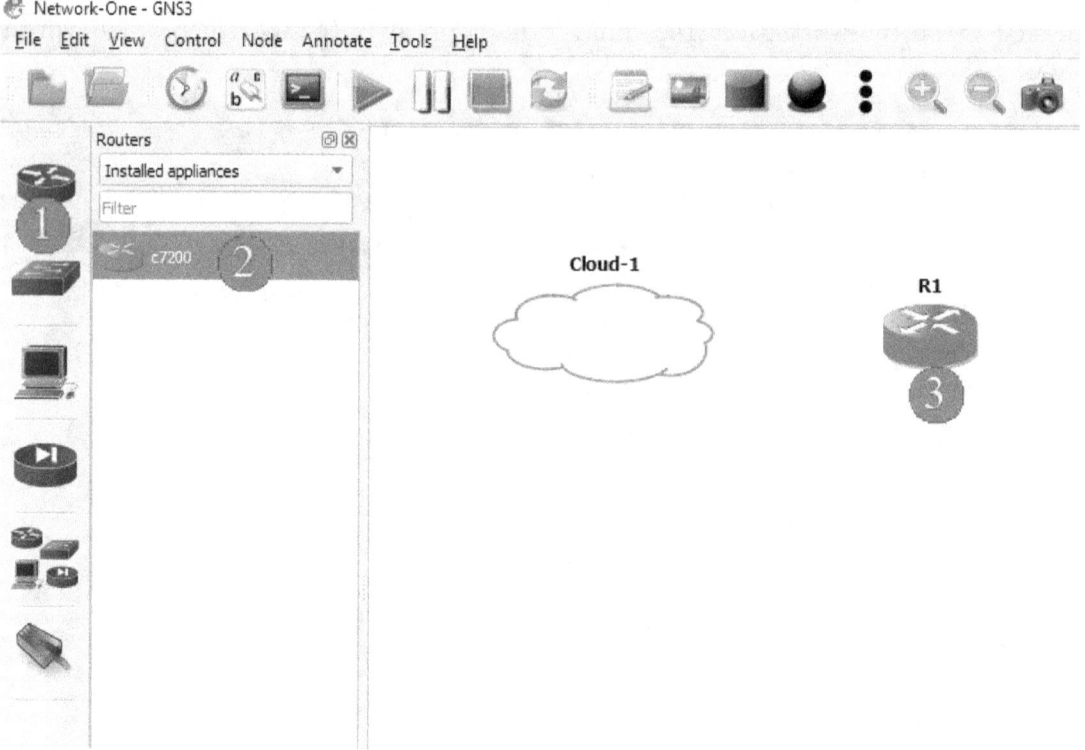

Figure 6.3: Creating a router

In the next, we will drop the Ethernet switch into the workspace. In order to create an ethernet switch, click on the Browse switches (1), choose Ethernet switch (2) and then drag and drop it into the workspace as shown in figure 6.4.

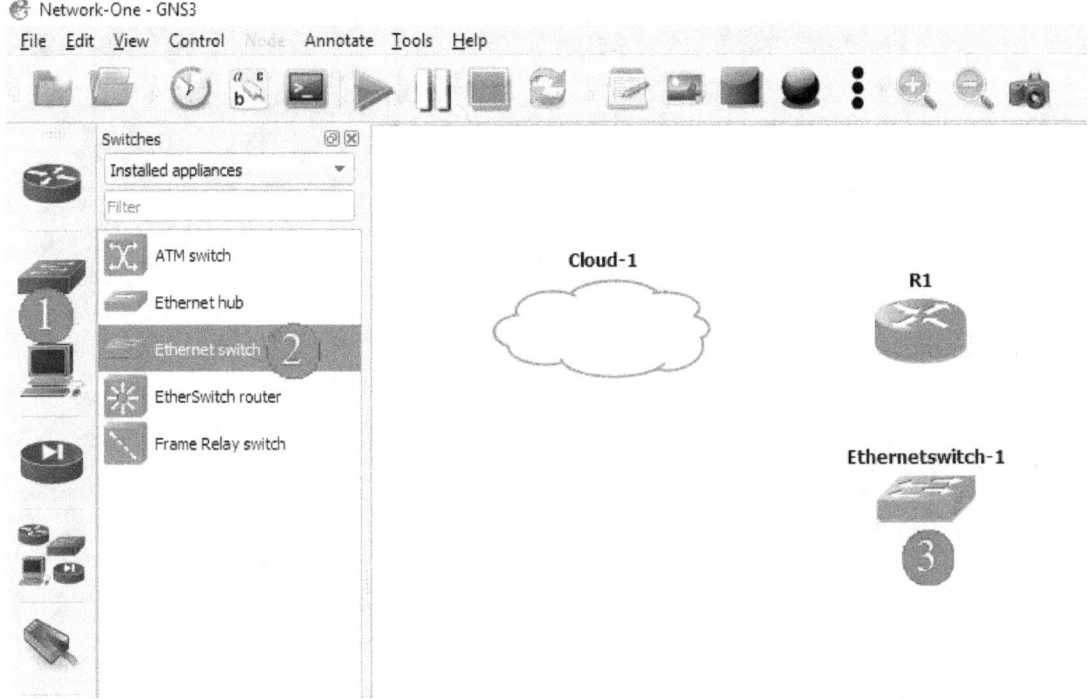

Figure 6.4: Creating an Ethernet switch

Virtualize Network Test-Labs

In a similar way, we will add one appliance (Windows 7) into the workspace by clicking on the Browse End Devices (1), choosing Windows 7 (2) and dragging and dropping into the workspace as shown in figure 6.5.

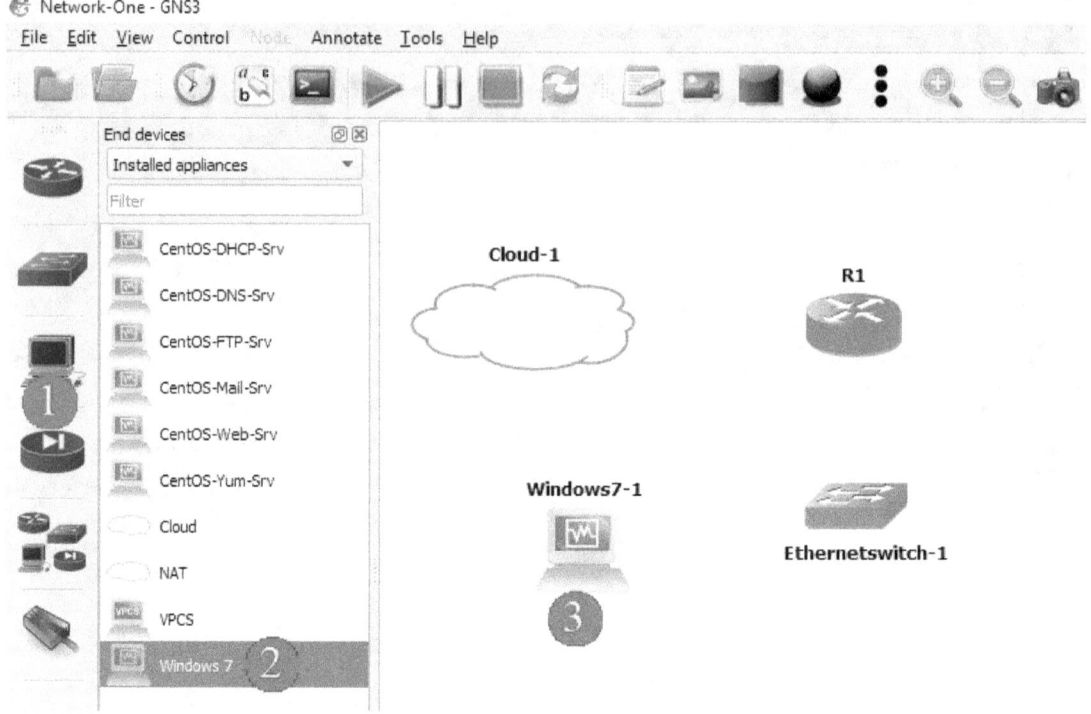

Figure 6.5: Creating Windows 7 (end device)

Configuring the Windows 7 (End device)

Before we give connections to the devices, we need to configure the appliance to allow the GNS3 to use any configured VirtualBox Adaptor. For this, right-click on the Windows 7 placed in the workspace and click on the Configure as indicated in figure 6.6.

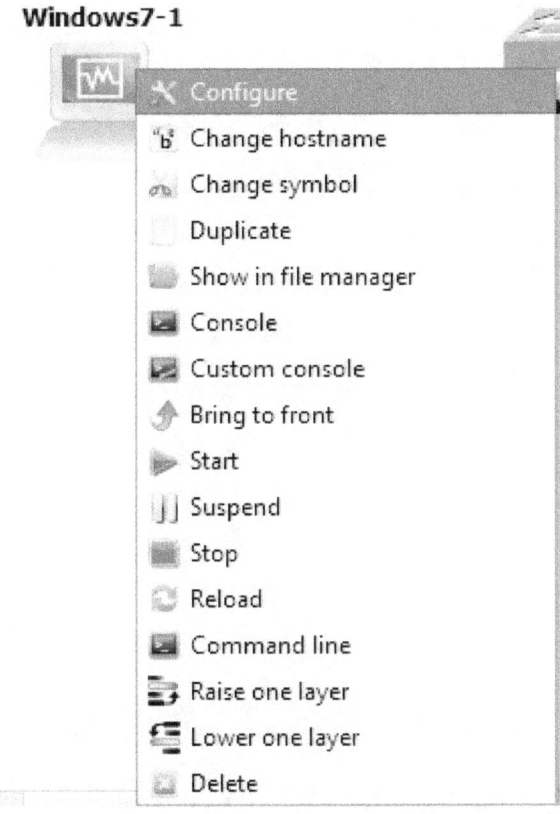

Figure 6.6: Configuring Windows 7

Upon clicking the configure option, the following window would be displayed. Choose the Network Tab (1), tick "Allow GNS3 to use any configured VirtualBox adaptor" (2), apply the setting and click "OK".

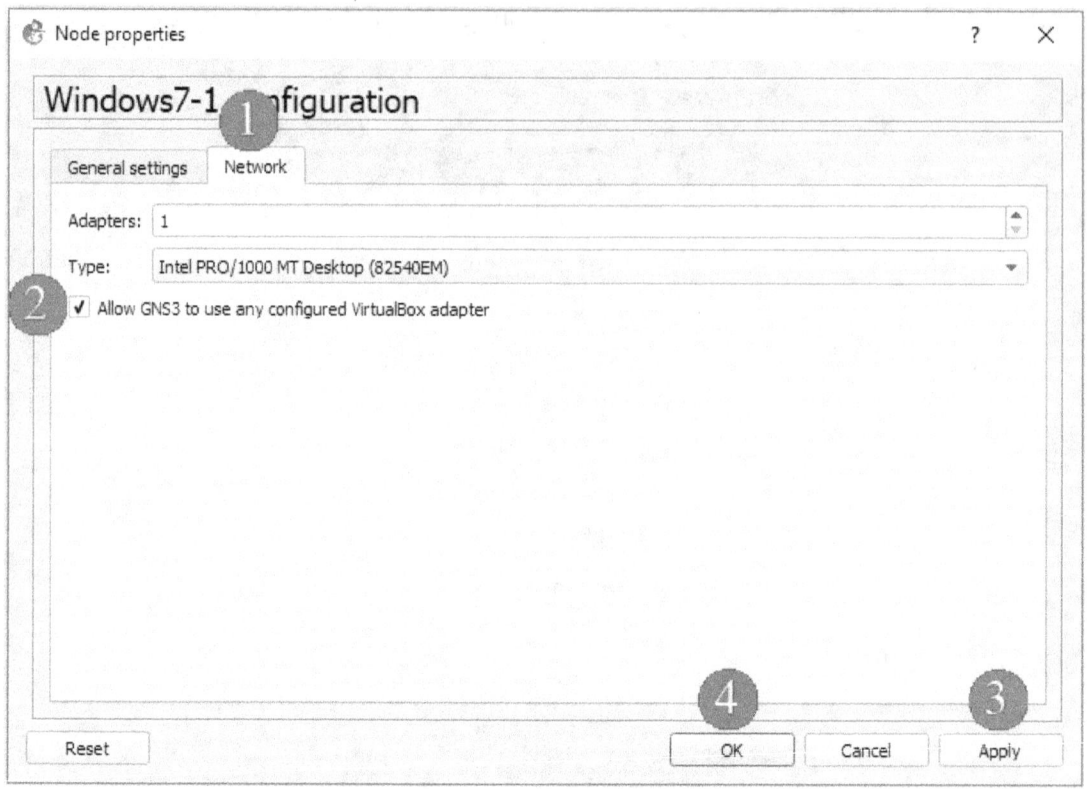

Figure 6.7: Allow GNS3 to use any configured VirtualBox adaptor

Creating Links Between the Devices

In order to create the links between the devices, click on the "Add a Link" button and take the mouse to the workspace where the devices are placed. The mouse cursor would change to a plus like sign (+), with that left-click on the Cloud-1 and the "Ethernet" option would appear. Click on the "Ethernet" option and then take your cursor to the router (R1) and left-click. Two interfaces as options would appear to choose from in order to connect the Cloud-1 (1) and the router (R1). Just to follow, choose FastEthernet0/0 and the connection between the Cloud-1 and the router (R1) would be complete with that.

To connect the router (R1) and the Ethernetswitch-1, click on the router and choose the other interface which is not in use (fastEthernet0/1) and then when you click on the Ethernetswitch-1, you would be shown a number of interfaces to choose. Just to follow choose Ethernet0. This completes the connection between the router (R1) and the Ethernetswitch-1.

Finally, to complete the connection between the Ethernetswitch-1 and the Windows 7-1, after clicking Ethernetswitch-1, choose Ethernet1 from the options and then choose Ethernet0 from Windows 7-1.

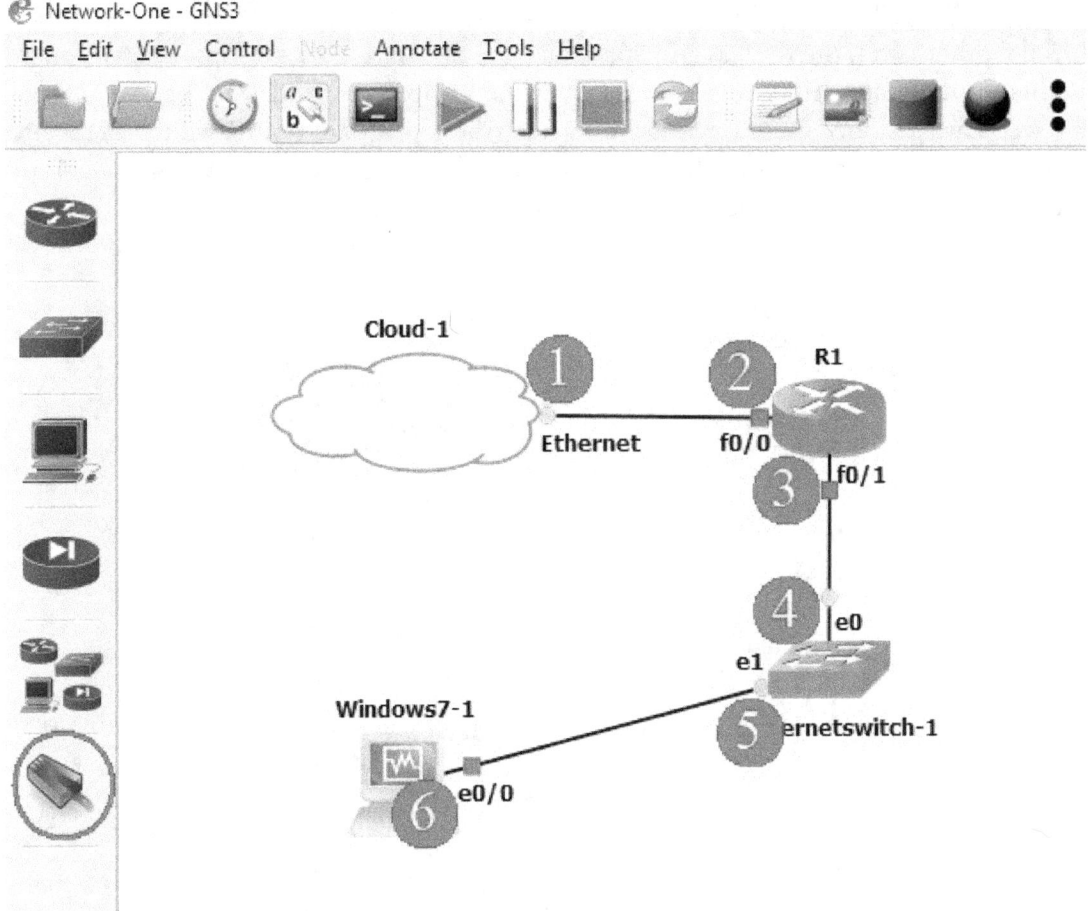

Figure 6.8: Complete links between the devices

Once the adding of the links is completed, press the Esc key on the keyboard to enable you to carry out other tasks. At this point your cursor must be changed to the normal one.

Status of the Devices and Nodes

In the GNS3 workspace, the Cloud and the generic Ethernet Switches are always on (started) by default. The links of connections on these devices and nodes are shown by green circular points indicating that the devices are started or kept on.

On the other hand, the routers and appliances are not started by default. The red square points on the connection links indicate that the devices and nodes are powered-off or not yet started. Once these devices are started, the red square points would change to green circular points. In the following figure 6.9, the router (R1) and Windows 7-1 are off, which is why the links bear red square points.

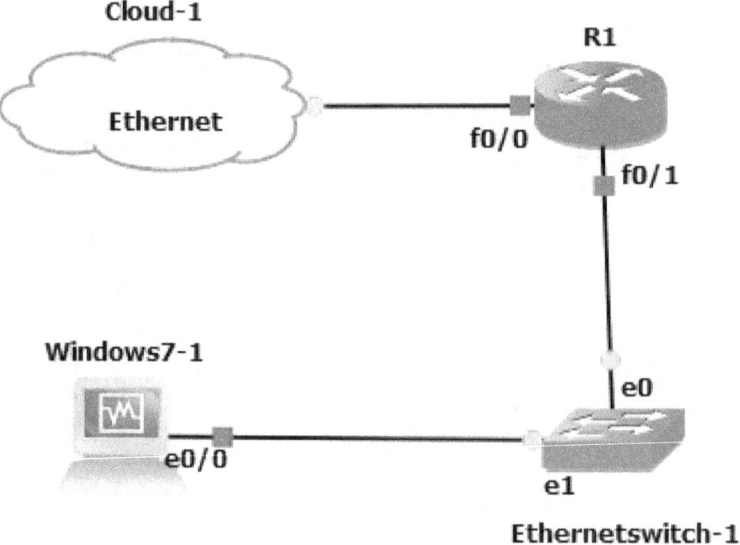

Figure 6.9: Status of the devices and nodes

Verifying the Network Adaptors

To start using the devices placed in the workspace, we have to start the devices whichever are required, but before that it is important to verify the network adaptors assigned to the appliances. A single network adaptor must not be assigned to more than one appliance.

To verify, launch the Oracle VM VirtualBox Manager, choose the appliance for which the adaptor is to be verified, right-click on the selected appliance which is used in the GNS3 workspace and choose the Settings.

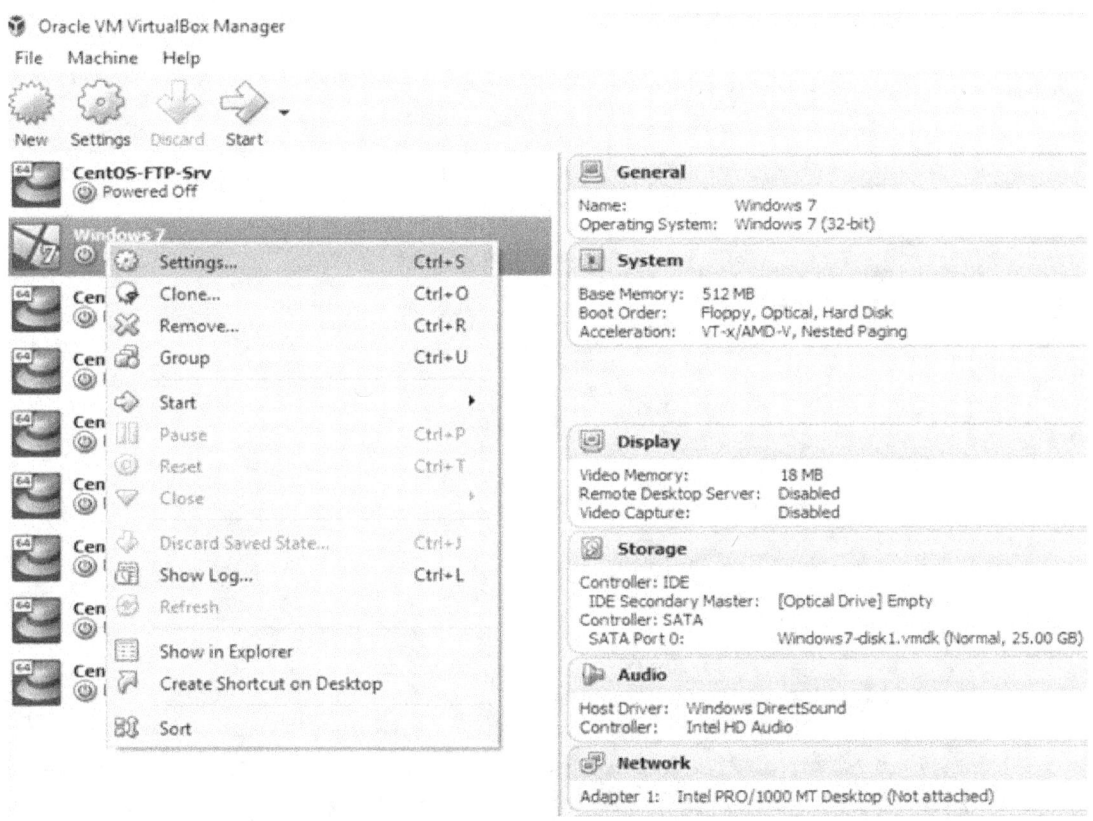

Figure 6.10: Settings option

In the Settings window, select Network (1) and then on the Adaptor 1 tab, choose "Host-only Adaptor". In the next, choose the VirtualBox Host-only Ethernet Adaptor whichever is not assigned to other appliances. Check the "Cable connected" option and click "OK" button.

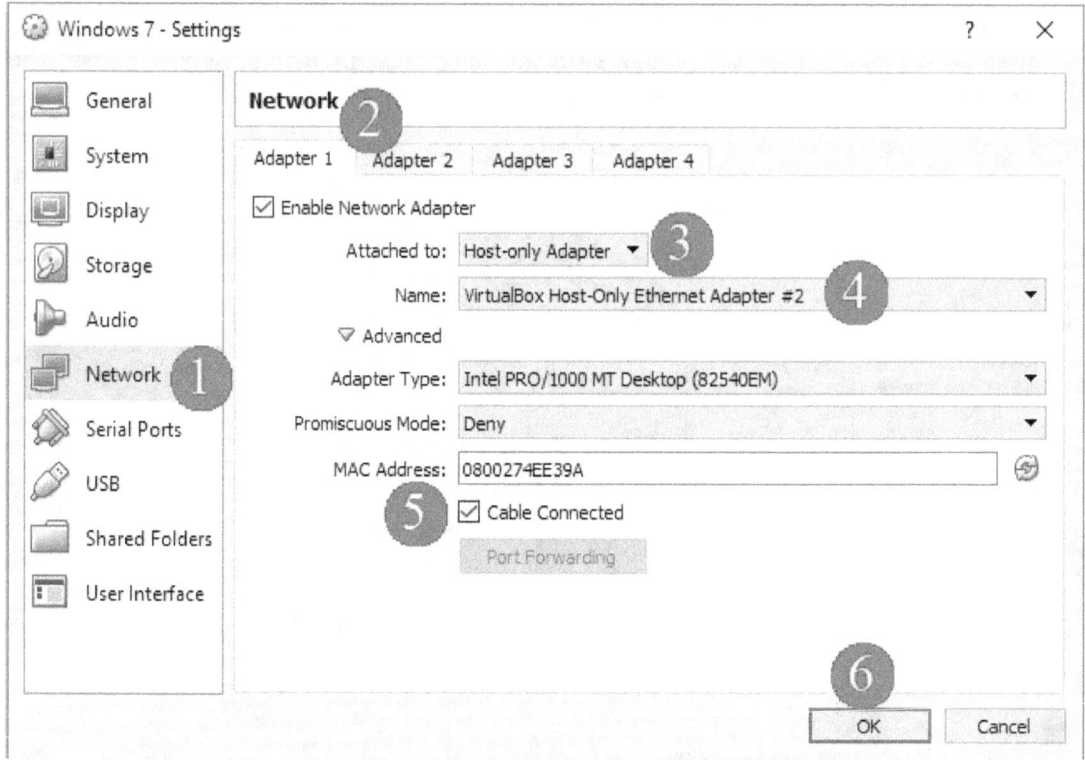

Figure 6.11: Settings window

In the above figure 6.11, the VirtualBox Host-only Adaptor #2 must not be assigned to any other appliances since it is assigned to Windows 7. If you have multiple appliances used on the GNS3 network, the adaptor must be verified for any possible double assignment to avoid problems.

Starting the Devices

To be able to make use of the devices, we have to start the devices. The devices can be started all at a time or one by one. To start the devices all at a time, the play-like button (Start/resume all nodes) must be clicked. This will start or resume all the suspended or stopped nodes placed in the GNS3 network.

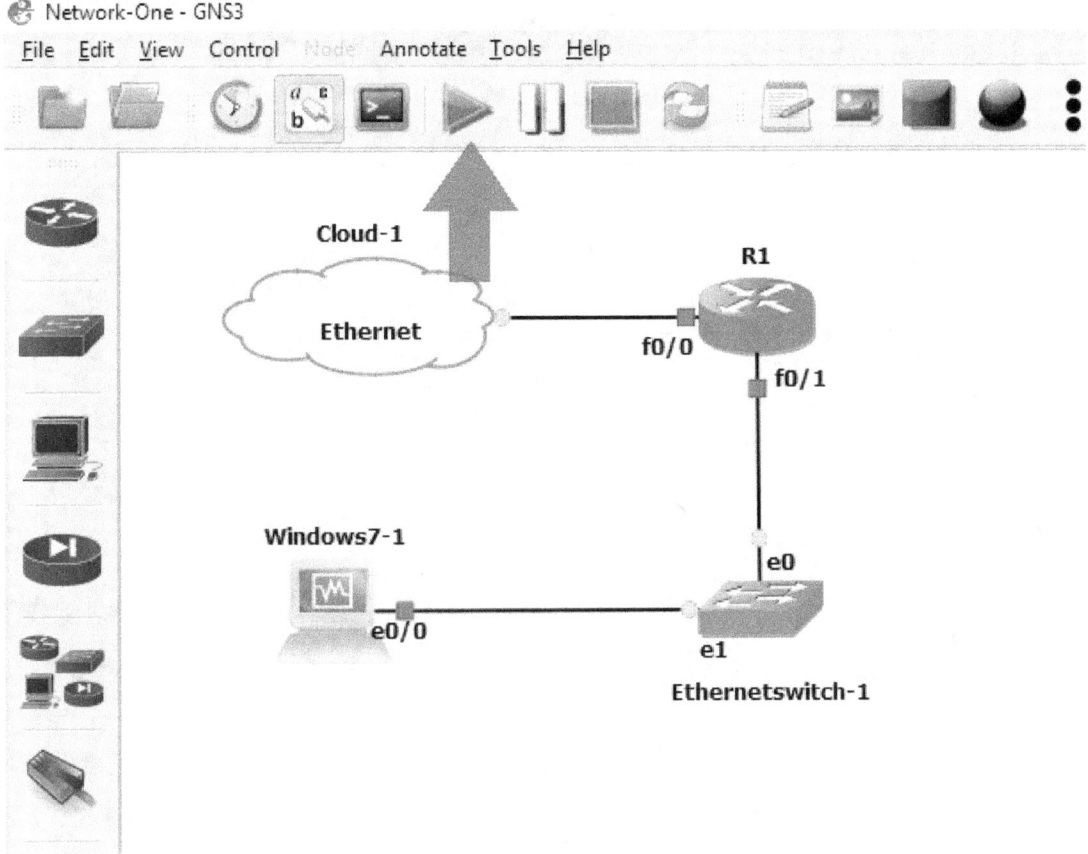

Figure 6.12: Starting or resuming all the nodes

If we want to start the nodes individually, we have to right-click the node to be started and choose the "Start" option as indicated in the figure below.

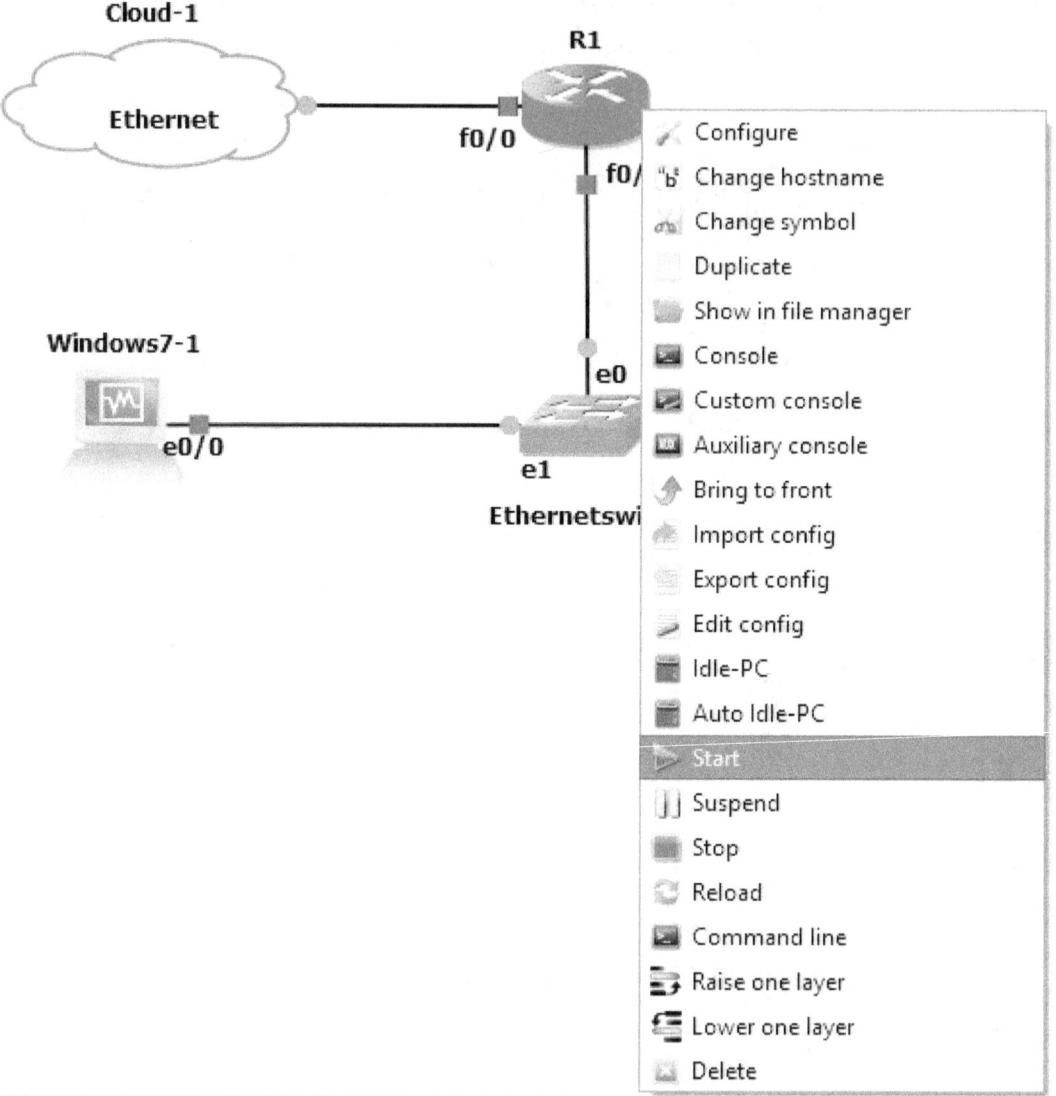

Figure 6.13: Starting the selected node individually

Finally, if we have started all the required nodes, the points on the connection links would appear as green circular points as in the following figure.

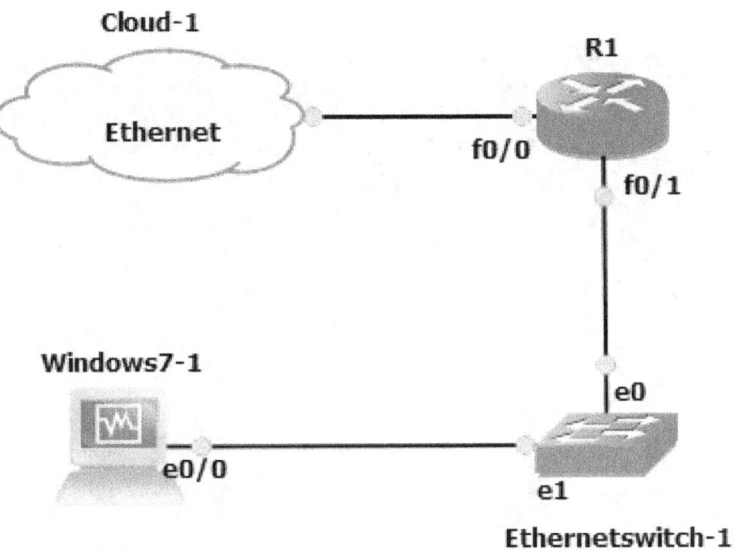

Figure 6.14: All the nodes started

Since the Oracle VM VirtualBox Manager and the GNS3 are linked, when the individual virtual machines are started from the GNS3 network, the virtual machines' operating systems would start to boot and appear as shown in the figure below.

Figure 6.15: Started Virtual Machine linked to the GNS3

Further Reading

Configuring the GNS3 Topology. (n.d.). Retrieved from https://www.freeccnaworkbook.com/workbooks/ccna/configuring-the-free-ccna-workbook-gns3-topology

Connecting GNS3 to Real Networks. (2016, March 14). Retrieved from http://www.smartpctricks.com/2014/06/connecting-gns3-real-networks.html

GNS3 Graphical User Interface. (n.d.). Retrieved from https://docs.gns3.com/1NjJlvu176VG4mq7qAl4wDo79P7pmOaiaa-c7kW5htuo/index.html

Network device simulation with GNS3. (n.d.). Retrieved from https://frinx.io/ftpp/network-device-simulation-with-gns3

Your First GNS3 Topology. (n.d.). Retrieved from https://docs.gns3.com/1wr2j2jEfX6ihyzpXzC23wQ8ymHzID4K3Hn99-qqshfg/

Chapter 7
Configure and Test Network

Once the creation of the network topology in the GNS3 is completed, it is time for us to be able to access the nodes and start configuring. In this chapter, based on the network topology created in the previous chapter, we will access the nodes and configure, so that the virtual network becomes functional. Finally, the configured network created in the GNS3 will be tested for the functionality.

Network Scenario

Before we go onto accessing and configuring the nodes, let us consider the following network scenario to get a clear picture of the sample network. In this network, the cloud which is connected to the ethernet adaptor of the host computer is treated as a connection to the internet. On the interface 0/1 of the router (R1) the IP address assigned is 172.168.30.1/24 and the other consideration is, the Windows 7 device would be assigned the IP address dynamically from the DHCP service configured on the router (R1), where NAT is also configured on the same router.

Finally, when the configurations are completed, the Windows 7 device should be able to browse and access the web services hosted outside of this network.

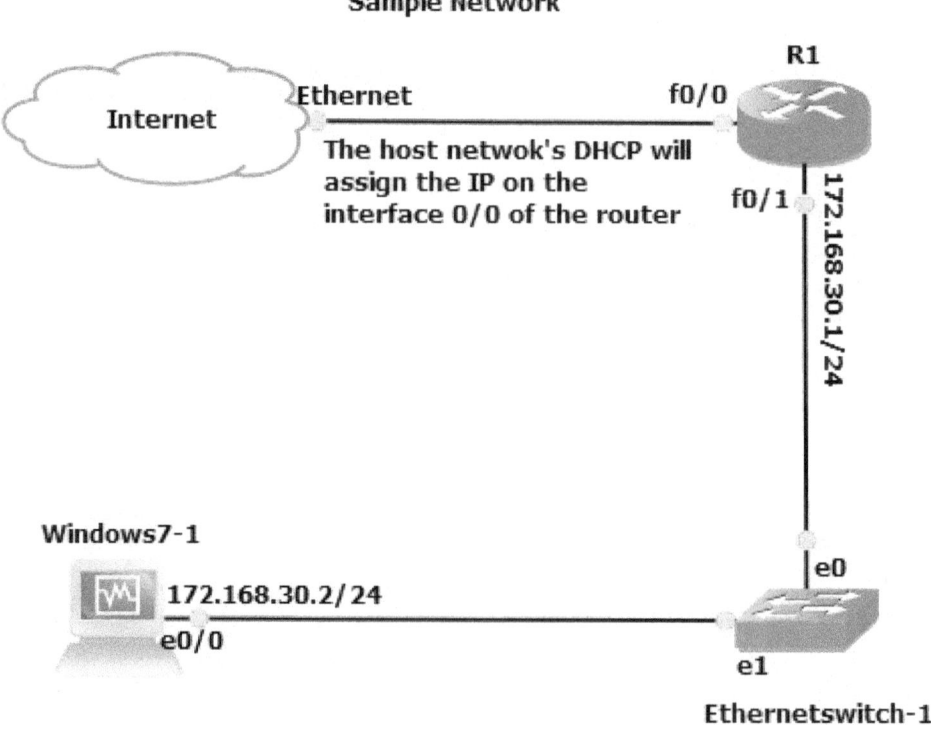

Figure 7.1: Network scenario

Accessing and Configuring Router

Once the router is being started, to configure it we have access to it. Unlike the virtual machines, the routers when started doesn't show up for access immediately. We can have access to the router's console by right-clicking the router and choosing the "Console" option.

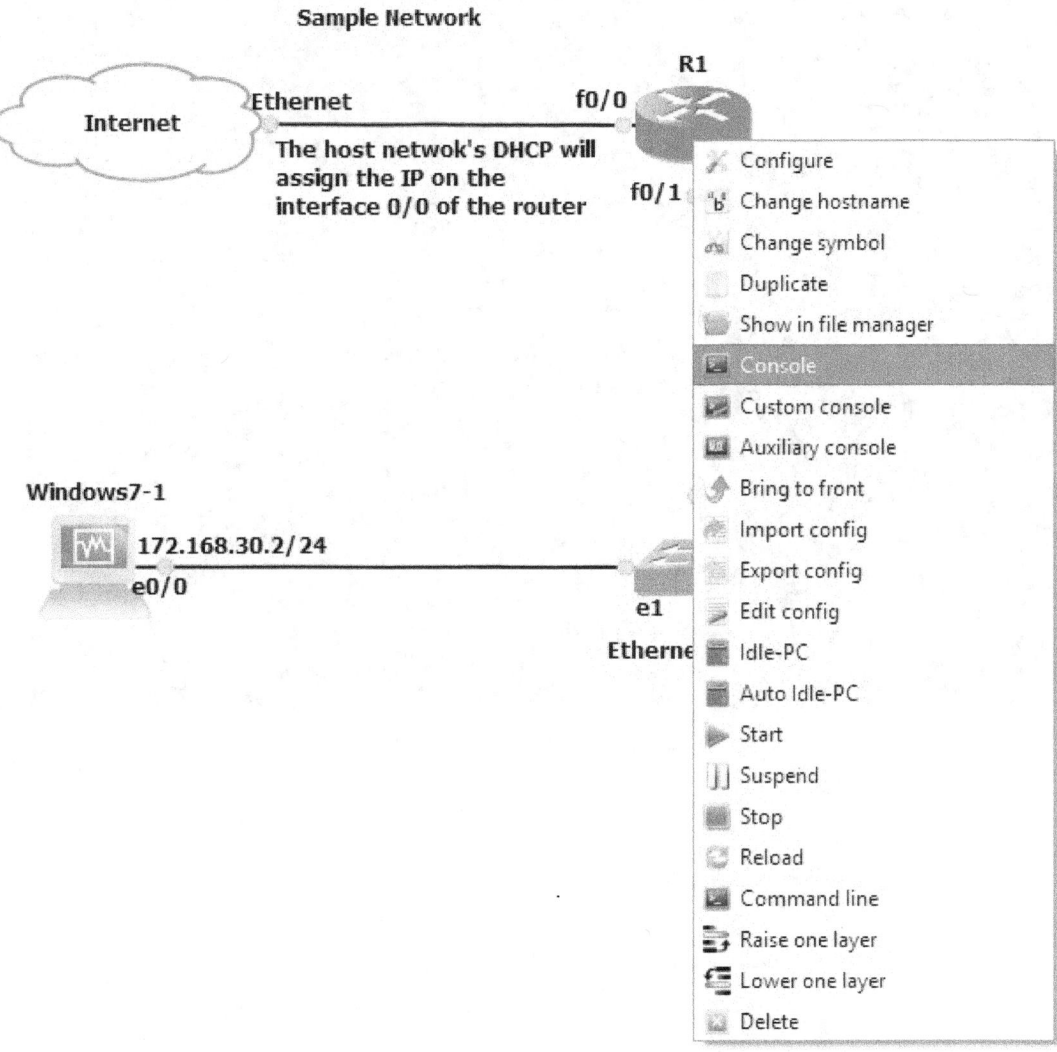

Figure 7.2: Opening the router's console for access

By clicking on the console option, the selected router's console would be opened for making configuration changes to the particular router. If the configurations have to be made, we can make it using the console.

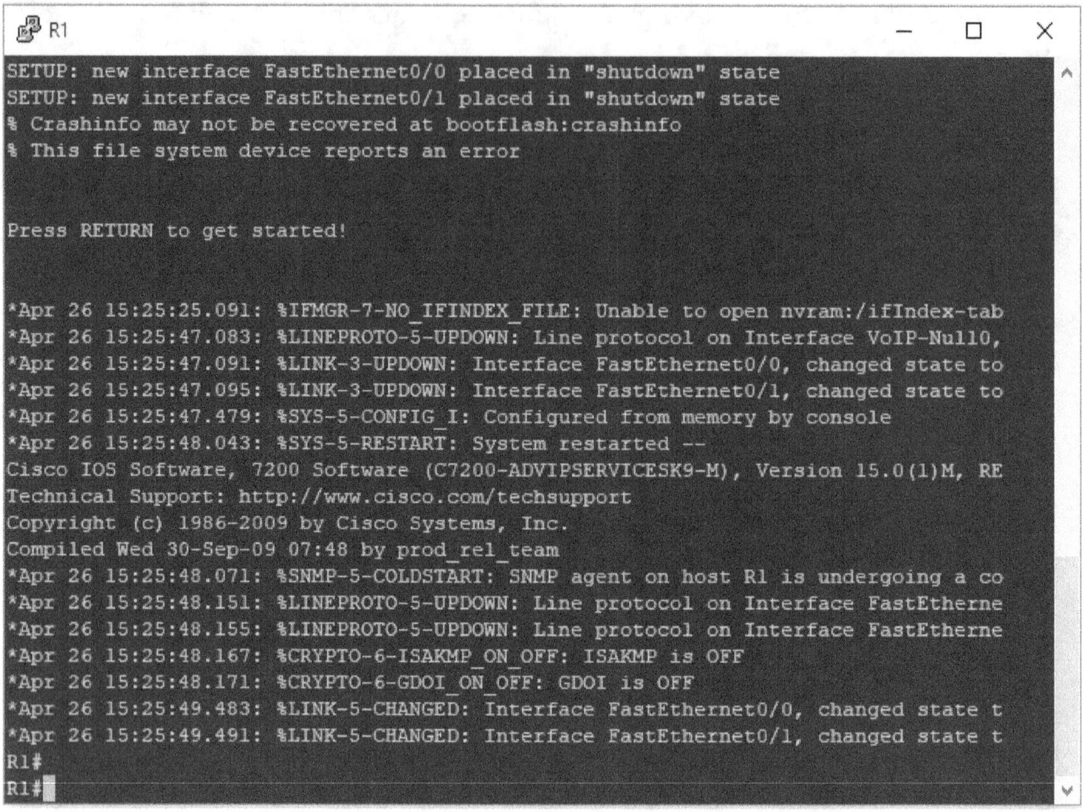

```
R1                                                              —   □   ×
SETUP: new interface FastEthernet0/0 placed in "shutdown" state
SETUP: new interface FastEthernet0/1 placed in "shutdown" state
% Crashinfo may not be recovered at bootflash:crashinfo
% This file system device reports an error


Press RETURN to get started!

*Apr 26 15:25:25.091: %IFMGR-7-NO_IFINDEX_FILE: Unable to open nvram:/ifIndex-tab
*Apr 26 15:25:47.083: %LINEPROTO-5-UPDOWN: Line protocol on Interface VoIP-Null0,
*Apr 26 15:25:47.091: %LINK-3-UPDOWN: Interface FastEthernet0/0, changed state to
*Apr 26 15:25:47.095: %LINK-3-UPDOWN: Interface FastEthernet0/1, changed state to
*Apr 26 15:25:47.479: %SYS-5-CONFIG_I: Configured from memory by console
*Apr 26 15:25:48.043: %SYS-5-RESTART: System restarted --
Cisco IOS Software, 7200 Software (C7200-ADVIPSERVICESK9-M), Version 15.0(1)M, RE
Technical Support: http://www.cisco.com/techsupport
Copyright (c) 1986-2009 by Cisco Systems, Inc.
Compiled Wed 30-Sep-09 07:48 by prod_rel_team
*Apr 26 15:25:48.071: %SNMP-5-COLDSTART: SNMP agent on host R1 is undergoing a co
*Apr 26 15:25:48.151: %LINEPROTO-5-UPDOWN: Line protocol on Interface FastEtherne
*Apr 26 15:25:48.155: %LINEPROTO-5-UPDOWN: Line protocol on Interface FastEtherne
*Apr 26 15:25:48.167: %CRYPTO-6-ISAKMP_ON_OFF: ISAKMP is OFF
*Apr 26 15:25:48.171: %CRYPTO-6-GDOI_ON_OFF: GDOI is OFF
*Apr 26 15:25:49.483: %LINK-5-CHANGED: Interface FastEthernet0/0, changed state t
*Apr 26 15:25:49.491: %LINK-5-CHANGED: Interface FastEthernet0/1, changed state t
R1#
R1#
```

Figure 7.3: The router's console

The other way to access the router is by using the "Console connect to all nodes" button. However, when we use this button, the consoles of all the nodes would be opened up for us.

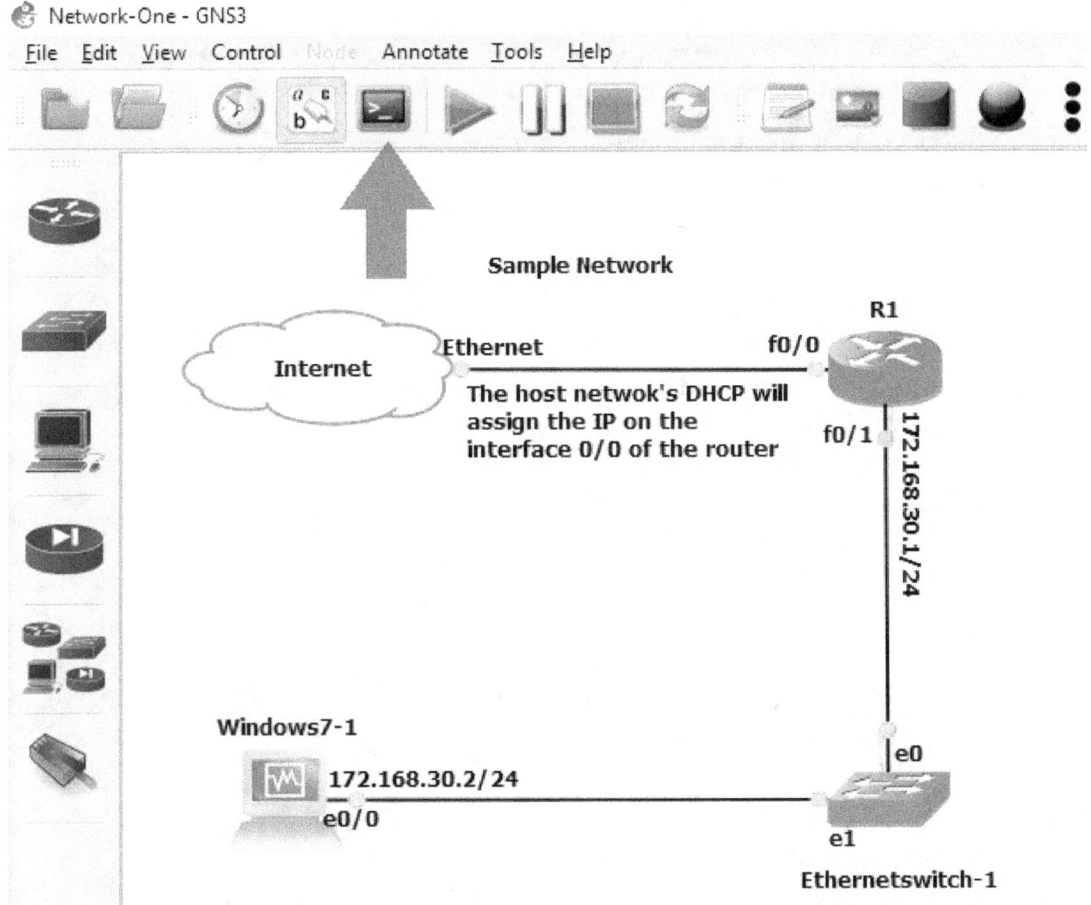

Figure 7.4: The "Console connect to all nodes" button

Configuring Router's Interface 0/0

To configure the router's interfaces, we will use the console and the following commands can be used for configuring the first interface to get an IP address assigned from the host network's DHCP. Although, technically, assigning IP address to a router is not recommended for a production environment, we are doing here since we are not having access to the real ISP. The host network is assumed as an ISP for our virtual network.

```
R1# conf t
R1(config)# interface fastEthernet 0/0
R1(config-if)# ip address dhcp
R1(config-if)# no shutdown
R1(config-if)# end
R1# wr
```

R1# show ip interface brief

Configuring Router's Interface 0/1

As per the scenario we have, assign 172.168.30.1/24 on to the router R1's interface fa 0/1 which is connected to the switch.

```
R1#conf t
R1(config)#interface fastEthernet 0/1
R1(config-if)#ip address 172.168.30.1 255.255.255.0
R1(config-if)#no shutdown
R1(config-if)#end
R1#wr
```

Configuring DHCP Service

For the devices used in the workspace to receive the IP addresses from the router, the following commands can be used to configure the DHCP service on the router.

```
R1#conf t
R1(config)#ip dhcp pool internal-clients
R1(dhcp-config)#network 172.168.30.0 255.255.255.0
R1(dhcp-config)#default-router 172.168.30.1
R1(dhcp-config)#dns-server aaa.bbb.ccc.ddd
R1(dhcp-config)#end
R1#wr
```

> *In the above in the place of aaa.bbb.ccc.ddd, you are expected to use the DNS server's IP address of your network.*

Configuring NAT

The following commands can be used for configuring the NAT on the router so that the devices which are assigned IP addresses by the DHCP service configured on the router would be able to make a request to the computers on the internet.

```
R1#conf t
R1(config)#access-list 1 permit 172.168.30.0 0.0.0.255
R1(config)#ip nat inside source list 1 interface fastEthernet 0/0 overload
R1(config)#interface fastEthernet 0/1
R1(config-if)#ip nat inside
R1(config-if)#exit
R1(config)#interface fastEthernet 0/0
R1(config-if)#ip nat outside
R1(config-if)#end
R1#wr
```

Testing the Network

The basic configuration required is completed and the client device (Windows 7) in the GNS3 network should be able to get the IP address assigned dynamically and also should be able to browse the internet.

For the verification, use the ipconfig command in the Windows 7 virtual machine's command prompt. The details of the IP address assigned would be shown in the output section of the command prompt as shown below.

Figure 7.5: Assigned IP details on the Windows 7 device

The same concept of creating a network topology in GNS3, configuring and testing the network can be applied to other networks of similar nature.

Further Reading

ProTechGurus. (2016, July 16). How to Connect Router to Cloud in GNS3. Retrieved from https://protechgurus.com/connect-router-cloud-in-gns3/

ProTechGurus. (2016, August 31). How To Use VPCS in GNS3. Retrieved from https://protechgurus.com/how-to-use-vpcs-in-gns3/

Step By Step Using And Configuring GNS3 Cisco Router simulator. (2010, May 25). Retrieved from https://www.routemybrain.com/step-by-step-using-and-configuring-gns3-cisco-router-simulator/

VPCs Tutorial. (2014, August 16). Retrieved from https://rednectar.net/archives/vpcs-tutorial/

Wilkins, S. (2012, July 11). Basic Configuration for GNS3 Labs. Retrieved from https://www.pluralsight.com/blog/tutorials/basic-configuration-for-gns3-labs

Your First Cisco GNS3 Topology. (n.d.). Retrieved from https://docs.gns3.com/1d1huu6z9-wWGD_ipTSQZqy2mpaxiqzymu-YQo6at_Jg/index.html

Part B

Chapter 8
Network Interface Configuration

In the previous chapters, we have learned to prepare the environment for building a virtual network laboratory using the GNS3 and the VirtualBox. To continue from this chapter onwards, the learners are required to have the pre-requisite knowledge of installing the Linux Operating System and the basic administration (Linux System Administration). Once the Linux operating system installation is complete, we are required to configure the network interfaces in order to either connect to the internet or to the Local Area Network (LAN). If the system is not going to be connected to any sort of network then there is no reason to configure the interfaces at all. However, this situation is not going to happen. In this chapter, we will learn to configure the network interfaces by using different methods and different IP addressing styles.

> *If the pre-requisite knowledge is not being met, the learners are required to refer the books on the basics of Linux System Administration.*

Static vs Dynamic IP Addresses

While working to configure the IP addresses for a system, a question that should arise is, whether to assign a static or dynamic IP address. There are different times when we should be deciding to use static or dynamic, and each one deserves to be analyzed well.

The static IP addressing is normally used when your network doesn't have a working DHCP server and also in case if the particular system is intended to be configured as one of the servers. The other important point to take note of is, if the number of systems in your network is more, which would considerably take a long time to configure the IP addresses, then it is recommended to use the dynamic IP addresses.

On the other hand, the dynamic IP addresses are used in the situations where the number of client systems is more than manageable size. For this, the assigning, reassigning and modification of the IP addresses are done by the Dynamic Host Configuration Protocol (DHCP) Server. If the system is to be a server, then it is not recommended to configure for getting dynamic IP addresses as it would cause issues due to the changing nature of the IP addresses.

Methods of Configuring IP Addresses

There are several ways and methods by which the IP addresses can be configured on the systems. The following are some of the ways which we can use to assign or configure the IP addresses to a system using:

- The Network Interface file
- Network Setting via GUI
- NetworkManager Text User Interface

Whichever method you use for configuring the IP addresses, you have to be aware of some of the information related to your network. So, before you start looking into further, let's

Build a Virtual Network and Practice

assume the following information which can be used during the configuration:

- The pool of IP addresses for your network to be 192.168.30.0/24
- The IP Address to be assigned to the system is 192.168.30.2 with netmask 255.255.255.0
- Gateway IP address to be 192.168.30.1
- DNS server's IP Address to be 192.168.30.1

Using the Network Interface File

Each network interface has a corresponding file which stores the configuration information of that particular network interface. We just have to open the network interface configuration file and enter the network information in the file. The network interface configuration files for CentOS 7 is located in the "/etc/sysconfig/network-scripts" directory. The following command can be used to navigate to the network-scripts directory and list the contents of the directory:

    [root@localhost ~]# cd /etc/sysconfig/network-scripts/
    [root@localhost network-scripts]# ls

```
[root@localhost network-scripts]# ls
ifcfg-enp0s3    ifdown-ppp         ifup-ib       ifup-Team
ifcfg-lo        ifdown-routes      ifup-ippp     ifup-TeamPort
ifdown          ifdown-sit         ifup-ipv6     ifup-tunnel
ifdown-bnep     ifdown-Team        ifup-isdn     ifup-wireless
ifdown-eth      ifdown-TeamPort    ifup-plip     init.ipv6-global
ifdown-ib       ifdown-tunnel      ifup-plusb    network-functions
ifdown-ippp     ifup               ifup-post     network-functions-ipv6
ifdown-ipv6     ifup-aliases       ifup-ppp
ifdown-isdn     ifup-bnep          ifup-routes
ifdown-post     ifup-eth           ifup-sit
[root@localhost network-scripts]# vim ifcfg-enp0s3
```

Figure 8.1: Contents of network-scripts directory

When listing the contents of the directory, there must be files whose names are prefixed with ifcfg. In the above list, ifcfg-enp0s3 is the configuration file for the first ethernet on the system.

Open the file using any one of the text editors which you are comfortable to work with. By default, the BOOTPROTO is set to "dhcp" in order to get the dynamic IP address. The following figure shows the default contents of the ifcfg-enp0s3 file:

```
TYPE=Ethernet
BOOTPROTO=dhcp
DEFROUTE=yes
IPV4_FAILURE_FATAL=no
IPV6INIT=yes
IPV6_AUTOCONF=yes
IPV6_DEFROUTE=yes
IPV6_FAILURE_FATAL=no
IPV6_ADDR_GEN_MODE=stable-privacy
NAME=enp0s3
UUID=33c42567-354a-4555-b5f9-eed07b07fc56
DEVICE=enp0s3
ONBOOT=yes
PEERDNS=yes
PEERROUTES=yes
IPV6_PEERDNS=yes
IPV6_PEERROUTES=yes
```

Figure 8.2: Content of the interface ifcfg-enp0s3 file

To configure the static IP address on the interface, the "BOOTPROTO" have to be changed to "none" and enter the IP, gateway & DNS information. In addition, the "ONBOOT" have to be set to "yes", so that the networking services would be started every time the system is started. This saves us from having to start the networking services manually. The following file content shows the information entered according to our scenario.

```
TYPE=Ethernet
BOOTPROTO=none
DEFROUTE=yes
IPV4_FAILURE_FATAL=no
IPV6INIT=yes
IPV6_AUTOCONF=yes
IPV6_DEFROUTE=yes
IPV6_FAILURE_FATAL=no
IPV6_ADDR_GEN_MODE=stable-privacy
NAME=enp0s3
UUID=33c42567-354a-4555-b5f9-eed07b07fc56
DEVICE=enp0s3
ONBOOT=yes
IPADDR=192.168.30.2
PREFIX=24
GATEWAY=192.168.30.1
DNS1=192.168.30.1
PEERDNS=yes
PEERROUTES=yes
IPV6_PEERDNS=yes
IPV6_PEERROUTES=yes
```

Figure 8.3: Static configuration of the interface file

Once the required information is being entered into the network interface file, we must save, quit the file and then restart the networking service to bring the changes into effect.

Network Setting via GUI

We can very well configure the IP address for the system by going to the network Settings if the system you are working has the Graphical User Interface (GUI). For this go to Applications --> System Tools --> Settings --> Click on the Network. Then the following screen would be displayed:

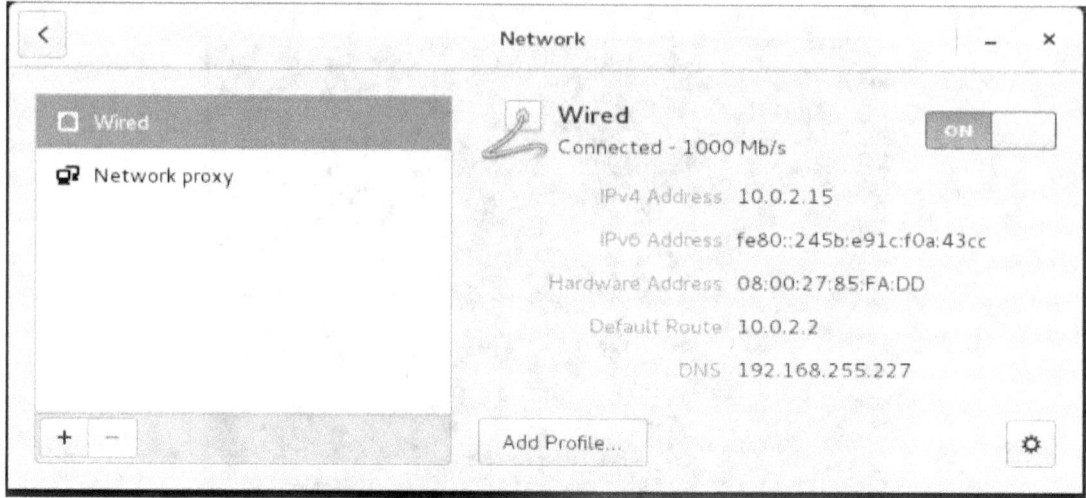

Figure 8.4: Choosing to configure from GUI

From the dialog box, click on the settings button after selecting Wired, and then the following would be displayed.

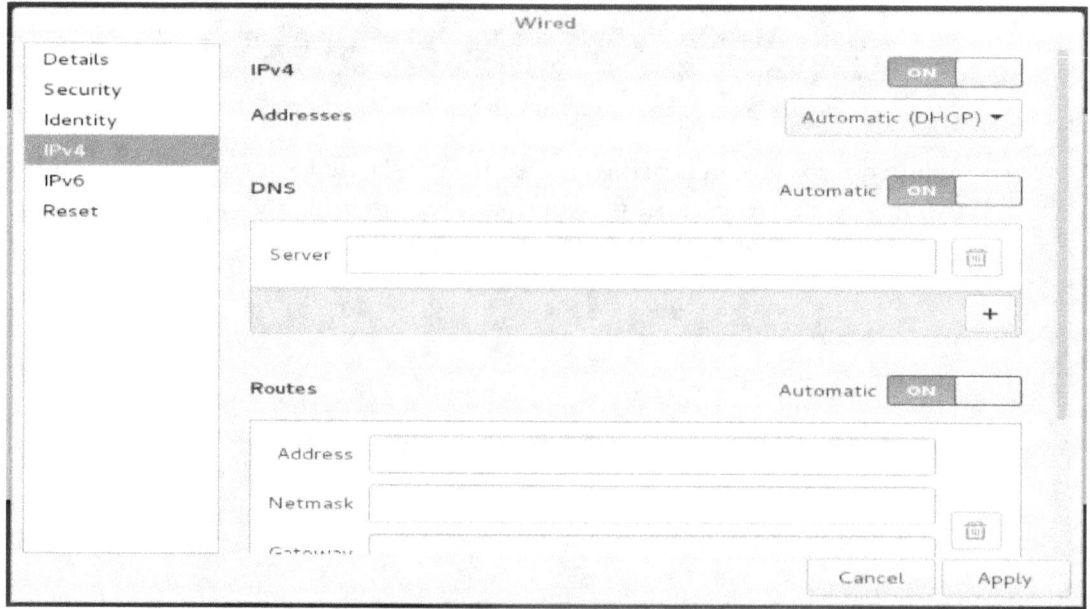

Figure 8.5: IPv4 settings

On the dialog box, keep the selection on the IPv4 and enter the information as shown:

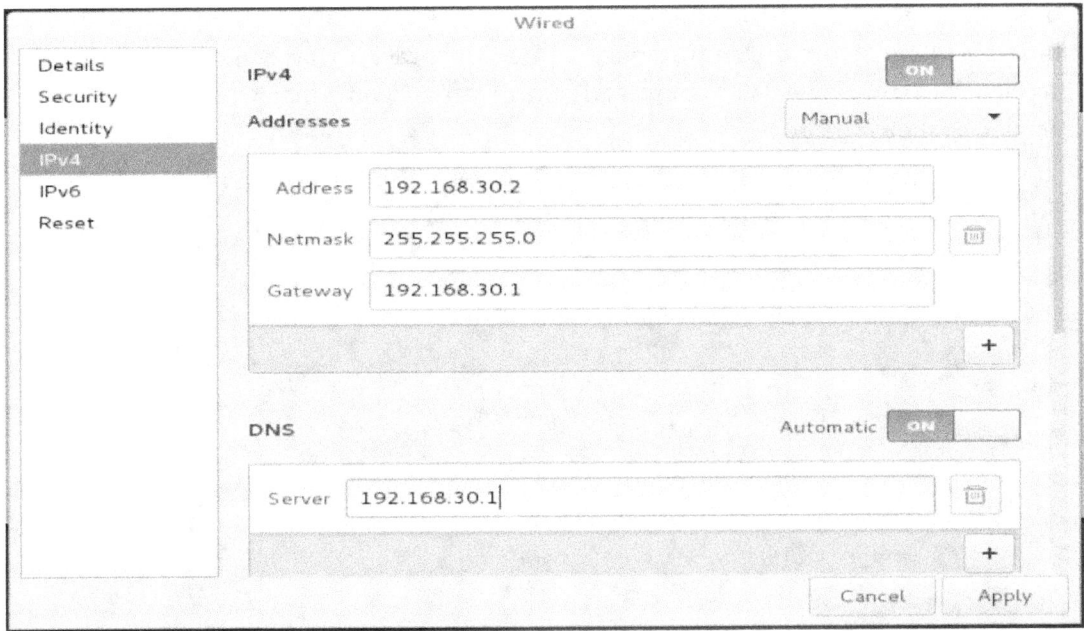

Figure 8.6: Specifying IPv4 options

To bring the changes into effect, click the apply button and then restart the networking services. Once the changes have taken effect, the settings would be similar to the following:

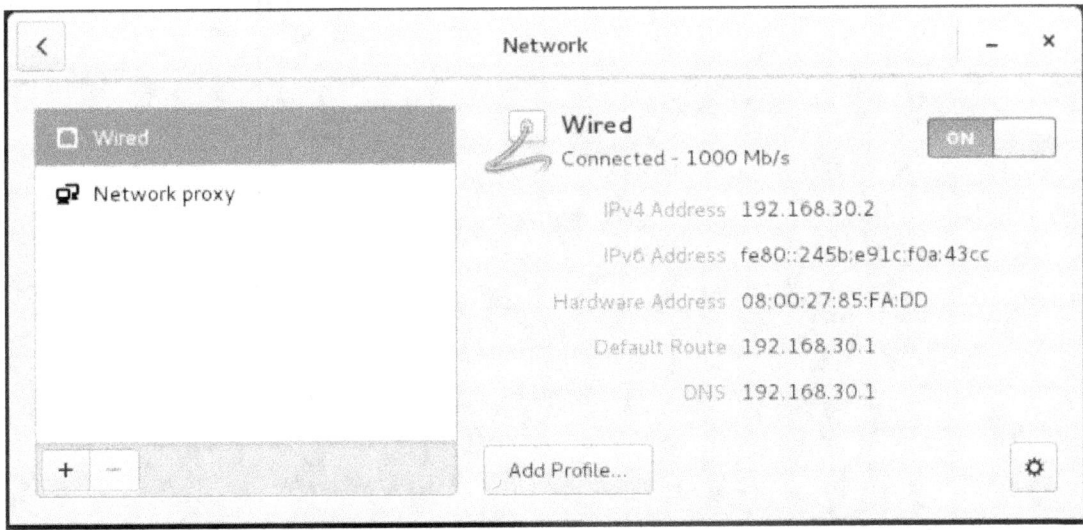

Figure 8.7: Configuration from GUI completed

The NetworkManager Text User Interface

Configuring the IP address using this method involves the use of a command nmtui, which brings up a Text User Interface (TUI). In order to launch the nmtui utility interface, just by typing the command nmtui on the terminal would bring up the interface as shown below:

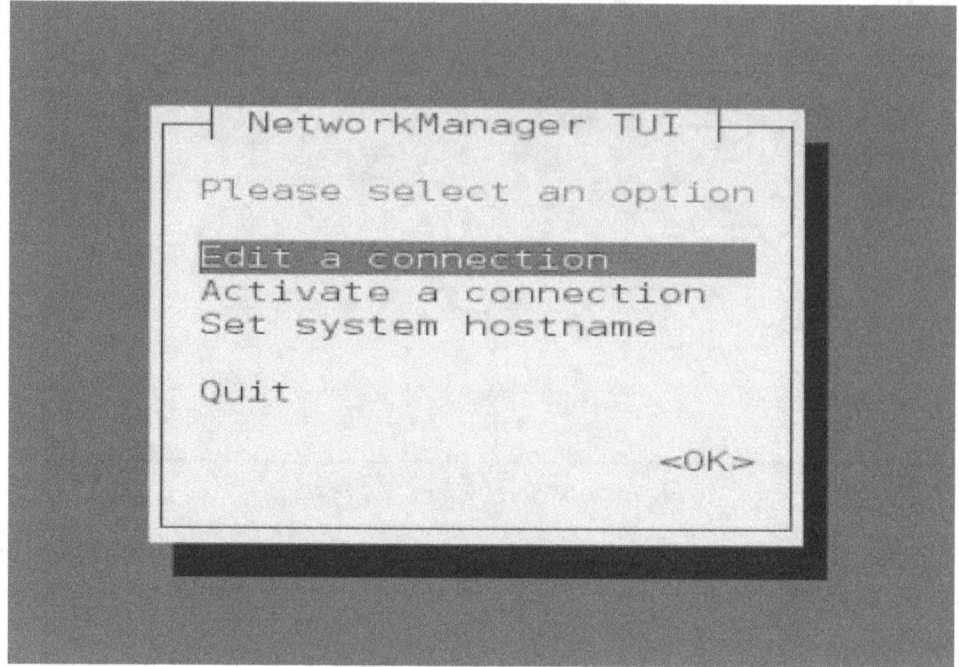

Figure 8.8: Choosing to edit a connection

From the three options, we have to select "Edit a connection" option by using the arrow keys on the keyboard. The selection using the mouse is not going to work since this is a Text User Interface. Once the selection is done, press Enter key and the following would be displayed:

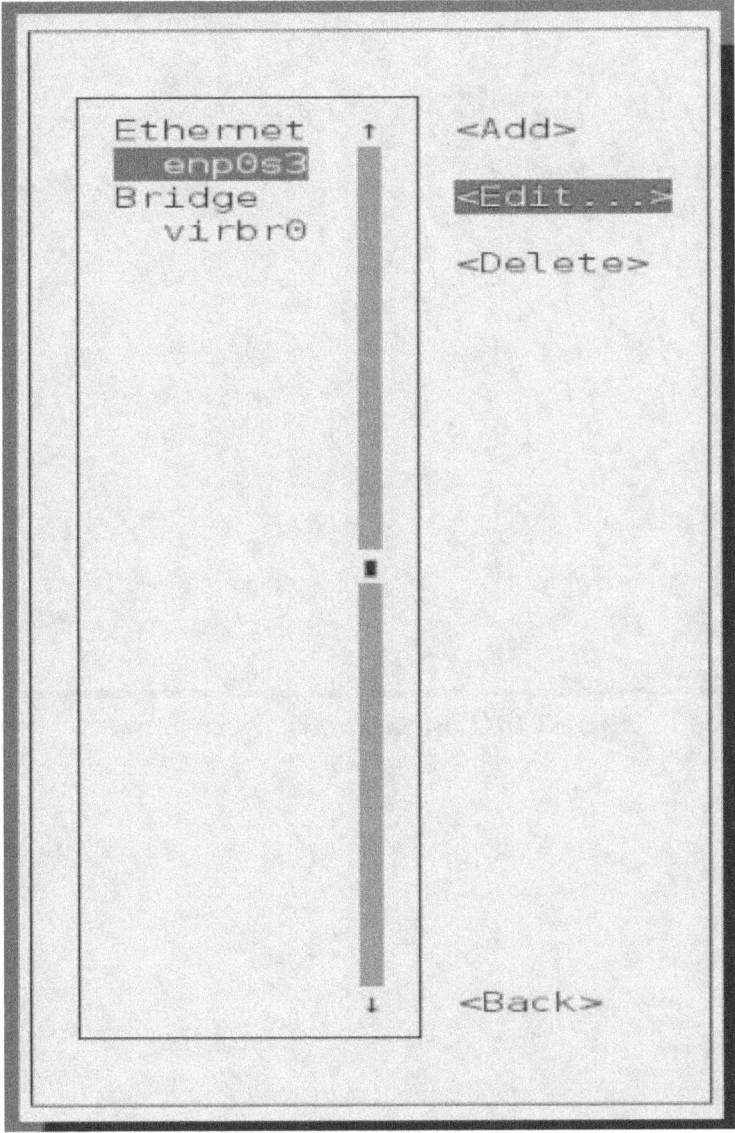

Figure 8.9: Editing the details of the enp0s3 interface

Select the intended network interface, then select 'Edit' using the arrow keys and then press [Enter] key on the keyboard. Then the following srceen would be shown:

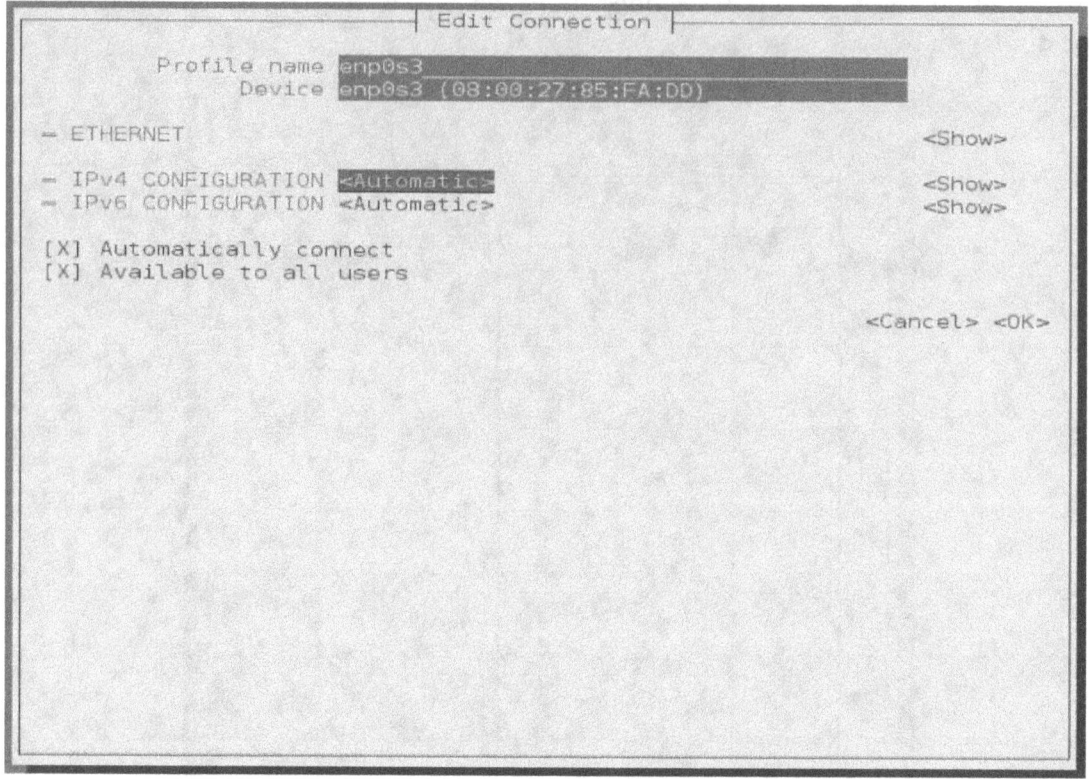

Figure 8.10: Choosing the configuration type

In the 'IPv4 Configuration' select "Manual" instead of "Automatic" and then expand the entry fields by selecting "Show" and pressing [Enter] to enter the network information.

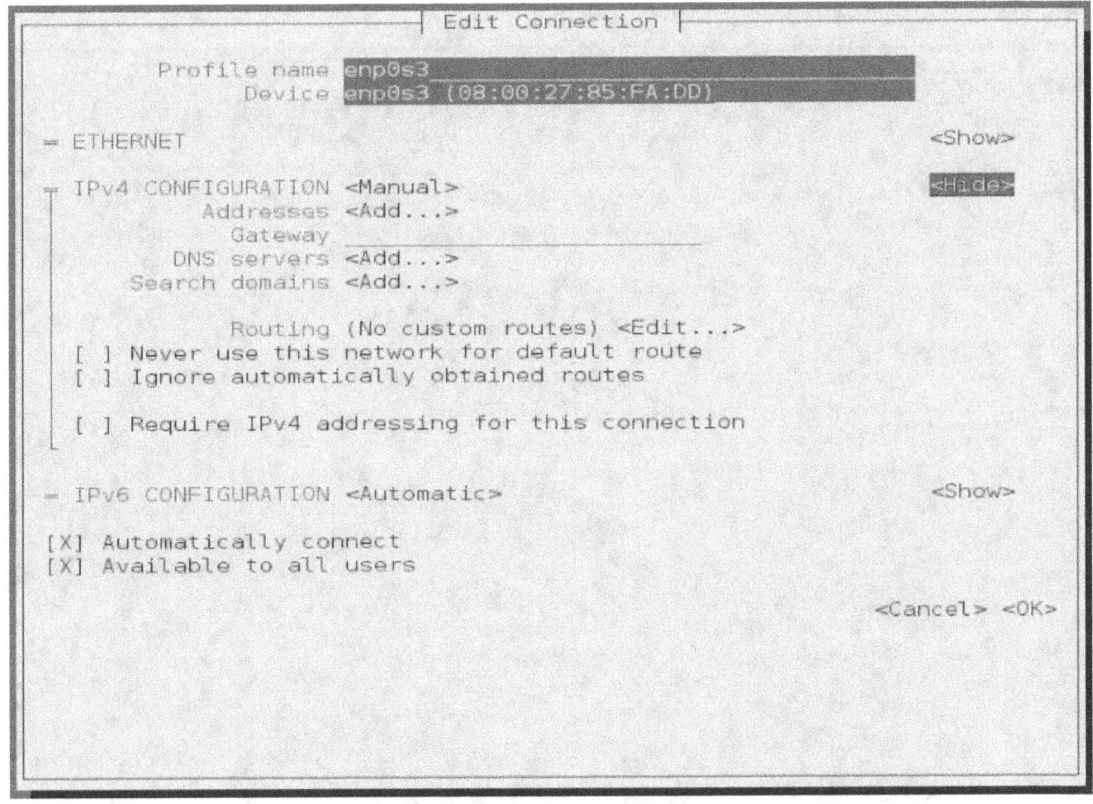

Figure 8.11: Expanding the configuration options

So, in the expanded fields, the network information can be entered accordingly as indicated in the following. Mark [x] next to Automatically connect by pressing the [spacebar] on the keyboard and then choose OK:

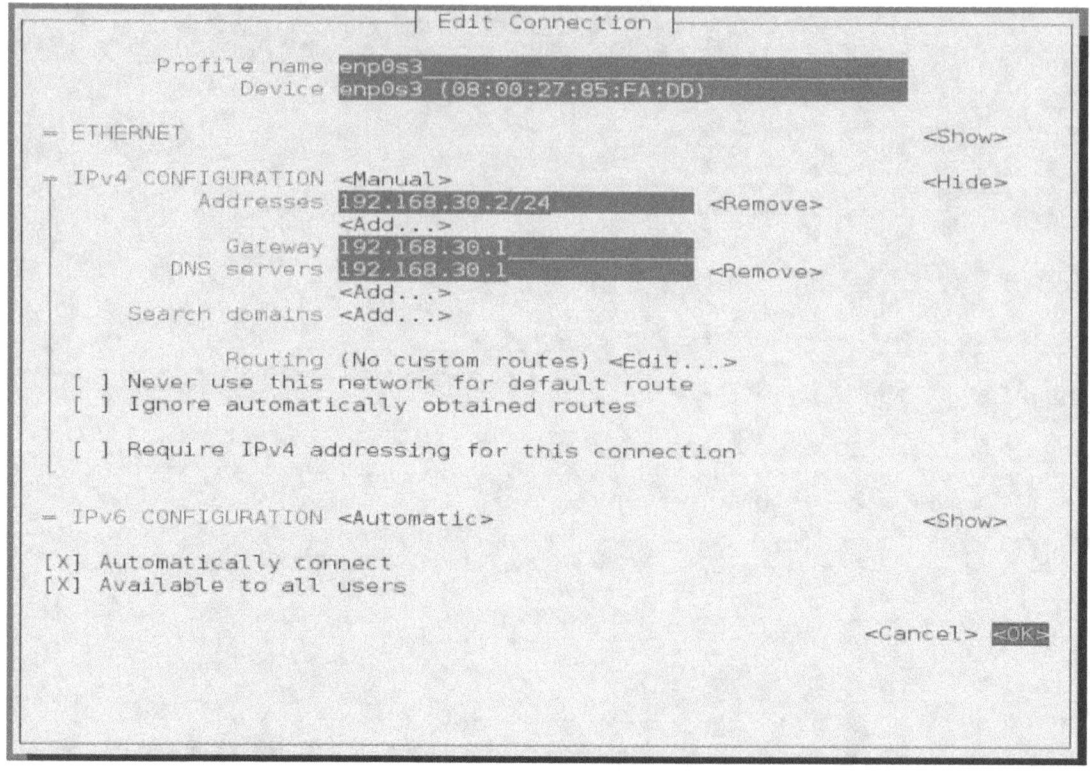

Figure 8.12: Completing the manual configuration

In the next, press [Esc] and then "quit" to complete the configuration.

> *In case if the nmtui utility is not available, you can install the net-tools package and then proceed further.*

Further Reading

A., Kalakoti. (2016, December 13). Static IP address configuration on Redhat / CentOS 7. Retrieved April 05, 2018, from https://www.techinformant.in/static-ip-address-configuration-in-linux-centos-7/

Centos 7 Network Config. (n.d.). Retrieved April 04, 2018, from https://www.psychz.net/client/question/en/centos-7-network-config.html

Configure static IP address on CentOS 7. (2017, September 24). Retrieved April 05, 2018, from https://www.linglom.com/networking/configure-static-ip-address-on-centos-7/

How to Configure Network Static IP Address and Manage Services on RHEL/CentOS 7.0. (n.d.). Retrieved April 05, 2018, from https://www.tecmint.com/configure-network-interface-in-rhel-centos-7-0/

J., Mutai. (2018, January 14). How to configure static IP address on CentOS. Retrieved April 05, 2018, from https://computingforgeeks.com/simple-way-to-configure-static-ip-address-on-centos-6-x-and-centos-7-server/

J., Mutai. (2018, March 02). Ifconfig vs ip usage guide on Linux. Retrieved April 05, 2018, from https://computingforgeeks.com/ifconfig-vs-ip-usage-guide-on-linux/

K. (2014, August 21). How to Setup network on centos 7. Retrieved April 05, 2018, from https://www.krizna.com/centos/setup-network-centos-7/

R. (2015, March 31). How to setup network after RHEL/CentOS 7 minimal installation. Retrieved April 05, 2018, from https://lintut.com/how-to-setup-network-after-rhelcentos-7-minimal-installation/

R. (2017, November 26). How to Configure Static IP Address in CentOS 7 / RHEL 7 / Fedora 27/26. Retrieved April 05, 2018, from https://www.itzgeek.com/how-tos/linux/centos-how-tos/how-to-configure-static-ip-address-in-centos-7-rhel-7-fedora-26.html

S. (2018, March 12). Configure IP address (Networking) in RHEL/CentOS 7. Retrieved April 05, 2018, from http://linuxtechlab.com/configure-ip-address-rhel-centos/

Chapter 9
Introduction to Firewall

In the earlier versions of the CentOS distribution, iptables was used as the firewall and with the recent developments, CentOS 7 uses the Firewalld as the default tool to manage the host-based firewall. Firewalld provides a way to configure dynamic firewall rules in Linux systems which can be applied instantly, without having to restart the firewall. In this chapter, we will look into the basics of firewalld and learn to manage ports, services, zones and use the rich rules.

Your Default Firewall

If you are using Linux distributions other than CentOS, firewalld may or may not be the default firewall on your system. If you wish to use the firewalld instead of iptables, consider disabling the iptables. Firewalld is considered to be incompatible with the iptables and it is recommended to avoid running both iptables and firewalld at the same time.

Disabling iptables

If iptables is your default firewall, all the three associated iptables' services must be disabled and masked. The individual iptables' services can be disabled and masked by following the given commands below.

Use the following commands for disabling and masking iptables service which is used for IPv4 configuration:

```
# systemctl disable iptables
# systemctl mask iptables
```

Use the following commands for disabling and masking ip6tables service which is used for IPv6 configuration:

```
# systemctl disable ip6tables
# systemctl mask ip6tables
```

Use the following commands for disabling and masking ebtables service which is used for software bridge configuration:

```
# systemctl disable ebtables
# systemctl mask ebtables
```

> *In order to avoid accidental or intentional enabling of the iptables' services by the users in a multi-user environment, it is recommended to mask the services completely so that the services can't be started or enabled.*

Enabling Firewalld

If you are working on a CentOS 7 system or higher version, the firewalld is the default firewall and it would be up and running by default. However, if your system had a firewall other than firewalld, then it is important for you to either install firewalld (if not present on your system), enable and start the firewalld services. The following commands can be used to check the status, unmask, start and enable the firewalld services on your system. To check the current status of firewalld service on your system, use the following command:

    #systemctl status firewalld

In order for you to be able to start a service which had been masked, we have to unmask it prior to its starting. So, to unmask the firewalld service, run the following command on your system:

    #systemctl unmask firewalld

Then you can proceed to start and enable the firewalld service by executing the following commands:

    #systemctl start firewalld
    #systemctl enable firewalld

> *Immediately after disabling and masking the iptables' services, you are required to restart your system and then only proceed with the enabling and starting of the firewalld services.*

Firewalld Zone Management

Firewalld is a zone-based firewall and in the firewalld, the zones can be configured to either accept or deny certain services or ports, which separate networks into different zones based on the level of trust the user has decided to place on the interfaces and traffic within that network.

The zones are the constructed rulesets for the various levels of trust and security scenario such as home, dmz, internal, etc. Each zone allows different network services and incoming traffic types while it denies the rest implicitly.

The firewalld zones can be made to associate with one or more network interfaces of the system. For example, with separate interfaces for both the internal network and the Internet, you can allow DHCP on an internal zone but only HTTP and SSH on the external zone. The interface which is not explicitly associated with any specific zone will be by default associated with default zone.

Listing Zones

The firewalld has a set of pre-configured zones such as block, dmz, drop, external, home, internal, public, trusted and work. In order to list the available zones on a system, the following command can be used:

$ firewalld-cmd --get-zones

```
[root@localhost ~]# firewall-cmd --get-zones
block dmz drop external home internal public trusted work
[root@localhost ~]#
```

Figure 9.1: Listing the available zones

In the above figure 9.1, the available zones are getting listed and it is important to know which services and ports are available through those zones. The following table describes the zones which are available by default:

Table 9.1

Zones	Description
block	Any incoming network connections are rejected with an icmp-host-prohibited message for IPv4 and icmp6-adm-prohibited for IPv6. Only network connections initiated from within the system (outgoing network connections) are possible.
dmz	For the systems in your demilitarized (dmz) zone which are publicly-accessible with limited access to your internal network. Only selected incoming connections are accepted.
drop	Any incoming network packets are dropped without sending a reply. Only outgoing network connections are possible.
external	For use on external networks with masquerading enabled, especially for the routers. You do not trust the other computers on the network to not harm your computer. So, only the selected incoming connections are accepted.
home	For computers in your home area, only selected incoming connections are accepted.
internal	For use on internal networks which you mostly trust that the other computers on the networks will not harm your computer. Only selected incoming connections are accepted.
public	For use in public areas, in which you do not trust the other computers

Default Zone

If you have not changed, the default zone in the firewall must be public zone. We can find out which zone is currently the default on your system by using the following command:

firewall-cmd --get-default-zone

```
[root@localhost ~]# firewall-cmd --get-default-zone
public
[root@localhost ~]#
```

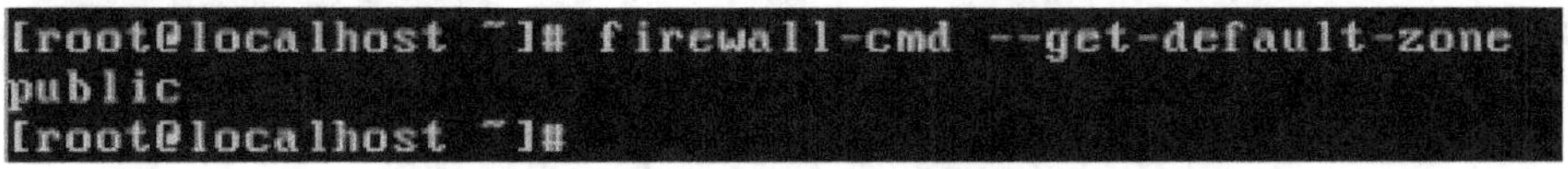

Figure 9.2: Getting the default zones

Active Zones

Since we haven't changed anything, the default zone will also be be the only "active" zone (the zone that is controlling the traffic for our interfaces). The active zones can be verified by using the following command:

firewall-cmd --get-active-zone

```
[root@localhost ~]#
[root@localhost ~]# firewall-cmd --get-active-zone
public
   interfaces: enp0s3
[root@localhost ~]# _
```

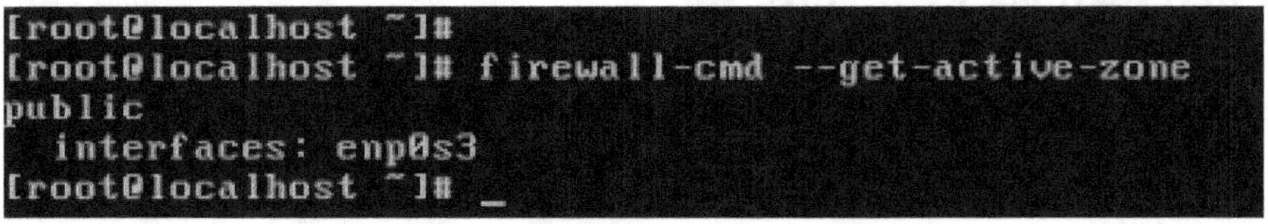

Figure 9.3: getting the active zones

In the above figure, one interface (enp0s3) of the system is being controlled by the firewall and is associated with the public zone.

Setting a Default Zone

You can change the default zone with the --set-default-zone option. In the example below, the default zone is set to work:

firewall-cmd --set-default-zone=work

```
[root@localhost ~]# firewall-cmd --set-default-zone=work
success
[root@localhost ~]#
[root@localhost ~]#
```

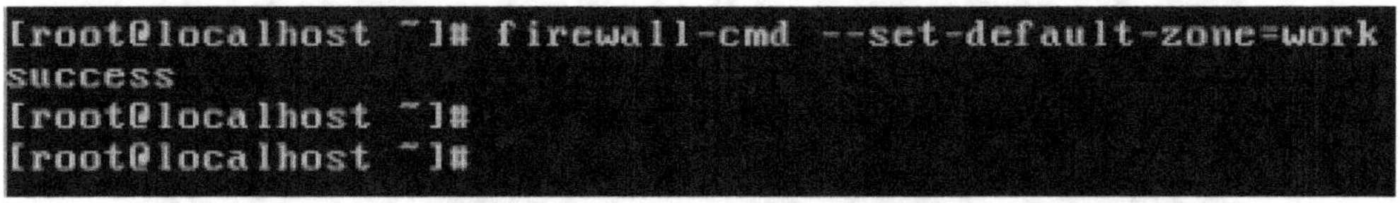

Figure 9.4: Setting the default zone

In the figure shown above, the default zone is being set to work zone from the public zone successfully.

Changing the Interface's Zone

We can also change the zone of an interface and whenever we change the zone of an interface, we will also be modifying the services that will be operational. In the example below, the zone of the interface enp0s3 will be changed to work.

firewall-cmd --zone=work --change-interface=enp0s3

```
[root@localhost ~]# firewall-cmd --zone=work --change-interface=enp0s3
The interface is under control of NetworkManager, setting zone to 'work'.
success
[root@localhost ~]#
```

Figure 9.5: Changing the interface's zone

> Whenever you are associating an interface to a new zone, be aware that you are probably modifying the services that will be operational. For instance, if we are moving to the "home" zone, which has SSH available, however, some zones would not have SSH service enabled by default. You should be able to figure out why your connection drops if it at all happens.

Viewing the Zone's Configuration

In the previous examples, we have changed the default zone to work and also, we have set the interface's zone to work. How do we know, what rules are associated with the work zone? To view the default zone's configuration, type the command shown in the following figure:

```
[root@localhost ~]# firewall-cmd --list-all
work (active)
  target: default
  icmp-block-inversion: no
  interfaces: enp0s3
  sources:
  services: ssh dhcpv6-client
  ports:
  protocols:
  masquerade: no
  forward-ports:
  source-ports:
  icmp-blocks:
  rich rules:

[root@localhost ~]#
```

Figure 9.6: Viewing the zone's configuration

Build a Virtual Network and Practice

From the above output, we can conclude that, the work zone is active and the interface enp0s3 is associated with this zone. In addition, we can also see that this zone allows for the normal operations associated with a DHCP client (for IP address assignment) and SSH (for remote administration).

The specific zone's associated configuration can also be listed and viewed by using the following command:

firewall-cmd --zone=home --list-all

```
[root@localhost ~]#
[root@localhost ~]# firewall-cmd --zone=home --list-all
home
  target: default
  icmp-block-inversion: no
  interfaces:
  sources:
  services: ssh mdns samba-client dhcpv6-client
  ports:
  protocols:
  masquerade: no
  forward-ports:
  source-ports:
  icmp-blocks:
  rich rules:

[root@localhost ~]#
```

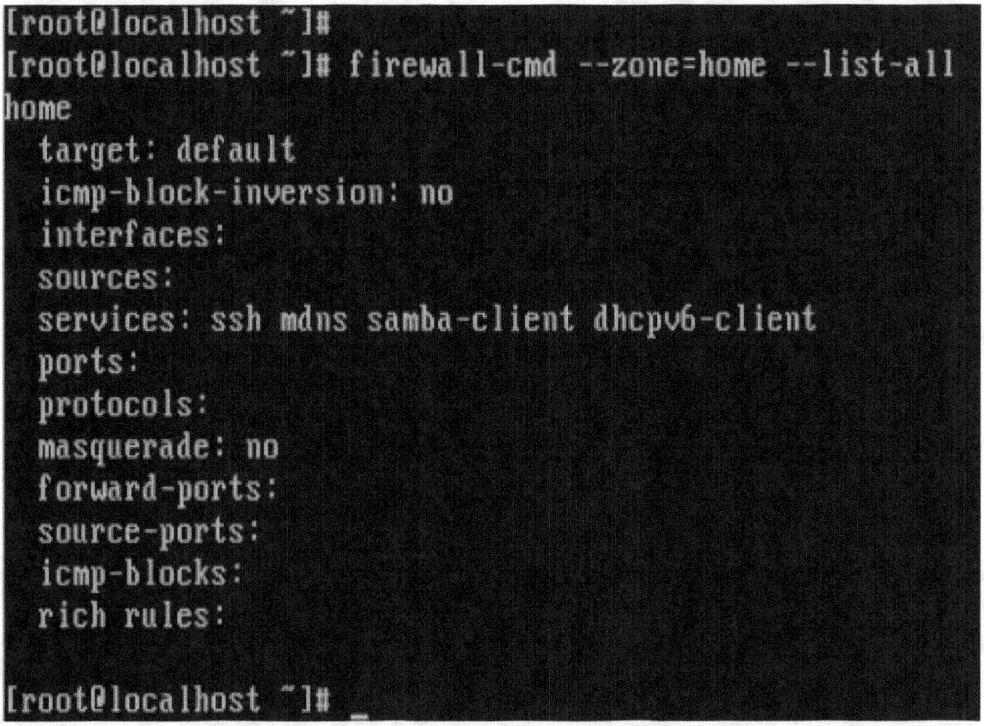

Figure 9.7: View specific zone's configuration

You can view all the zone's associated configuration by using the --list-all-zones option. Since the expected output is not going to fit in a single screen, you may consider using the pipe (|) for easy viewing.

firewall-cmd --list-all-zones | less

Interface's Associated Zones

In order to find out which zone is associated with the particular interface, use the following command:

firewall-cmd --get-zone-of-interface=enp0s3

```
[root@localhost ~]#
[root@localhost ~]# firewall-cmd --get-zone-of-interface=enp0s3
work
[root@localhost ~]#
```

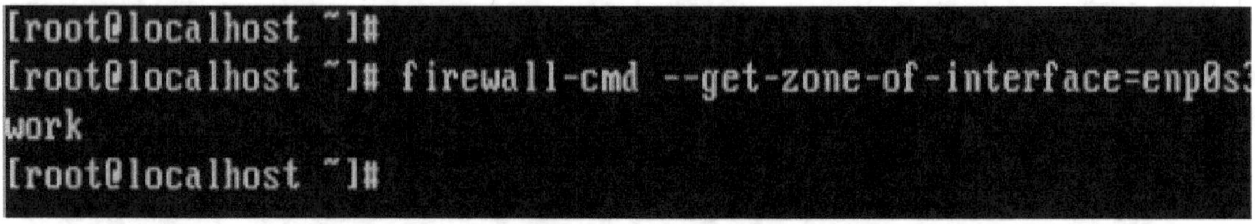

Figure 9.8: Checking zone's association with interface

In the above figure, the associated zone for the interface enp0ss3 is work.

Creating New Zones

In addition to the in-built zones, you can also create new zones which meet your requirements. The --new-zone option can be used along with the --permanent option to create a new zone. In the following example we create a zone called websrv:

firewall-cmd --new-zone=webzone --permanent

Then reload the firewalld and try to list the available zones as shown in the following:

firewall-cmd --reload
firewall-cmd --get-zones

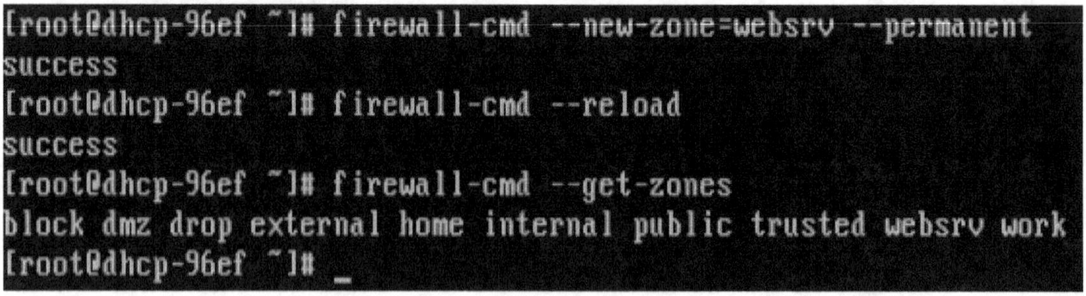

```
[root@dhcp-96ef ~]# firewall-cmd --new-zone=websrv --permanent
success
[root@dhcp-96ef ~]# firewall-cmd --reload
success
[root@dhcp-96ef ~]# firewall-cmd --get-zones
block dmz drop external home internal public trusted websrv work
[root@dhcp-96ef ~]#
```

Figure 9.9: Creating new zone

In the above figure, the newly created zone, websrv, get listed in addition to the available in-inbuilt zones.

Adding an Interface to a Zone

Once the creation of a zone is done, it can be associated with one of the interfaces. We have created a zone called "websrv" and want to associate it with the interface "enp0s3". For this we have to run the following commands respectively for the temporary and permanent association:

```
# firewall-cmd --permanent --zone=websrv --add-interface=enp0s3
# firewall-cmd --permanent --zone=websrv --add-interface=enp0s3 --permanent
```

Listing the Assigned Interfaces

The zones can be queried for the interfaces assigned to it. In the previous example, we have assigned the interface enp0s3 to the websrv zone. To query for the interfaces which are assigned to specific zones, use the following command:

```
# firewall-cmd --zone=websrv --list-interfaces
```

The expected output is "enp0s3" as we have just associated it with the websrv zone in the previous example.

Removing Interface from the Zone

From the zone, the associated interface can be removed using the --remove-interface option as shown in the following command:

```
# firewall-cmd --remove-interface=enp0s3 --zone=websrv
```

Service Management

Firewalld allows traffic based on the predefined rules for specific network services. You can create your own custom service rules and add them to any of the zones as required.

Getting the Services

In order to get a list of services available, which the firewall is aware of, use the following command:

```
# firewall-cmd --get-services
```

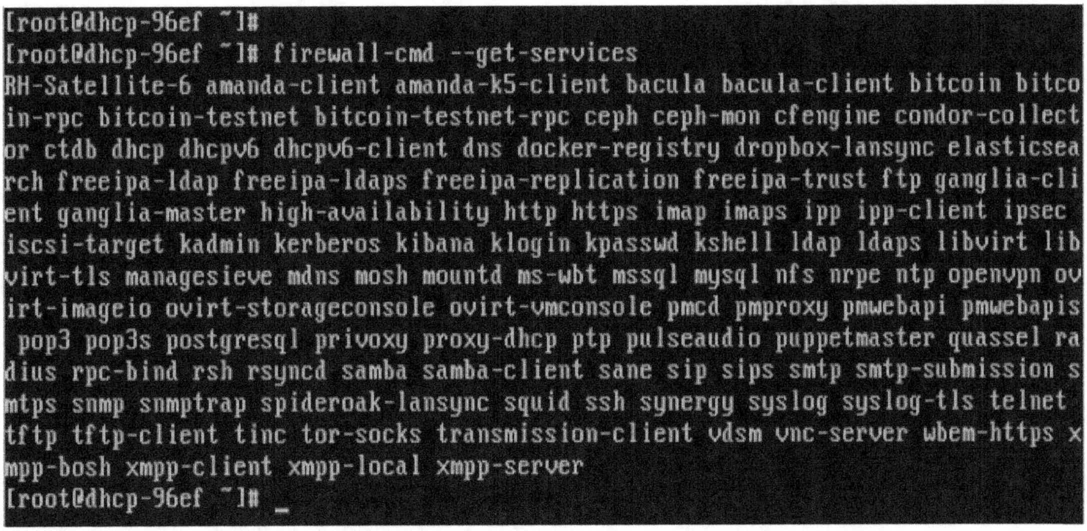

Figure 9.10: Listing the services

On the other hand, to get the list of services on a default zone for which the ports are opened, the following command can be used:

    # firewall-cmd --list-services

```
[root@dhcp-96ef ~]#
[root@dhcp-96ef ~]#
[root@dhcp-96ef ~]# firewall-cmd --list-services
ssh dhcpv6-client
[root@dhcp-96ef ~]#
```

Figure 9.11: Listing the default zone's services

To get the list of services of a particular zone, use --zone option as shown below:

    # firewall-cmd --list-services --zone=public
    # firewall-cmd --list-services --zone=websrv

```
[root@dhcp-96ef ~]#
[root@dhcp-96ef ~]# firewall-cmd --list-services --zone=public
dhcpv6-client ssh
[root@dhcp-96ef ~]#
[root@dhcp-96ef ~]# firewall-cmd --list-services --zone=websrv

[root@dhcp-96ef ~]#
[root@dhcp-96ef ~]#
```

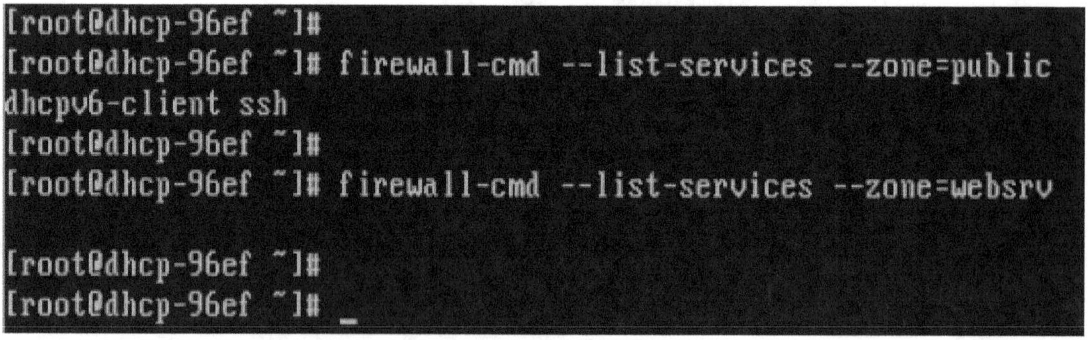

Figure 9.12: Listing specific zone's services

In the above figure, for the public zone, two services are listed while the websrv zone has no services as we have not added any service to the websrv zone after its creation.

Adding the Service

We can add the services to the zones as per our need. In the websrv zone, which we have created in addition to the in-built zones, there is no service added. Let's try to add the http service to this newly created zone, reload the firewall and list the services by following the sequence of commands shown below and see what happens:

    # firewall-cmd --zone=internal --add-service=http
    # firewall-cmd --reload
    # firewall-cmd --list-services --zone=websrv

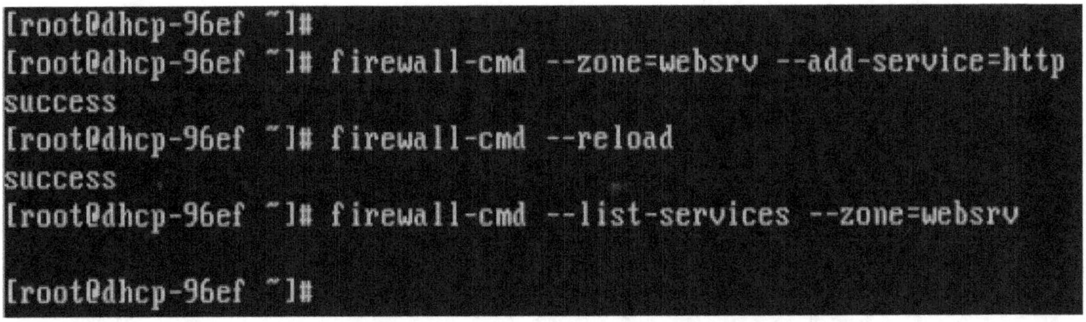

```
[root@dhcp-96ef ~]#
[root@dhcp-96ef ~]# firewall-cmd --zone=websrv --add-service=http
success
[root@dhcp-96ef ~]# firewall-cmd --reload
success
[root@dhcp-96ef ~]# firewall-cmd --list-services --zone=websrv

[root@dhcp-96ef ~]#
```

Figure 9.13: Adding services to the zone

In the above figure, we have followed the sequence of commands and successfully added the service to the websrv zone. However, the http service is not getting listed, which otherwise it should have been. What has happened here? The answer for not having listed any service lies in the next section.

Surviving the Next Reload or Reboot

In firewalld, the configurations can either be runtime or permanent. The addition or modification of the rules without the --permanent flag in the firewalld doesn't survive the next reload or the system reboot. Such rules are considered as the runtime rules and when the firewall is reloaded or when the system is rebooted, the old existing rules are taken into effect.

If a rule is added or modified with the --permanent flag, the rule survives or persists even after the reloading of the firewall or the system reboot. The --permanent flag can also be used to build up an entire set of rules over time that will be applied at once when the reload command is issued.

The following commands can be used to add the rules to both the runtime as well as the permanent configuration sets, reload and try listing the services:

    # firewall-cmd --zone=websrv --add-service=http --permanent
    # firewall-cmd --zone=websrv --add-service=http
    # firewall-cmd --list-services –zone=websrv

```
[root@dhcp-96ef ~]#
[root@dhcp-96ef ~]# firewall-cmd --zone=websrv --add-service=http
success
[root@dhcp-96ef ~]# firewall-cmd --reload
success
[root@dhcp-96ef ~]# firewall-cmd --list-services --zone=websrv

[root@dhcp-96ef ~]#
```

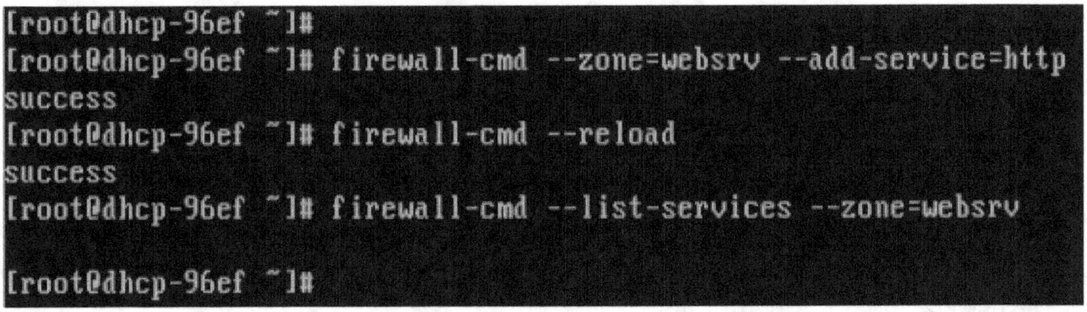

Figure 9.14: Adding services to be permanent

In the above figure, now we can see the service listed as expected because the "--permanent" flag has been used to create a persistent rule.

Removing the Services

In the previous examples, we have added the http service to the websrv zone. We will try to remove the http service from the websrv zone permanently. In order to remove the http service from the websrv zone, the following command can be used:

    # firewall-cmd --remove-service=http --zone=websrv --permanent

Similarly, runtime services can be removed from the websrv zone by using the following command:

    # firewall-cmd --remove-service=http --zone=websrv

Adding and Removing Multiple Services at Once

Multiple services can be added to the zones or removed from the zones as the runtime or permanent configuration at once. If we wanted to add the https and dns services to the websrv zone in addition to the already existing http service, the following commands can be used accordingly for temporary and permanent configurations respectively:

    # firewall-cmd --add-service={https,dns} --zone=websrv
    # firewall-cmd --add-service={https,dns} --zone=websrv --permanent

Similarly, if we wanted to remove the http, https and dns services from the websrv zone, the following commands can be used accordingly for temporary and permanent configurations respectively:

    # firewall-cmd --remove-service={http,https,dns} --zone=websrv
    # firewall-cmd --remove-service={http,https,dns} --zone=websrv --permanent

Port Management

The services which are included in the firewalld installation has the most common requirements for applications that we may use but there can be situations where those services do not fit our requirements.

Firewalld allows to manage the network ports directly when the service to be added is not available for the particular application and you can open the ports that a particular application uses in the zones.

On the other hand, even if a particular service is not installed in the system, ports can be either opened or closed in the firewall. For instance, even if the SSH service is not installed on a particular system, the port number 22 which is associated with SSH can be opened or closed in the firewall.

Opening Ports for the Zones

The port can be opened for the particular application by specifying the port or the range of ports used and the TCP or UDP protocol associated with that particular application. For example, if the application which we intend to use runs on port 5500 and uses TCP protocol, we can add to a zone permanently or temporarily as shown below:

```
# firewall-cmd --zone=websrv --add-port=5500/tcp --permanent
# firewall-cmd --zone=websrv --add-port=5500/tcp
```

If the protocol used is both TCP and UDP, then the following command can be used to add at once:

```
# firewall-cmd --zone=websrv --add-port=5500/{tcp,udp} --permanent
# firewall-cmd --zone=websrv --add-port=5500/{tcp,udp}
```

A sequential range of ports can also be opened for a zone by using the following command for the particular application:

```
# firewall-cmd --zone=websrv --add-port=5501-5505/udp --permanent
# firewall-cmd --zone=websrv --add-port=5501-5505/udp
```

A sequential range of ports for with both the TCP and UDP protocols can be opened for a zone by using the following command for the particular application:

```
# firewall-cmd --zone=websrv --add-port=5501-5505/{udp,tcp} --permanent
# firewall-cmd --zone=websrv --add-port=5501-5505/{udp,tcp}
```

Denying Ports for the Zones

If you wanted to deny certain ports by using the "--remove-port" option as shown in the following:

```
# firewall-cmd --zone=websrv --remove-port=5500/tcp --permanent
# firewall-cmd --zone=websrv --remove-port=5500/tcp
```

In the similar way, you can deny a range of ports with both the protocols as indicated below:

```
# firewall-cmd --zone=websrv --remove-port=1234-1239/{tcp,udp} --permanent
# firewall-cmd --zone=websrv --remove-port=1234-1239/{tcp,udp}
```

Listing the Opened Ports

The list of opened ports on a particular zone can be listed by using the following commands:

```
# firewall-cmd --list-ports --zone=websrv --permanent
# firewall-cmd --list-ports --zone=websrv
```

Masquerading

Masquerading is a form of NAT which allows internal computers to communicate to the external network, in which the range of private IP addresses can access network using public IP thereby hiding the local network behind a firewall.

In order to configure a NAT, set the interfaces to required zones, and set masquerade on the zone that will hide the others behind (the zone which is associated with the internet facing interface).

Assuming that our system has two interfaces eth0 (internet facing) and eth1(internal network), we will configure NAT to enable the internal network to use eth1 as their gateway to reach the Internet. This way, all the packets will get your firewall's IP address as the source address. Accordingly, associate the interfaces to the corresponding zones as shown in the following commands:

```
# firewall-cmd --zone=internal --add-interface=eth1 --permanent
# firewall-cmd --zone=external --add-interface=eth0 --permanent
# firewall-cmd --reload
```

Verify whether the interfaces are associated correctly with the corresponding zones or not as mentioned below:

```
# firewall-cmd --list-all --zone=external
# firewall-cmd --list-all --zone=internal
```

In the outputs of the above commands, the interfaces eth1 and eth0 must be associated with the internal and external zones respectively. If the association is correctly done, check if the masquerade is enabled for the external zone or not by running the following command:

```
# firewall-cmd --zone=external --query-masquerade
```

In case, if the output says not enabled, you can enable it by using the following command and reload:

```
# firewall-cmd --zone=external --add-masquerade --permanent
# firewall-cmd –reload
```

Now, the internal clients must be able to use the internal interface as their gateway to access the internet.

> *In case if there is a need to remove masquerading from the external zone, the command "firewall-cmd --zone=external --remove-masquerade --permanent".*

Port Forwarding

The port forwarding can be used to forward the traffic that comes to a specific port to another port that a service listens to on the same system or to a different machine with same or different port number for which a NAT must be configured. Port forwarding is a way to forward inbound network traffic of a specific port to another internal address or to an alternative port.

For example, to forward the traffic that comes to TCP port 22 to TCP port 3753 permanently, use the following commands accordingly:

```
# firewall-cmd --zone=external --add-forward-port=port=22:proto=tcp:toport=3753 --permanent
# firewall-cmd --reload
# firewall-cmd --zone=external --list-all
```

To forward the traffic to a different internal system which has the service running, use the following commands (after configuring NAT):

```
# firewall-cmd --permanent --zone=external --add-forward-port=port=22:proto=tcp:toport=3753:toaddr=172.168.30.3
# firewall-cmd --reload
# firewall-cmd --zone=external --list-all
```

Rich Rules

Configuring Services and ports are good for the basic firewall configuration but at times we need to add custom firewall rules to any zone for any port, protocol, address and action. The rich rule in firewalld provides a greater level of control with more options not just to allow some ports and services in a zone. The firewalld's rich rules can also be used to configure logging, masquerading, port forwarding, and rate limiting. In this part, we will learn to manage the rich rules with examples.

Rich Rules Command

The rich rules command, follows the syntax given below to manage the rich rules in the firewalld :

```
# firewall-cmd    [Option]    [Rule]
```

In the above syntax, firewall-cmd is the main command and the [Option] is the type of operation that we intend to perform on a rule. Some of the options for specifying the operations to the rule in firewalld is mentioned in the table below with the descriptions.

Table 9.2:

Option	Description
--add-rich-rule='[RichRule]'	Adds the specified rule to the default zone if the zone is not specified with the --zone option. If the rule is intended to be added to a particular zone it must be specified with --zone option. In order to add rule permanently use --permanent option.

Option	Description
--query-rich-rule='[RichRule]'	Finds out if the specified rule is added in default zone or not. To query the rule in other zones, the zone must be specified with --zone option.
--remove-rich-rule='[RichRule]'	Removes the specified rule from default zone if the zone is not specified. In order to remove the rule from other zones, the zone must be specified as an argument with the --zone option. The --permanent option can be used to permanently remove the rule from the zones.
--list-rich-rules	List all the rules from default zone and the other zones if the name of the zone is provided as an argument with --zone option.

Adding a Rich Rule

A zone can have multiple rules and the rule that matches first gets applied and the actions are taken. In the following example, we will add a rule to allow packets from the network 172.168.30.0/24 to only 192.168.30.2/32 through the TCP ports 8080-8090.

```
# firewall-cmd --permanent --zone=websrv --add-rich-rule='rule family=ipv4 source address=172.168.30.0/24 destination address=192.168.30.2/32 port port=8080-8090 protocol=tcp accept'
# firewall-cmd --reload
# firewall-cmd --zone=websrv --list-rich-rules
```

In the next, we will add a rule to the websrv zone which will reject all the traffic from certain IP address (172.168.30.10):

```
# firewall-cmd --permanent --zone=websrv --add-rich-rule='rule family=ipv4 source address=172.168.30.10/24 reject'
# firewall-cmd --reload
```

The following example shows how to limit the incoming SSH connections to 3 per minute:

```
# firewall-cmd --permanent --add-rich-rule='rule service name=ssh limit value=3/m accept'
```

The rich rules can also be used to log messages to a log file, and this message logging can also be rate limited. In this example, the SSH connections coming from 172.168.30.0/24 would be logged 30 per minute, whose log level is of the 'info' level or more important with "ssh" as the prefix of the lines logged.

```
# firewall-cmd --permanent --add-rich-rule='rule family=ipv4 source address=172.168.30.0/24 service name=ssh log prefix=ssh level=info limit value=30/m accept'
```

NAT using Rich Rule

The NAT works in the similar fashion to that of the normal but the only difference is, instead of specifying the interface, a range of IP address is being used which gives more granular control. In the following example, the traffic coming from the 172.168.30.0/24 would be masqueraded:

```
# firewall-cmd --permanent --zone=external --add-rich-rule='rule family=ipv4 source address=172.168.30.0/24 masquerade'
```

Port Forwarding using Rich Rule

When it comes to the port forwarding also, the same granular level of control is being given to that of NAT by not having to specify the interface. The following command adds a rich rule which could forward the traffic originating from 172.168.30.0/24 to the port 2222 of 192.168.30.2.

```
# firewall-cmd --permanent --zone=external --add-rich-rule='rule family=ipv4 source address=172.168.30.0/24 forward-port port=22 protocol=tcp to-port=2222 to-addr=192.168.30.2'
```

Listing Rich Rules

The following command can be used to list the rich rules on the default zone and the specified zones respectively:

```
# firewall-cmd --list-rich-rules
# firewall-cmd --list-rich-rules --zone=external
```

Removing Rich Rules

To remove the rich rule from the default zone and the specified zone, we have to specify which rule to be removed along with the --remove-rich-rule option. The following commands remove the rich rules from the default zone and the websrv zone respectively.

```
# firewall-cmd --permanent --remove-rich-rule='rule family=ipv4 source address=172.168.30.0/24 destination address=192.168.30.2/32 port port=8080-8090 protocol=tcp accept'
# firewall-cmd --permanent --zone=websrv --remove-rich-rule='rule family=ipv4 source address=172.168.30.0/24 destination address=192.168.30.2/32 port port=8080-8090 protocol=tcp accept'
```

Further Reading

Chapter 5. Using Firewalls. (n.d.). Retrieved from https://access.redhat.com/documentation/en-us/red_hat_enterprise_linux/7/html/security_guide/sec-using_firewalls#sec-Introduction_to_firewalld

Docile, E. (2017, December 24). Introduction to firewalld and firewall-cmd command on Linux. Retrieved May 4, 2018, from https://linuxconfig.org/introduction-to-firewalld-and-firewall-cmd-command-on-linux

Firewalld. (n.d.). Retrieved from https://fedoraproject.org/wiki/Firewalld?rd=FirewallD

Firewalld Basic concepts Explained with Examples. (2018, February 03). Retrieved from https://www.computernetworkingnotes.com/rhce-study-guide/firewalld-basic-concepts-explained-with-examples.html

Firewalld.zones. (n.d.). Retrieved from https://www.firewalld.org/documentation/man-pages/firewalld.

zones.html

How to Set Up a Firewall Using FirewallD on CentOS 7. (2018, March 15). Retrieved from https://cloudwafer.com/blog/how-to-set-up-a-firewall-using-firewalld-on-centos-7/

J., Ellingwood. (2018, March 02). How to Set Up a Firewall Using FirewallD on CentOS 7 | DigitalOcean. Retrieved from https://www.digitalocean.com/community/tutorials/how-to-set-up-a-firewall-using-firewalld-on-centos-7

How to Use Firewalld Rich Rules and Zones for Filtering and NAT. (2017, February 22). Retrieved from https://www.rootusers.com/how-to-use-firewalld-rich-rules-and-zones-for-filtering-and-nat/

Linux Firewalld Port-Forward and NAT. (2017, April 30). Retrieved from https://akm111.wordpress.com/2017/04/30/linux-firewalld-port-forward-and-nat/

RHEL7: How to get started with Firewalld. (n.d.). Retrieved from https://www.certdepot.net/rhel7-get-started-firewalld/

RHEL7: How to get started with Firewalld. (n.d.). Retrieved from https://www.certdepot.net/rhel7-get-started-firewalld/

Set Up FirewallD on CentOS 7. (2018, April 27). Retrieved from https://www.rosehosting.com/blog/set-up-and-configure-a-firewall-with-firewalld-on-centos-7/

Using FirewallD to Manage Your Firewall on CentOS 7. (n.d.). Retrieved May 4, 2018, from https://www.vultr.com/docs/using-firewalld-to-manage-your-firewall-on-centos-7

Chapter 10
Virtual Network Lab

Learning to set up and implement a Server would come at a cost, if we have not learnt how to virtualize a network in the preceding chapters. Here onwards, instead of setting up a real network with the expensive server hardware and network hardware devices, with the help of GNS3 and VirtualBox, we will create our own virtual network laboratory where we will spend much of our time creating, configuring and testing the servers. In this chapter, we will create our final envisioned Virtual Network Lab for carrying out the installation, configuration and testing of the rest of the servers setup.

Requirements and Presumptions

Before proceeding, I presume that the GNS3 and the Oracle VM VirtualBox Manager are installed and configured on your system following the steps carefully and correctly through Chapter 1 to Chapter 7, which we are going to use. If you have not followed along, you are asked to carry out the installation and configuration of GNS3 and Oracle VM VirtualBox Manager in order to move forward. In addition, it is also presumed that the CentOS 7 operating system is installed in the virtual machine created using the VirtualBox and the clones have been made to be configured as individual servers as shown in the following figure 10.1.

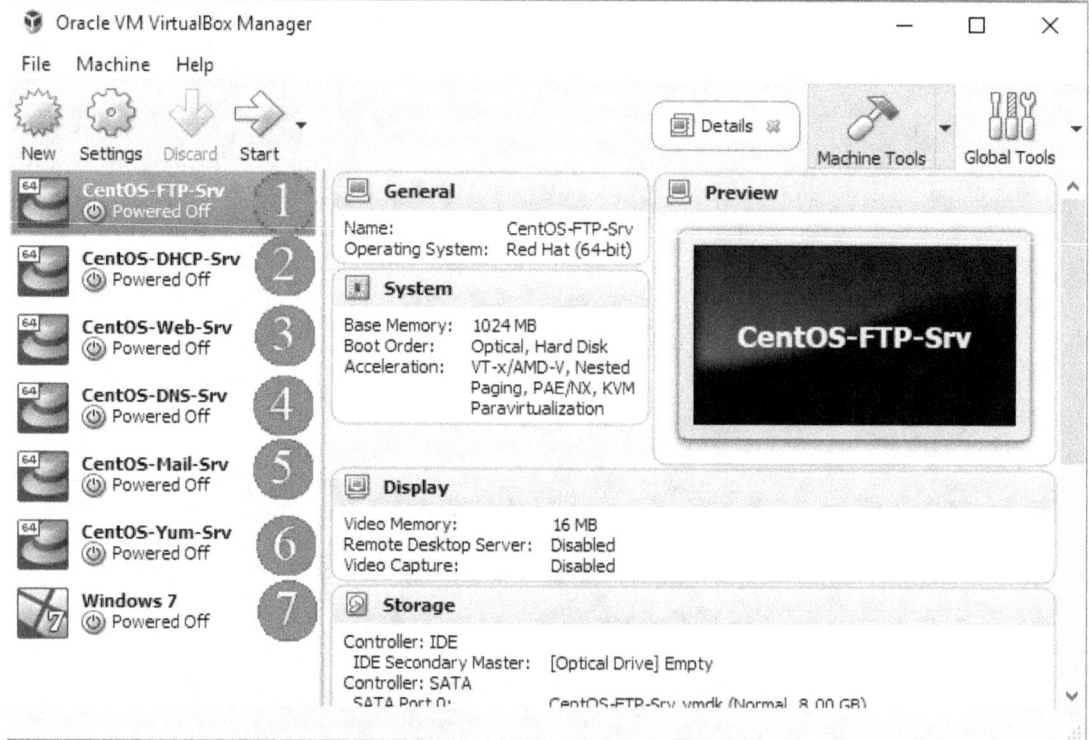

Figure 10.1: Cloned Virtual Machines

As shown in the figure 10.1, at least 7 virtual machines are required, which includes 6 numbers of CentOS 7-based virtual machines; CentOS-FTP-Srv, CentOS-DHCP-Srv, CentOS-Web-Srv, CentOS-DNS-Srv, CentOS-Mail-Srv and CentOS-Yum-Srv, and one Windows 7.

Each of those virtual machines with the operating system installed will be used for configuring FTP, DHCP, Web, DNS, Mail and Yum Server, and the Windows 7 will be just used as a client for testing the functionality of the configured servers.

In the next, since we are going to make use of seven virtual machines, we need to have a minimum of seven VirtualBox Host-Only Ethernet Adaptors. If you have less than 7 or no adaptors at all, create the required number of adaptors.

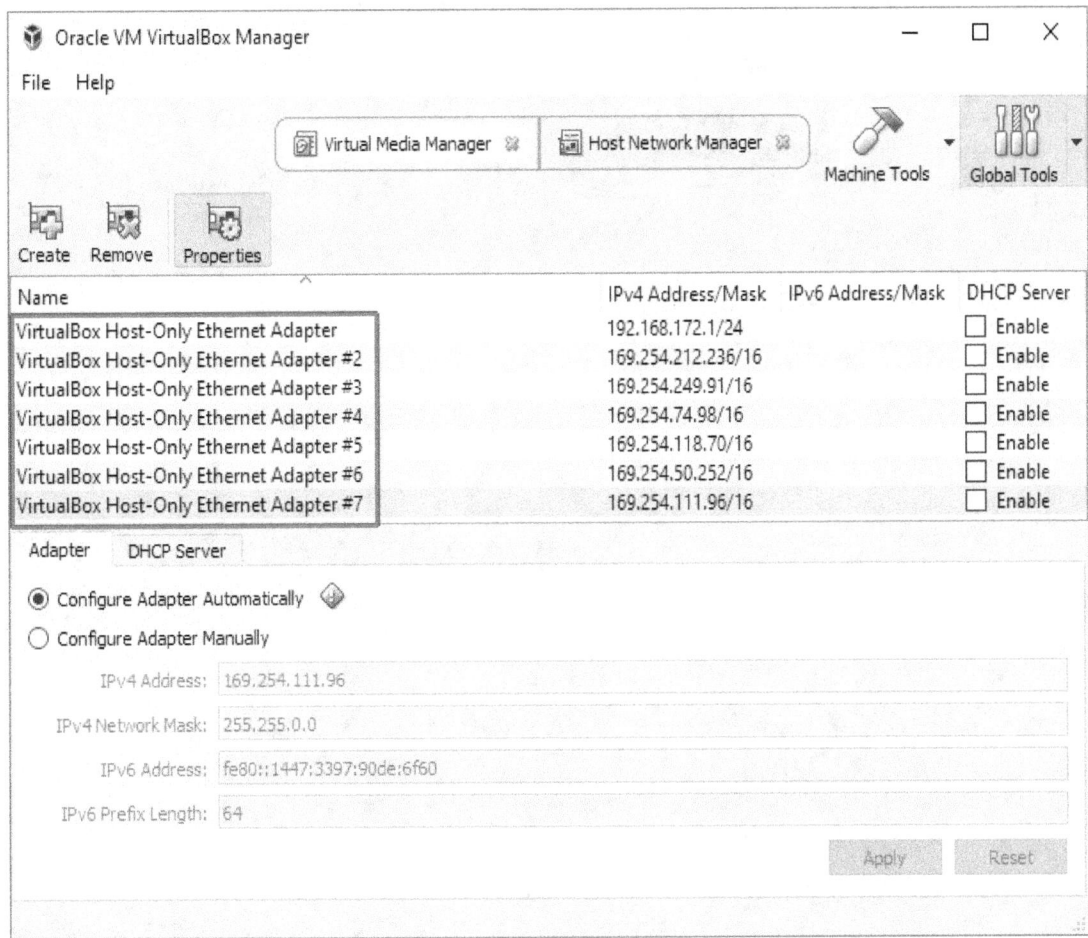

Figure 10.2: List of VirtualBox Host-Only Ethernet Adaptors

In the GNS3, make sure that the VirtualBox VM templates are populated as shown in the figure below. Otherwise, we will not be able to add those devices to the GNS3 workspace.

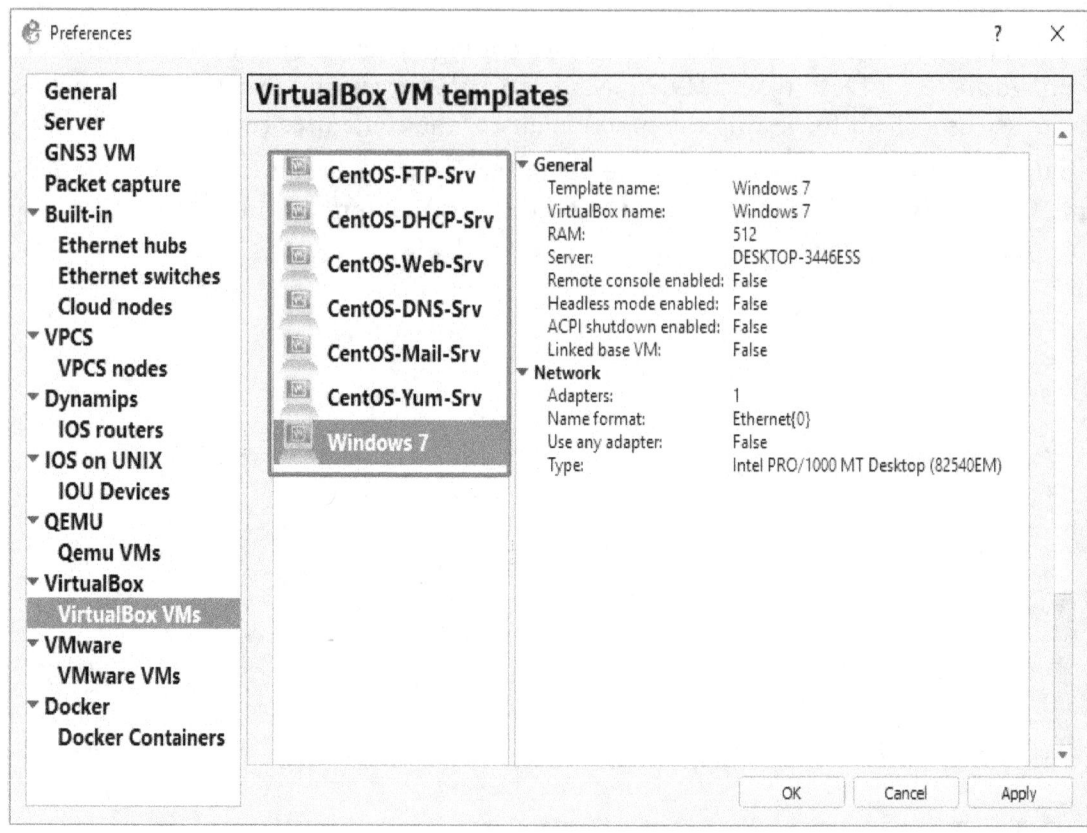

Figure 10.3: Populated VirtualBox VM templates

Creating Envisioned Virtual Network

Launch the GNS3 application and create a new project with the name "EVN" and save it to the default location.

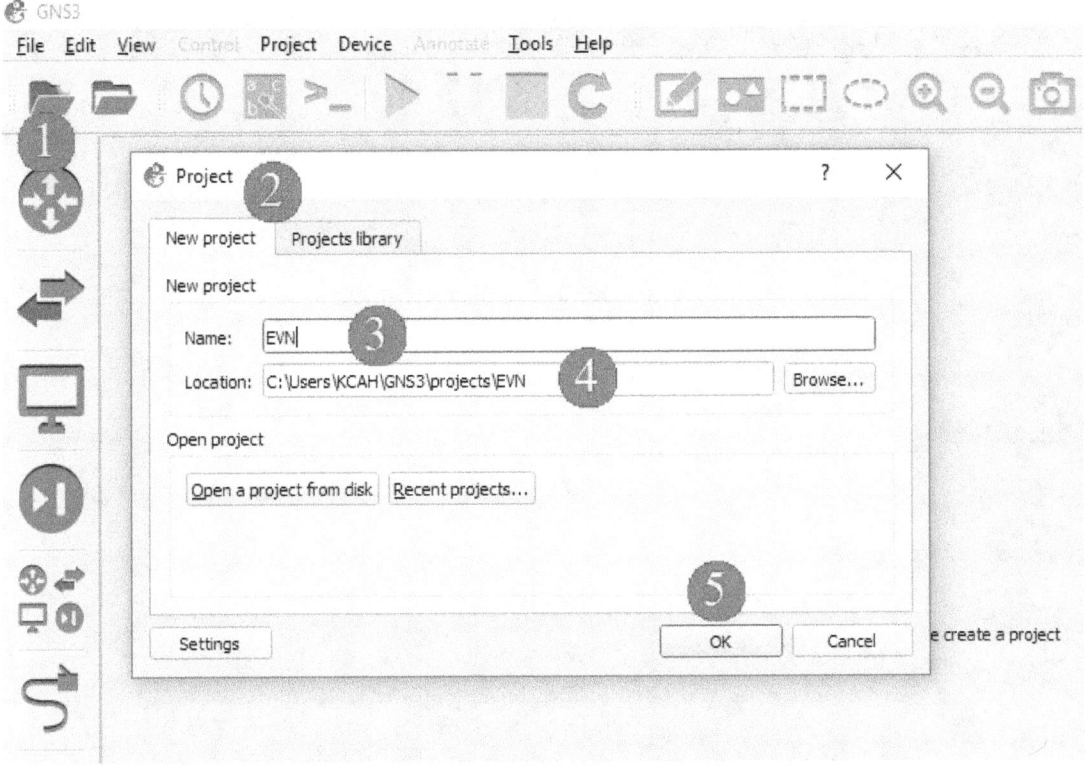

Figure 10.4: Creating a new project

Clicking on the tool "add the note" in the toolbar would enable you to add notes in the workspace. Add the note in the workspace to give some information regarding the virtual network lab which we are trying to build as shown in the following figure.

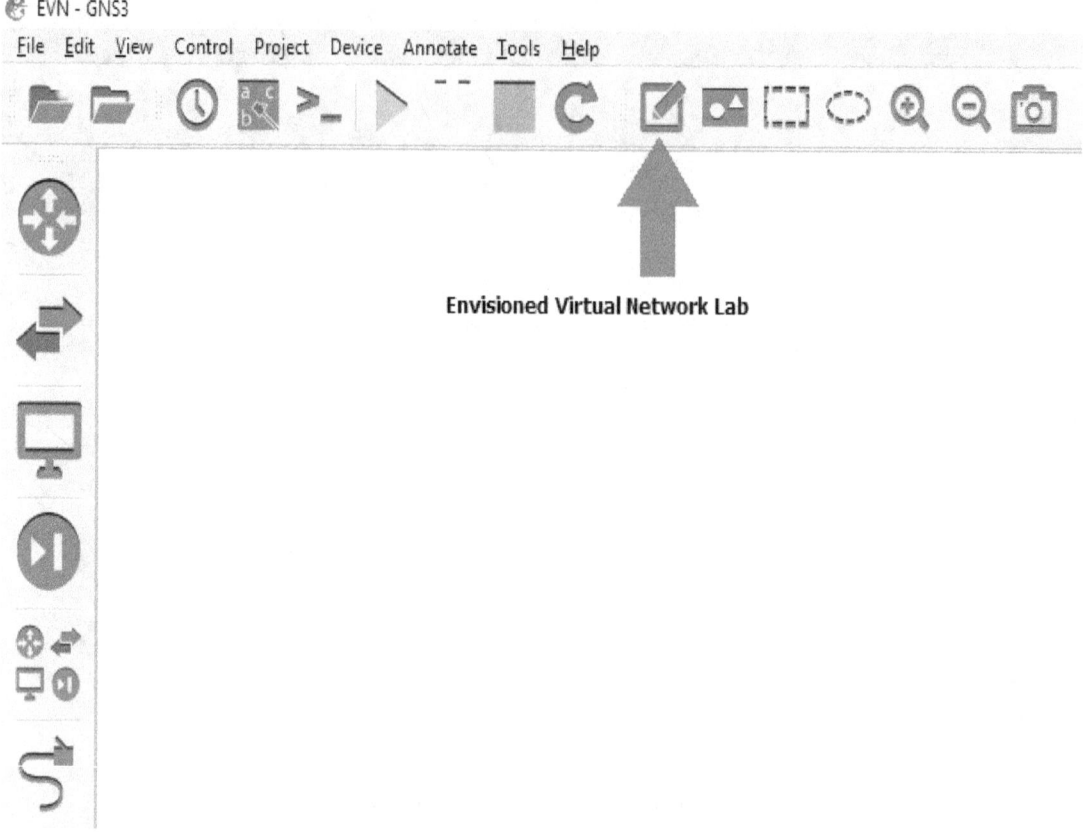

Figure 10.5: Adding a note to the workspace

Build a Virtual Network and Practice

Drag and drop all the virtual machines and devices indicated with numbers to the GNS3 workspace to represent the servers, client and network devices.

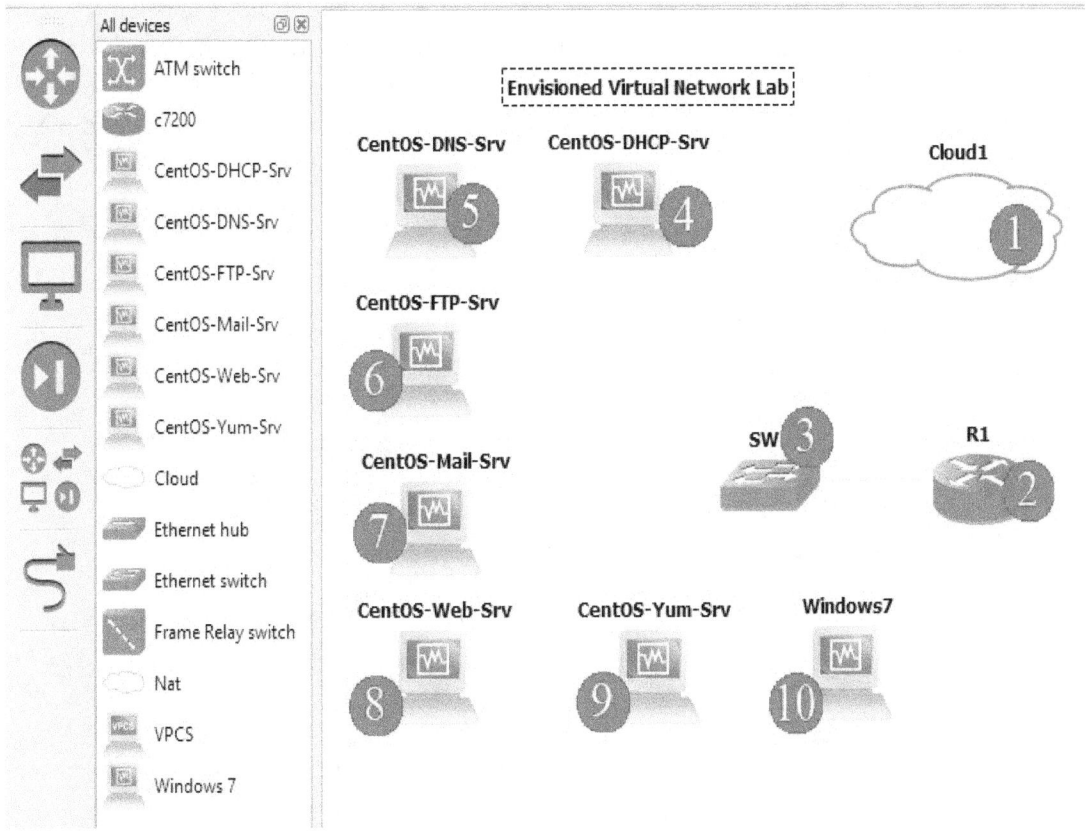

Figure 10.6: Workspace with devices and virtual machines

In the next step, before we start interconnecting those devices, configure all the virtual machines to allow the GNS3 to use any configured virtualbox adaptor by right clicking on the individual virtual machine templates placed on the GNS3 workspace and choosing the "Configure" option. The following figure shows configuration done only for the CentOS-DNS-Srv. It must be done similarly for CentOS-FTP-Srv, CentOS-DHCP-Srv, CentOS-Mail-srv, CentOS-Web-Srv, CentOS-Yum-Srv and Windows 7 respectively.

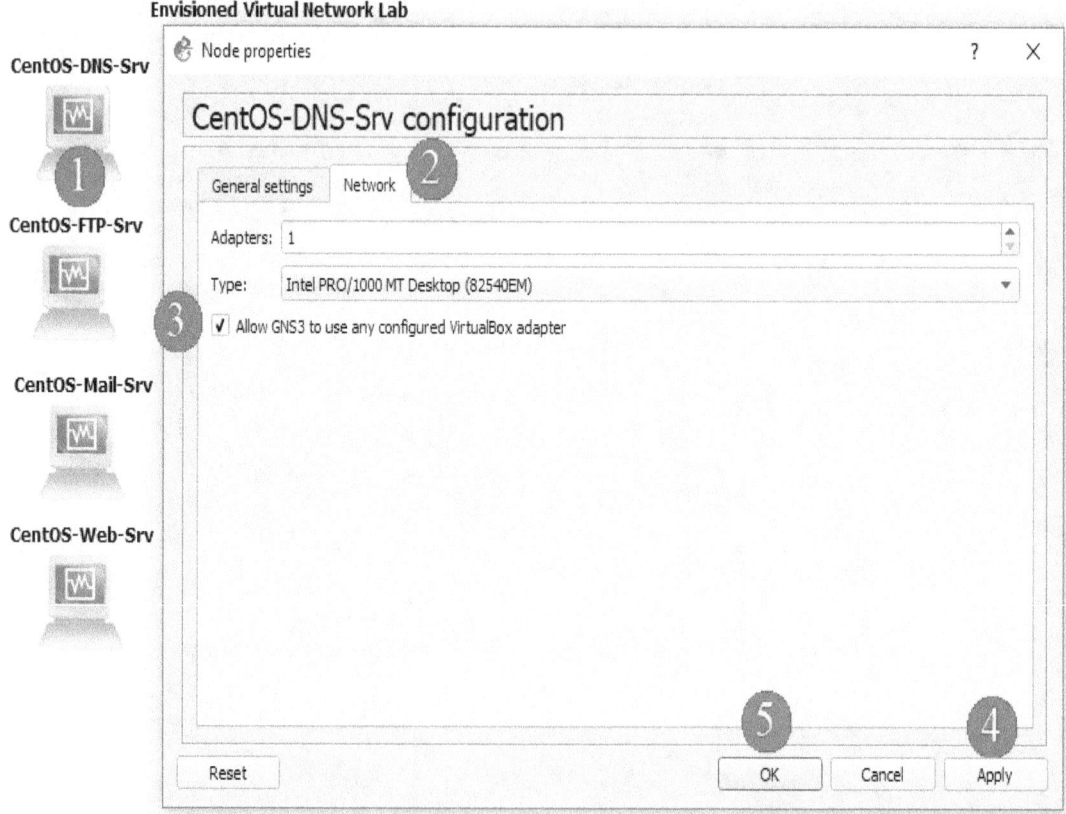

Figure 10.7: Allowing GNS3 to use any configured VirtualBox adaptor

Build a Virtual Network and Practice

Then make connections between those devices as indicated in the figure below. Take note of the interfaces especially the router's interfaces. The router's interface f0/0 and f0/1 are external and internal facing respectively.

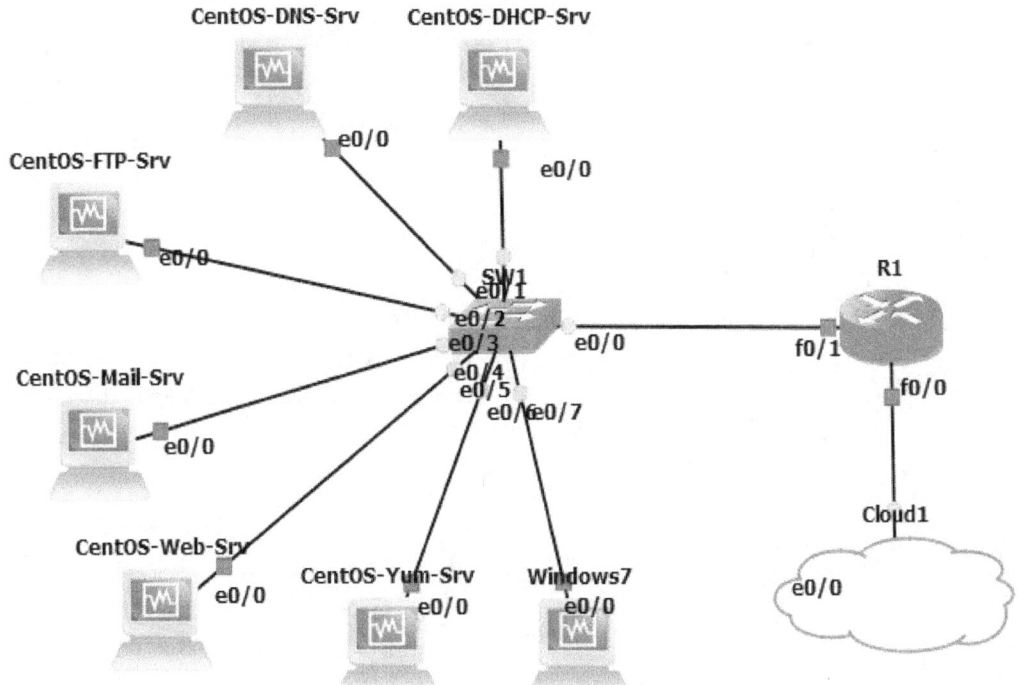

Figure 10.8: Connections and interfaces

> *If you do not want to see the interface details, you can toggle it (ON/OFF) by clicking the Show/hide interface labels tool in the toolbar.*

Adaptor Assignment in VirtualBox

In total, there are seven VirtualBox Host-Only Ethernet adaptors. After launching the Oracle VM VirtualBox Manager, select individual Virtual machines and assign the VirtualBox Host-Only Adaptor one by one. The same adaptor must not be assigned to two virtual machines and also remember to assign all the virtual machines with adaptors. The following figure shows VirtualBox Host-Only adaptor assignment for CentOS-FTP-Srv only.

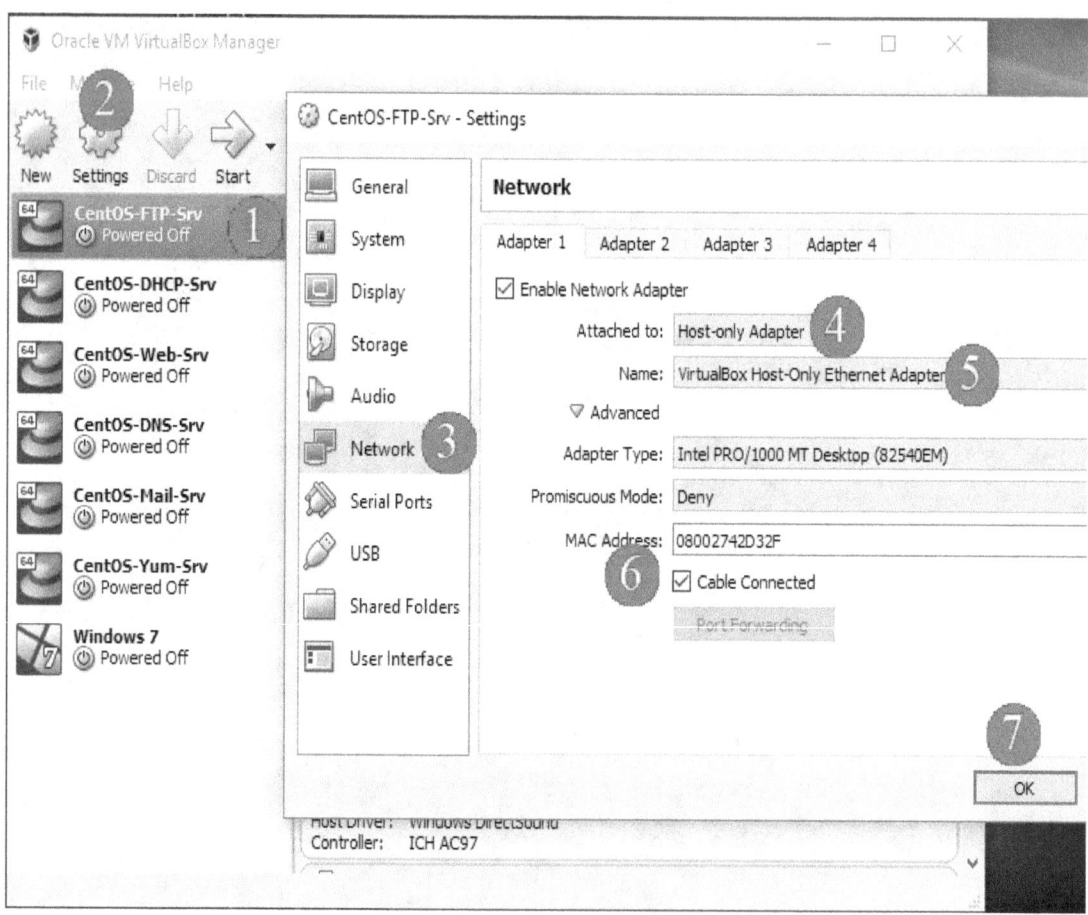

Figure 10.9: Assigning Adaptors

Build a Virtual Network and Practice

IP Addressing

In the following figure, the Cloud1 is considered as the Internet (ISP) connected to the router R1's interface f0/0 (192.168.150.30/24). The router's interface f0/1 with IP address 172.168.30.1/24 is connected to the internal network (172.168.30.0/24).

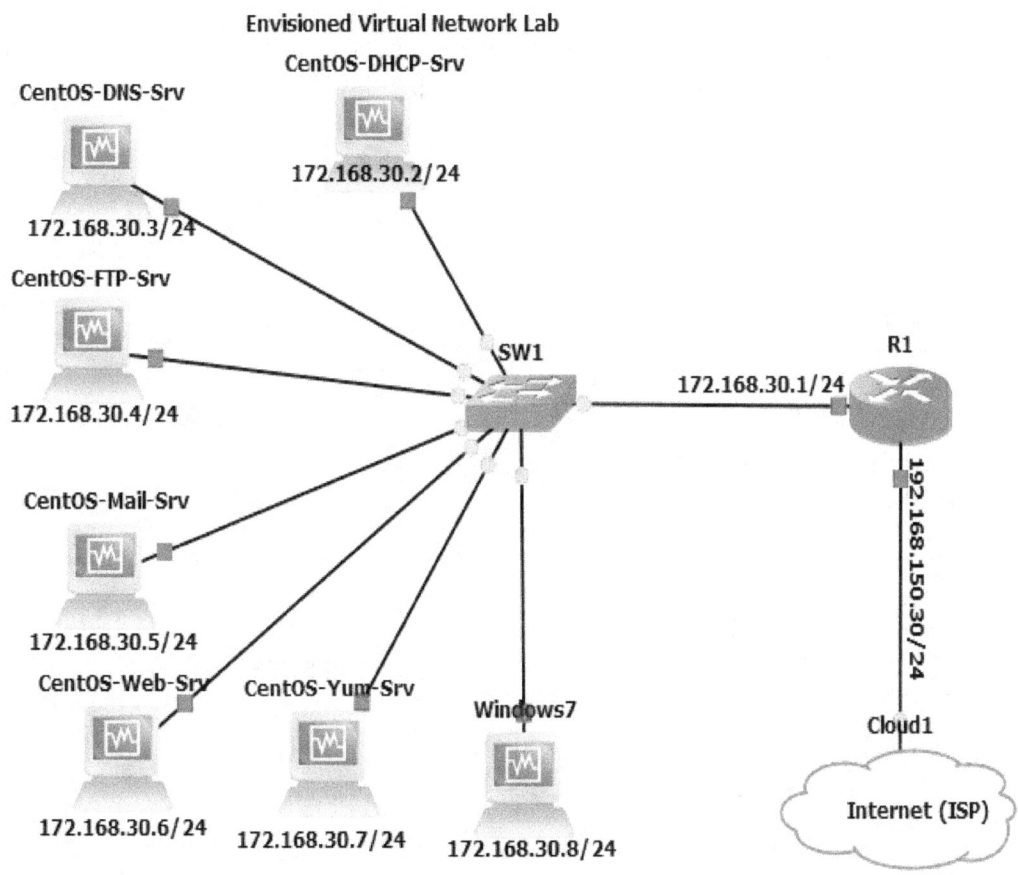

Figure 10.10: IP addressing scheme

Configure the Router's Interfaces

After right clicking on the router (R1) and choosing Start, the router's interfaces can be configured according to the IP addressing scheme shown in the figure 10.10. To configure the router's interfaces, we will use the console after starting the router and the following commands can be used for configuring the first interface to get IP address (192.168.150.30/24 is assumed and practically it can be different) assigned from the host network's DHCP. Although, technically, assigning an IP address to a router is not recommended for a production environment, we are doing here since we are not having access to the real ISP. The host network is assumed as an ISP for our virtual network.

```
R1# conf t
R1(config)# interface fastEthernet 0/0
R1(config-if)# ip address dhcp
R1(config-if)# no shutdown
R1(config-if)# end
R1# wr
R1# show ip interface brief
```

As per the scenario we have, assign 172.168.30.1/24 on to the router R1's interface fa 0/1 which is connected to the switch. Use the following commands to configure the router R1's second interface f0/1:

```
R1#conf t
R1(config)#interface fastEthernet 0/1
R1(config-if)#ip address 172.168.30.1 255.255.255.0
R1(config-if)#no shutdown
R1(config-if)#end
R1#wr
```

Configure NAT on Router

The following commands can be used for configuring the NAT on the router so that the devices in the 172.168.30.0/24 would be able to make a request to the computers on the internet.

```
R1#conf t
R1(config)#access-list 1 permit 172.168.30.0 0.0.0.255
R1(config)#ip nat inside source list 1 interface fastEthernet 0/0 overload
R1(config)#interface fastEthernet 0/1
R1(config-if)#ip nat inside
R1(config-if)#exit
R1(config)#interface fastEthernet 0/0
R1(config-if)#ip nat outside
R1(config-if)#end
R1#wr
```

The creation of the Virtual Network Lab is completed with the required configurations. We will be using this Virtual Network Lab in the subsequent chapters for installing, configuring and testing the servers.

Further Reading

Canepa, G. (n.d.). Cloning, exporting, importing, and removing virtual machines in VirtualBox. Retrieved from https://www.systemcodegeeks.com/virtualization/virtualbox/cloning-exporting-importing-removing-virtual-machines-virtualbox/

Host-only Networking in VirtualBox. (n.d.). Retrieved from http://condor.depaul.edu/glancast/443class/docs/vbox_host-only_setup.html

Host-only Networking in VirtualBox. (n.d.). Retrieved from http://condor.depaul.edu/glancast/443class/docs/vbox_host-only_setup.html

ProTechGurus. (2016, July 29). How To Clone Virtual Machine in VirtualBox. Retrieved from https://protechgurus.com/clone-virtual-machine-virtualbox/

Import VirtualBox VM template to GNS3. (2016, January 24). Retrieved from http://www.it-tutorials.net/import-virtualbox-vm-template-to-gns3/

Integrating GNS3 and VirtualBox. (n.d.). Retrieved from https://digi.ninja/blog/gns_vbox_basic_lab.php

Using VirtualBox linked clones in the GNS3 network simulator. (2017, January 03). Retrieved from http://www.brianlinkletter.com/using-virtualbox-linked-clones-in-the-gns3-network-simulator/

VMs in GNS3: Add VirtualBox servers to your network lab. (2018, March 09). Retrieved from https://www.ictshore.com/gns3/vms-in-gns3-virtualbox/

Configuring the GNS3 Topology. (n.d.). Retrieved from https://www.freeccnaworkbook.com/workbooks/ccna/configuring-the-free-ccna-workbook-gns3-topology

Connecting GNS3 to Real Networks. (2016, March 14). Retrieved from http://www.smartpctricks.com/2014/06/connecting-gns3-real-networks.html

Your First GNS3 Topology. (n.d.). Retrieved from https://docs.gns3.com/1wr2j2jEfX6ihyzpXzC23wQ8ymHzID4K3Hn99-qqshfg/

Chapter 11
Setting Up a DHCP Server

A DHCP Server is a network server which can assign IP addresses, gateway information and other required network parameters to its clients automatically. It depends on the standard Dynamic Host Configuration Protocol to respond to the broadcast queries of the clients. This enables the clients to have a proper communication in the network.

If you are a network administrator overlooking a considerable network size, manually configuring the network clients would be taking away a much of your interest in the job. Instead, the network client configuration can be practically automated by implementing a DHCP server in your network. Besides saving time and effort, errors are avoided.

The DHCP server can automatically assign each client with a unique dynamic IP address, which changes when the client's lease for that IP address expires and all the problems associated with the manual configuration vanishes in a blink.

In this chapter, we will learn to set up a CentOS as a DHCP server for a network and then set the clients to use the service and finally the functionality of the DHCP server would be tested and verified.

Static and Dynamic Hosts

When a computer uses a static IP address, it is manually configured by the administrator or the user to use a specific IP address. The static IP assignment can result in two computers configured with the same IP address at times. Implementing DHCP to dynamically assign IP addresses minimizes these conflicts but there are situations where the static assignment is desirable.

Static addresses are best suited for assigning to those hosts in the network whose IP address must not desired to change frequently, which includes servers, routers, switches, etc.

Network Scenario

Learning to set up and implement a DHCP Server would come at a cost, if we did not learn how to virtualize a network in the preceding chapters. Here onwards, instead of setting up a DHCP Server in a real network with expensive server hardware and network devices, we will use the "Envisioned Virtual Network Lab" created in Chapter 10. In this scenario, we want our DHCP server to assign a dynamic IP address to the clients in the network 172.168.30.0/24 ranging from 172.168.30.11 to 172.168.30.20. Since the servers require static IP assignment, it is only the Windows 7 which should be assigned with the dynamic IP address.

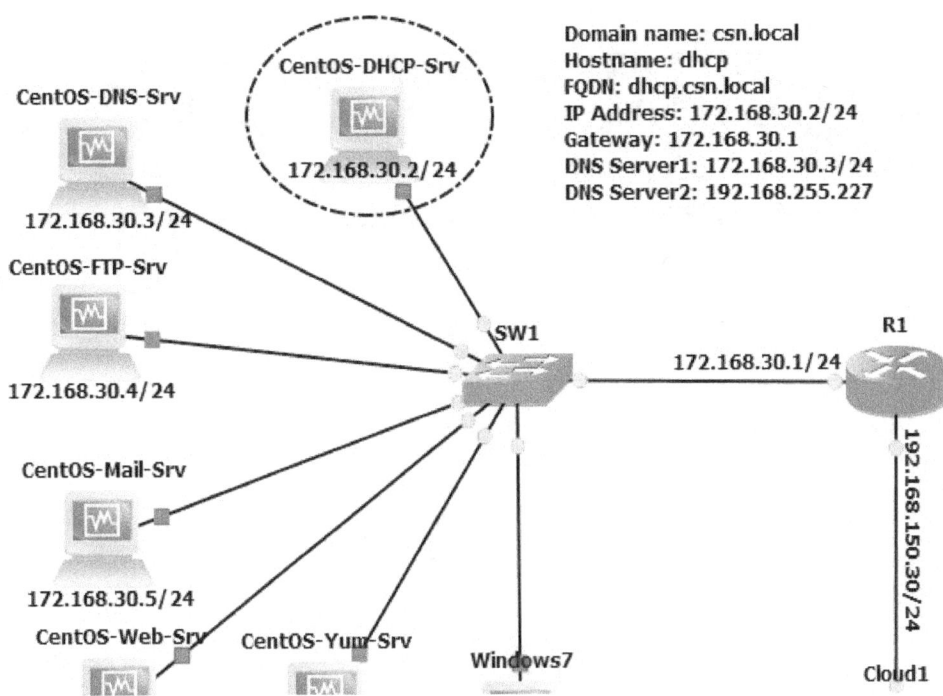

Figure 11.1: Base network with DHCP details

Configuring the DHCP Server Details

Taking into consideration the details of the DHCP Server shown in the figure 11.1, the DHCP server details have to be configured. In order to configure, we have to start the DHCP server from the GNS3 workspace by right-clicking and choosing to start.

> *It is advised not to either start or shutdown the DHCP server directly from the VirtualBox interface while working on the GNS3 as this action would lead to issues. So, start or shutdown from the GNS3 User Interface only. While trying to start any of the severs not just limited to CentOS-DHCP-Srv (DHCP Server) from the GNS3, sometimes you may get error messages and you won't be able to start. In such cases, start the server directly from the VirtualBox interface and once the starting is complete, login and give a proper shutdown. This happens when the server was improperly shutdown previously. After starting and shutting down from the VirtualBox, then go to the GNS3 workspace and start from there.*

When you try to start the server from the GNS3, you might be issued with a security alert, choose the options and allow access as shown in the figure 11.2.

Figure 11.2: Windows Security Alert

If the starting of the DHCP server is successful, the link status of the devices would change to green circular bullets and also the screen of the CentOS-DHCP-Srv (DHCP Server) would be available for login. Then you can login to the system as the root and then continue to configure the details.

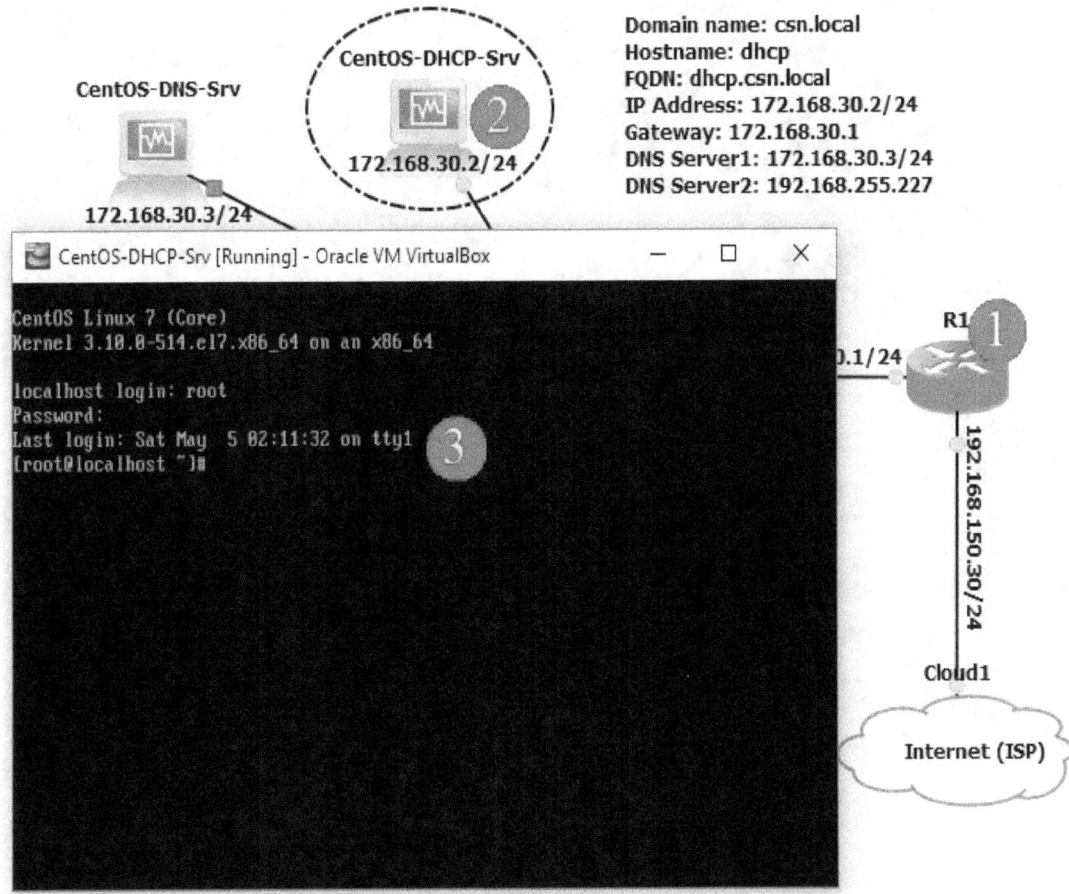

Figure 11.3: Virtual Network Lab with started DHCP and router

After successfully logging in to the server, configure the hostname by using the nmtui utility as shown in the figure below:

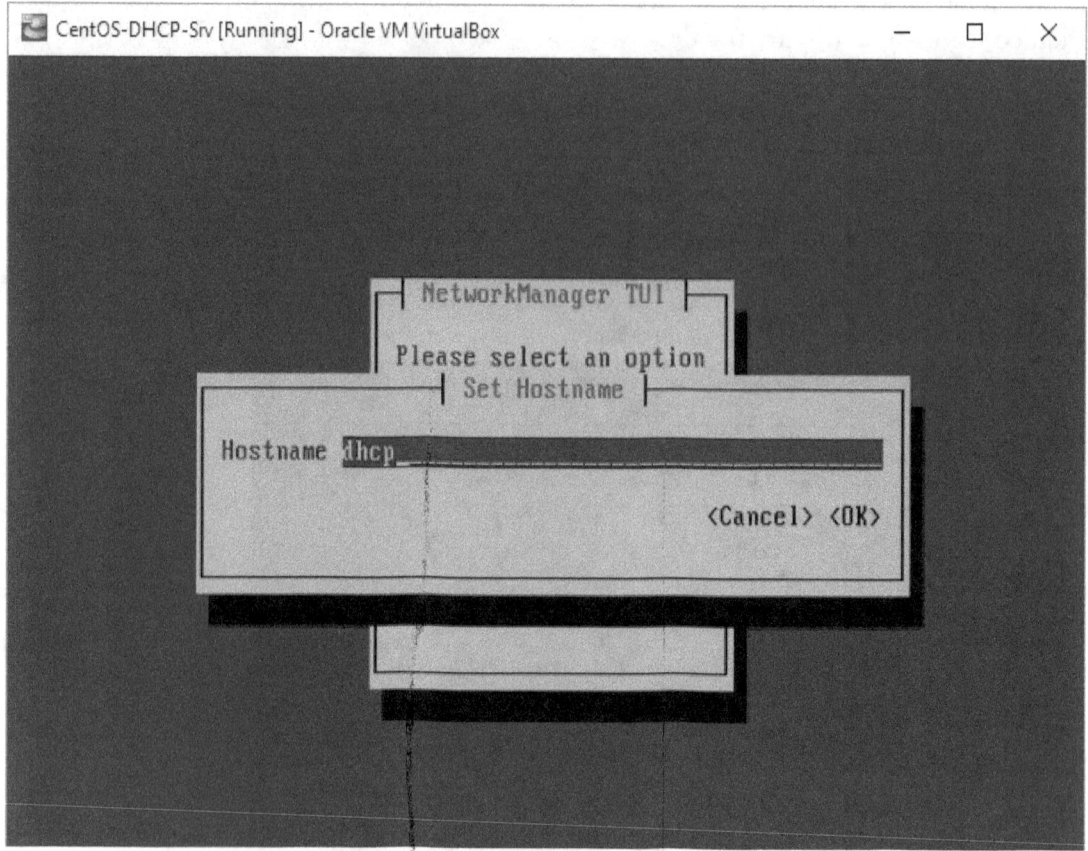

Figure 11.4: Setting the hostname

Build a Virtual Network and Practice

In the next, configure the IP address details using the nmtui as indicated in the figure 11.5 and figure 11.6.

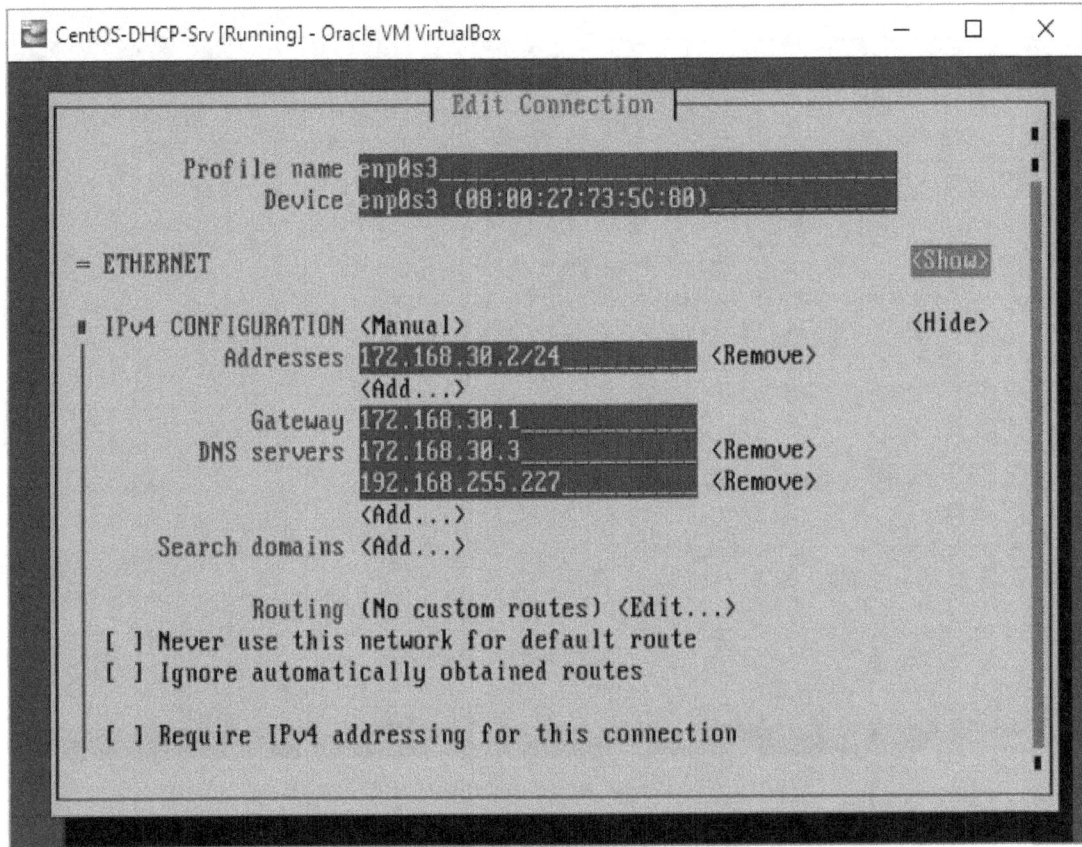

Figure 11.5: Ethernet IPv4 Setting for DHCP

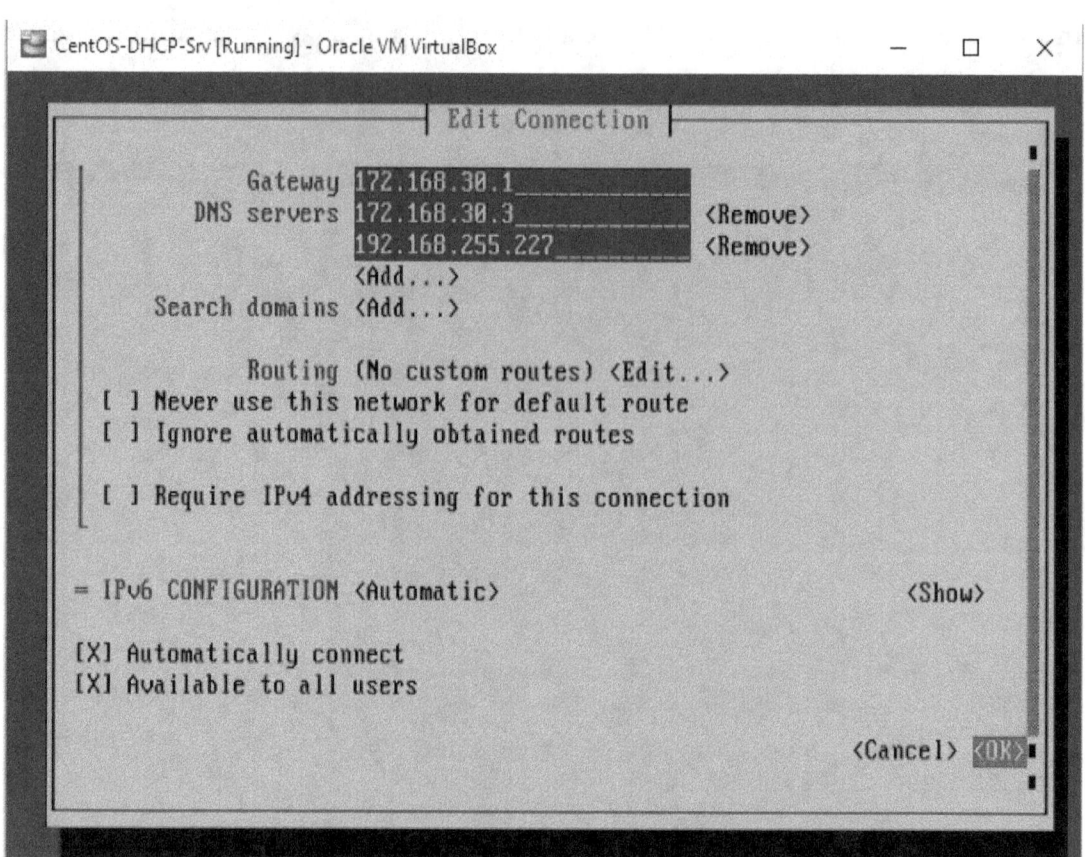

Figure 11.6: Allowing to automatically connect

Once the required manual settings are completed, you must be able to ping the router's IP address (172.168.30.1) as shown below:

```
CentOS-DHCP-Srv [Running] - Oracle VM VirtualBox
[root@localhost ~]# ping 172.168.30.1
PING 172.168.30.1 (172.168.30.1) 56(84) bytes of data.
64 bytes from 172.168.30.1: icmp_seq=2 ttl=255 time=44.7 ms
64 bytes from 172.168.30.1: icmp_seq=3 ttl=255 time=8.41 ms
64 bytes from 172.168.30.1: icmp_seq=4 ttl=255 time=6.48 ms
64 bytes from 172.168.30.1: icmp_seq=5 ttl=255 time=9.35 ms
64 bytes from 172.168.30.1: icmp_seq=6 ttl=255 time=9.59 ms
64 bytes from 172.168.30.1: icmp_seq=7 ttl=255 time=6.35 ms
64 bytes from 172.168.30.1: icmp_seq=8 ttl=255 time=7.32 ms
^C
--- 172.168.30.1 ping statistics ---
8 packets transmitted, 7 received, 12% packet loss, time 7013ms
rtt min/avg/max/mdev = 6.350/13.181/44.731/12.935 ms
[root@localhost ~]#
```

Figure 11.7: Verifying the connection

Before starting to install the packages, it is important to verify whether your router can connect to the internet or not by pinging the 8.8.8.8 after opening the terminal.

```
R1#ping 8.8.8.8

Type escape sequence to abort.
Sending 5, 100-byte ICMP Echos to 8.8.8.8, timeout is 2 seconds:
!!!!!
Success rate is 100 percent (5/5), round-trip min/avg/max = 112/120/136 ms
R1#
```

Figure 11.8: Verifying the connection to the Internet

> *If the pinging is not successful, try to check the configuration on the router and if the configurations are correctly done, try to reload or restart the router. Since we are using the dynamic IP address on the router's first interface f0/0, the lease might have expired.*

Installing DHCP Package

To configure a DHCP server you need to install the dhcp package from the repository. The dependency packages would be installed automatically when the dhcp package is installed. First install dhcp packages using a yum package manager on your to-be DHCP Server by using the following command:

yum install dhcp -y

Configure DHCP Server

While installing, DHCP creates an empty configuration file /etc/dhcp/dhcpd.conf. It also provides a sample configuration file at /usr/share/doc/dhcp*/dhcpd.conf.sample, which is very useful for configuring the DHCP server.

So, if you want to use the sample contents from the dhcpd.conf.sample file, copy the content of the sample configuration file to the main configuration file /etc/dhcp/dhcpd.conf.

cp /usr/share/doc/dhcp-4.2.5/dhcpd.conf.sample /etc/dhcp/dhcpd.conf

Otherwise, if you wish to continue configuring DHCP server without using the sample file, open the dhcp.conf file using the following command:

vi /etc/dhc/dhcpd.conf

The contents of the dhcpd.conf is similar to the figure 11.9 shown below, if you have not used the sample configuration file.

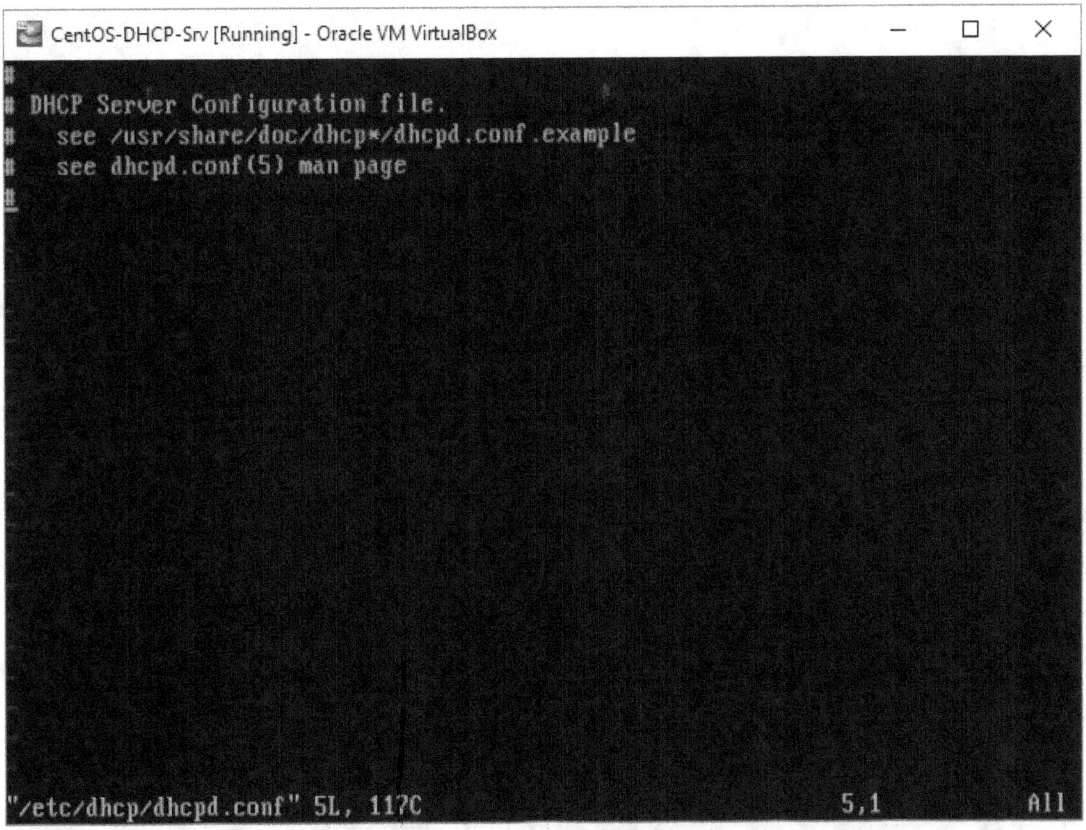

Figure 11.9: Contents of dhcpd.conf file

Parameter Configuration

After opening the configuration file, first configure the basic options which is common to all supported networks as shown in the following:

    option domain-name "csn.local";
    option domain-name-servers 172.168.30.3, 192.168.255.227;
    default-lease-time 600;
    max-lease-time 7200;
    authoritative;

IP Subnet Declaration

Then specify the subnet details as per our network plan. For this example, we are configuring DHCP for 172.168.30.0/24 LAN network to assign the IP within the range of 172.168.30.11 to 172.168.30.20 to the clients.

    subnet 172.168.30.0 netmask 255.255.255.0 {
        option routers   172.168.30.1;

```
        option subnet-mask      255.255.255.0;
        option domain-search    "csn.local";
        option domain-name-servers    172.168.30.3, 192.168.255.227;
    range   172.168.30.11   172.168.30.20;
}
```

Assign Static IP Address to Host

In some cases, we need to assign a fixed IP address to an interface each time it is requested from DHCP. We can also assign a fixed IP on the basis of MAC address (hardware Ethernet) of that interface. As an example, imagine that, we will configure the DHCP to assign the fixed IP 172.168.30.12 to a Windows10 client whose MAC address is 08:00:27:C5:E2:32. So, we have to use the following block of statement to configure:

```
host Windows10 {
    hardware ethernet 08:00:27:C5:E2:32;
    fixed-address 172.168.30.12;
}
```

After configuring all the options and parameters, the dhcpd.conf configuration file must at least contain the following details:

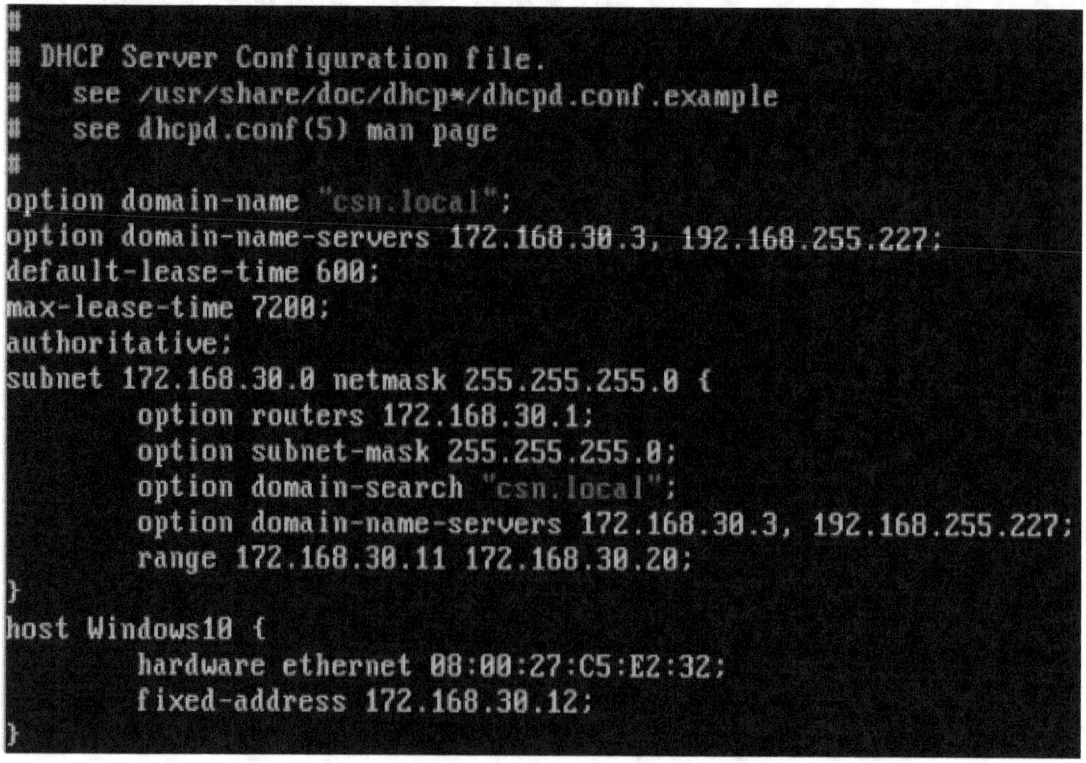

```
#
# DHCP Server Configuration file.
#   see /usr/share/doc/dhcp*/dhcpd.conf.example
#   see dhcpd.conf(5) man page
#
option domain-name "csn.local";
option domain-name-servers 172.168.30.3, 192.168.255.227;
default-lease-time 600;
max-lease-time 7200;
authoritative;
subnet 172.168.30.0 netmask 255.255.255.0 {
        option routers 172.168.30.1;
        option subnet-mask 255.255.255.0;
        option domain-search "csn.local";
        option domain-name-servers 172.168.30.3, 192.168.255.227;
        range 172.168.30.11 172.168.30.20;
}
host Windows10 {
        hardware ethernet 08:00:27:C5:E2:32;
        fixed-address 172.168.30.12;
}
```

Figure 11.10: Snapshot of the dhcpd.conf configuration

Start and Enable DHCP Service

After making all the above-mentioned configuration, you can start and enable the dhcp service by using following commands:

    # systemctl enable dhcpd
    # systemctl start dhcpd

The dhcpd should start successfully, if everything was configured properly till this point. If not, it is time to troubleshoot and get it up and running.

At this stage we have a running DHCP server which is ready for accepting requests and assign them a proper IP address but we also have to configure our clients to accept the dynamic configuration.

Setup Client System

The configuration of the DHCP server is complete and now we will try to test its functionality in our Virtual Network Lab. The DHCP server must assign an IP address to the clients within the range of 172.168.30.11 to 172.168.30.20.

Here, in our network, Windows 7 is going to be the client and we have to remove manually configured IP addresses on the Windows 7 if there is any, in order to accept the dynamic IP address.

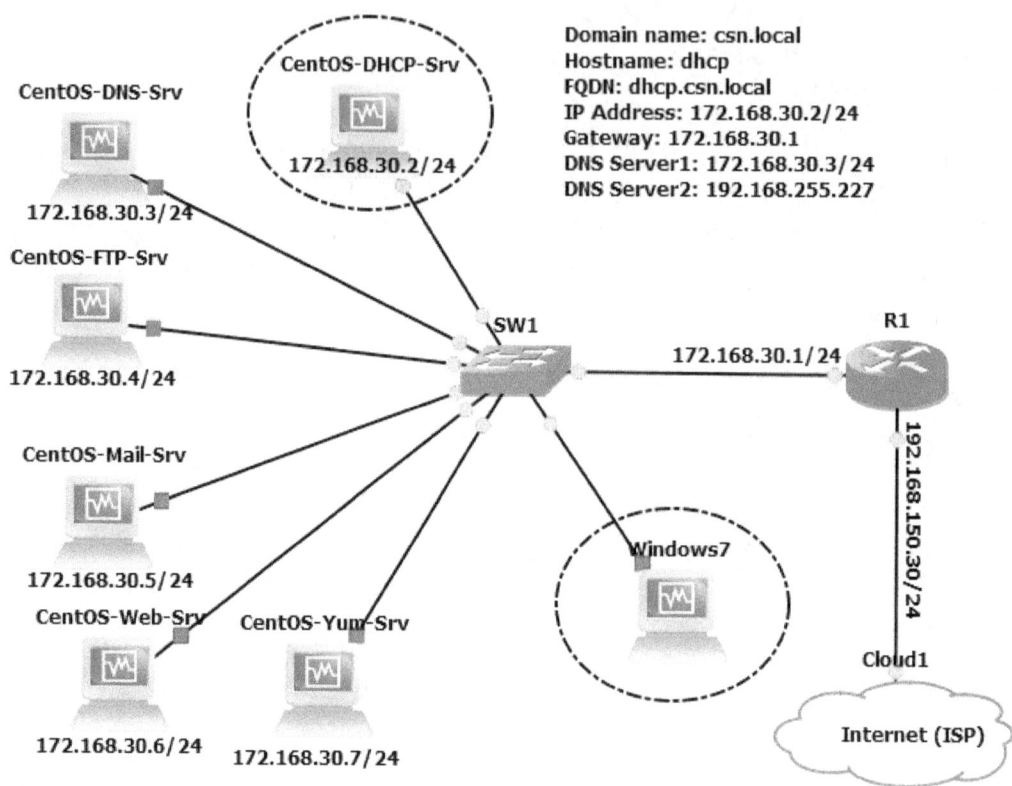

Figure 11.11: Windows 7 client not started

You can start the Windows 7 from the GNS3 workspace and then login to the Windows 7 client system using the available username and password if any.

The following figure shows the Windows 7 client started from the GNS3 along with DHCP Server and the router.

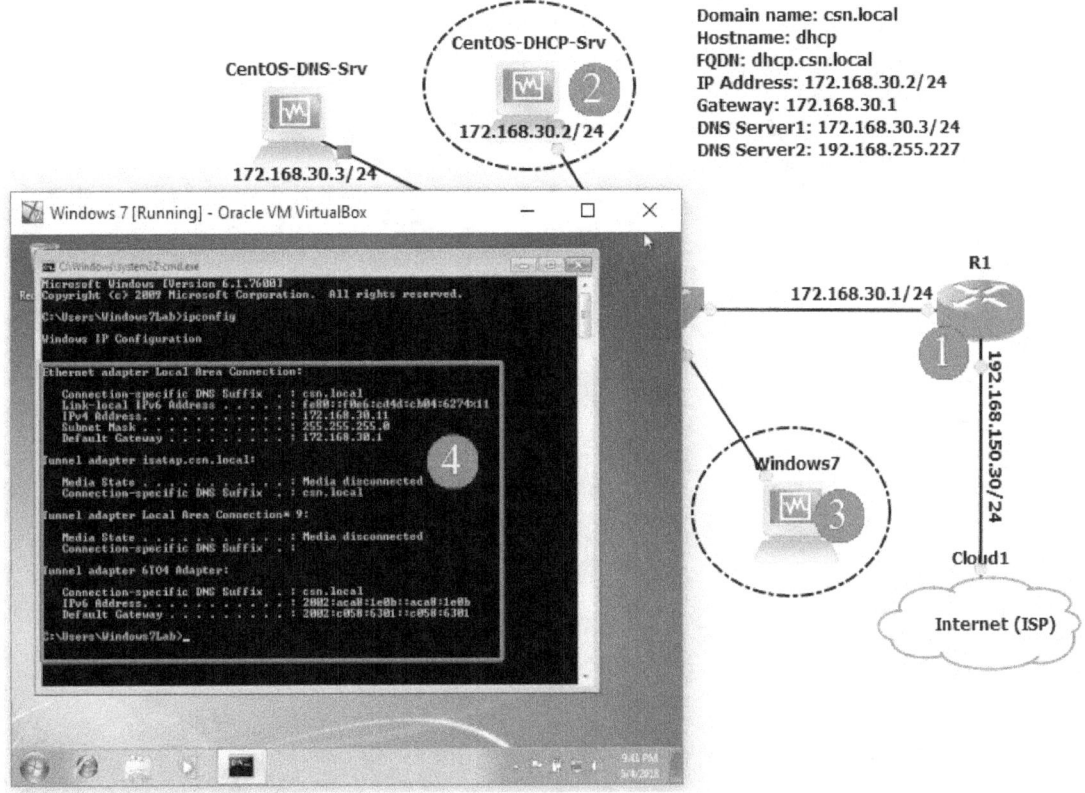

Figure 11.12: Windows 7 client up and running with IP from DHCP

The DHCP Server which we have configured is functional since the Windows 7 client is getting IP address assigned by the DHCP server.

> *If you have configured a DHCP service on the router which is placed in the workspace, disable the DHCP service on the Router to avoid assigning IP from it.*

Further Reading

S. (2017, October 28). Configuring DHCP Server in RHEL7/ Cent OS 7. Retrieved from http://www.linuxbookcenter.com/configuring-dhcp-in-rhel7-centos-7/

How to Configure DHCP Server on CentOS/RHEL 7/6/5. (2017, March 18). Retrieved from https://tecadmin.net/configuring-dhcp-server-on-centos-redhat/

How to Setup the Hostname and FQDN on CentOS / RHEL. (2017, September 27). Retrieved from https://www.webhostinghero.com/how-to-setup-the-hostname-and-fqdn-on-centos-rhel/

Install and Configure DHCP Server on CentOS 7/6/5 Linux Systems. (2016, December 12). Retrieved from http://www.mimastech.com/2016/12/11/install-and-configure-dhcp-server-on-centos-765-linux-systems/

What is a DHCP Server? | Learn What They Are & How They Work. (n.d.). Retrieved from https://www.infoblox.com/glossary/dhcp-server/

Chapter 12
Setting Up an FTP Server

The FTP is one of the most commonly used protocols found on the Internet today. Its purpose is to reliably transfer files between computer hosts on a network without requiring the users to log directly into the remote host or have knowledge of how to use the remote system. It allows users to access files on remote systems using a standard set of simple commands. The vsftpd is an FTP server software that comes with most of the popular Linux distributions. In this chapter, you will learn to install, configure and test the functionality of the configured FTP server in the Virtual Network.

Network Scenario

To learn to implement an FTP Server, we will continue to use the Virtual Network Lab which we created and used in the previous chapter. In the same Virtual Network Lab, we have implemented the DHCP server, here onwards without removing the DHCP server and the rest of the configurations, we will implement the FTP server in our Virtual Network Lab.

In this scenario, we want our FTP server to allow the clients in the network to be able to transfer the files between the client and the server. The details required for the FTP server is indicated in the following figure:

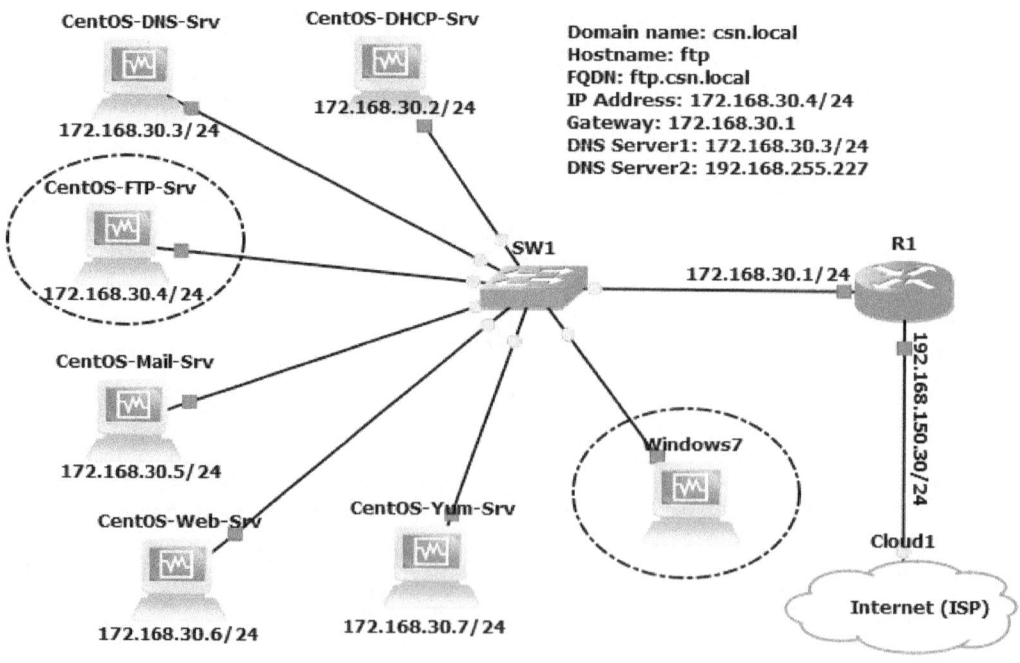

Figure 12.1: Base network with FTP Server details

Configuring the FTP Server Details

Taking into consideration the details of the FTP Server shown in the figure 12.1, the FTP server details have to be configured. In order to configure, we have to start the FTP server (CentOS-FTP-Srv) from the GNS3 workspace by right-clicking and choosing to start.

> *It is advised not to either start or shutdown the FTP server directly from the VirtualBox interface while working on the GNS3 as this action would lead to issues. So, start or shutdown from the GNS3 User Interface only. While trying to start any of the severs not just limited to CentOS-FTP-Srv (FTP Server) from the GNS3, sometimes you may get error messages and you won't be able to start. In such cases, start the server directly from the VirtualBox interface and once the starting is complete, login and give a proper shutdown. This happens when the server was improperly shutdown previously. After starting and shutting down from the VirtualBox, then go to the GNS3 workspace and start from there.*

When you try to start the server from the GNS3, you might be issued with a security alert, choose the options and allow access as shown in the figure 12.2.

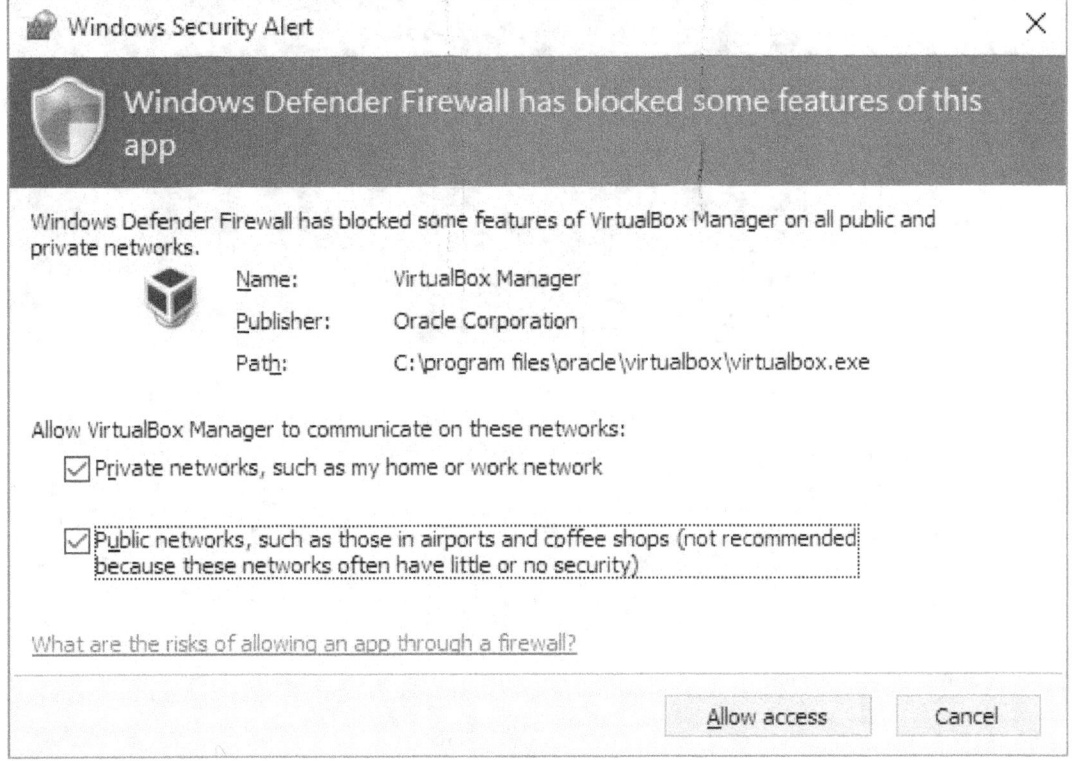

Figure 12.2: Windows Security Alert

If the starting of the FTP server is successful, the link status of the devices would change to green circular bullets and also the screen of the CentOS-FTP-Srv (FTP Server) would be available for login. Then you can login to the system as the root and then continue to configure the details.

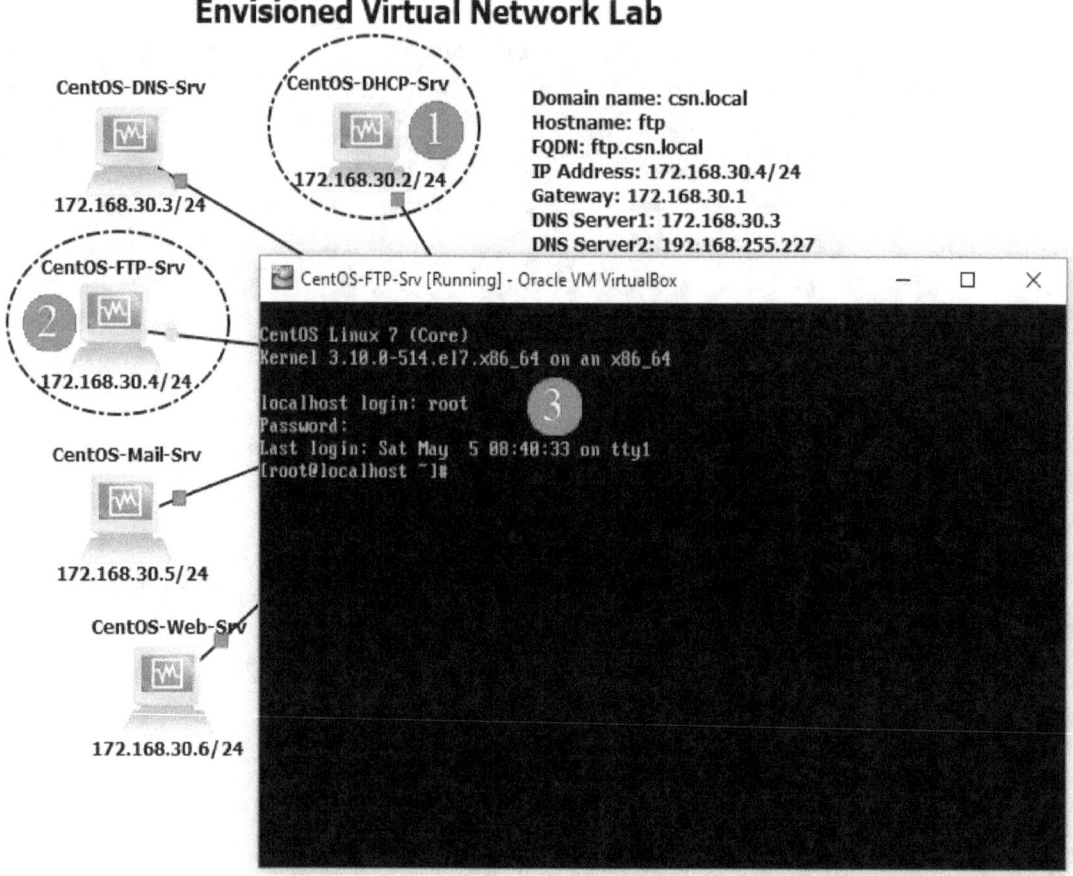

Figure 12.3: Virtual Network with FTP server and router running

> As we are working in a virtual network, running multiples virtual machines would drastically slow down the system. Since the configuration of the DHCP server is completed, you can shut it down from the GNS3 workspace to release system resources for faster processing. At this point, there is no need for DHCP to be running.

After successfully logging in to the server, configure the hostname by using the nmtui utility as shown in the figure below:

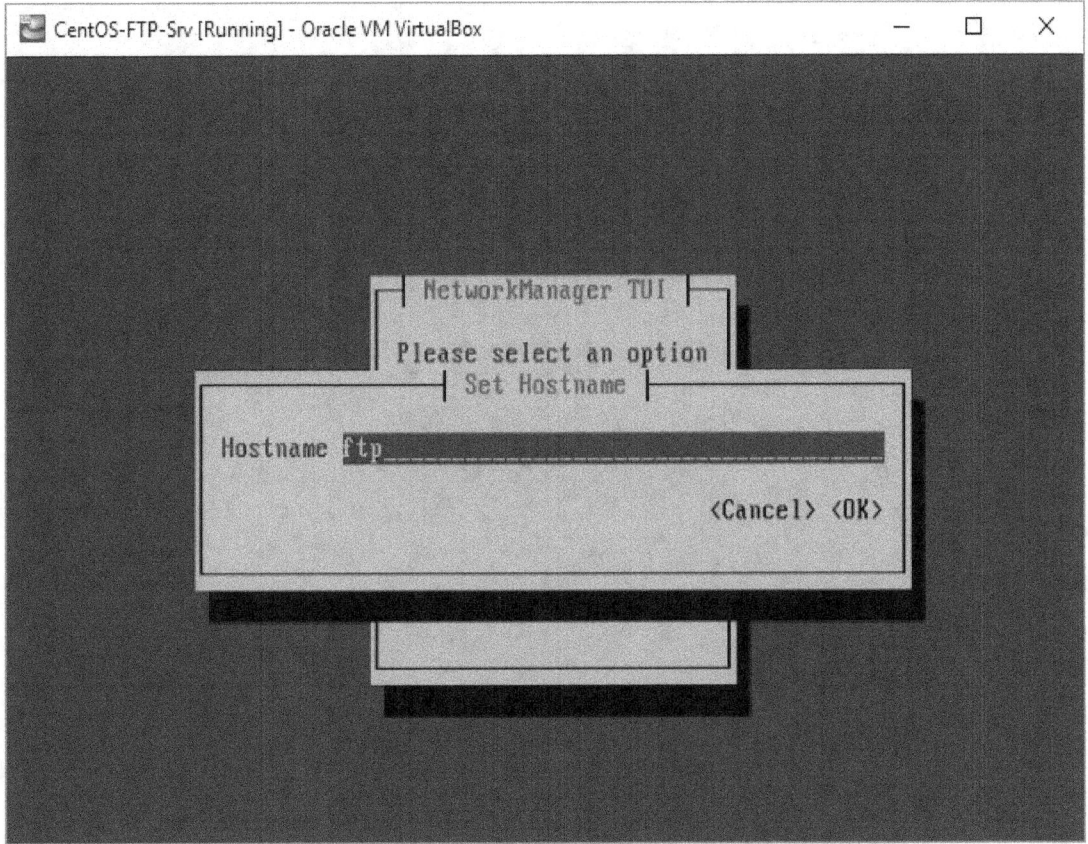

Figure 12.4: Setting the hostname

In the next, configure the IP address details using the nmtui as indicated in the figure 12.5 and figure 12.6.

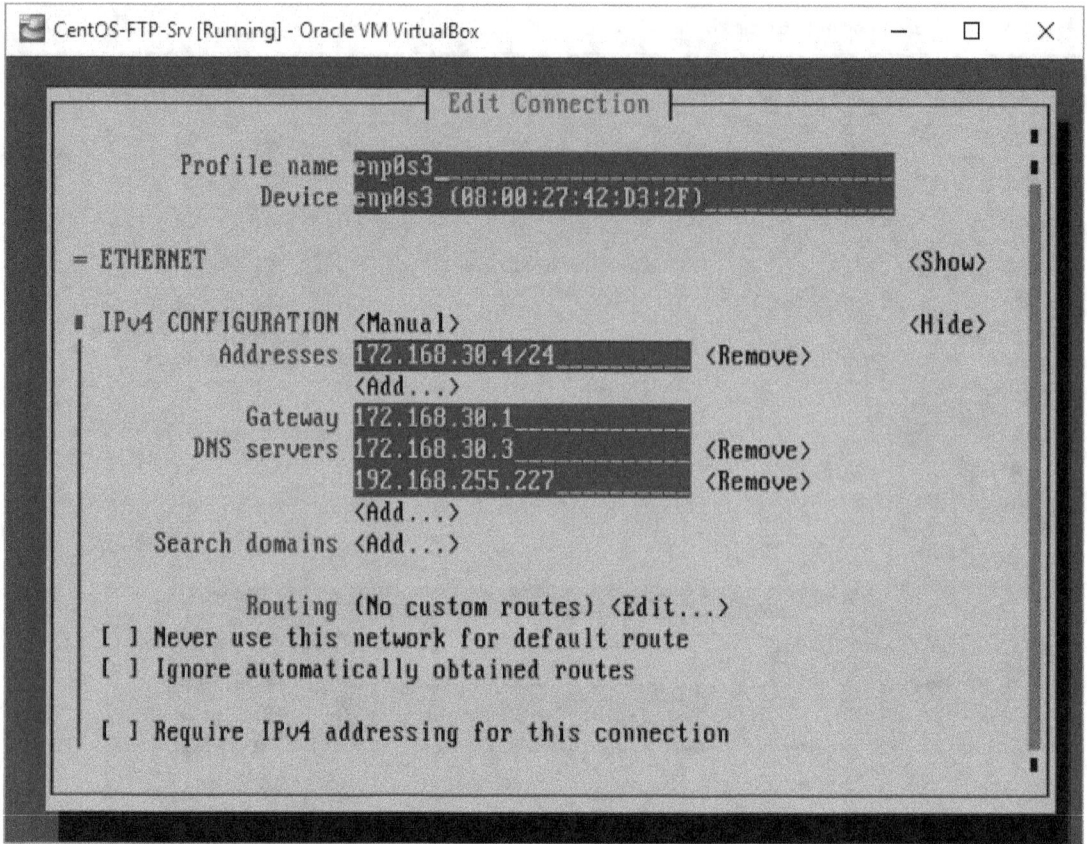

Figure 12.5: Ethernet IPv4 Setting for FTP Server

Build a Virtual Network and Practice

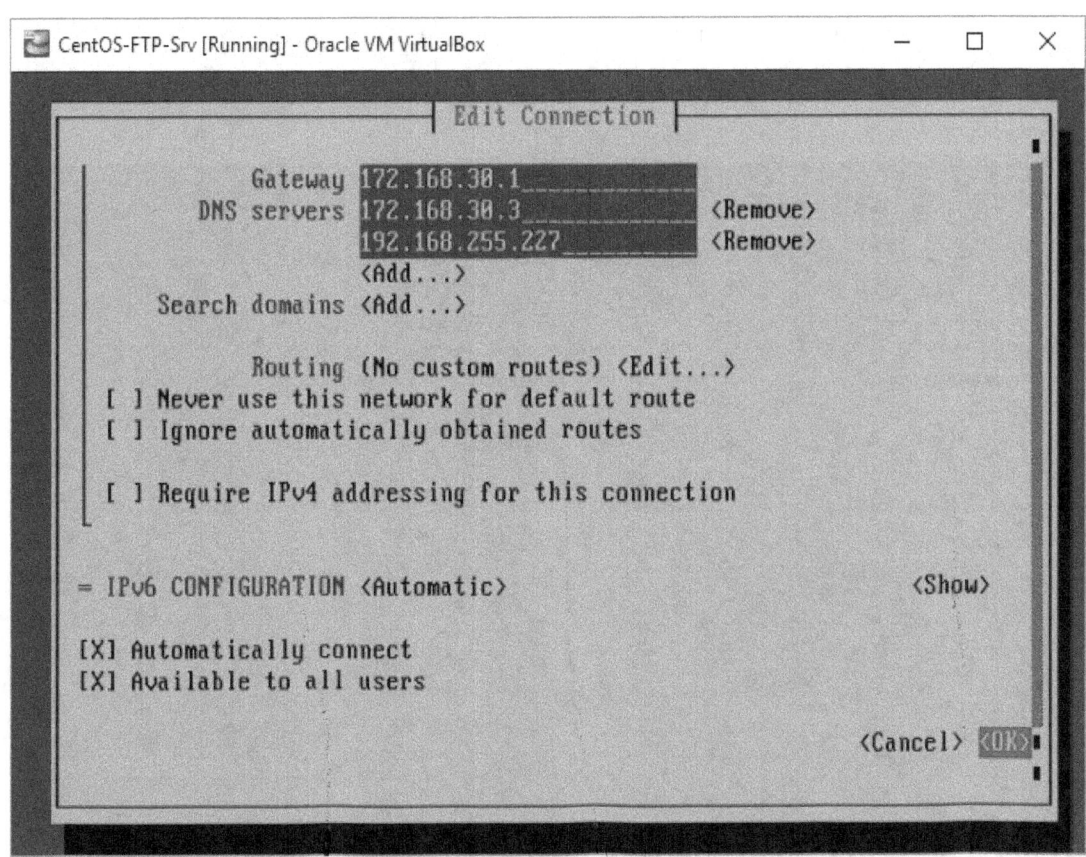

Figure 12.6: Allowing to automatically connect

Once the required manual settings are completed, you must be able to ping the router's IP address (172.168.30.1) as shown below from the FTP Server:

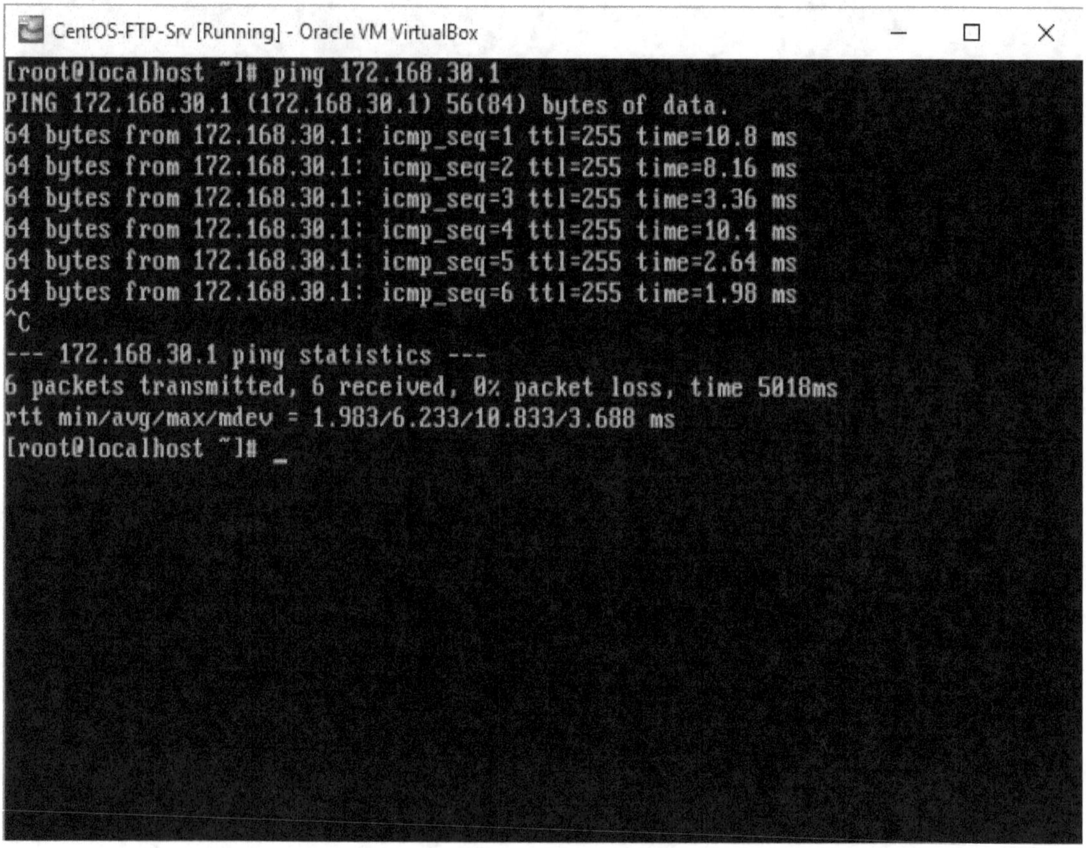
CentOS-FTP-Srv [Running] - Oracle VM VirtualBox
[root@localhost ~]# ping 172.168.30.1
PING 172.168.30.1 (172.168.30.1) 56(84) bytes of data.
64 bytes from 172.168.30.1: icmp_seq=1 ttl=255 time=10.8 ms
64 bytes from 172.168.30.1: icmp_seq=2 ttl=255 time=8.16 ms
64 bytes from 172.168.30.1: icmp_seq=3 ttl=255 time=3.36 ms
64 bytes from 172.168.30.1: icmp_seq=4 ttl=255 time=10.4 ms
64 bytes from 172.168.30.1: icmp_seq=5 ttl=255 time=2.64 ms
64 bytes from 172.168.30.1: icmp_seq=6 ttl=255 time=1.98 ms
^C
--- 172.168.30.1 ping statistics ---
6 packets transmitted, 6 received, 0% packet loss, time 5018ms
rtt min/avg/max/mdev = 1.983/6.233/10.833/3.688 ms
[root@localhost ~]# _

Figure 12.7: Verifying the connection

Before starting to install the packages for the FTP server, it is important to verify whether our router can connect to the internet or not by pinging the 8.8.8.8 after opening the console of the router.

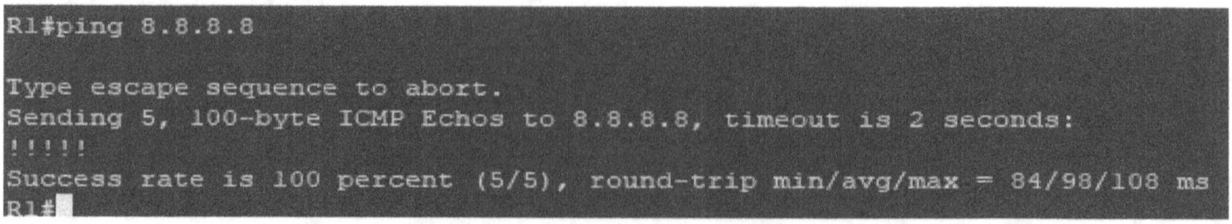
R1#ping 8.8.8.8
Type escape sequence to abort.
Sending 5, 100-byte ICMP Echos to 8.8.8.8, timeout is 2 seconds:
!!!!!
Success rate is 100 percent (5/5), round-trip min/avg/max = 84/98/108 ms
R1#

Figure 12.8: Verifying the connection to the Internet

If the pinging is not successful, try to check the configuration on the router and if the configurations are correctly done, try to reload or restart the router. Since we are using the dynamic IP address on the router's first interface f0/0, the lease might have expired.

Installing vsftpd (FTP) Package

To configure an FTP server, you need to install the vsftpd package from a repository with a root user's privilege. The other dependency packages would be installed automatically when the vsftpd package is installed. First install vsftpd package using a yum package manager on your to-be FTP Server by using the following command:

```
# yum install vsftpd -y
```

Files Installed with vsftpd

The vsftpd package installs its configuration and related files, as well as FTP directories onto the system (/usr/sbin/vsftpd). The following are the list of files and directories related to the vsftpd configuration:

- */etc/pam.d/vsftpd:* The Pluggable Authentication Modules (PAM) configuration file for vsftpd. This file specifies the requirements a user must meet to login to the FTP server.
- */etc/vsftpd/vsftpd.conf:* It is the main configuration file for the vsftpd daemon and the behavior of the FTP server depends on the directives we set in this configuration file.
- */etc/vsftpd/ftpusers:* This file can contain a list of users which are not allowed to log into FTP Server.
- */etc/vsftpd/user_list:* This file can contain a list of users and it can be configured to either deny or allow access to the users listed in this file, depending on whether the userlist_deny directive is set to YES (default) or NO in /etc/vsftpd/vsftpd.conf. If /etc/vsftpd/user_list is used to grant access to users, the usernames listed must not appear in /etc/vsftpd/ftpusers.
- */var/ftp/:* The directory containing files served by vsftpd. It also contains the /var/ftp/pub/ directory which can contain files meant to be served to the anonymous users.

Configuration Options for vsftpd

All the configurations of vsftpd is handled by its configuration file, /etc/vsftpd/vsftpd.conf. The behavior of the vsftpd depends on how the configurations are set on the /etc/vsftpd/vsftpd.conf file.

Each directive is on its own line within the file and follows the following format, <directive>=<value>. For each directive, replace directive with a valid directive and value with a valid value.

> *There must not be any spaces between the directive, equal symbol, and the value in a directive. Comment lines must be preceded by a hash sign (#) and are ignored by the daemon.*

The following is a list of some of the important directives within /etc/vsftpd/vsftpd.conf which control the overall behavior of the vsftpd daemon. All directives not explicitly found or commented out within vsftpd's configuration file are set to their default value.

Directive	Value	Description
anonymous_enable	YES	Controls whether anonymous logins are permitted or not. If enabled, both the usernames ftp and anonymous are recognized as anonymous logins.
local_enable	YES	Controls whether local logins are permitted or not. If enabled, normal user accounts in /etc/passwd would be allowed to login.
write_enable	YES	This controls whether any FTP commands which change the file system are allowed or not. These commands are: STOR, DELE, RNFR, RNTO, MKD, RMD, APPE and SITE.
local_umask	022	The value that the umask for file creation is set to for local Users.
dirmessage_enable	YES	Activate directory messages which are given to the users when they go to certain directories.
xferlog_enable	YES	Activate logging of file uploads and downloads.
anon_upload_enable	YES	If set to YES, anonymous users will be allowed to upload files under certain conditions. For this to work, the option write_enable must be activated, and the anonymous ftp user must have write permission on desired upload locations.
anon_mkdir_write_enable	YES	If set to YES, anonymous users will be permitted to create new directories under certain conditions. For this to work, the option write_enable must be activated, and the anonymous ftp user must have write permission on the parent directory.

Directive	Value	Description
userlist_enable	YES/NO	If enabled, vsftpd will load a list of usernames, from the file name given by userlist_file. If a user tries to log in using a name in this file, they will be denied before they are asked for a password. This may be useful in preventing cleartext passwords being transmitted. See also userlist_deny.
chroot_local_user	YES/NO	If set to YES, local users will be (by default) placed in a chroot() jail in their home directory after login. Warning: This option has security implications, especially if the users have upload permission, or shell access. Only enable if you know what you are doing. Note that these security implications are not vsftpd specific. They apply to all FTP daemons which offer To put local users in chroot() jails.
local_max_rate	local_max_rate=1000	The maximum data transfer rate permitted, in bytes per second, for locally authenticated users. Default: 0 (unlimited)
anon_max_rate	anon_max_rate=1000	The maximum data transfer rate permitted, in bytes per second, for anonymous clients. Default: 0 (unlimited)
no_anon_password	YES/NO	When enabled, this prevents vsftpd from asking for an anonymous password – the anonymous user will log straight in.

Configure FTP Server

Assuming that we wanted to configure an FTP server, which will allow anonymous users to use the ftp server, the required configuration changes must be made in its configuration file. The configuration file of the vsftpd is /etc/vsftpd/vsftpd.conf and the configuration adjustments must be made here in this file by opening the configuration file as shown below:

```
# vim /etc/vsftpd/vsftpd.conf
```

After opening the configuration file, look for the following lines and set the values accordingly to control the behavior of the vsftpd daemon as desired:

```
anonymous_enable=YES
local_enable=YES
write_enable=YES
```

> *In a similar way, the other configuration directives and values can be changed to suite the nature of the FTP server we want in your network. Whatever the configuration directives are enabled and set by default, suites most of our requirements.*

Start and Enable the vsftpd Service

Execute the following commands to start vsftpd service and also to enable the vsftpd service to run on boot, without having to start manually every time the system is restarted:

```
# systemctl start vsftpd.service
# systemctl enable vsftpd.service
```

The vsftpd should start successfully, if everything was configured properly till this point. If not, it is time to troubleshoot and get it up and running.

Adjusting the Firewall

Since the FTP uses the port 20 and 21, we have to open the ports in the firewall accordingly to allow the traffic and make the FTP service available in the network.

```
# firewall-cmd --permanent --zone=public --add-port=20-21/tcp
# firewall-cmd --permanent --zone=public --add-service=ftp
# firewall-cmd --reload
```

SELinux

If you want to allow ftp to read and write files in the users' home directories, you must turn on the ftp_home_dir boolean. Disabling the SELinux is not a part of a solution and it is not recommended.

```
# setsebool -P ftp_home_dir 1
```

Managing FTP Server with Filezilla

The FTP server is configured and it is up and running along with the DHCP Server, router and the Windows 7. The scenario in the following figure is, the Windows 7 depends on the DHCP server for getting the valid IP address assigned. If the client (Windows 7) need to access the Internet, the router is required to be there up and running. Now, to access the FTP server from the Windows 7, an FTP client is required to be there installed on the Windows 7.

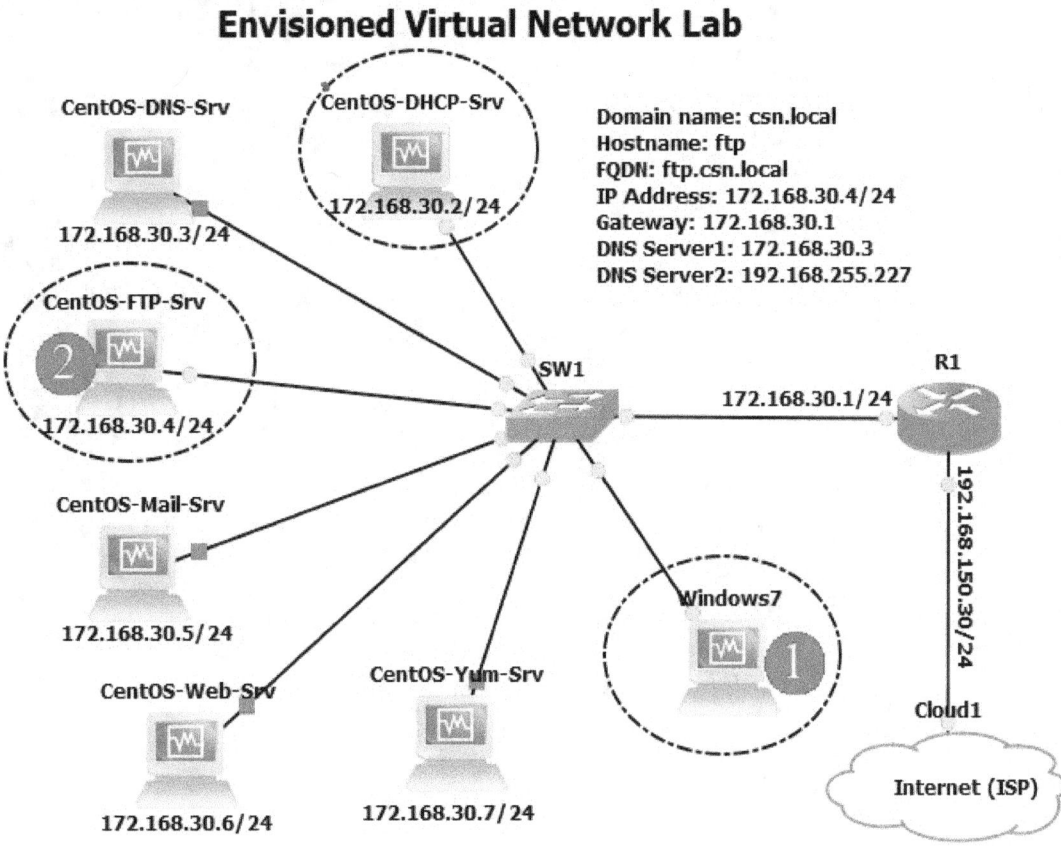

Figure 12.9: Virtual Network with servers and client running

After logging into the Windows 7, download Filezilla (FTP client for the Windows platform) from its official page and install it.

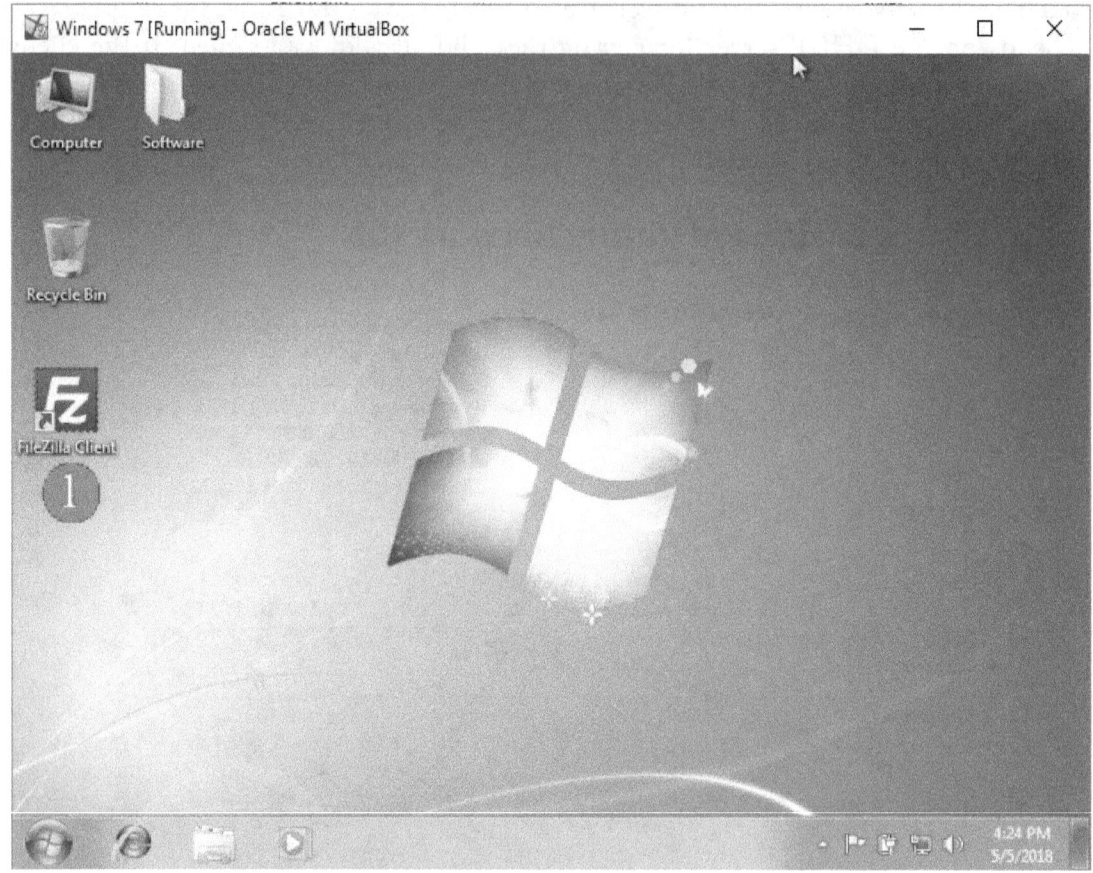

Figure 12.10: Filezilla downloaded and installed on Windows 7

After downloading and installing the Filezilla on the Windows 7, you can launch the Filezilla as the Administrator and then fill the details as indicated in the following figure.

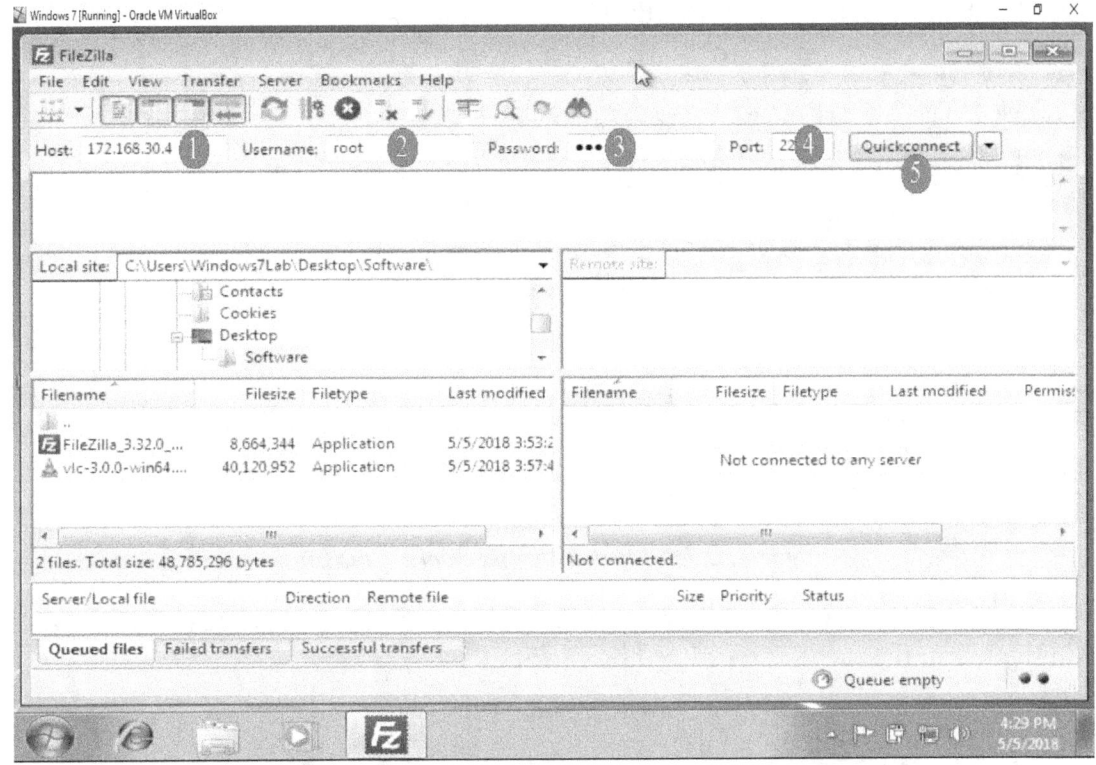

Figure 12.11: Specifying the user and server details

In the above figure, the information provided is as mentioned below:

Host: 172.168.30.4 [IP Address of the FTP Server]
User: root [User of the FTP Server]
Password: **** [The root user's password]
Port: 22 [Port used to communicate between Filezilla and the Server]

After specifying the required details correctly, clicking the "Quickconnect" button would let Filezilla connect to the FTP Server. When the following dialog box appears, choose the appropriate option for you and proceed.

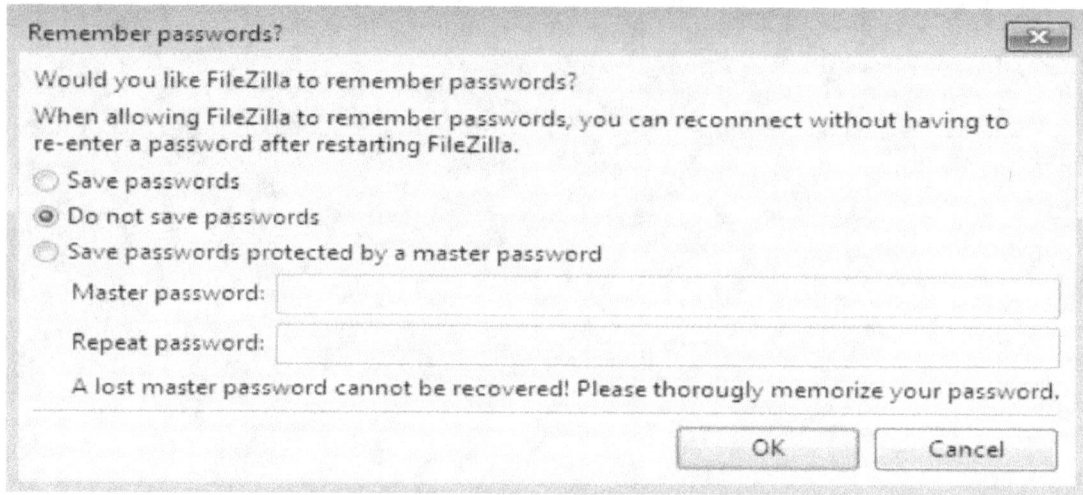

Figure 12.12: Options for password handling

For the security reasons, the following screen pops up. So, choose to trust the host and add the key to the cache and proceed by clicking "OK".

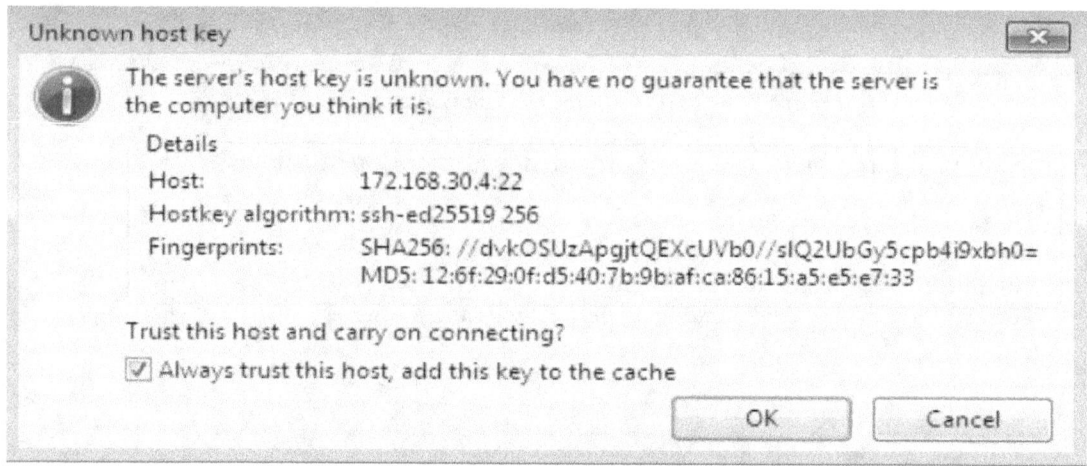

Figure 12.13: Choosing to trust the host

After that, the connection process would be complete and the root user's home directory would be displayed on the right side of the Filezilla's interface while the contents of the localhost (Windows 7) is being displayed on the left side.

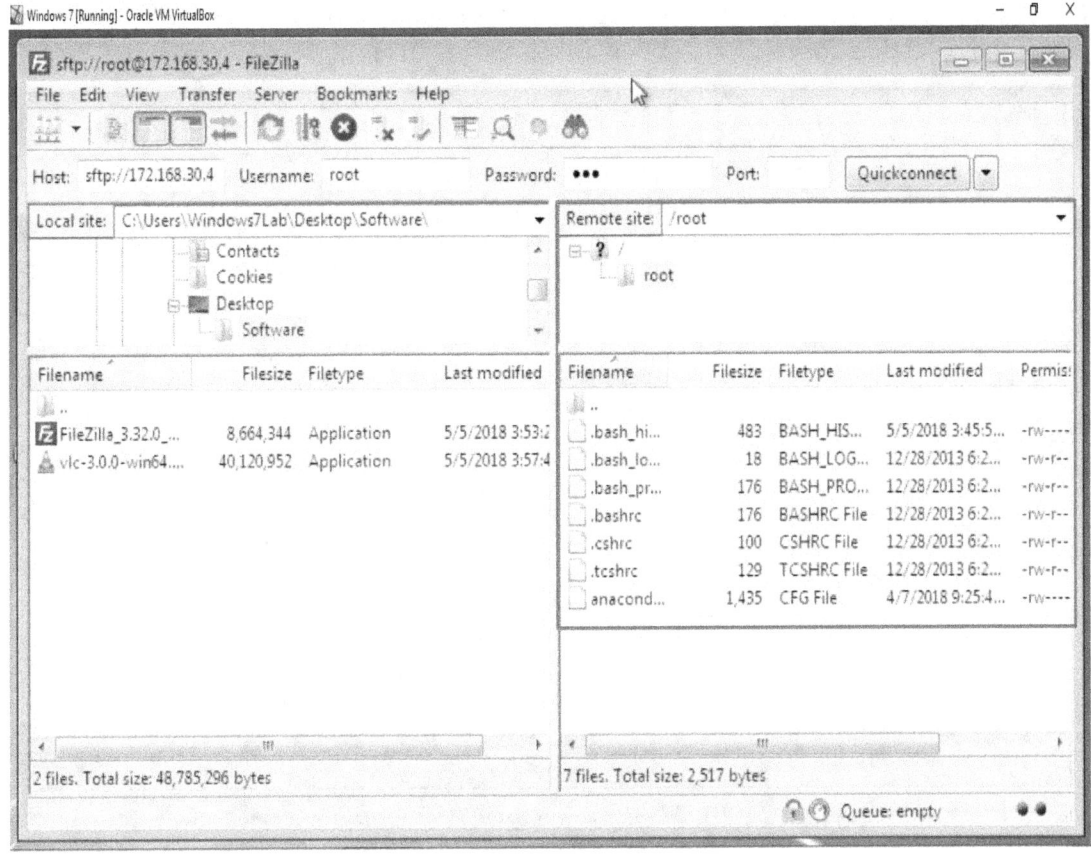

Figure 12.14: Displaying the destination directory's content

Just as an example, I have kept a folder with the name "Software" on the Windows 7 desktop, which has two files. My intention here is to upload those two files to the FTP's /var/ftp/pub directory using the Filezilla.

For, this we have to navigate to the /var/ftp/pub directory and initially there will be no files in the pub directory.

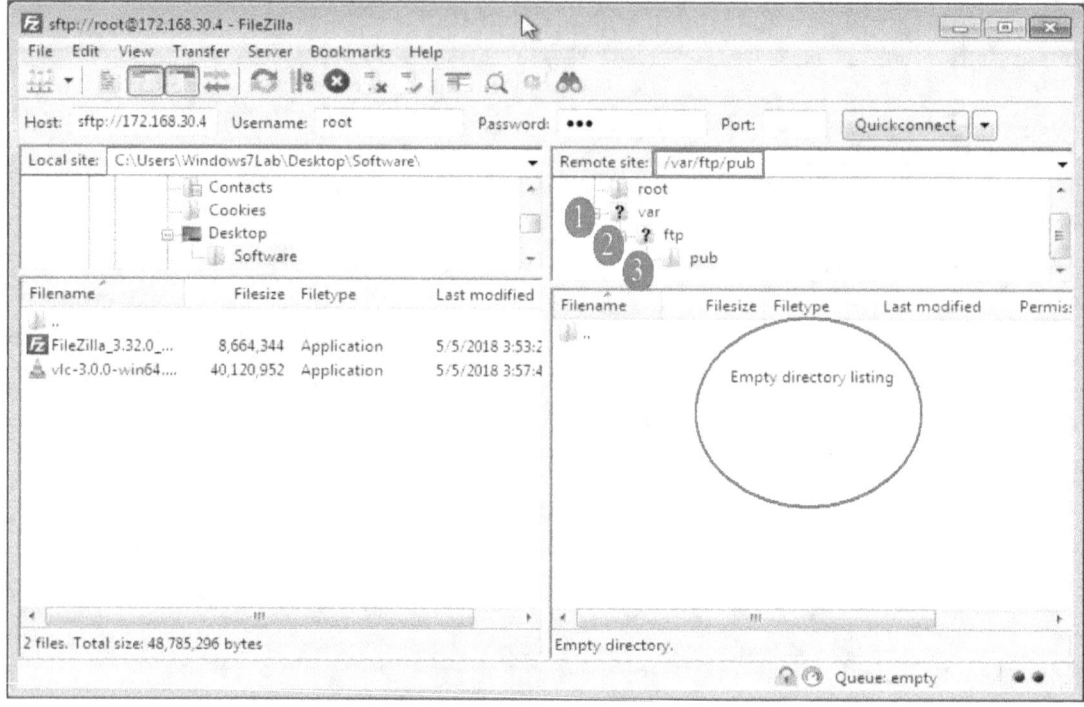

Figure 12.15: Navigating to /var/html/pub directory

We will try to upload those two files from the Software folder in the Desktop of the Windows 7 to the /var/ftp/pub directory, so that the files would be accessible to the clients. For this, the files must be selected and then drag and drop into the /var/ftp/pub directory. The files will be uploaded to the pub directory and then will be available for the clients to download via browser and use.

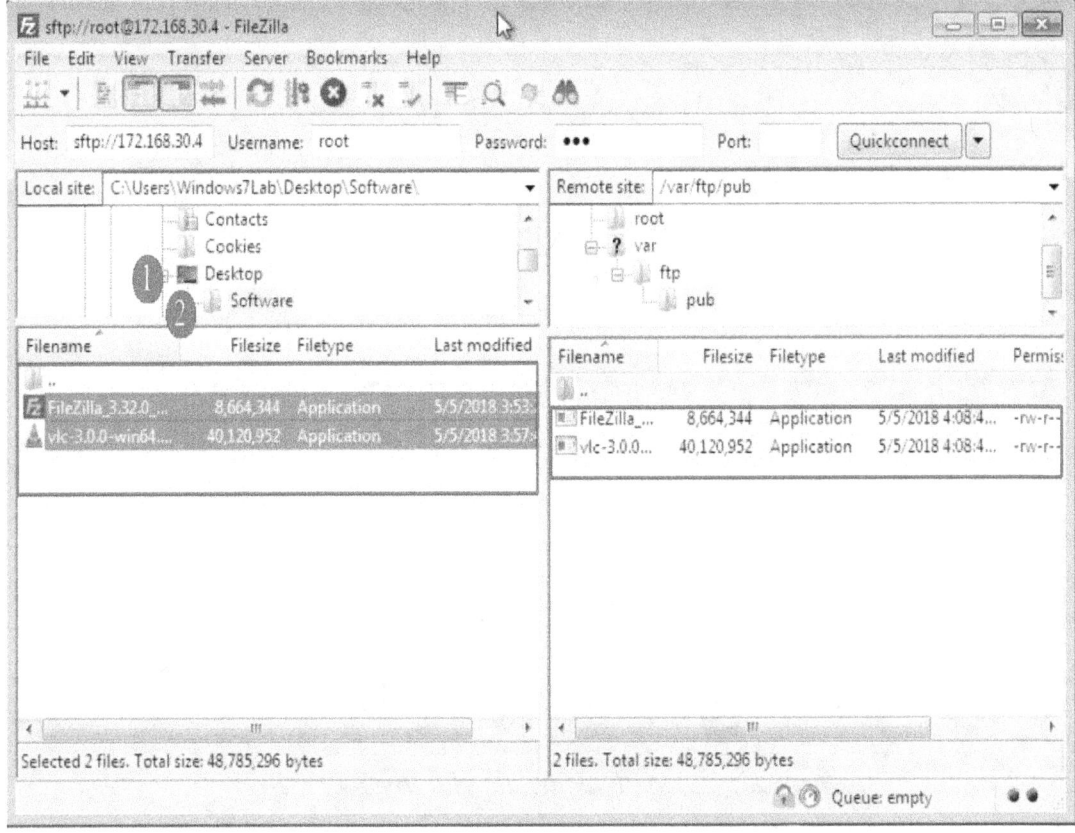

Figure 12.16: Uploading the files

Once the uploading of the files is completed you can quit the Filezilla.

Accessing from the Clients

To access the files available on the FTP server, the clients can use the internet browsers and specify the address as indicated in the following:

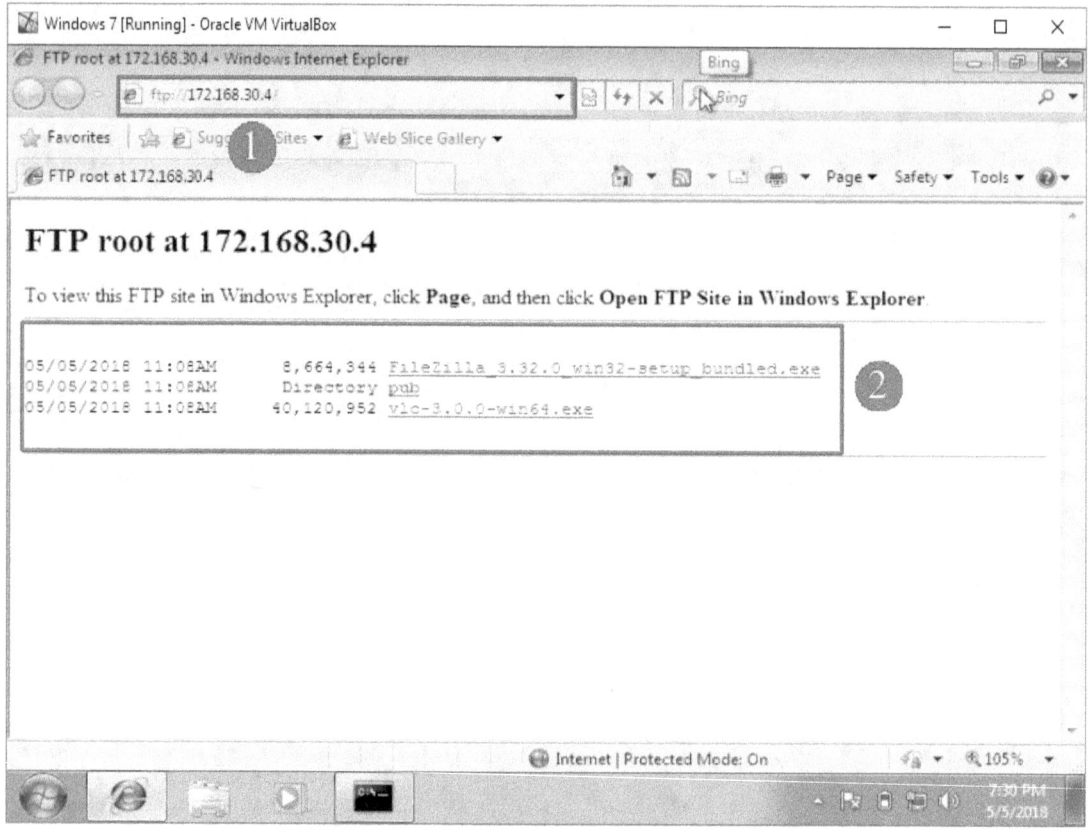

Figure 12.17: Accessible files stored in the FTP Server

Now, the files which we have uploaded are available for download by using the internet browsers from the clients.

Further Reading

Beginner's guide to SELinux. (2018, March 12). Retrieved from https://linuxtechlab.com/beginners-guide-to-selinux/

A. (n.d.). CentOS / RHEL 7: How to install and configure ftp server (vsftpd). Retrieved from https://www.thegeekdiary.com/centos-rhel-7-how-to-install-and-configure-ftp-server-vsftpd/

Install and Configure FTP Server on CentOS 7. (2015, January 21). Retrieved from https://www.unixmen.com/install-configure-ftp-server-centos-7/

L., Abrams. (n.d.). Introduction to the File Transfer Protocol (FTP). Retrieved from https://www.bleepingcomputer.com/tutorials/introduction-to-ftp/

Pock, D. (2017, December 06). How to set up vsftpd on CentOS 7. Retrieved from https://www.liquidweb.com/kb/how-to-install-and-configure-vsftpd-on-centos-7/

Setup FTP server on centos 7 (VSFTP). (2017, March 26). Retrieved from https://www.krizna.com/centos/setup-ftp-server-centos-7-vsftp/

Chapter 13
Setting Up a Mail Server

Today, e-mail is used by almost all the internet users for the purpose of communication on any matters and issues regardless of their organization sizes. If your organization is a newly established one, you might be asked to create one for your organization by the management.

In this chapter, you will learn to set up an e-mail server in CentOS to be able to send and receive e-mails using the Postfix, Dovecot and the SquirrelMail. Finally, the functionality of the configured Mail Server will be tested and verified.

Network Scenario

To learn to set up the Mail Server, we will continue to use the Virtual Network Lab which we created and used in the previous chapters. In the same virtual network Lab, we have implemented the DHCP server, FTP Server and here onwards, without removing the DHCP server, FTP Server and the rest of the configurations, we will implement the Mail server in our Virtual Network Lab.

In this scenario, we want our users to be allowed to send and receive e-mails to and from the other users using the configured mail server for the organization (domain name).

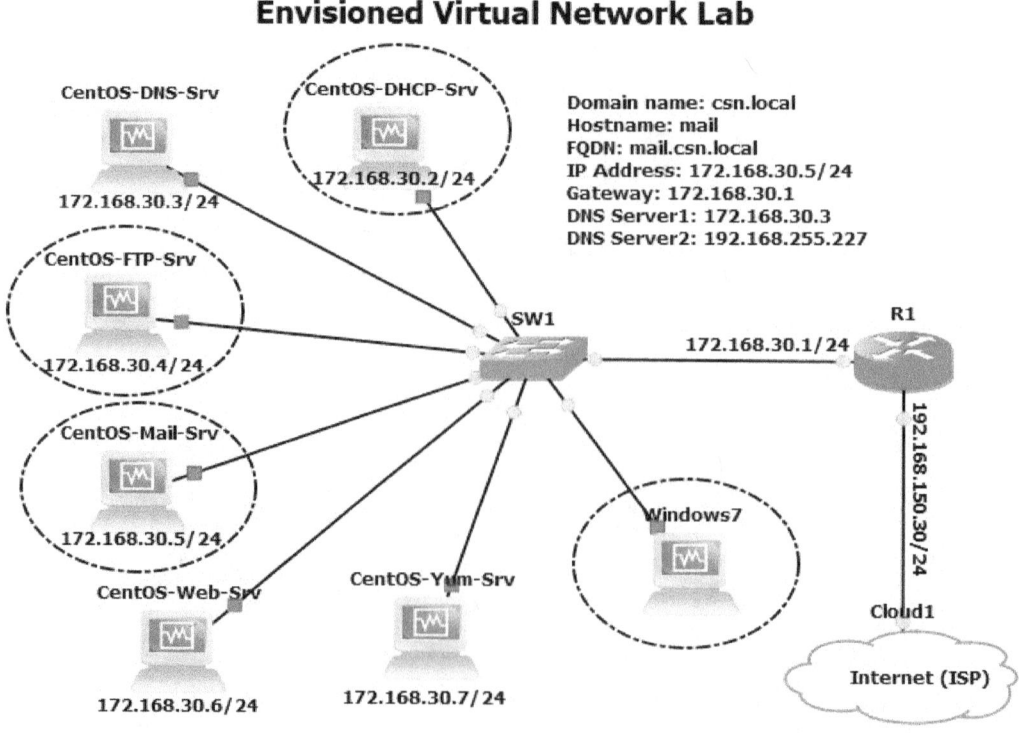

Figure 13.1: Base network with Mail Server details

Configuring the Mail Server Details

Taking into consideration the details of the Mail Server shown in the figure 13.1, the Mail server details have to be configured. In order to configure, we have to start the Mail server (CentOS-Mail-Srv) from the GNS3 workspace by right-clicking and choosing to start.

> *It is advised not to either start or shutdown the Mail server directly from the VirtualBox interface while working on the GNS3 as this action would lead to issues. So, start or shutdown from the GNS3 Interface only. While trying to start any of the severs not just limited to CentOS-Mail-Srv (Mail Server) from the GNS3, sometimes you may get error messages and you won't be able to start. In such cases, start the server directly from the VirtualBox interface and once the starting is complete, login and give a proper shutdown. This happens when the server was improperly shutdown previously. After starting and shutting down from the VirtualBox, then go to the GNS3 workspace and start from there.*

When you try to start the server from the GNS3, you might be issued with a security alert, choose the options and allow access as shown in the figure 13.2.

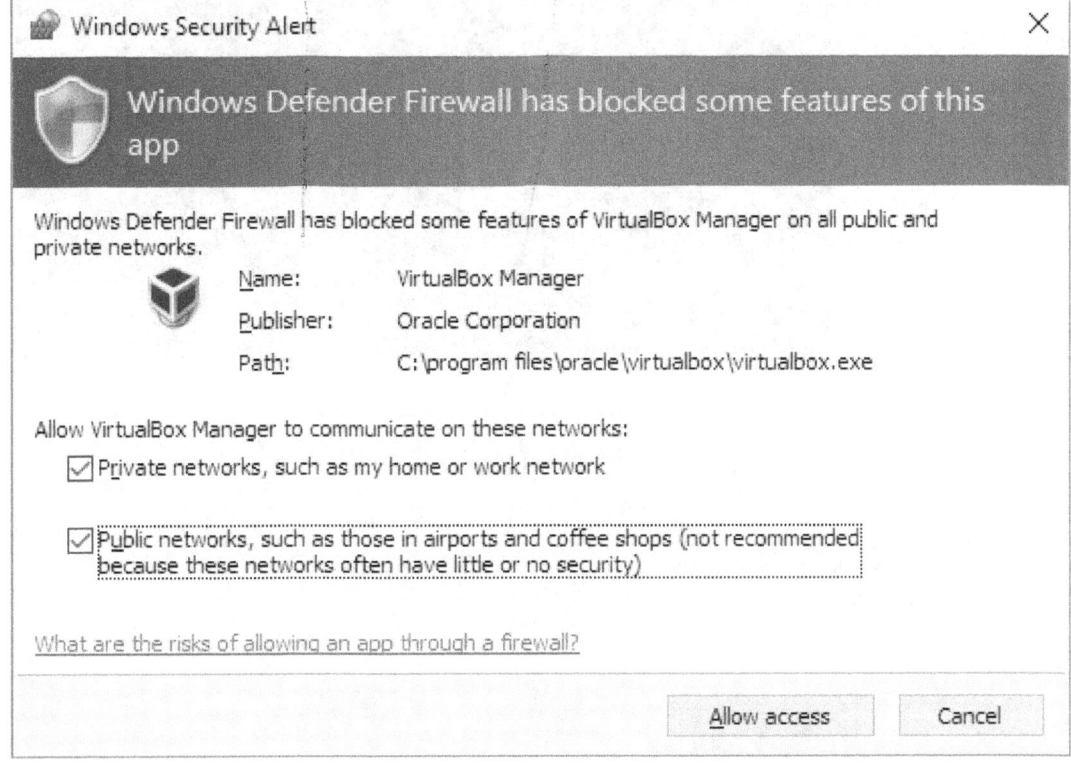

Figure 13.2: Windows Security Alert

If the starting of the Mail server is successful, the link status of the devices would change to green circular bullets and also the screen of the CentOS-Mail-Srv (Mail Server) would be available for login. Then you can login to the system as the root and then continue to configure the details.

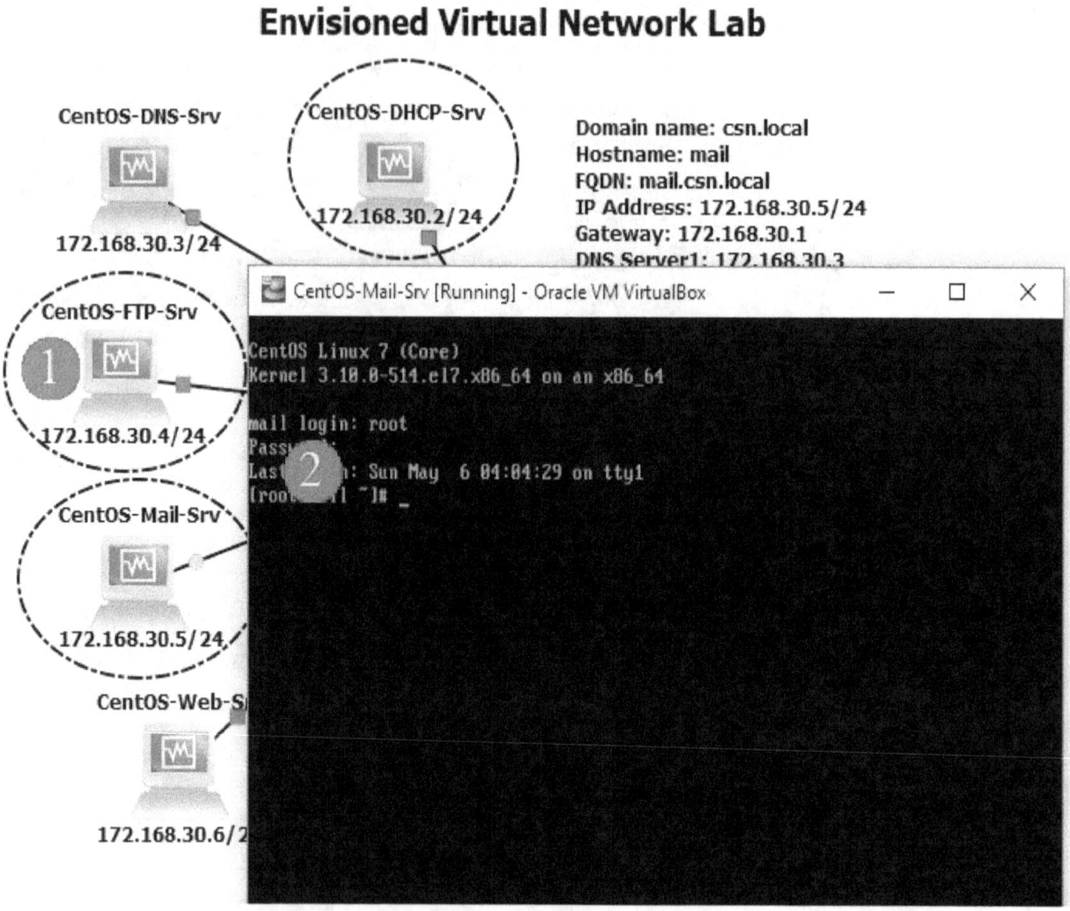

Envisioned Virtual Network Lab

CentOS-DNS-Srv
172.168.30.3/24

CentOS-DHCP-Srv
172.168.30.2/24

Domain name: csn.local
Hostname: mail
FQDN: mail.csn.local
IP Address: 172.168.30.5/24
Gateway: 172.168.30.1
DNS Server1: 172.168.30.3

CentOS-FTP-Srv
172.168.30.4/24

CentOS-Mail-Srv
172.168.30.5/24

CentOS-Web-Srv
172.168.30.6/24

```
CentOS Linux 7 (Core)
Kernel 3.10.0-514.el7.x86_64 on an x86_64

mail login: root
Password:
Last login: Sun May 6 04:04:29 on tty1
[root@mail ~]#
```

Figure 13.3: Virtual Network with Mail server and router running

As we are working in a virtual network, running multiples virtual machines would drastically slow down the system. Since the configuration of the DHCP server is completed, you can shut it down from the GNS3 workspace to release system resources for faster processing. At this point, there is no need for DHCP to be running.

After successfully logging in to the server, configure the hostname by using the nmtui utility as shown in the figure below:

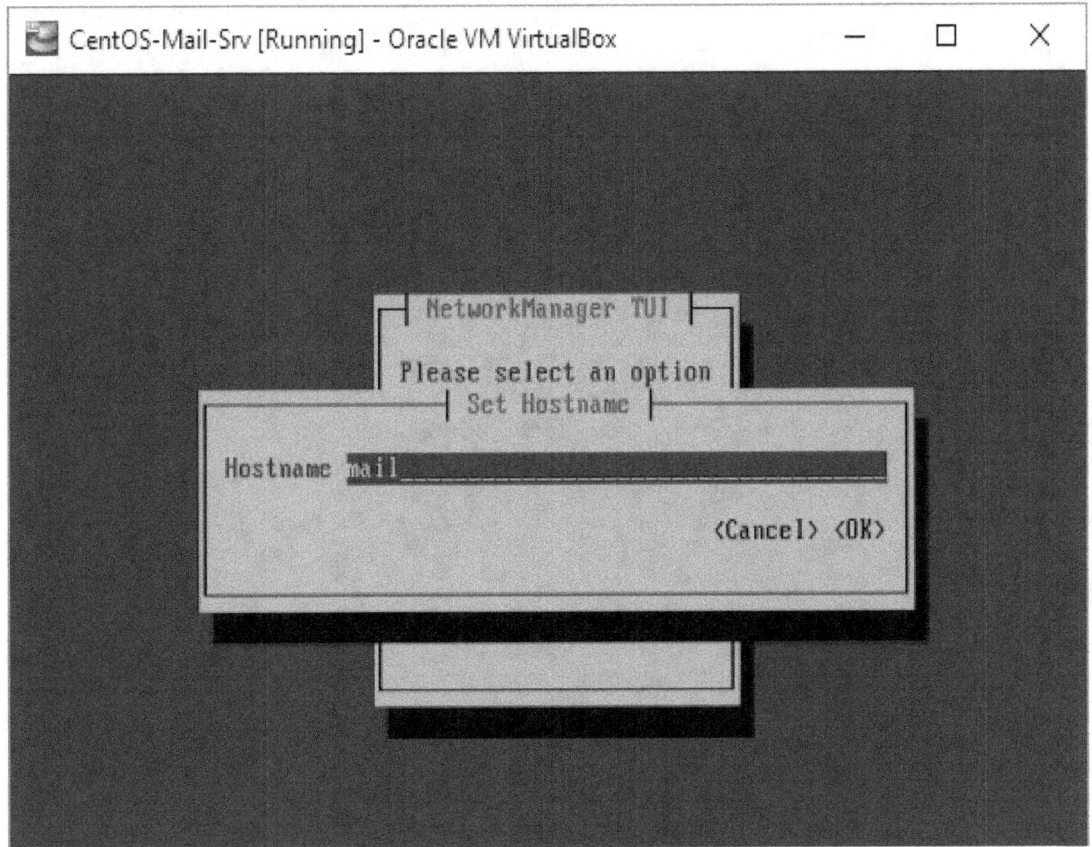

Figure 13.4: Setting the hostname

In the next, configure the IP address details using the nmtui as indicated in the figure 13.5 and figure 13.6.

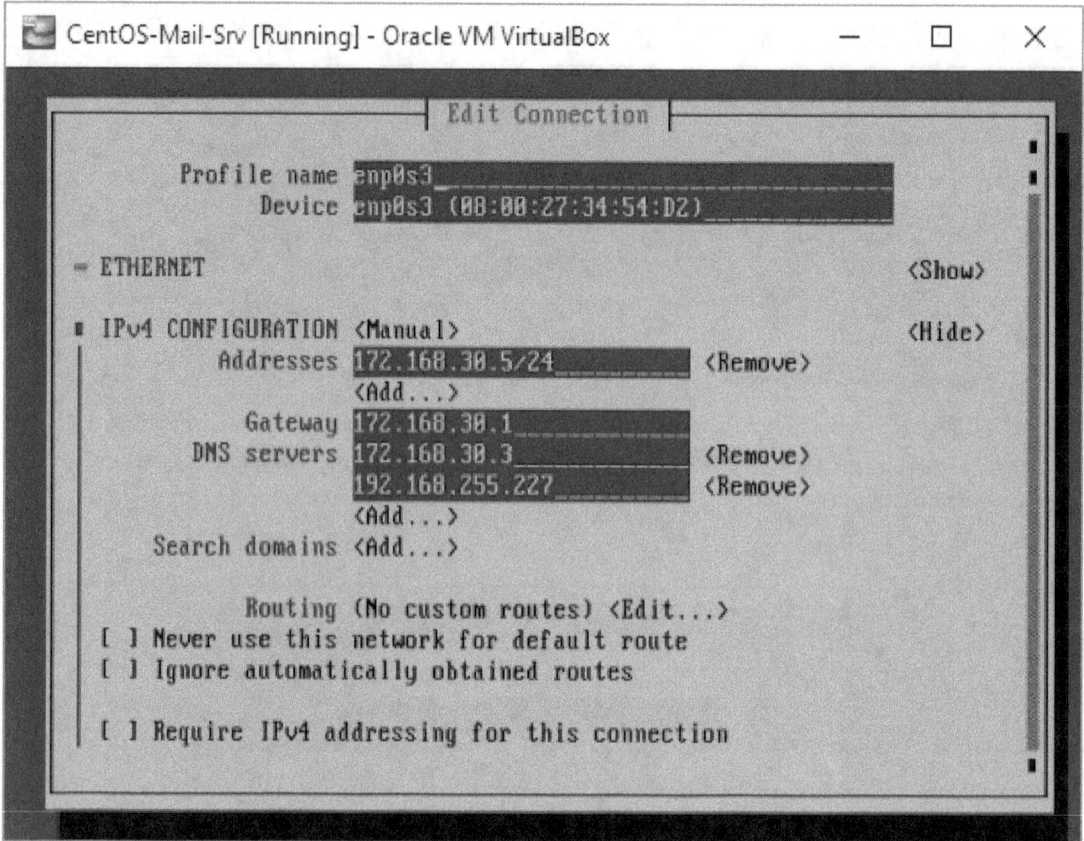

Figure 13.5: Ethernet IPv4 Setting for Mail Server

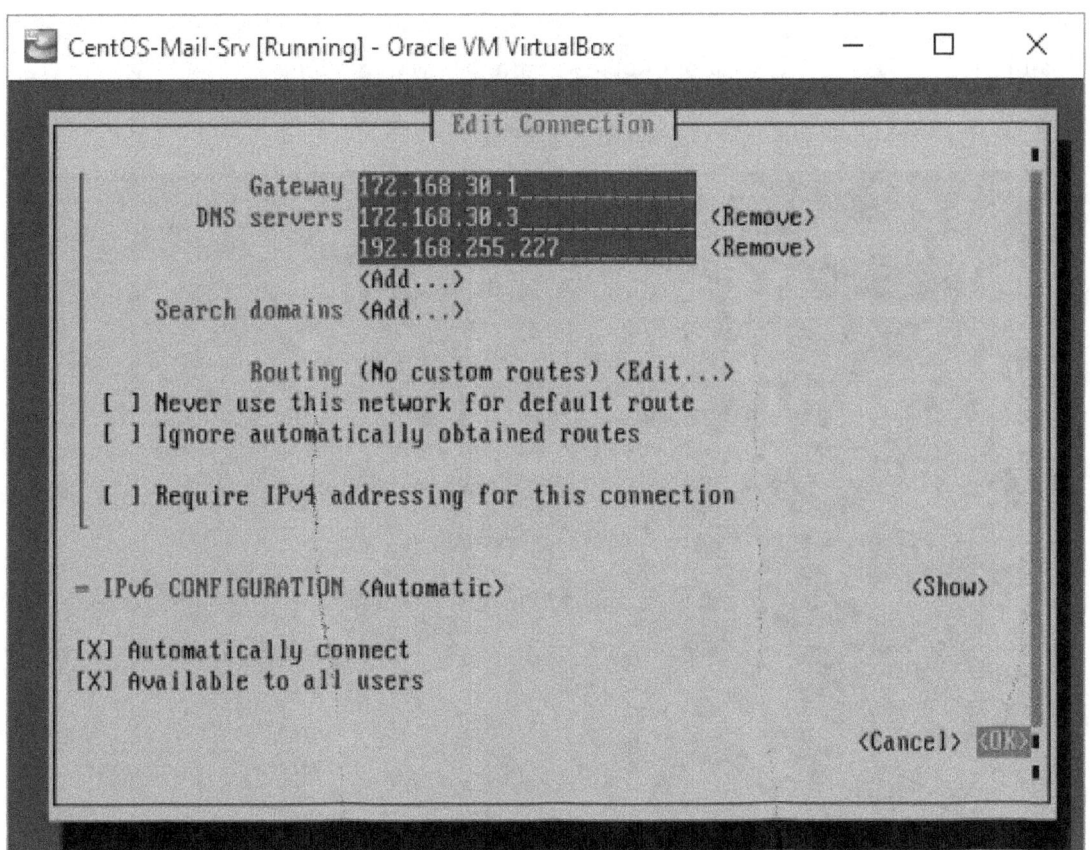

Figure 13.6: Allowing to automatically connect

Once the required manual settings are completed, you must be able to ping the router's IP address (172.168.30.1) as shown below from the Mail Server:

```
[root@mail ~]# ping 172.168.30.1
PING 172.168.30.1 (172.168.30.1) 56(84) bytes of data.
64 bytes from 172.168.30.1: icmp_seq=1 ttl=255 time=12.2 ms
64 bytes from 172.168.30.1: icmp_seq=2 ttl=255 time=5.17 ms
64 bytes from 172.168.30.1: icmp_seq=3 ttl=255 time=5.54 ms
64 bytes from 172.168.30.1: icmp_seq=4 ttl=255 time=10.5 ms
64 bytes from 172.168.30.1: icmp_seq=5 ttl=255 time=5.91 ms
64 bytes from 172.168.30.1: icmp_seq=6 ttl=255 time=10.7 ms
64 bytes from 172.168.30.1: icmp_seq=7 ttl=255 time=1.86 ms
64 bytes from 172.168.30.1: icmp_seq=8 ttl=255 time=7.95 ms
^C
--- 172.168.30.1 ping statistics ---
8 packets transmitted, 8 received, 0% packet loss, time 7011ms
rtt min/avg/max/mdev = 1.864/7.501/12.256/3.283 ms
[root@mail ~]#
```

Figure 13.7: Verifying the connection

Before starting to install the packages for the Mail server, it is important to verify whether our router can connect to the internet or not by pinging the 8.8.8.8 after opening the console of the router.

```
R1#ping 8.8.8.8

Type escape sequence to abort.
Sending 5, 100-byte ICMP Echos to 8.8.8.8, timeout is 2 seconds:
!!!!!
Success rate is 100 percent (5/5), round-trip min/avg/max = 220/234/244 ms
R1#
```

Figure 13.8: Verifying the connection to the Internet from the router

> If the pinging is not successful, try to check the configuration on the router and if the configurations are correctly done, try to reload or restart the router. Since we are using the dynamic IP address on the router's first interface f0/0, the lease might have expired.

Adding Hosts Entry

Open the hosts file using your favourite editor to add hostname entry in /etc/hosts file as shown below for resolution. The format for making an entry is:

[IP Address of the Mail Server] [FQDN of the Mail Server] [Mail Server's Hostname]
[root@mail ~]# vim /etc/hosts

The following figure shows the entry being made in the /etc/hosts file of the mail server:

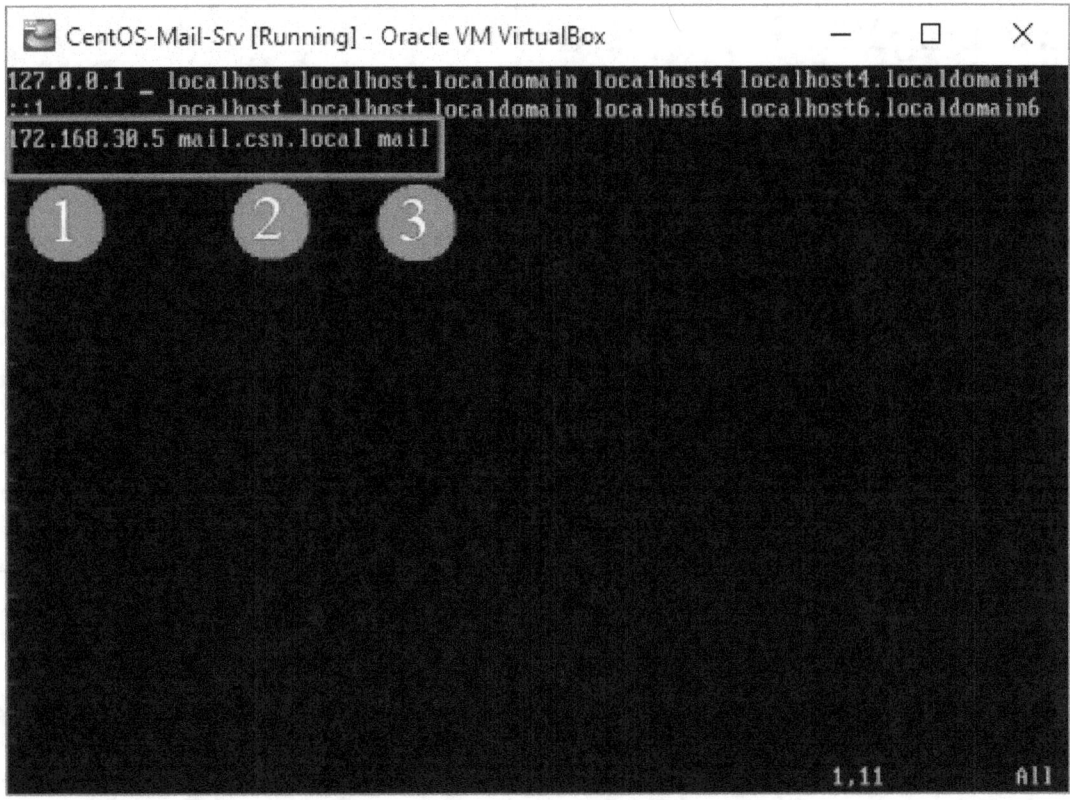

Figure 13.9: Entry in the /etc/hosts file

Disable SELinux

Although it is not recommended to disable the SELinux permanently, for time being we will disable the SELinux in order to avoid the troubles. We will enable it in the later part and we will try to troubleshoot.

[root@mail ~]# setenforce 0
[root@mail ~]# sed -i 's/SELINUX=enforcing/SELINUX=disabled/g' /etc/selinux/config

Firewall Adjustment

Allow the Apache default port 80 through your firewall and also IMAP port 143 and reload the firewall to take the changes into effect.

    [root@mail ~]# firewall-cmd --permanent --zone=public --add-port=80/tcp
    [root@mail ~]# firewall-cmd --permanent --zone=public --add-port=143/tcp
    [root@mail ~]# firewall-cmd --reload

Installing Postfix

Postfix is a secure, easy to administer open source mail transfer agent (MTA). We will install Postfix using the following command:

    [root@mail ~]# yum install postfix -y

Configuring Postfix

The main.cf is the configuration file for the Postfix and to configure it, open and edit /etc/postfix/main.cf file.

    [root@mail ~]# vim /etc/postfix/main.cf

After opening the configuration file, the configuration changes have to be made as indicated in the following lines:

The line number 75 is commented by default, you can uncomment it by removing the # from the beginning of the line. Then replace the host.domain.tld with your mail server's FQDN.

    myhostname = mail.csn.local

Uncomment the line number 83 and set the domain name for the server.

    mydomain = csn.local

Go to the line number 99, 113 and 119 and uncomment if those lines are commented by default.

    myorigin = $mydomain
    inet_interfaces = all
    inet_protocols = all

By default, the line number 164 is uncommented, comment it by putting # at the beginning of the line.

    # mydestination = $myhostname, localhost.$mydomain, localhost

After commenting line number 164, uncomment the line number 165.

mydestination = $myhostname, localhost.$mydomain, localhost, $mydomain

Go to the line 264, uncomment it and specify your network's IP range. So, in our example, the network range is 172.168.30.0/24.

mynetworks = 172.168.30.0/24, 127.0.0.0/8

Finally, uncomment line 419 by removing the # sign from the beginning of the line, save the changes and quit the file.

home_mailbox = Maildir/

Start and Enable Postfix

After saving and quitting the file, enable and start the postfix server using the following commands:

[root@mail ~]# systemctl enable postfix
[root@mail ~]# systemctl start postfix

Dovecot Installation

Dovecot is an open source IMAP and POP3 mail server for Unix-like systems. To install dovecot on the CentOS-Mail-Srv, use the following command as the root user:

[root@mail ~]# yum install dovecot -y

Configuring Dovecot

To configure the Dovecot, the configurations have to be made in /etc/dovecot/dovecot.conf, /etc/dovecot/conf.d/10-mail.conf, /etc/dovecot/conf.d/10-auth.conf and /etc/dovecot/conf.d/10-master.conf files. You can open and edit /etc/dovecot/dovecot.conf configuration file as indicated in the following:

[root@mail ~]# vim /etc/dovecot/dovecot.conf

By default, the line number 24 comes commented, you can uncomment it by removing the # from the beginning of the line and save and quit the file.

protocols = imap pop3 lmtp

Open and edit the file /etc/dovecot/conf.d/10-mail.conf file as indicated below:

[root@mail ~]# vim /etc/dovecot/conf.d/10-mail.conf

You can uncomment the line number 24 by removing the # sign from the beginning to the line as shown below:

mail_location = maildir:~/Maildir

Open and edit the file /etc/dovecot/conf.d/10-auth.conf as indicated below:

    [root@mail ~]# vim /etc/dovecot/conf.d/10-auth.conf

Uncomment line number 10 and in line number 100, add the keyword "login" as indicated in the following respectively:

    disable_plaintext_auth = yes
    auth_mechanisms = plain login

Open and edit the file /etc/dovecot/conf.d/10-master.conf as indicated in the following:

    [root@mail ~]# vim /etc/dovecot/conf.d/10-master.conf

Uncomment both line number 91 and 92 and add postfix as user and group in the way shown below:

    user = postfix
    group = postfix

Start and Enable Dovecot

After making the required changes in the configuration files of the Dovecot, start the service and enable it.

    [root@mail ~]# systemctl enable dovecot
    [root@mail ~]# systemctl start dovecot

Installing SquirrelMail

The Postfix and the Dovecot will enable us to send and receive mails by using the command line, which most of us, including the technical personnel would loath to do it. In order to ease our work, the SquirrelMail comes into the picture as a rescuer literally. We will use the SquirrelMail to easily send or receive mails, which is a browser-based webmail client.

The squirrelmail can be installed in a variety of ways. We will use the RPM file of the Squirrelmail for CentOS distribution. To install the Squirrelmail, we need to install the dependency files as shown below:

    [root@mail ~]# yum install –y httpd hunspell hunspell-en mod_php php-mbstring tmpwatch deltarpm perl

To download the squirrelmail rpm file for the CentOS based distributions, run the following command on the terminal:

    [root@mail ~]# cd /root
    [root@mail ~]# wget https://dl.fedoraproject.org/pub/epel/7/x86_64/Packages/s/squirrel-mail-1.4.22-16.el7.noarch.rpm

> *If the wget utility is not installed, run the command "yum install –y wget" on the terminal. It is used for downloading the files from the internet to the current directory. Also, if the download link is broken, you can download the squirrelmail rpm file from other links as well.*

Assuming that the rpm file for the squirrelmail is downloaded and saved in the /root directory, run the following commands to get the squirrelmail installed:

```
[root@mail ~]# cd /root
[root@mail ~]# rpm –ivh squirrelmail-1.4.22-16.el7.noarch.rpm
```

Configuring SquirrelMail

After the installation of the Squirrelmail is successful, navigate to /usr/share/squirrelmail/config/ directory and run the following command to configure the SquirrelMail:

[root@mail ~]# cd /usr/share/squirrelmail/config/
[root@mail config]# ls
config_default.php config_local.php config.php conf.pl index.php
[root@mail config]# ./conf.pl

When you run the script, the following menu will be shown. Enter choice number "1" to set your organizational details and press [Enter]:

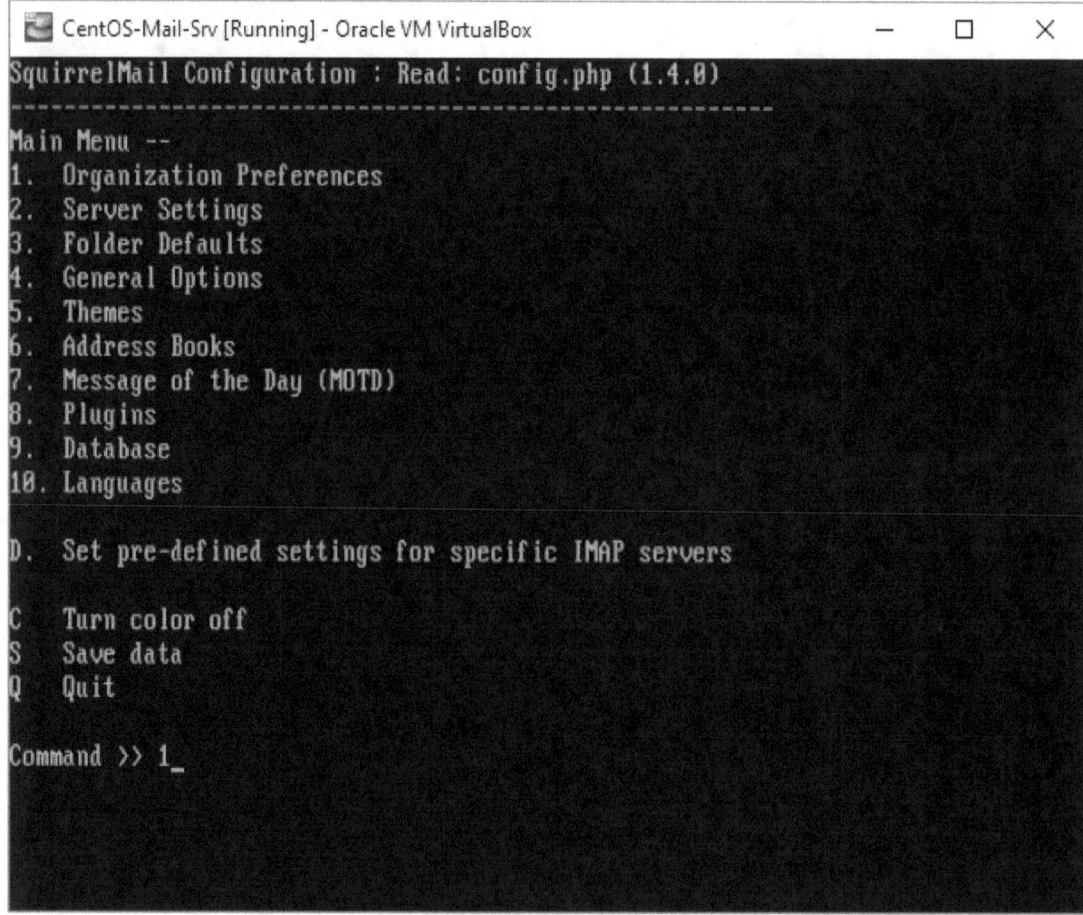

Figure 13.10: Choosing to set Organization Preferences

The following menu will be displayed. Again enter "1" and press [Enter] key to modify your Organization name. By default, the Organization name is kept as SquirrelMail, but that is not our organization name. We will change it to Computer System and Network (CSN).

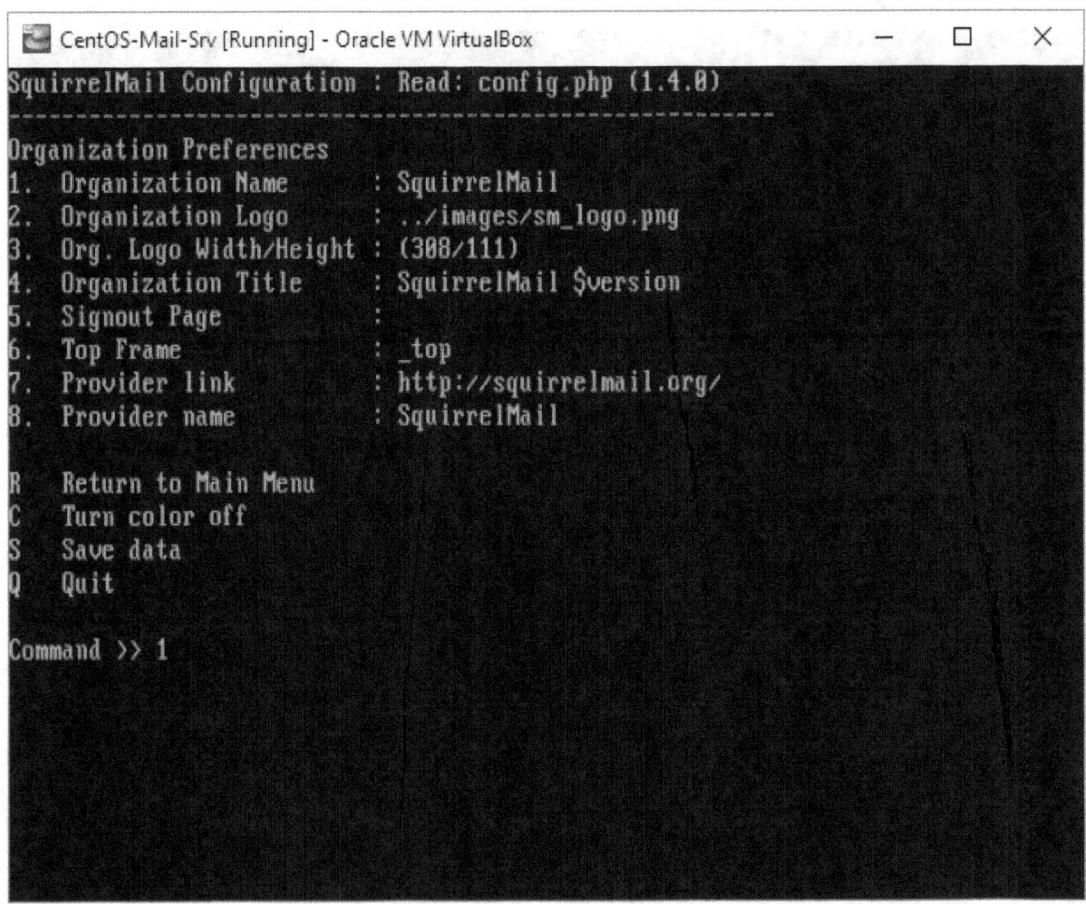

Figure 13.11: Choosing to change the organization name

In the next screen, considering that our organization's name is Computer System and Network (CSN), enter Computer System and Network (CSN) in the prompt and press [Enter] key.

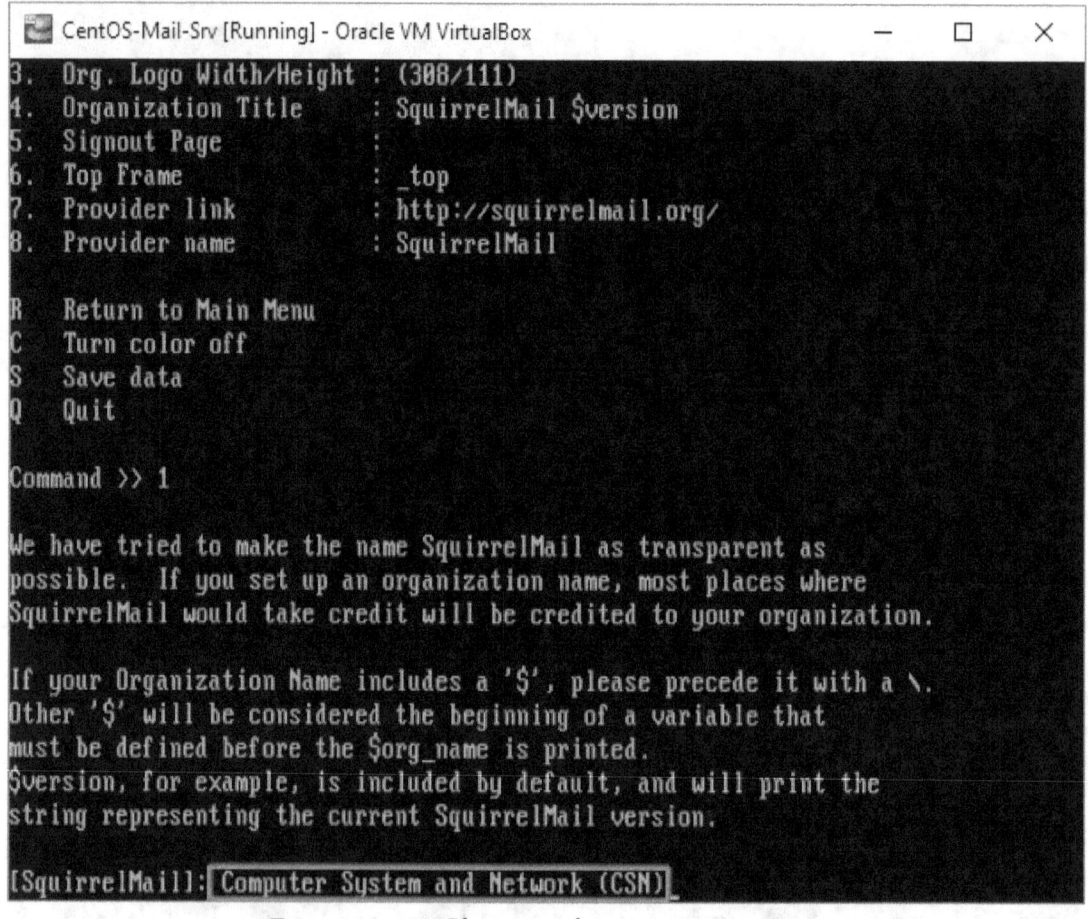

Figure 13.12: Changing the organization name

The name of your organization would change to what you have provided in the previous step and the change will be shown as under. You have the option to change the organization's logo and other details as well. By default, the logo provided is the SquirrelMail logo which is stored in the images directory. Next, we will opt to change the provider's link by putting our web link. For that enter the choice number 7 in the prompt and press [Enter] key.

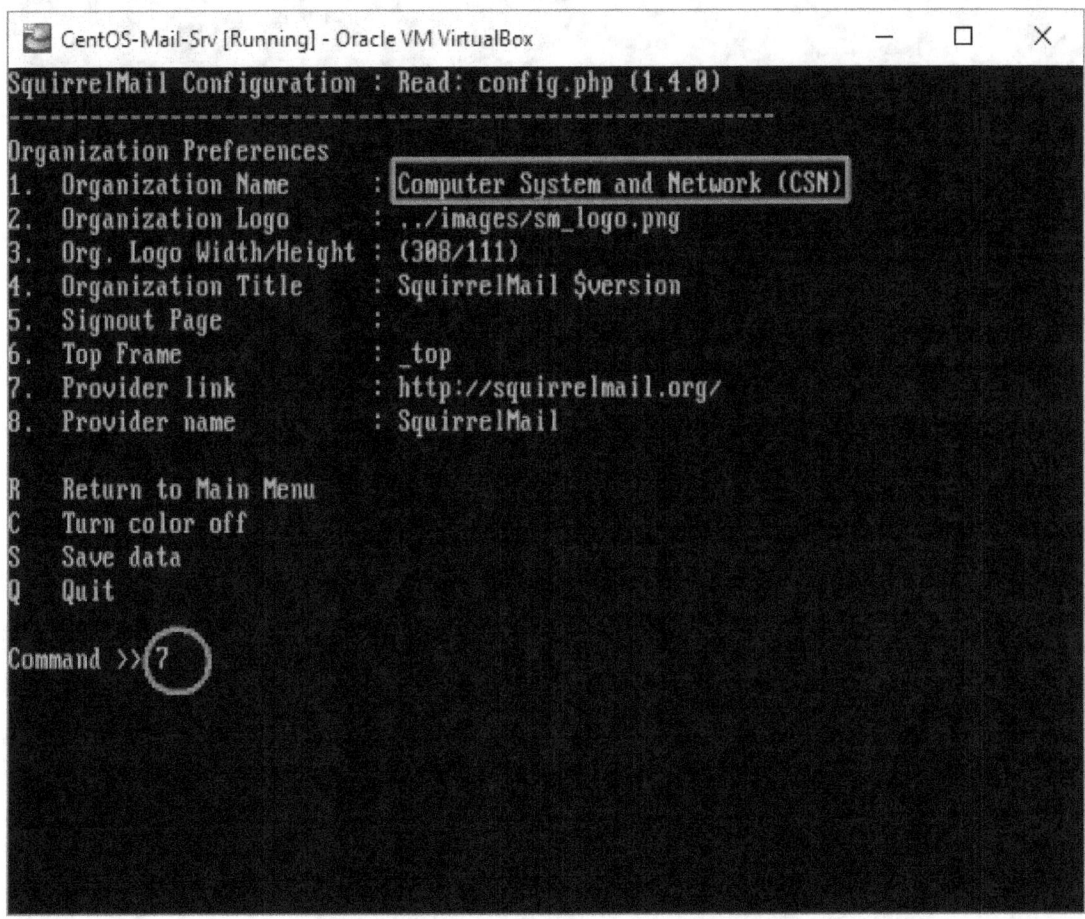

Figure 13.13: To change the provider link

Then it displays a prompt to enter the link which is related to our organization other than the SquirrelMail's link. In the following, http://www.csn.local is being entered. To proceed, press the [Enter] key.

Figure 13.14: Changing the provider link

The changes we have made so far is recorded but we still need to change the name of the provider to Computer System and Network (CSN) from SquirrelMail. For that, the choice number 8 has to be entered and press the [Enter] key.

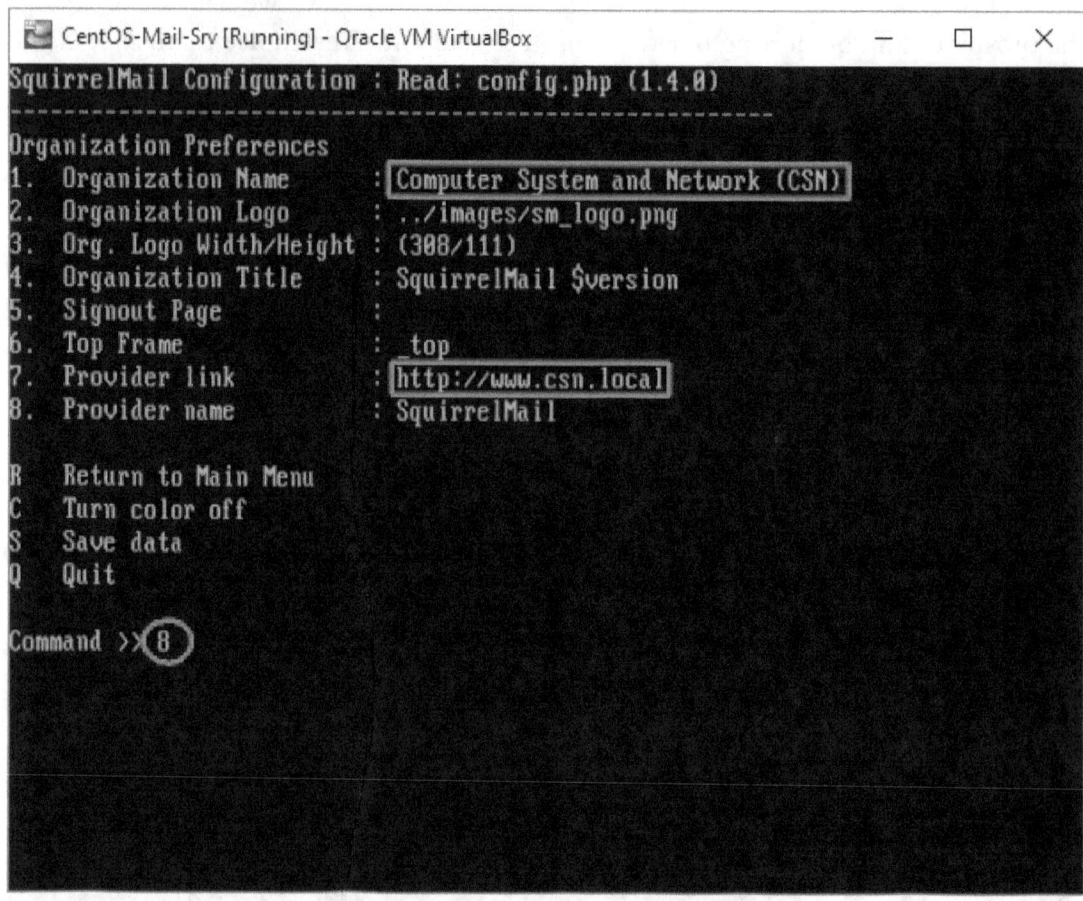

Figure 13.15: To change the provider name

The default provider name is set to SquirrelMail and to change, in the prompt enter Computer System and Network (CSN) and press [Enter] key.

Figure 13.16: Changing provider name

We have made changes in multiple options and to save those changes type "S" and press [Enter] key as indicated below:

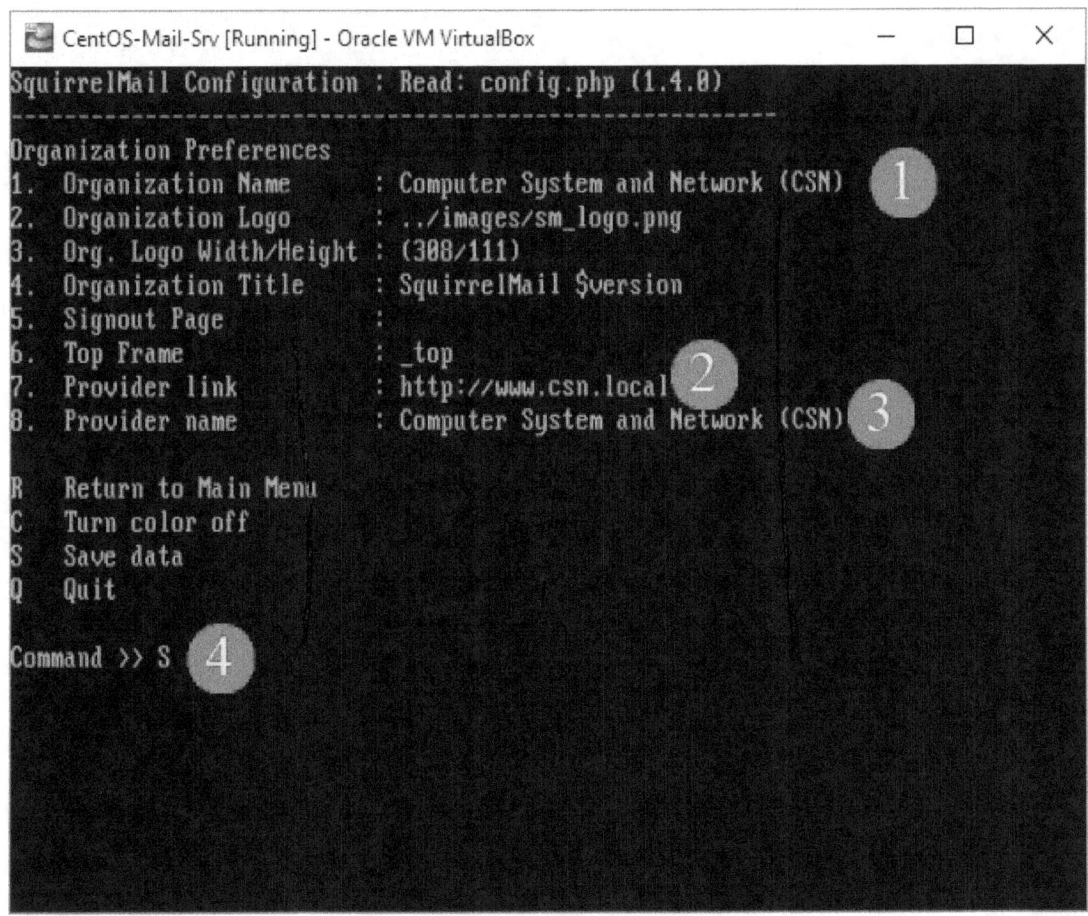

Figure 13.17: Saving the changes

Once the changes are saved, it would prompt you to press [Enter] key to continue. To go to the main menu, type "R" in the prompt and press [Enter] key.

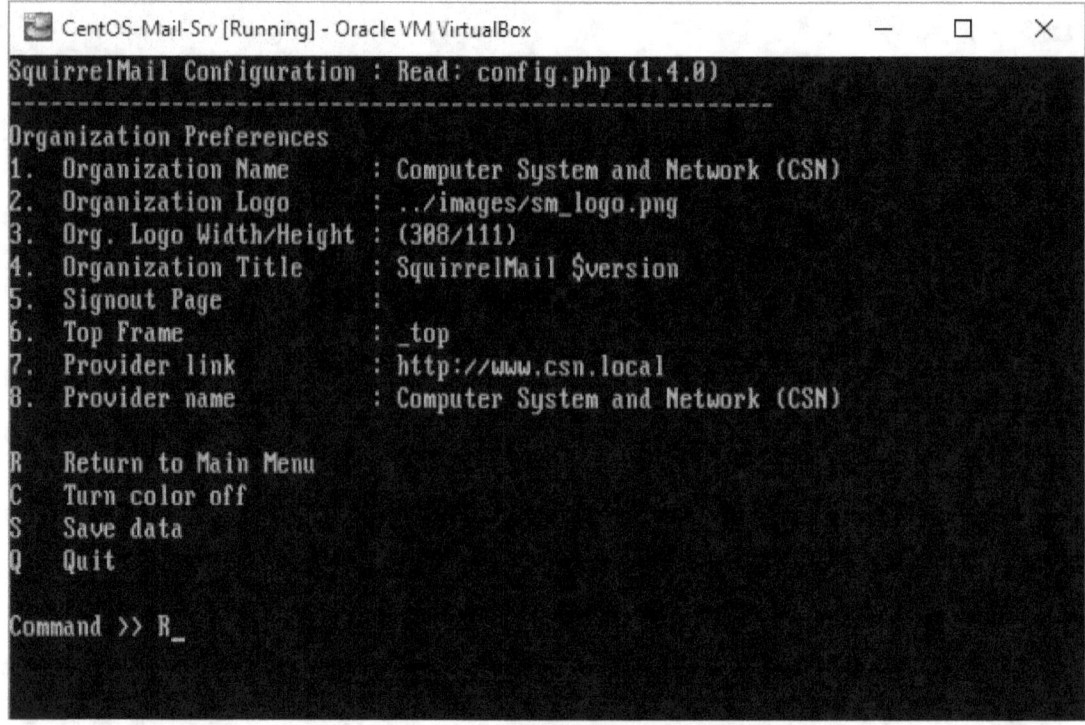

Figure 13.18: Returning to the main menu

Build a Virtual Network and Practice

We modified some of the organizational details and now we will try to change the server settings. For this, we have to enter the choice number 2 and continue.

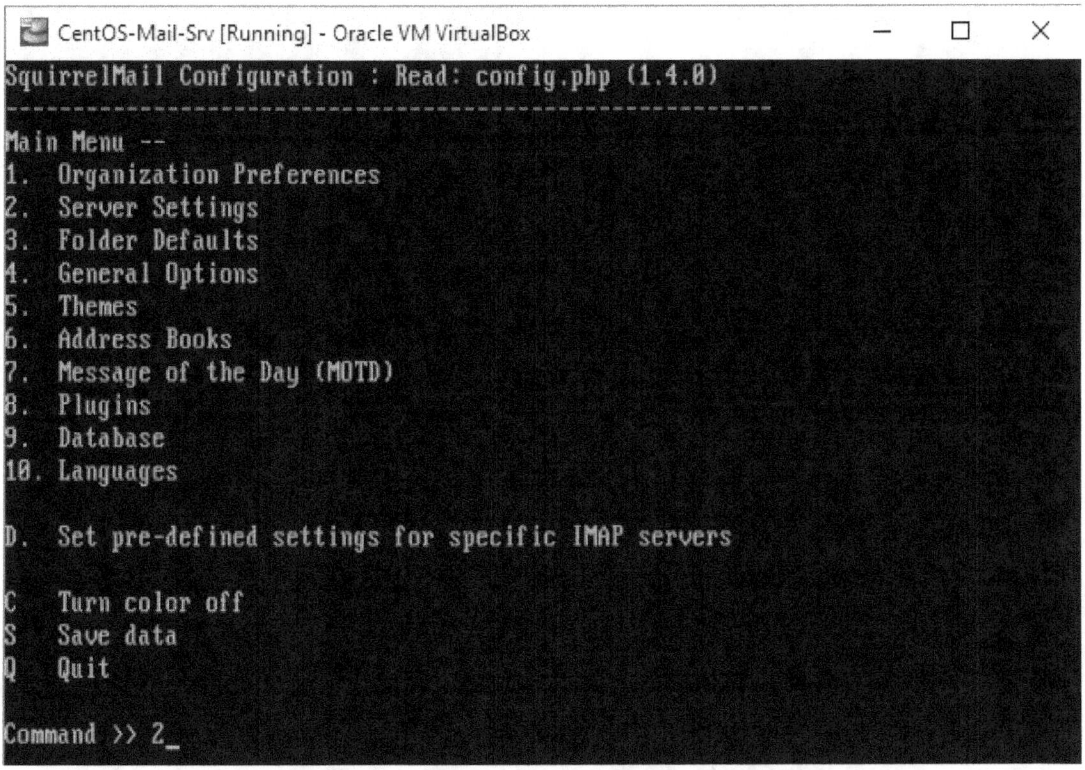

```
CentOS-Mail-Srv [Running] - Oracle VM VirtualBox
SquirrelMail Configuration : Read: config.php (1.4.0)
---------------------------------------------------------
Main Menu --
1.  Organization Preferences
2.  Server Settings
3.  Folder Defaults
4.  General Options
5.  Themes
6.  Address Books
7.  Message of the Day (MOTD)
8.  Plugins
9.  Database
10. Languages

D.  Set pre-defined settings for specific IMAP servers

C   Turn color off
S   Save data
Q   Quit

Command >> 2_
```

Figure 13.19: Opting to change server settings

Here we will change the domain to what we have, csn.local, which means at the end of each email address, csn.local would appear as the suffix as in tashi@csn.local. For that we have to choose option number 1 and press [Enter].

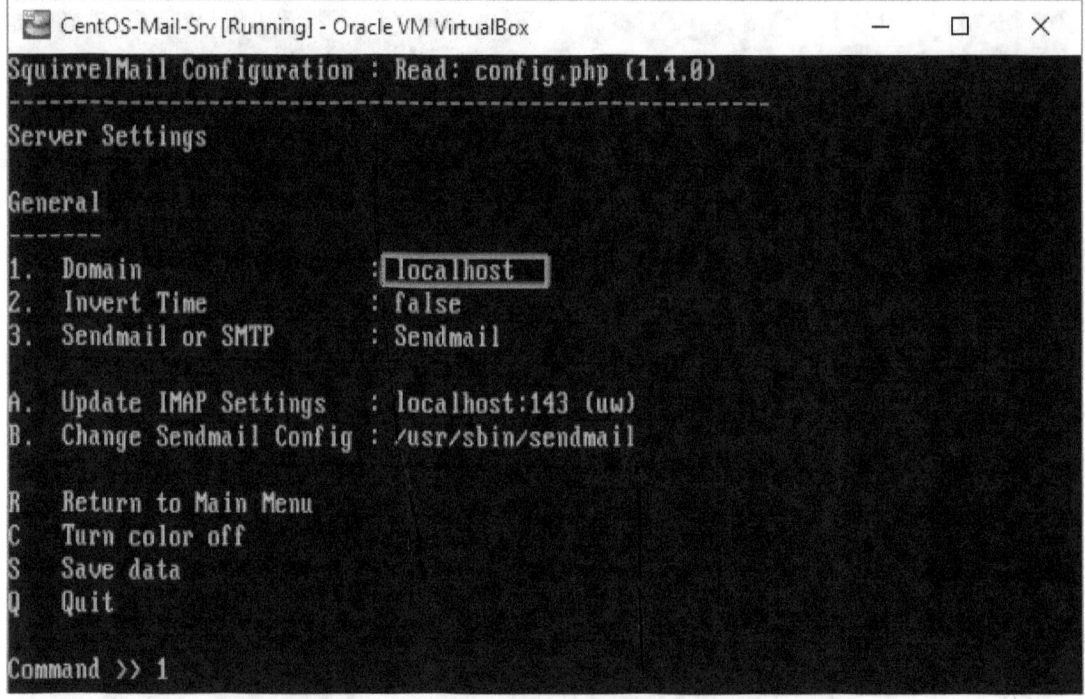

Figure 13.20: To change the domain portion

In the prompt, enter the domain which we have decided to use, csn.local and press [Enter] to proceed.

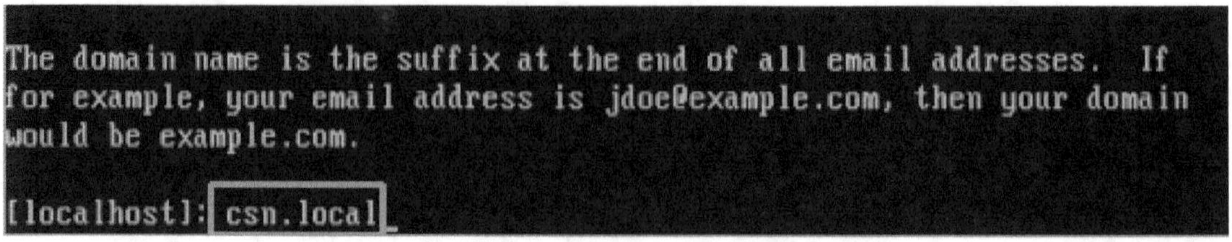

Figure 13.21: Changing the domain

In the next, we can change the option of sending the mail from the default Sendmail to SMTP by choosing option number 3.

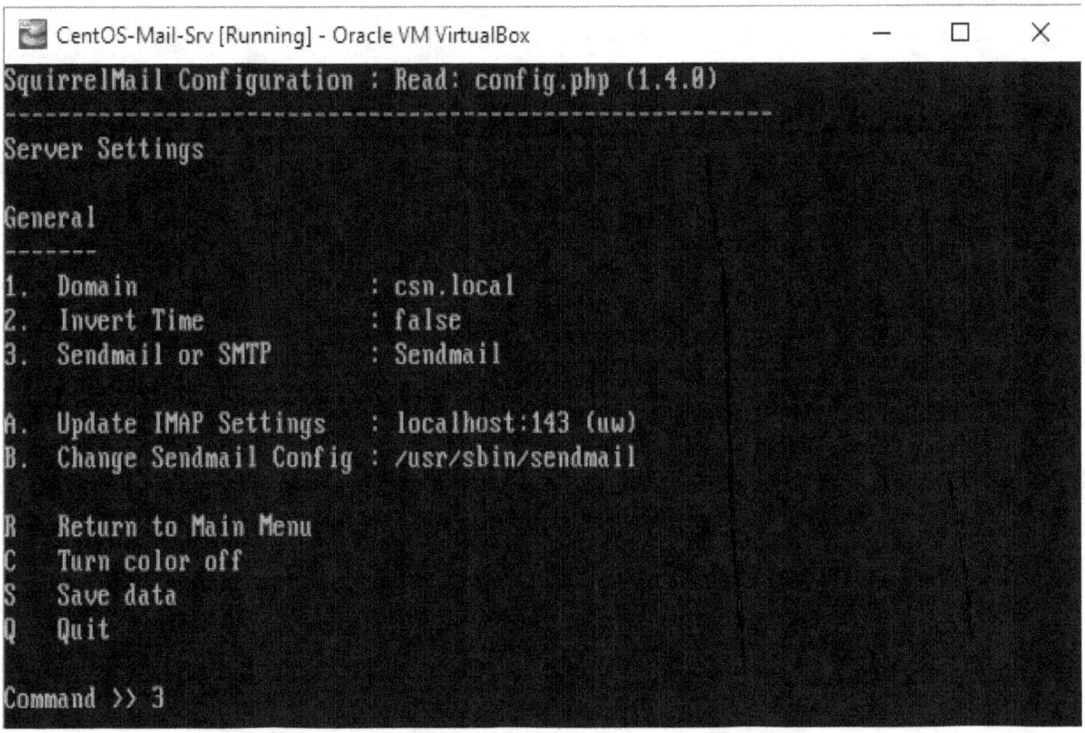

Figure 13.22: Opting to change the mail sending method

In the prompt, the choice number for the SMTP must be entered and press [Enter] to continue.

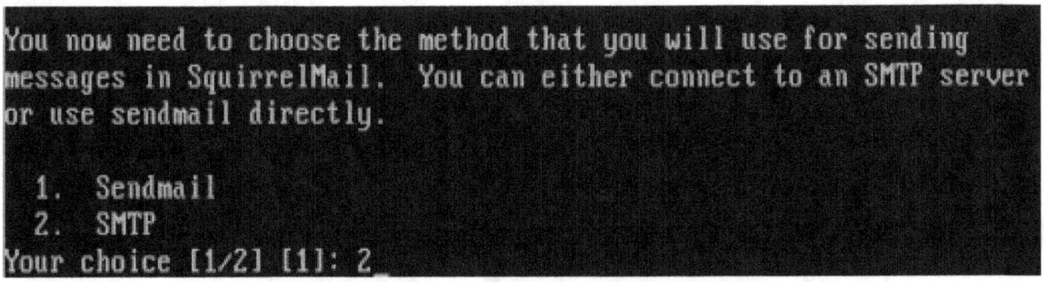

Figure 13.23: Choosing SMTP method

Then save the server setting which we have proposed by typing "S" in the prompt and press [Enter] key to continue.

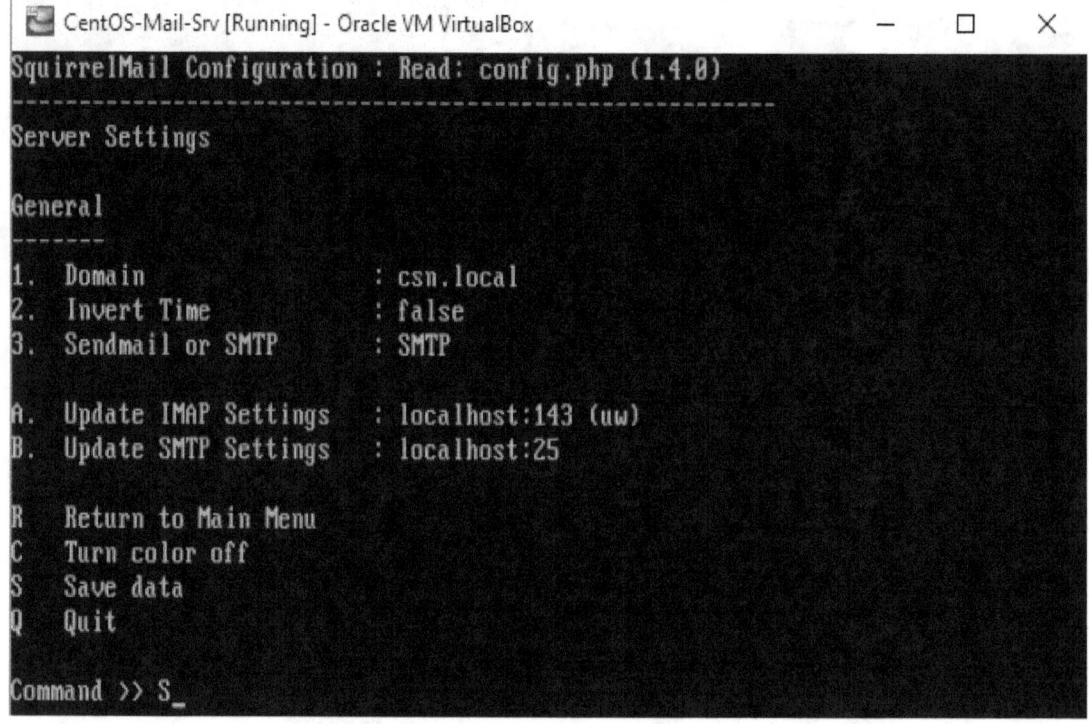

Figure 13.24: Saving the server settings

Then you would be prompted to press the [Enter] key to continue and then in the prompt type "Q" to quit.

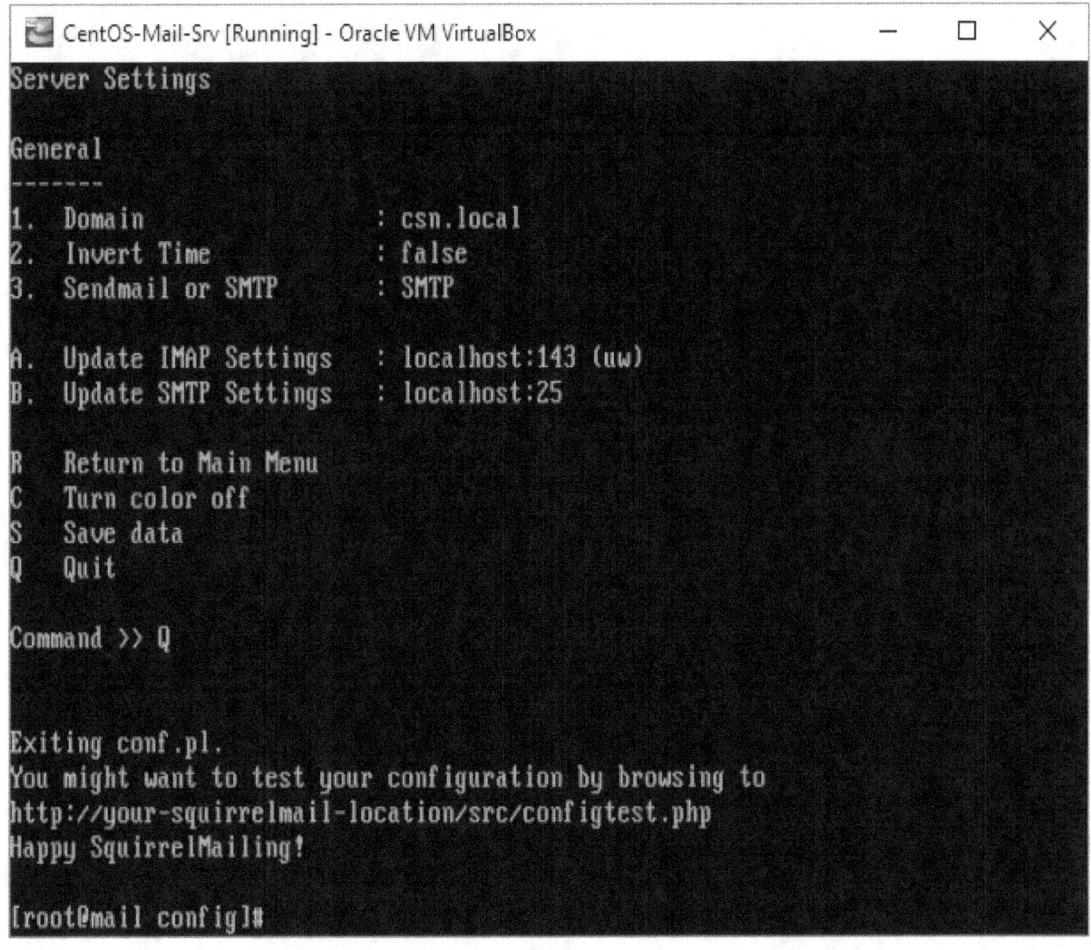

Figure 13.25: End of SquirrelMail configuration

Creation of vhost for squirrelmail

We will have to create the vhost for the SquirrelMail in the Apache's configuration file /etc/httpd/conf/httpd.conf.

    [root@mail ~]# vim /etc/httpd/conf/httpd.conf

Add the following lines at the end of the httpd.conf file:

```
Alias /webmail /usr/share/squirrelmail
<Directory /usr/share/squirrelmail>
Options Indexes FollowSymLinks
RewriteEngine On
AllowOverride All
DirectoryIndex index.php
Order allow,deny
Allow from all
</Directory>
```

Start and Enable Apache

Start and enable the Apache service by using the following commands:

    [root@mail ~]# systemctl start httpd
    [root@mail ~]# systemctl enable httpd

Creating Mail User Accounts

In order to use the mail service, we have to create the mail user accounts on the mail server itself. In this case we are creating two users namely "tashi" and "wangchuk" with their respective passwords.

    [root@mail ~]# useradd tashi
    [root@mail ~]# passwd tashi
    [root@mail ~]# useradd wangchuk
    [root@mail ~]# passwd wangchuk

Accessing the Webmail

For testing purpose, we will try to access it from the Windows 7 placed in the GNS3 network. In the browser's URL field type http://172.168.30.5/webmail after launching any browser installed on Windows 7. Since we have not set up the DNS server, we have to use the Mail Server's IP address at this time. The following screen should appear and then enter the username and password of the user which we have created in the previous step.

Figure 13.26: Logging into the SquirrelMail

The figure shown below is the view of user tashi's mail inbox. Initially there will be no mail and if users send email to user tashi, then it will be stored in the INBOX.

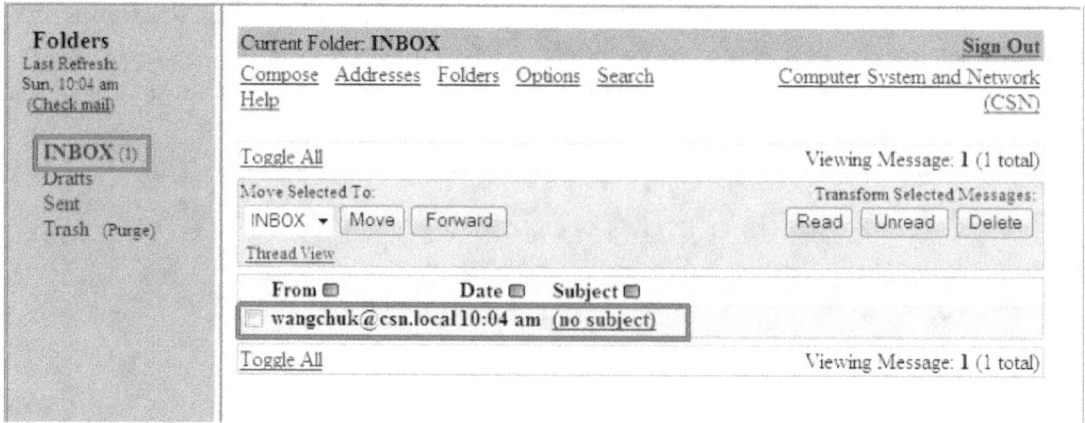

Figure 13.27: Viewing e-mails

Now, the users can login and use the email server setup for sending and receiving the mails using the SquirrelMail, Postfix and the Dovecot.

Further Reading

Email with Postfix, Dovecot and MariaDB on CentOS 7. (2015, July 16). Retrieved from https://www.linode.com/docs/email/postfix/email-with-postfix-dovecot-and-mariadb-on-centos-7/

How to Add Antivirus and Spam Protection to Postfix Mail Server with ClamAV and SpamAssassin – Part 3. (n.d.). Retrieved from https://www.tecmint.com/integrate-clamav-and-spamassassin-to-protect-postfix-mails-from-viruses/

How to Configure Postfix and Dovecot with Virtual Domain Users in Linux – Part 2. (n.d.). Retrieved from https://www.tecmint.com/configure-postfix-and-dovecot-with-virtual-domain-users-in-linux/

How to Install and Configure RoundCube Webmail Client with Virtual Users in Postfix – Part 4. (n.d.). Retrieved from https://www.tecmint.com/install-and-configure-roundcube-webmail-for-postfix-mail-server/

How to set up a mail server with PostfixAdmin on CentOS 7. (2018, January 29). Retrieved from https://www.rosehosting.com/blog/how-to-set-up-a-mail-server-with-postfixadmin-on-centos-7/

How to Setup an Email Server on CentOS 7. (n.d.). Retrieved from https://hostpresto.com/community/tutorials/how-to-setup-an-email-server-on-centos7/

How to Setup Postfix Mail Server and Dovecot with Database (MariaDB) Securely – Part 1. (n.d.). Retrieved from https://www.tecmint.com/setup-postfix-mail-server-and-dovecot-with-mariadb-in-centos/

How to Use Sagator, an Antivirus/Antispam Gateway, to Protect Your Mail Server. (n.d.). Retrieved from https://www.tecmint.com/install-sagator-antivirus-antispam-protection-postfix-mail-server/

Setup A Local Mail Server in CentOS 7. (2015, July 24). Retrieved from https://www.unixmen.com/setup-a-local-mail-server-in-centos-7/

Chapter 14
Setting Up a Web Server

A web server delivers the content over the Hypertext Transfer Protocol (HTTP). When you visit a website using your browser from your system, you are communicating with the web server, requesting for web pages, which the server has hosted. Many governmental, non-profit, educational or business organizations, make use of the Web for gathering and disseminating information in an efficient and inexpensive way.

If there is a need, you can as well develop website and host using the Apache HTTP Web Server software made available from the Apache project with the support of other technologies. Apache HTTP Web Server is a free software, distributed by the Apache Software Foundation, which promotes various free and open source web technologies. In this chapter, you will learn to install, configure and test the functionality of the configured Apache HTTP Web server in the Virtual Network with the help of GNS3 and VirtualBox.

Network Scenario

To implement the Apache HTTP Web Server, we will use the Virtual Network Lab which we have created and used in the earlier chapters. In the same virtual network Lab, we have implemented the DHCP Server, FTP Server and Mail Server; here onwards, without removing those configurations and setup, we will implement the Web Server in our Virtual Network Lab. The details required for the FTP server is indicated in the figure 14.1.

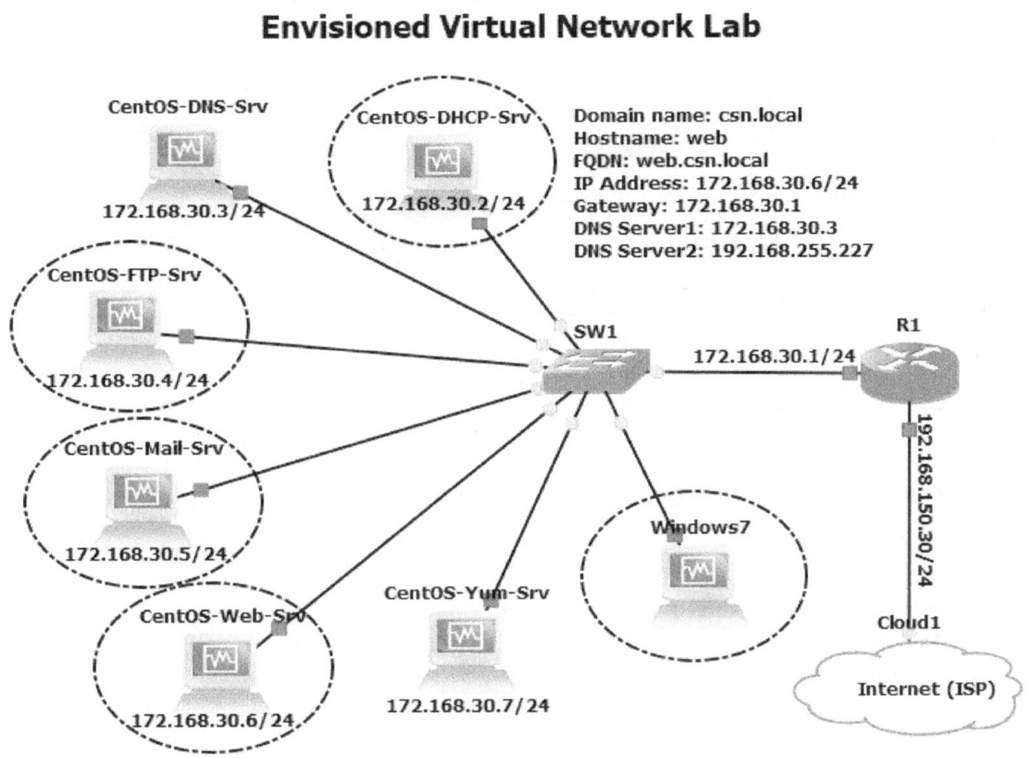

Build a Virtual Network and Practice

Envisioned Virtual Network Lab

Figure 14.1: Base network with Web Server details

Configuring the Web Server Details

Taking into consideration the details of the Web Server shown in figure 14.1, the Web server details have to be configured. In order to configure, we have to start the Web Server from the GNS3 workspace by right-clicking and choosing to start.

> *It is advised not to either start or shutdown the Web Server directly from the VirtualBox interface while working on the GNS3 as this action would lead to issues. So, start or shutdown from the GNS3 Interface only. While trying to start any of the severs not just limited to CentOS-Web-Srv (Web Server) from the GNS3, sometimes you may get error messages and you won't be able to start. In such cases, start the server directly from the VirtualBox interface and once the starting is complete, login and give a proper shutdown. This happens when the server was improperly shutdown previously. After starting and shutting down from the VirtualBox, then go to the GNS3 workspace and start from there.*

When you try to start the server from the GNS3, you might be issued with a security alert, choose the options and allow access as shown in the figure 14.2.

Figure 14.2: Windows Security Alert

Build a Virtual Network and Practice

If the starting of the Web server is successful, the link status of the devices would change to green circular bullets and also the screen of the CentOS-Web-Srv (Web Server) would be available for login. Then you can login to the system as the root and then continue to configure the details.

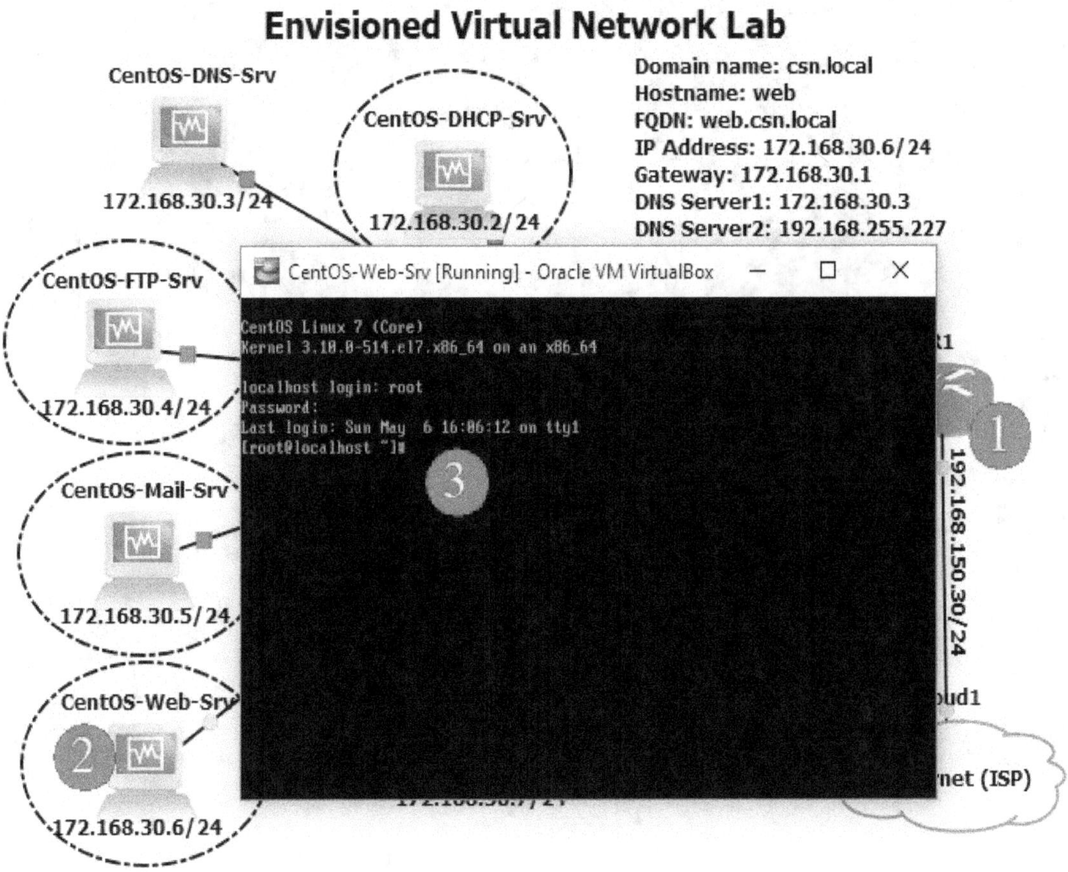

Figure 14.3: Virtual Network Lab with started Web Server and router

> *As we are working in a virtual network, running multiples virtual machines would drastically slow down the system. Since the configuration of the DHCP server is completed, you can shut it down from the GNS3 workspace to release system resources for faster processing. At this point, there is no need for DHCP to be running.*

After successfully logging in to the server, configure the hostname by using the nmtui utility as shown in the figure below:

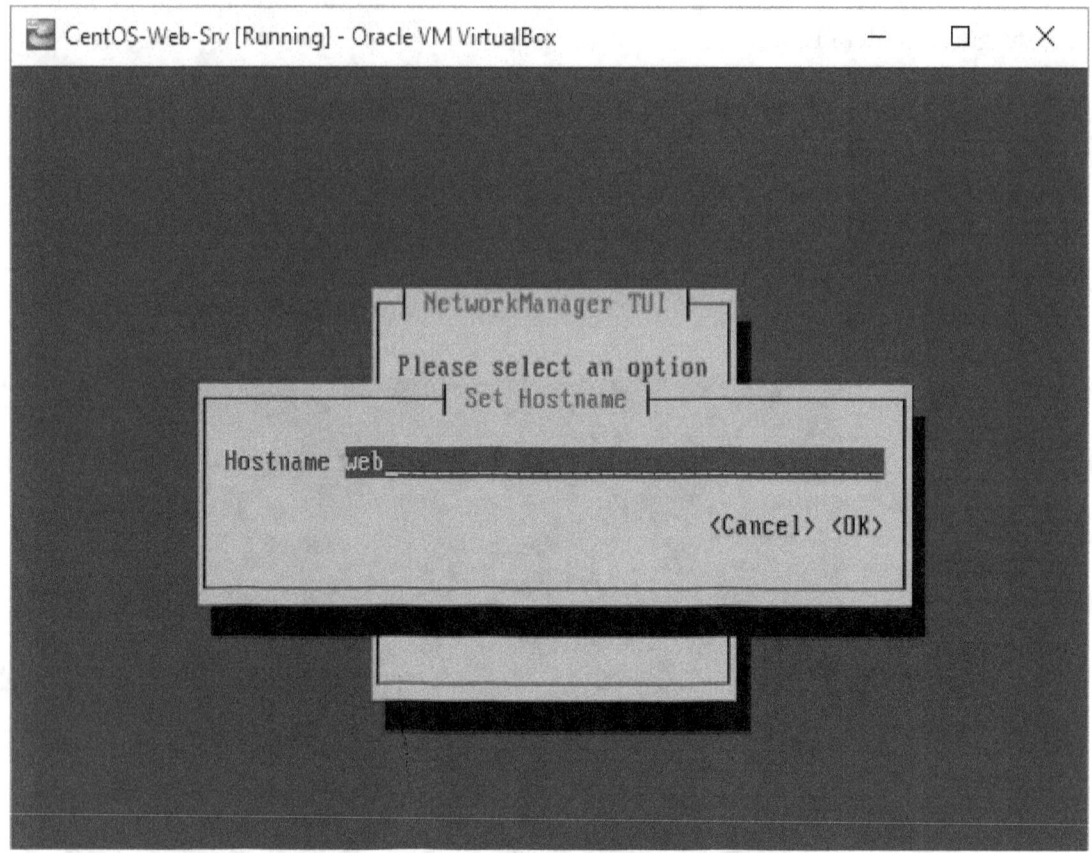

Figure 14.4: Setting the hostname

Build a Virtual Network and Practice

In the next, configure the IP address details using the nmtui as indicated in the figure 14.5 and figure 14.6.

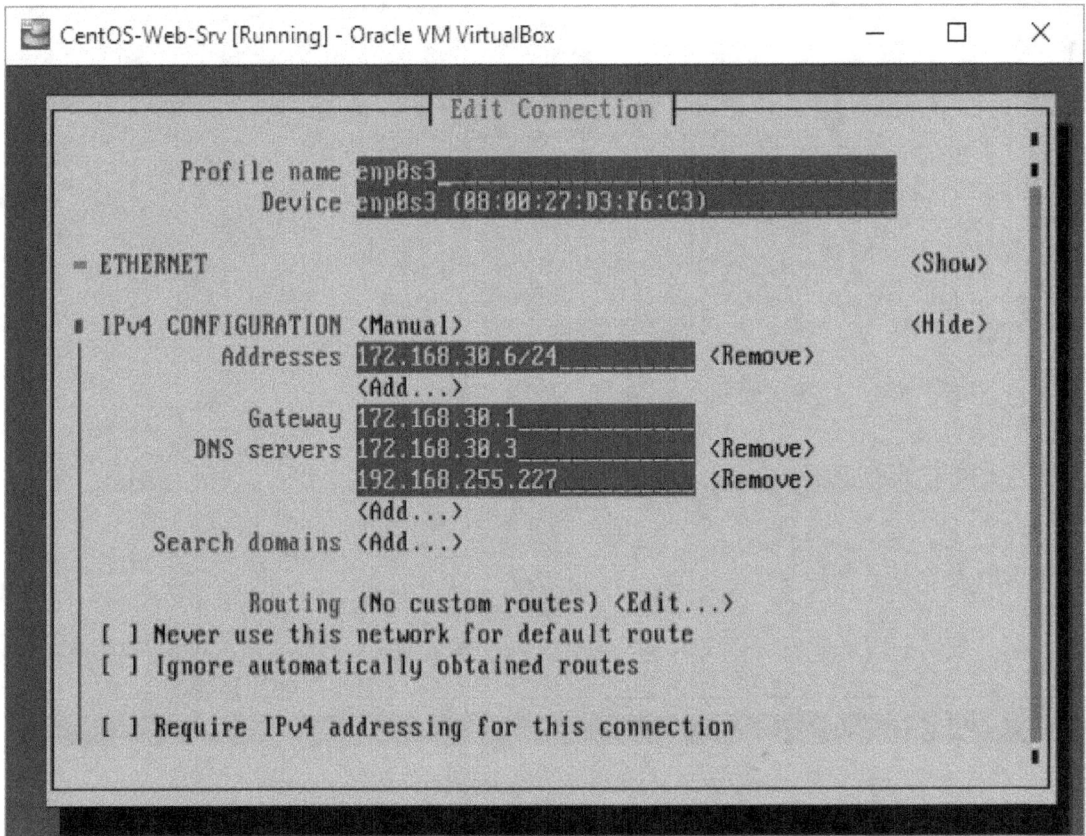

Figure 14.5: Ethernet IPv4 Setting for Web Server

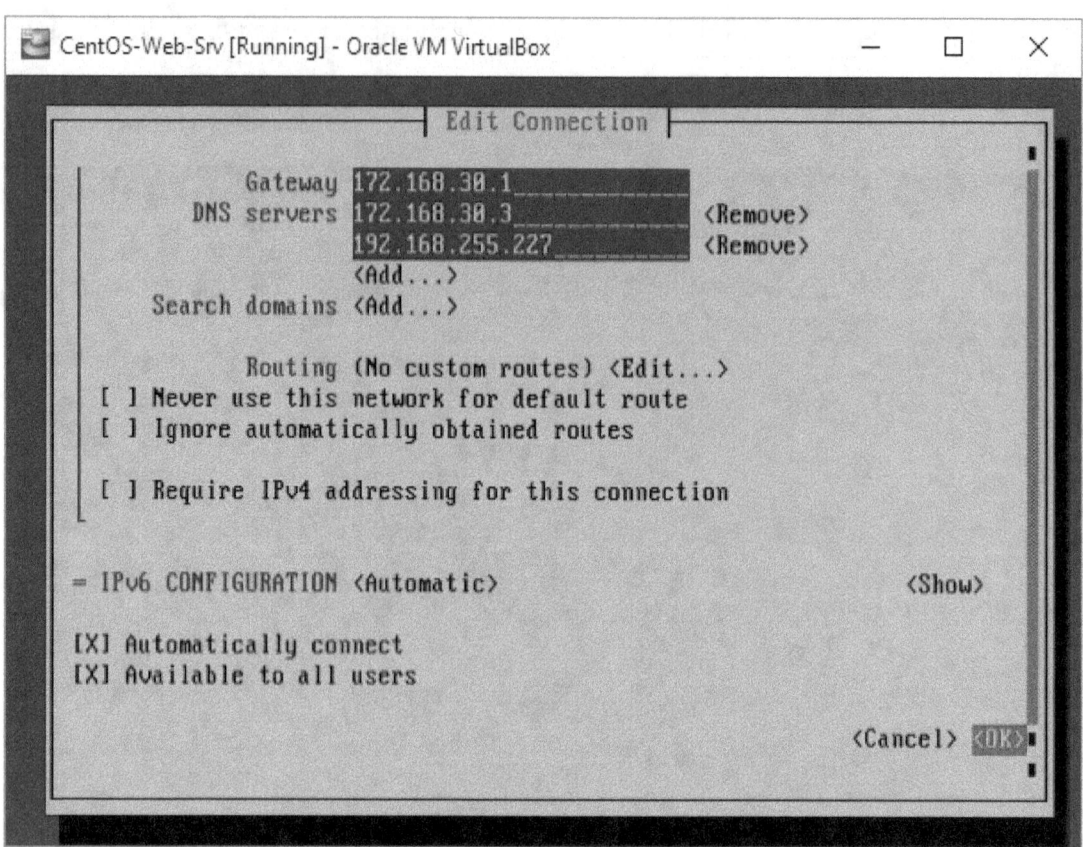

Figure 14.6: Allowing to automatically connect

Once the required manual settings are completed, you must be able to ping the router's IP address (172.168.30.1).

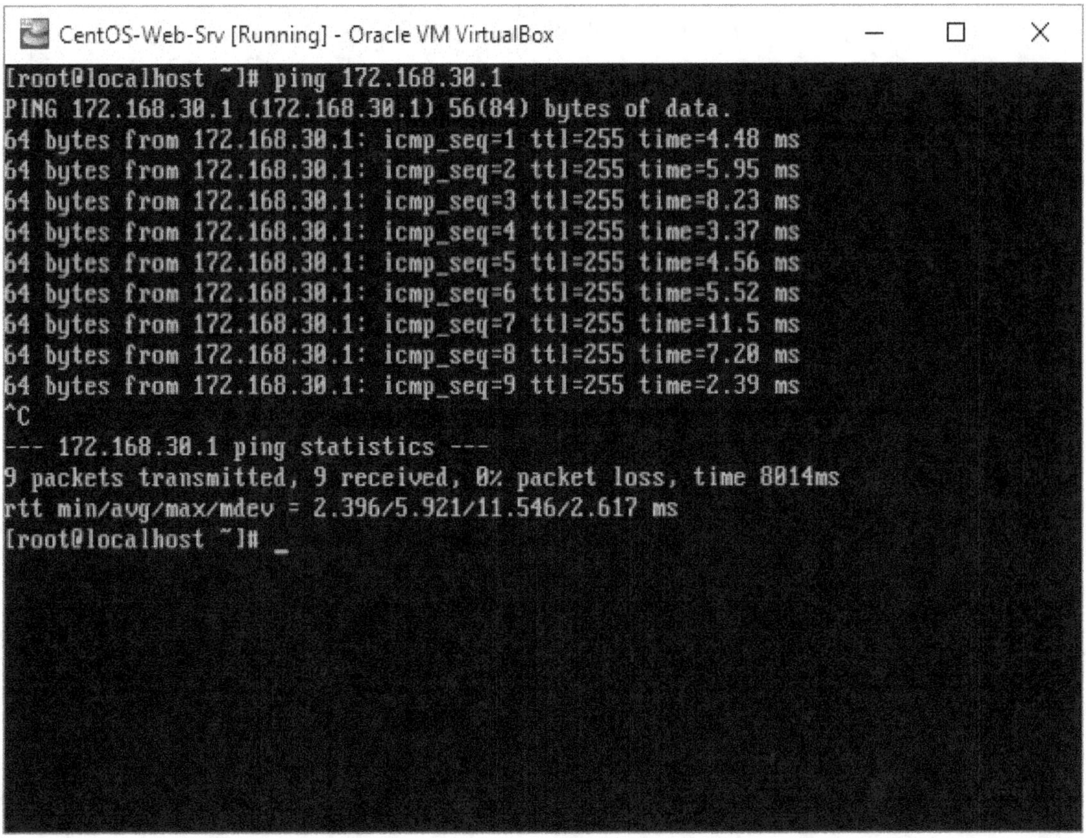
CentOS-Web-Srv [Running] - Oracle VM VirtualBox
[root@localhost ~]# ping 172.168.30.1
PING 172.168.30.1 (172.168.30.1) 56(84) bytes of data.
64 bytes from 172.168.30.1: icmp_seq=1 ttl=255 time=4.48 ms
64 bytes from 172.168.30.1: icmp_seq=2 ttl=255 time=5.95 ms
64 bytes from 172.168.30.1: icmp_seq=3 ttl=255 time=8.23 ms
64 bytes from 172.168.30.1: icmp_seq=4 ttl=255 time=3.37 ms
64 bytes from 172.168.30.1: icmp_seq=5 ttl=255 time=4.56 ms
64 bytes from 172.168.30.1: icmp_seq=6 ttl=255 time=5.52 ms
64 bytes from 172.168.30.1: icmp_seq=7 ttl=255 time=11.5 ms
64 bytes from 172.168.30.1: icmp_seq=8 ttl=255 time=7.20 ms
64 bytes from 172.168.30.1: icmp_seq=9 ttl=255 time=2.39 ms
^C
--- 172.168.30.1 ping statistics ---
9 packets transmitted, 9 received, 0% packet loss, time 8014ms
rtt min/avg/max/mdev = 2.396/5.921/11.546/2.617 ms
[root@localhost ~]# _

Figure 14.7: Verifying the connection

Before starting to install the packages, it is important to verify whether our router can connect to the internet or not by pinging the 8.8.8.8 after opening the console.

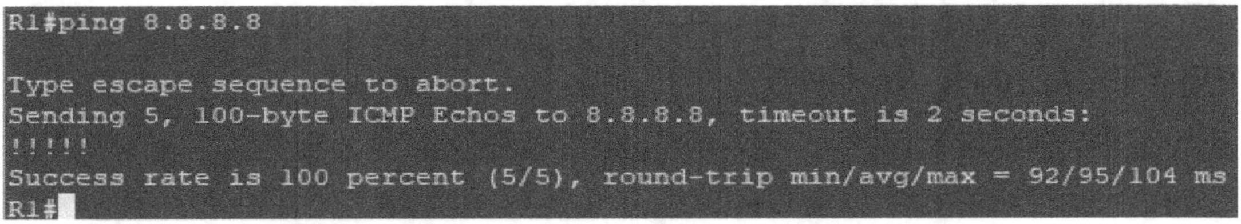
R1#ping 8.8.8.8
Type escape sequence to abort.
Sending 5, 100-byte ICMP Echos to 8.8.8.8, timeout is 2 seconds:
!!!!!
Success rate is 100 percent (5/5), round-trip min/avg/max = 92/95/104 ms
R1#

Figure 14.8: Verifying the connection to the Internet

If the pinging is not successful, try to check the configuration on the router and if the configurations are correctly done, try to reload or restart the router. Since we are using the dynamic IP address on the router's first interface f0/0, the lease might have expired.

Install Apache Web Server Package

You can install the Apache HTTP Web Server package provided from official repositories or the local yum repositories using the following command:

yum install -y httpd

Configuring the Web Server

The configuration file httpd.conf for the webserver is located in the /etc/httpd/conf/ directory. Before making any changes to the configuration file it is always safe to keep a backup of the original configuration file. To keep a backup of the httpd.conf file, run the following command in the terminal with the root privilege:

cp /etc/httpd/conf/httpd.conf /etc/httpd/conf/httpd.conf.bak

The open the /etc/httpd/conf/httpd.conf file using the vi editor by using the following command:

vi /etc/httpd/conf/httpd.conf

After opening the configuration file, make changes accordingly as indicated in the following:

In the line number 86 change the administrator's email address as indicated.

ServerAdmin root@csn.local

You can uncomment the line number 95 and change the server name according to the domain we have chosen.

ServerName www.csn.local:80

In the line number 119, mention the absolute path to the directory from where the web server will serve the documents.

DocumentRoot "/var/www/html/web"

In line 164, add file name that can access only with directory's name.

DirectoryIndex index.html index.cgi index.php

Add the following to the end to hide the server information from being added to the http header (server's response header).

ServerTokens Prod

Keep alive is a method to allow the same TCP connection for HTTP conversation instead of opening a new one with each new request.

KeepAlive On

After changing the configuration settings as indicated, we have to create a directory (web) to contain our web files. Run the following command to create a folder with the name "web":

mkdir /var/www/html/web

Then inside the web folder create a file with the name "index.html" whose extension is .html.

touch /var/www/html/web/index.html

Open the index.html file and add the following lines to the index.html file. This index.html file is going to be considered as our sample webpage.

```html
# vim /var/www/html/web/index.html
<html>
    <head>
            <title>
            Sample Web Page
            </title>
    </head>
<body>
    <h1>Welcome to CSN's Sample Page</h1>
            <br>
            Username: <input type= "text">
            <br>
            Password: <input type= "password">
            <br>
            <input type= "button" value= "Submit">
</body>
</html>
```

After adding the above lines, save and quit the file.

> *We are creating only a single file just as an example. The real website designed would involve a huge number of pages and the use of the database as well.*

Start and Enable Apache

In order to have the effect of the configuration changes we have to start or restart the httpd service by using the following commands:

systemctl start httpd
systemctl enable httpd

Installing MariaDB

CentOS 7.0 switched from MySQL to MariaDB for its default database management system. To install MariaDB database use the following command:

> # yum install -y mariadb mariadb-server

Start and Enable MariaDB

Start and enable the MariaDB by using the following commands:

> # systemctl start mariadb
> # systemctl enable mariadb

Securing MySQL/MariaDB server

The mysql_secure_installation script enables you to improve the security of your MySQL/MariaDB installation by setting a password for the root account, disabling root account from accessing the MySQL/MariaDB from outside the localhost, removing the anonymous user accounts and the test database which is accessible by all the users.

Once the MySQL / MariaDB installation is complete, you can type mysql_secure_installation command at the terminal to secure the database server.

> [root@web ~]# mysql_secure_installation

When the script is run, the following message would appear, prompting for the root user's password. Since, this is the first time, we have no password for the root user account. To login, just press [Enter] key.

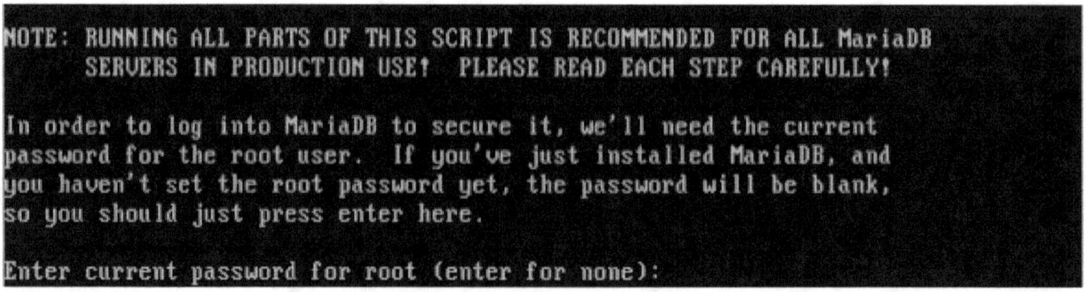

```
NOTE: RUNNING ALL PARTS OF THIS SCRIPT IS RECOMMENDED FOR ALL MariaDB
      SERVERS IN PRODUCTION USE!  PLEASE READ EACH STEP CAREFULLY!

In order to log into MariaDB to secure it, we'll need the current
password for the root user.  If you've just installed MariaDB, and
you haven't set the root password yet, the password will be blank,
so you should just press enter here.

Enter current password for root (enter for none):
```

Figure 14.9: Prompting for the root password

Next, it would ask whether to set the root user's password or not. So, to make it secure, we should set the password for the root user account. For this, type "Y" in the prompt and press [Enter] key.

```
OK, successfully used password, moving on...

Setting the root password ensures that nobody can log into the MariaDB
root user without the proper authorisation.

Set root password? [Y/n] Y_
```

Figure 14.10: Choosing to set the root password

After creating the password for the root account, it would ask whether to remove the anonymous users or not. Definitely we must say yes by typing "Y" in the prompt and pressing [Enter] key.

```
New password:
Re-enter new password:
Password updated successfully!
Reloading privilege tables..
 ... Success!


By default, a MariaDB installation has an anonymous user, allowing anyone
to log into MariaDB without having to have a user account created for
them.  This is intended only for testing, and to make the installation
go a bit smoother.  You should remove them before moving into a
production environment.

Remove anonymous users? [Y/n] Y_
```

Figure 14.11: Removing anonymous users

After removing the anonymous users, it will ask whether to allow remote login of the root user from other than the localhost. Type "Y" and continue to disallow.

```
 ... Success!

Normally, root should only be allowed to connect from 'localhost'.  This
ensures that someone cannot guess at the root password from the network.

Disallow root login remotely? [Y/n] Y_
```

Figure 14.12: Disabling remote login of the root account

Then to remove the test database, type "Y" in the prompt and press [Enter] to continue.

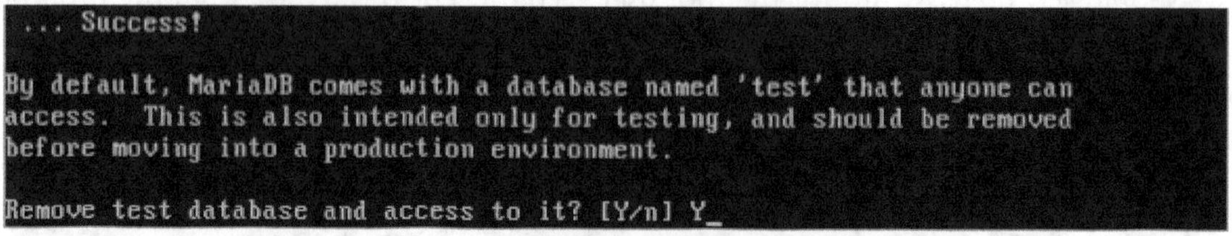

Figure 14.13: Removing test database and access to it

Finally, type "Y" to reload the privilege to take the changes into effect.

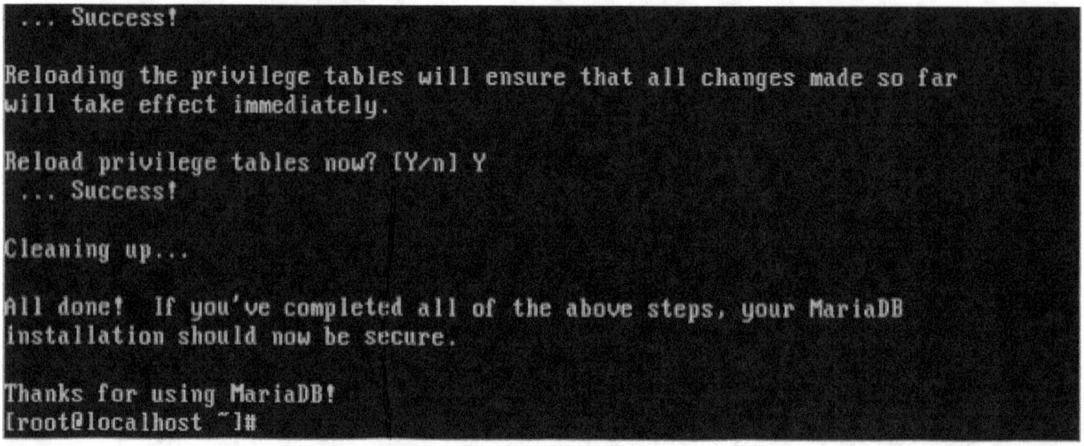

Figure 14.14: Secure installation complete

Creating Database for the Web Server

Since we are not hosting a full-fledged website, we are not going to use the database in our example. However, we will learn to create a database, database user and the password for the database user in case we have to create one in the future as indicated in the following:

> Database name: web
> Database username: webuser
> Database user's password: P@sSw0rD

After the secure installation is complete, login to MySQL/MariaDB by using the following command at the terminal:

> [root@web ~] # mysql -u root -p

Provide the root MySQL's root user's password which you have created during the secure installation process.

Now, create the database for Web Server, database user and the password for the database user as indicated in the following:

CREATE DATABASE web;
CREATE USER 'webuser'@'localhost' IDENTIFIED BY 'P@sSw0rD';
GRANT ALL PRIVILEGES ON web.* TO 'webuser'@'localhost';
exit

Install and Configure PHP

PHP is responsible for processing code to display dynamic content for the web. It can run scripts, connect to our MySQL/MariaDB databases to get information, and hand the processed content over to the web server to display. Use the following command to install PHP and other dependent packages:

[root@web ~] # yum install php php-mysql php-dba php-devel php-gd php-mbstring

After installation of PHP and its packages, you can restart Apache HTTP web server.

[root@localhost ~] # systemctl restart httpd.service

Firewall Adjustment

In the firewall, we have to allow the traffic though to enable the http service run properly.

firewall-cmd --permanent --zone=public --add-service=http
firewall-cmd --reload

Testing the Web Server

On the Linux (L) platform, we have completed installing Apache (A), MySQL/MariaDB(M) and PHP (P), collectively known as the LAMP stack. In addition, we have also configured the firewall to allow the httpd traffic through. We have a running Web Server which is ready to serve the sample page we have created if there are requests coming in. To test the functionality of the configured Apache HTTP Web Server, we will try to access the Web Server from Windows 7 via the web browser.

You can start the Windows 7 from the GNS3 workspace and then login to the Windows 7 client system using the available username and password if any. Then from the internet browser, try to access the web server by typing http://172.168.30.6 in the URL field.

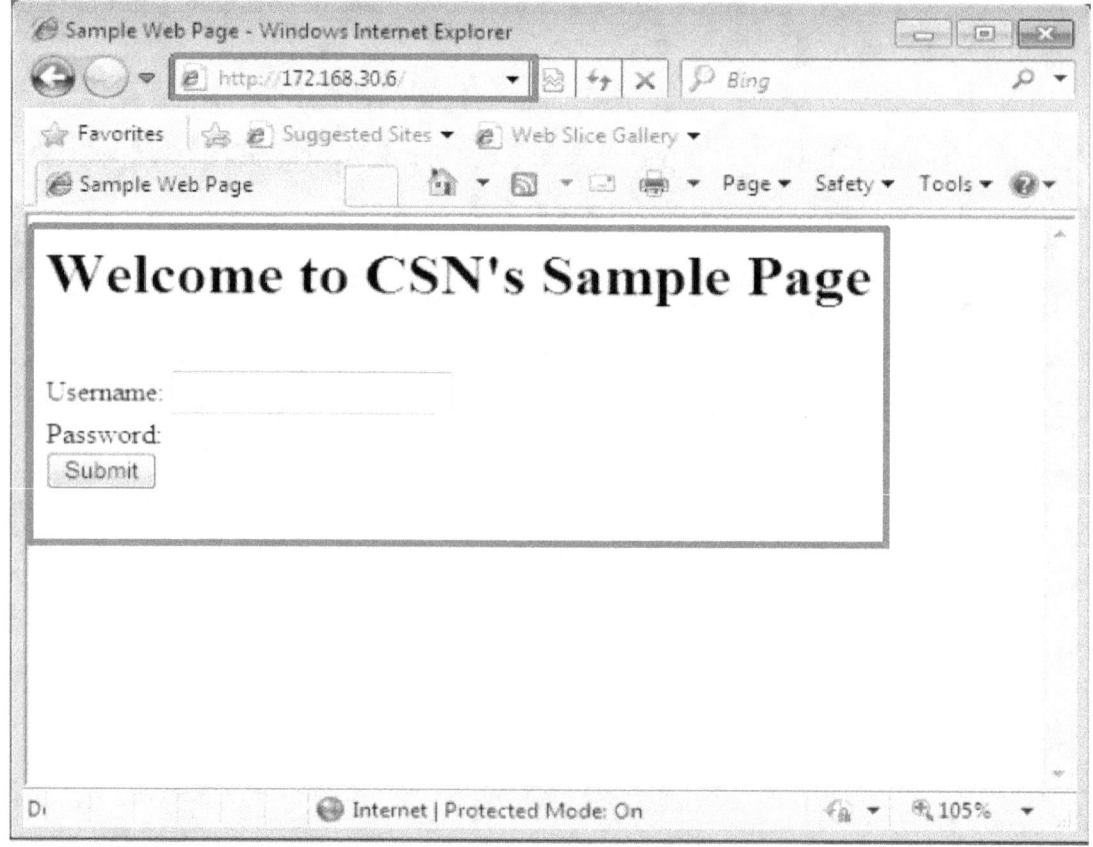

Figure 14.15: Accessing the sample web page

> In case, the web page is not accessible, try disabling the SELinux although it is not recommended. We will learn to configure the SELinux in the later chapter. If the page is not accessible even after the SELinux is disabled, then try to troubleshoot other configurations.

Further Reading

How to Configure Apache HTTP Web server on RHEL7 / CentOS7. (2016, January 01). Retrieved from http://www.learnitguide.net/2016/03/how-to-configure-apache-http-web-server.html

A., Pawar. (2018, February 18). How to Install Linux, Apache, MySQL, PHP (LAMP) stack On CentOS 7. Retrieved from http://devopstechie.com/how-to-install-linux-apache-mysql-php-lamp-stack-on-centos-7/

Mitchell, B. (n.d.). An Overview of the Apache Web Server. Retrieved from https://www.lifewire.com/definition-of-apache-816509

Setting up an Apache Web Server (httpd) on CentOS/RHEL 7. (n.d.). Retrieved from https://codingbee.net/tutorials/open-source-software/apache-web-server/setting-up-an-apache-web-server-httpd-on-centos

SSL Configuration to enable HTTPS Apache Web Server on Linux. (2016, January 01). Retrieved from http://www.learnitguide.net/2016/03/ssl-configuration-to-enable-https.html

Chapter 15
Setting Up a DNS Server

The Domain Name System (DNS) is a system, which allows the resolution of the human-friendly names to unique IP addresses. A DNS server has a database of IP addresses and their associated hostnames which translates those human-friendly hostnames to IP addresses whenever requested. You can very well use the IP addresses of the hosts, which you wanted to access but remembering the IP addresses for several hosts would be troublesome.

Berkeley Internet Name Domain (BIND) is an open source software used as DNS servers across the internet, which provides the ability to perform name to IP conversion there by resolving the DNS queries for the users. The DNS uses UDP protocol and the port used is 53.

In this Chapter, we will setup and implement a DNS server using the BIND name server software on the CentOS 7 platform to resolve the hostnames to IP address.

Network Scenario

To implement the DNS Server using BIND, just like the earlier times, we will use the Virtual Network Lab which we have created and used in the earlier chapters. In the same virtual network Lab, we have implemented the DHCP server, FTP Server, Mail Server and Web Server; here onwards, without removing those configurations and setup, we will implement the DNS server in our Virtual Network Lab. The details required for the DNS server is indicated in the figure 15.1.

Build a Virtual Network and Practice

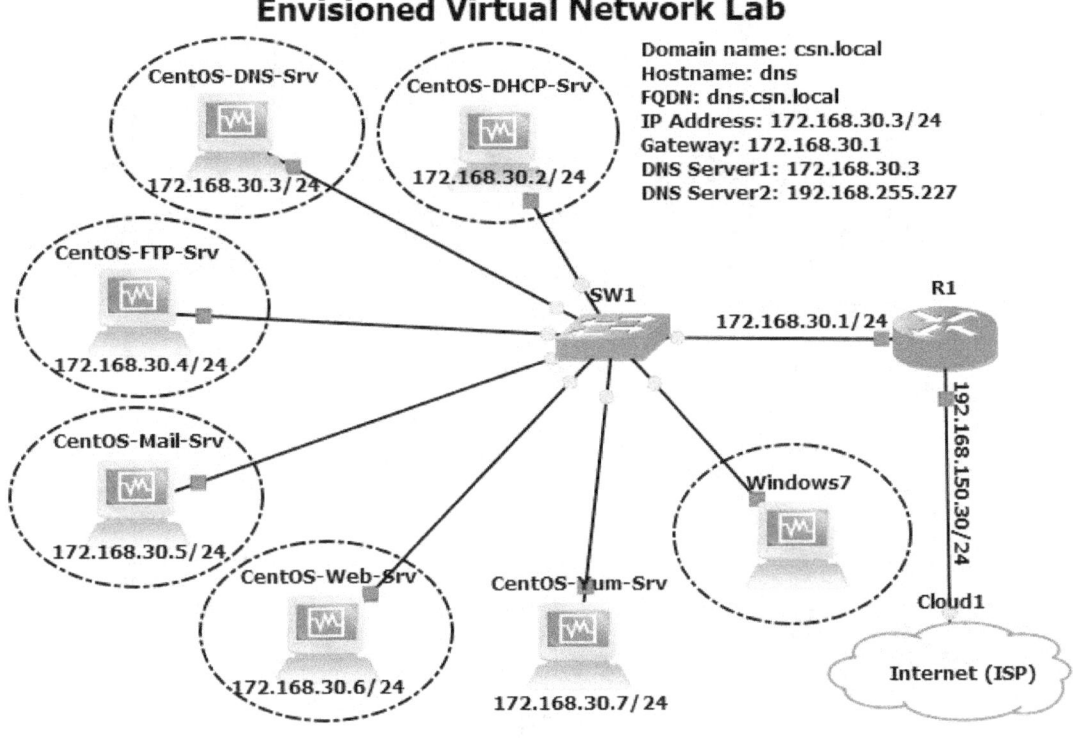

Figure 15.1: Base network with DNS Server details

Configuring the DNS Server Details

Taking into consideration the details of the DNS Server shown in the figure 15.1, the DNS server details have to be configured. In order to configure, we have to start the DNS Server from the GNS3 workspace by right-clicking and choosing to start.

> *It is advised not to either start or shutdown the DNS Server directly from the VirtualBox Interface while working on the GNS3 as this action would lead to issues. So, start or shutdown from the GNS3 Interface only. While trying to start any of the severs not just limited to CentOS-DNS-Srv (DNS Server) from the GNS3, sometimes you may get error messages and you won't be able to start. In such cases, start the server directly from the VirtualBox interface and once the starting is complete, login and give a proper shutdown. This happens when the server was improperly shutdown previously. After starting and shutting down from the VirtualBox, then go to the GNS3 workspace and start from there.*

When you try to start the server from the GNS3, you might be issued with a security alert, choose the options and allow access as shown in the figure 15.2.

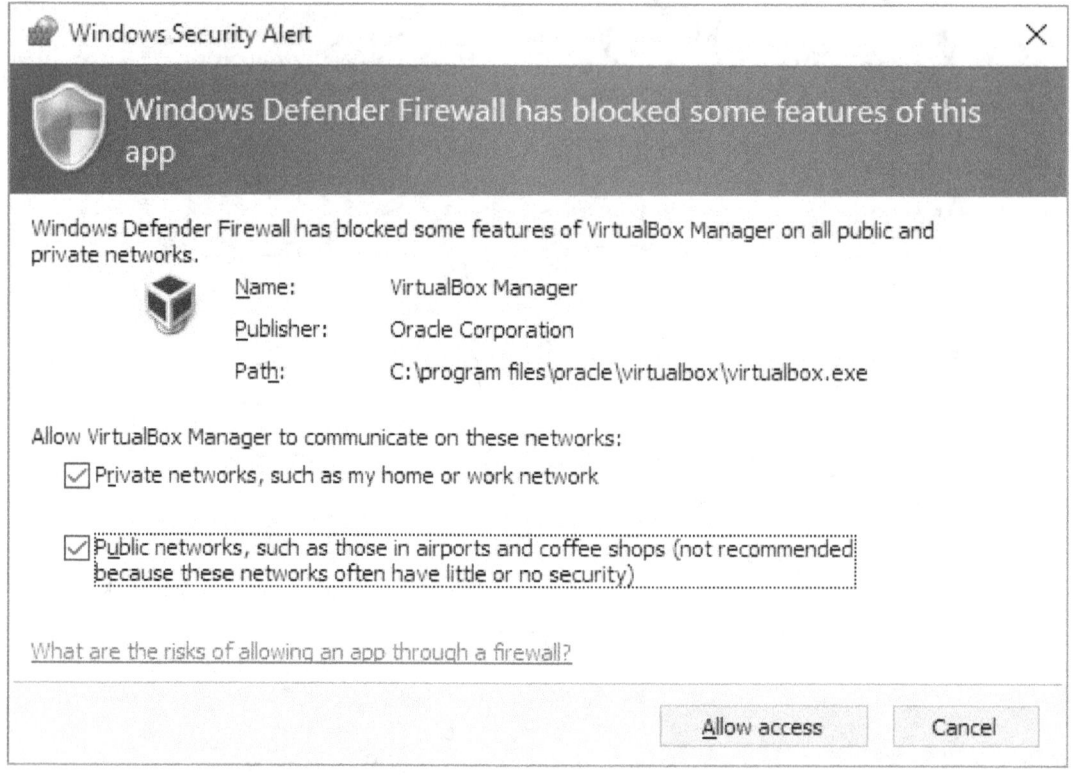

Figure 15.2: Windows Security Alert

Build a Virtual Network and Practice

If the starting of the DNS server is successful, the link status of the devices would change to green circular bullets and also the screen of the CentOS-DNS-Srv (DNS Server) would be available for login. Then you can login to the system as the root and then continue to configure the details.

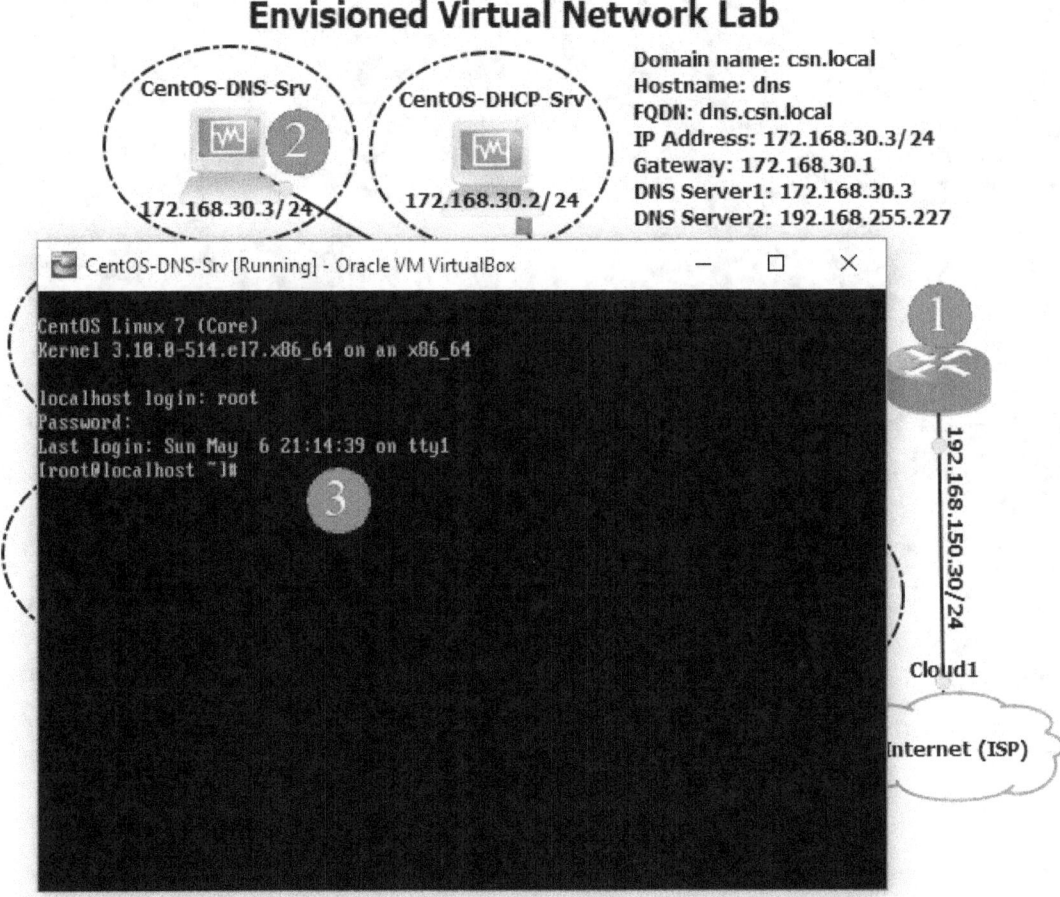

Figure 15.3: Virtual Network Lab with started DNS Server and router

> As we are working in a virtual network, running multiples virtual machines would drastically slow down the system. Since the configuration of the DHCP server is completed, you can shut it down from the GNS3 workspace to release system resources for faster processing. At this point, there is no need for DHCP to be running.

After successfully logging in to the server, configure the hostname by using the nmtui utility as shown in the figure below:

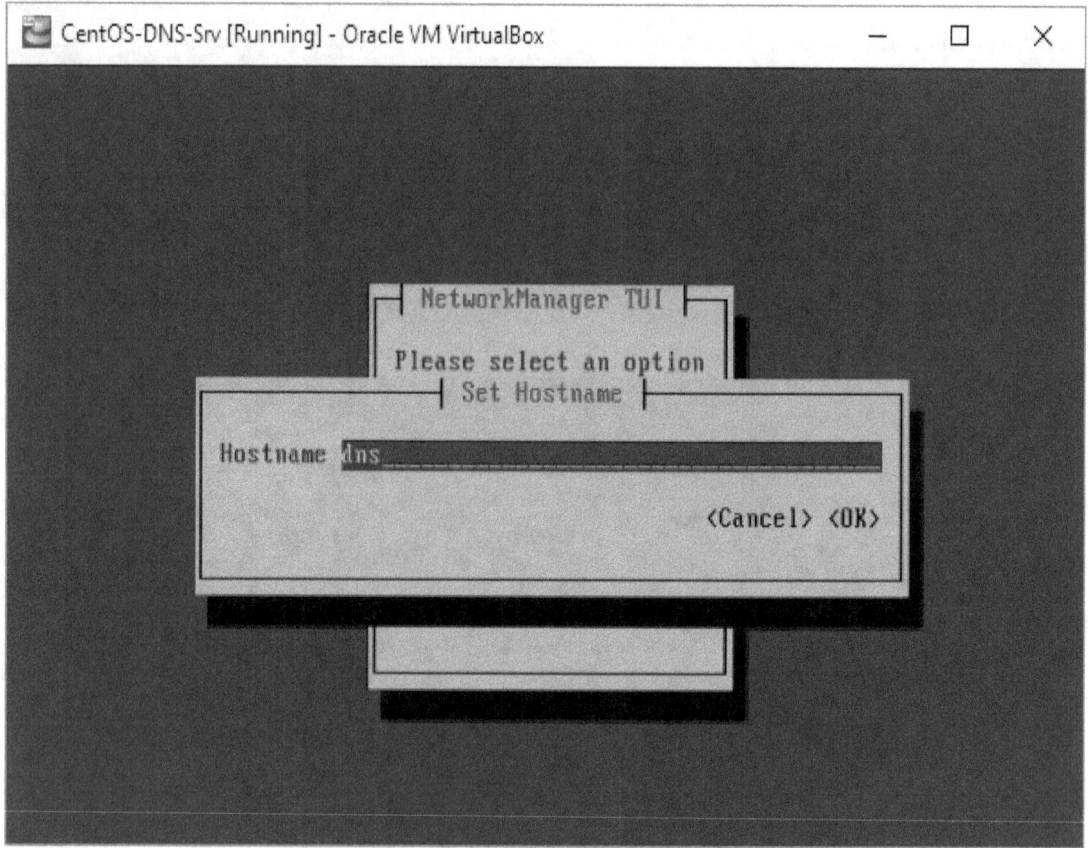

Figure 15.4: Setting the hostname

Build a Virtual Network and Practice

In the next, configure the IP address details using the nmtui as indicated in the figure 15.5 and figure 15.6.

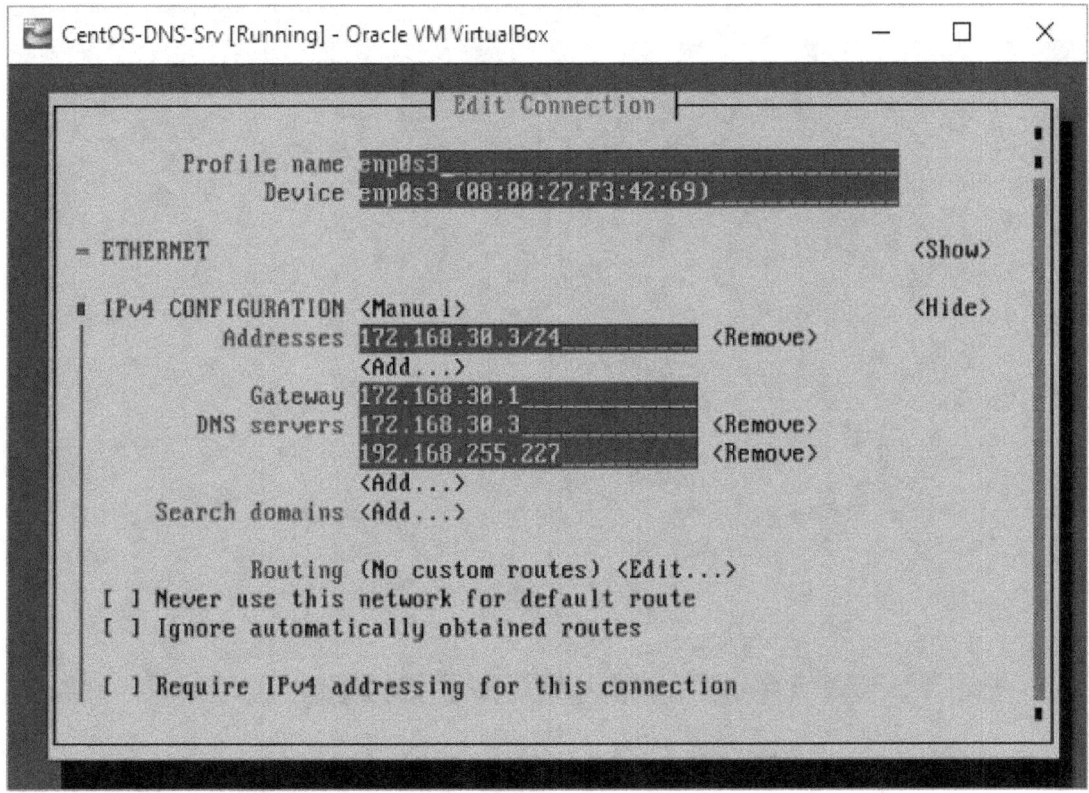

Figure 15.5: Ethernet IPv4 Setting for DNS Server

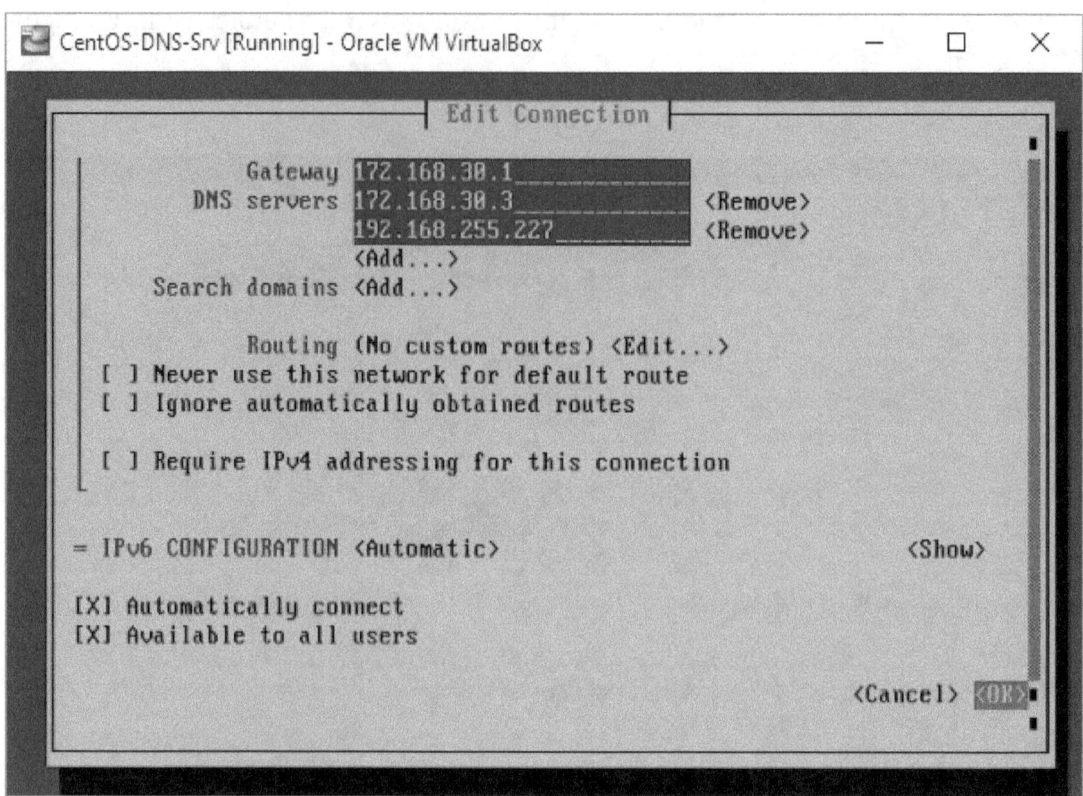

Figure 15.6: Allowing to automatically connect

Build a Virtual Network and Practice

Once the required manual settings are completed, you must be able to ping the router's IP address (172.168.30.1) as shown below:

```
[root@dns ~]# ping 172.168.30.1
PING 172.168.30.1 (172.168.30.1) 56(84) bytes of data.
64 bytes from 172.168.30.1: icmp_seq=1 ttl=255 time=8.30 ms
64 bytes from 172.168.30.1: icmp_seq=2 ttl=255 time=13.1 ms
64 bytes from 172.168.30.1: icmp_seq=3 ttl=255 time=8.28 ms
64 bytes from 172.168.30.1: icmp_seq=4 ttl=255 time=11.4 ms
64 bytes from 172.168.30.1: icmp_seq=5 ttl=255 time=6.57 ms
64 bytes from 172.168.30.1: icmp_seq=6 ttl=255 time=13.1 ms
64 bytes from 172.168.30.1: icmp_seq=7 ttl=255 time=9.89 ms
64 bytes from 172.168.30.1: icmp_seq=8 ttl=255 time=2.58 ms
64 bytes from 172.168.30.1: icmp_seq=9 ttl=255 time=6.92 ms
64 bytes from 172.168.30.1: icmp_seq=10 ttl=255 time=10.1 ms
^C
--- 172.168.30.1 ping statistics ---
10 packets transmitted, 10 received, 0% packet loss, time 9019ms
rtt min/avg/max/mdev = 2.583/9.047/13.191/3.085 ms
[root@dns ~]#
```

Figure 15.7: Verifying the connection

Before starting to install the packages, it is important to verify whether our router can connect to the internet or not by pinging the 8.8.8.8 after opening the console.

```
R1#ping 8.8.8.8

Type escape sequence to abort.
Sending 5, 100-byte ICMP Echos to 8.8.8.8, timeout is 2 seconds:
!!!!!
Success rate is 100 percent (5/5), round-trip min/avg/max = 212/219/228 ms
R1#
```

Figure 15.8: Verifying the connection to the Internet

> *If the pinging is not successful, try to check the configuration on the router and if the configurations are correctly done, try to reload or restart the router. Since we are using the dynamic IP address on the router's first interface f0/0, the lease might have expired.*

Install BIND DNS Server Package

BIND is available from the default CentOS software repository and there is no need to install EPEL repositories. The bind-utils is extremely useful for testing and troubleshooting DNS related issues. Therefore, install both the bind and bind-utils packages using the following command:

```
[root@dns ~]# yum -y install bind bind-utils
```

Configuring BIND

The configuration file of bind is /etc/named.conf. Open the /etc/named.conf file using any editor and modify or add the lines which are only bolded in the following content of the /etc/named.conf file:

```
options {
    listen-on port 53 { 127.0.0.1; any; };
    listen-on-v6 port 53 { ::1; any; };
    ######################################################################
    # The above two bolded lines instruct the DNS server to listen on UDP port 53 for queries.   #
    ######################################################################
    directory       "/var/named";
        dump-file           "/var/named/data/cache_dump.db";
        statistics-file "/var/named/data/named_stats.txt";
        memstatistics-file "/var/named/data/named_mem_stats.txt";
        allow-query     { localhost; any; };
        allow-query-cache { localhost; any; };
    ######################################################################
    # The above two lines allow the localhost and any network machines to query the DNS Server #
    # and the cache responses.                                                                  #
    ######################################################################
    recursion yes;
        dnssec-enable yes;
        dnssec-validation yes;
        bindkeys-file "/etc/named.iscdlv.key";
        managed-keys-directory "/var/named/dynamic";
        pid-file "/run/named/named.pid";
        session-keyfile "/run/named/session.key";
};

logging {
        channel default_debug {
                file "data/named.run";
                severity dynamic;
        };
};

zone "." IN {
```

```
        type hint;
        file "named.ca";
};

zone "csn.local" IN {
    type master;
    file "forward.csn.local";
    allow-update { none; };
};
#####################################################################
# The bolded lines specify the name of the forward zone file, that is forward.chn.local for the   #
# domain chn.local. The master indicates that this is the Primary DNS Server for the              #
# chn.local domain. Since it is the primary DNS, it doesn't have to get any zone updates.         #
#####################################################################
zone "30.168.172.in-addr.arpa" IN {
    type master;
    file "30.168.172";
    allow-update { none; };
};
#####################################################################
# The bolded lines above specify the name of the reverse lookup zone file, that is 30.168.172.   #
# The master type indicates this is the Primary DNS Server, it doesn't have to get any zone      #
# updates.                                                                                        #
#####################################################################
include "/etc/named.rfc1912.zones";
include "/etc/named.root.key";
```

After the making the necessary modifications in the /etc/named.conf file, we can verify if all the syntaxes are written correctly or not by using the following command. The following command would give no output if the syntaxes are correct, however, the error messages will be displayed.

```
[root@dns ~]# named-checkconf /etc/named.conf
```

Creating Forward Zone file

Once the zone files are indicated in the /etc/named.conf file, we have to create the zone files. By default, the location of the zone file is /var/named. Create a forward lookup zone file with the name forward.csn.local under /var/named directory and add the details of the zone file as follows:

```
[root@dns ~]# vim /var/named/forward.csn.local

$TTL        1D
@           IN      SOA     dns.csn.local.      root.csn.local. (
                                    2018050700      ; serial
                                    4H              ; refresh
                                    30M             ; retry
                                    2W              ; expire
                                    1H )            ; minimum
            IN      NS              dns.csn.local.
            IN      MX      10      mail.csn.local.
dns         IN      A               172.168.30.3
ftp         IN      A               172.168.30.4
mail        IN      A               172.168.30.5
web         IN      A               172.168.30.6
www.csn.local.  IN  CNAME           web.csn.local.
```

After saving and quitting, test the zone file for any syntax error using the command shown below:

```
[root@dns ~]# named-checkzone    csn.local    /var/named/forward.csn.local
```

Zone File Parameter Values

The following are some of the Start of Authority (SOA) parameters, values and the format explained to be used in the zone files:

- **Time to Live (TTL):** The Time to Live ($TTL) configures the time to live for the information it provides. The TTL set for the cache information is one day which is equivalent to 86400 seconds and the cache information available with the master DNS server will expire after 24 hours. Which means, a caching name server can use previously queried results to answer questions until the TTL value expires.

- **Serial Number:** Every time you edit a zone file, you must increment this number for the zone file to push the changes correctly. Slave servers will check whether the master DNS server's serial number for a zone is larger than the one they have on their system or not. If the serial number is larger than they have, the slave servers will request for the new zone file to update, if not, it will continue to serve using the original zone file. So, it is very important for us to remember to change the serial number whenever updates are made on the Primary DNS zone files. The format followed by the users for writing the serial number is YYYYMMDDXX. The

YYYYMMDD is for the date followed by XX. The XX is a number which can be starting from 00.

- **Refresh Interval:** This is the amount of time that the slave DNS Server will wait before polling the master for zone file changes. In our example, after every 4 hours slave will contact master DNS server for updates.

- **Retry Interval:** If slave DNS is not able to contact master DNS for checking the updates when the refresh time is up, then in every after 30 minutes it will retry to contact master DNS server for updates.

- **Expire Interval:** The cached information which is available with slave DNS servers will expire after 2 weeks if the slave DNS is not able to contact the primary Server and it will no longer respond as an authoritative source for this zone.

- **Minimum Time to Live (TTL):** The amount time, another DNS Server is allowed to cache any resource records from this server's database file.

Creating Reverse Zone file

Create reverse lookup zone file with a name 30.168.172 under /var/named directory and nter the details as shown under:

```
[root@dns ~]# vim /var/named/30.168.172

$TTL      1D;
@   IN    SOA    dns.csn.local.   root.csn.local. (
                                  2018050700    ; serial
                                  4H            ; refresh
                                  30M           ; retry
                                  2W            ; expire
                                  1H )          ; minimum
    IN    NS     dns.csn.local.
3   IN    PTR    dns.csn.local.
4   IN    PTR    ftp.csn.local.
5   IN    PTR    web.csn.local.
6   IN    PTR    mail.csn.local.
```

After saving and quitting, test the zone file for any syntax error as shown below:

[root@dns ~]# named-checkzone   30.168.172   /var/named/30.168.172

> *The configuration of the zone files and the main configuration file was based on the assumption that the hostnames of FTP, Web, Mail and DNS Servers are ftp, web, mail and dns respectively. If the hostnames are not set for the servers, set it and restart the NetworkManager by using "systemctl restart NetworkManager" command.*

Starting and Enabling the named Service

The named is the daemon for the BIND DNS server. Once zone files are created and configured, start and enable the named service as shown under:

```
[root@dns ~]# systemctl start named
[root@dns ~]# systemctl enable named
```

If you are not able to start the named service, look for the errors in the configuration files and the zone files and troubleshoot.

Firewall Adjustment

Both network and host firewalls must allow incoming TCP and UDP traffic over port 53. Standard DNS requests occur over UDP port 53. However, if the response size is over 512 bytes, as the case may be with DNSSEC, the request need to be sent over TCP port 53. Zone transfers between the primary and secondary name servers will occur over TCP port 53. Use the following commands to open the TCP and UDP port 53.

```
[root@dns ~]# firewall-cmd --permanent --zone=public --add-port=53/{tcp,udp}
[root@dns ~]# firewall-cmd --permanent --zone=public --add-service=dns
[root@dns ~]# firewall-cmd --reload
```

Testing the Functionality of DNS Server

The functionality of the configured DNS Server can be tested from a Linux system if it has the bind-utils package installed. You can type the following commands on the terminal and look for the output.

    # dig www.csn.local
    # dig -x 172.168.30.6

On the other hand, you can open the browser and look for http://www.csn.local, ftp://ftp.csn.local, and http://mail.csn.local/webmail. The DNS Server must be able to resolve the hostnames and the pages would be displayed accordingly.

The following figure shows the name resolution provided for the web server and the web server can be accessed just by specifying the hostname mapped in the DNS.

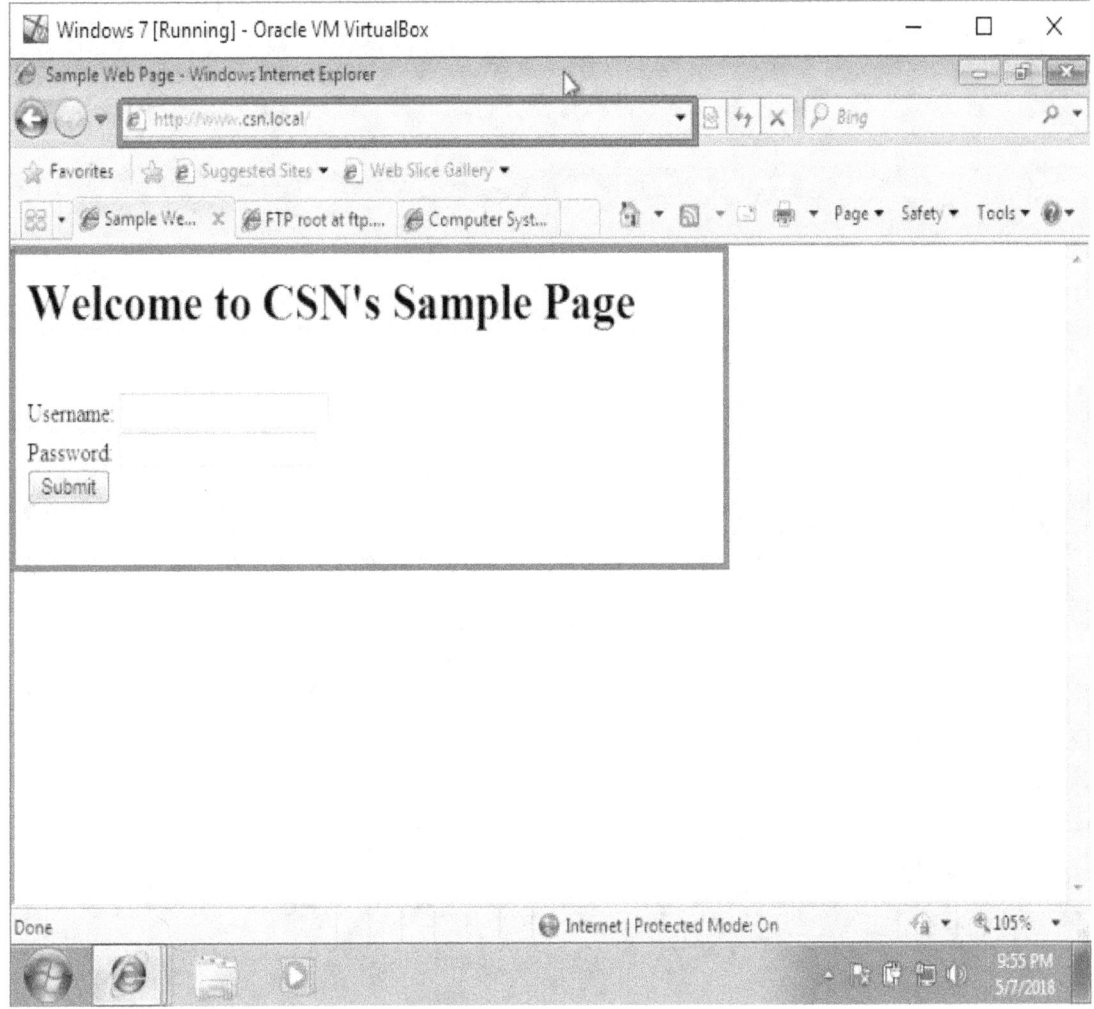

Figure 15.9: Web Server's hostname getting resolved

In the following figure, it shows the name resolution provided for the FTP server and uploaded sample files kept for download is accessible to the clients.

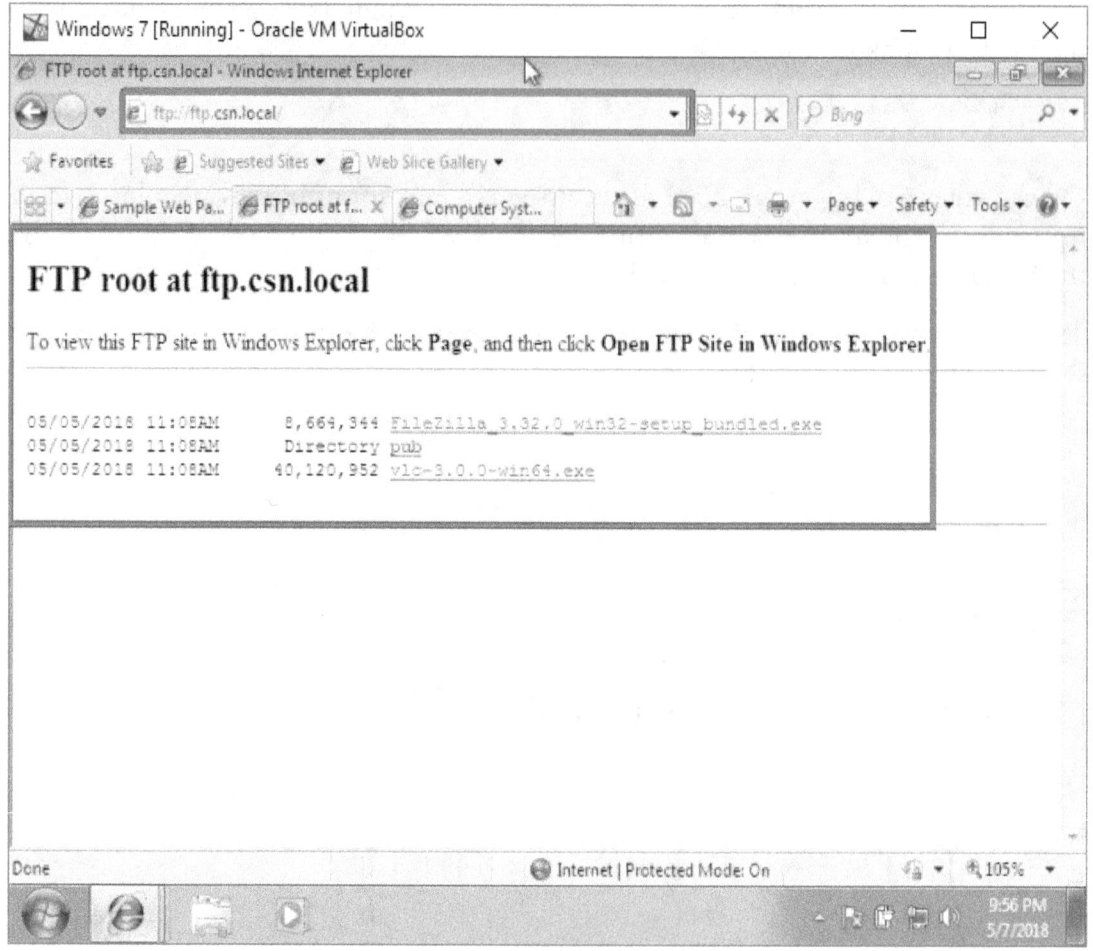

Figure 15.10: FTP Server's hostname getting resolved

Similarly, the name resolution for the Mail server is also working properly and now the clients can access the mail successfully.

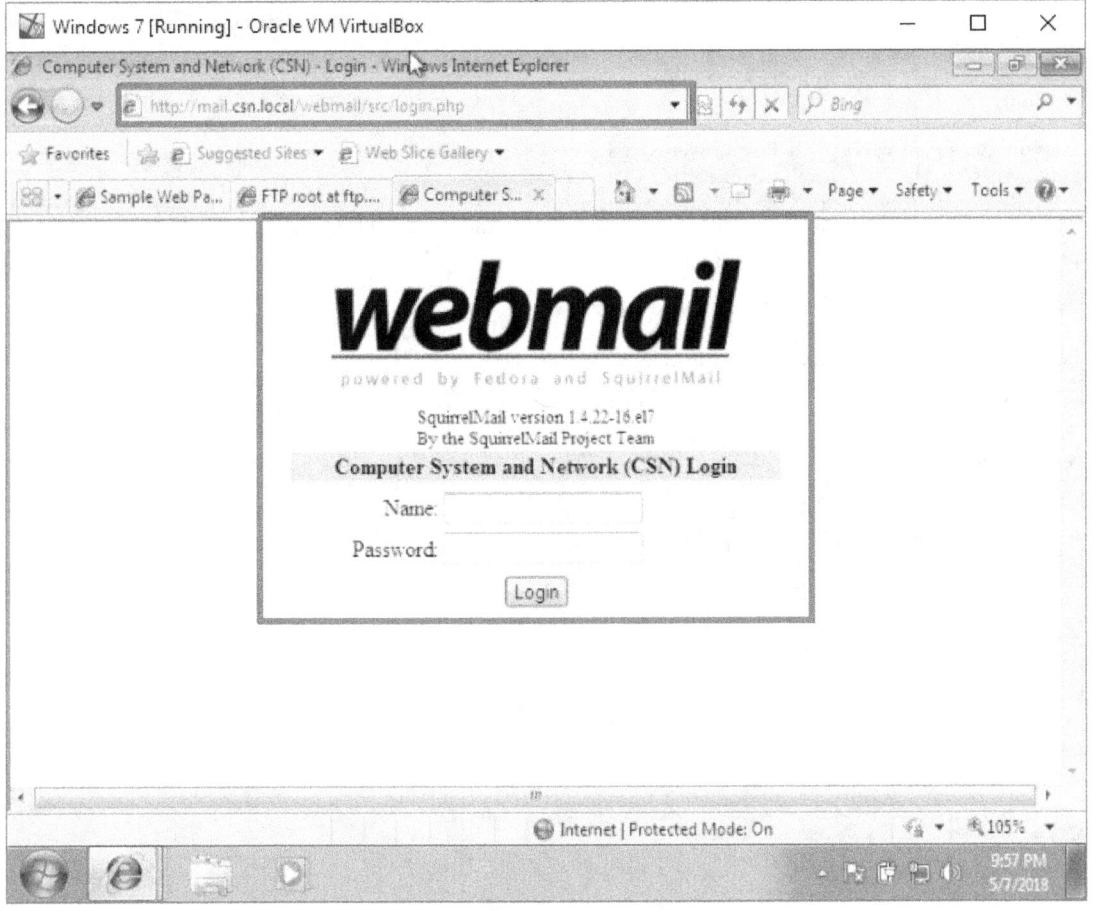

Figure 15.11: Mail Server's hostname getting resolved

> *In case, the web page is not accessible, try disabling the SELinux although it is not recommended. We will learn to configure the SELinux in the later chapter. If the page is not accessible even after the SELinux is disabled, then try to troubleshoot other configurations.*

Further Reading

6. DNS Sample BIND Configurations. (n.d.). Retrieved from http://www.zytrax.com/books/dns/ch6/

An Introduction to DNS Terminology, Components, and Concepts | DigitalOcean. (2017, October 10). Retrieved from https://www.digitalocean.com/community/tutorials/an-introduction-to-dns-terminology-components-and-concepts

BIND. (n.d.). Retrieved from https://www.isc.org/downloads/bind/

Configure DNS (BIND) Server on CentOS 7 / RHEL 7. (2017, October 09). Retrieved from https://www.itzgeek.com/how-tos/linux/centos-how-tos/configure-dns-bind-server-on-centos-7-rhel-7.html

DNS Server Configuration on RHEL/CentOS 7 in 10

Easy Steps. (2017, January 24). Retrieved from https://www.techinformant.in/dns-server-configuration-on-rhelcentos-7/

How Domain Name Servers Work. (2000, April 01). Retrieved from https://computer.howstuffworks.com/dns.htm

How to Configure BIND as a Private Network DNS Server on CentOS 7 | DigitalOcean. (2016, October 13). Retrieved from https://www.digitalocean.com/community/tutorials/how-to-configure-bind-as-a-private-network-dns-server-on-centos-7

How to Install and Configure DNS Server In CentOS 7. (n.d.). Retrieved from https://www.linuxhelp.com/how-to-install-and-configure-dns-server-in-centos-7/

Setting Up DNS Server On CentOS 7. (2015, July 13). Retrieved from https://www.unixmen.com/setting-dns-server-centos-7/

SOA (Start of Authority) Record. (n.d.). Retrieved from http://help.dnsmadeeasy.com/managed-dns/records/soa-start-authority-record/

SOA-Records (Start of authority). (n.d.). Retrieved from https://simpledns.com/help/soa-records

Stirnimann, D. (2016, May 03). DNS Zone File Time Value Recommendations. Retrieved from https://securityblog.switch.ch/2014/02/06/zone-file-recommendations/

What does serial / refresh / retry / expire / minimum / and TTL mean? (n.d.). Retrieved from http://knowledgelayer.softlayer.com/faq/what-does-serial-refresh-retry-expire-minimum-and-ttl-mean

SSL Configuration to enable HTTPS Apache Web Server on Linux. (2016, January 01). Retrieved from http://www.learnitguide.net/2016/03/ssl-configuration-to-enable-https.html

Chapter 16
Setting Up a YUM Repository

The Yellowdog Updater Modified (YUM) is an open source package management tool for RedHat Package Manager (RPM) based Linux systems. YUM enables the users and system administrator to install, update, remove or search software packages on systems easily. YUM also uses a number of third party repositories to install packages thereby resolving the dependencies of the packages automatically.

In this chapter, we will learn to install, configure and test the functionality of the configured YUM repository on a CentOS distribution.

Network Scenario

To create a YUM repository, we will use the Virtual Network Lab which we have created and used in the earlier chapters. In the same virtual network Lab, we have implemented the DHCP server, FTP Server, Mail Server, Web Server and DNS Server; here onwards, without removing those configurations and setup, we will configure the YUM repository in our Virtual Network Lab and test its functionality. The details required for the Yum Server is indicated in the following figure:

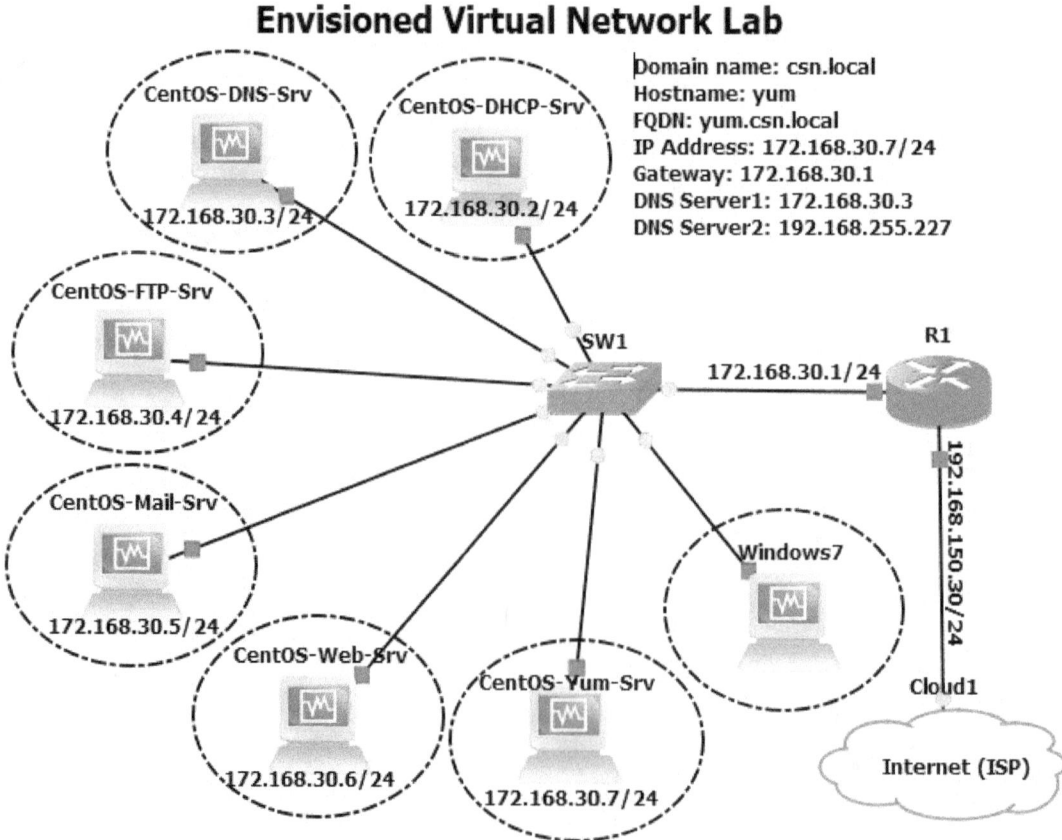

Figure 16.1: Base network with YUM Server details

Configuring the YUM Server Details

Taking into consideration the details of the YUM Server shown in the figure 16.1, the YUM server details have to be configured. In order to configure, we have to start the YUM Server from the GNS3 workspace by right-clicking and choosing to start.

> *It is advised not to either start or shutdown the YUM Server directly from the VirtualBox Interface while working on the GNS3 as this action would lead to issues. So, start or shutdown from the GNS3 Interface only. While trying to start any of the severs not just limited to CentOS-Yum-Srv (YUM Server) from the GNS3, sometimes you may get error messages and you won't be able to start. In such cases, start the server directly from the VirtualBox interface and once the starting is complete, login and give a proper shutdown. This happens when the server was improperly shutdown previously. After starting and shutting down from the VirtualBox, then go to the GNS3 workspace and start from there.*

When you try to start the server from the GNS3, you might be issued with a security alert, choose the options and allow access as shown in the figure 16.2.

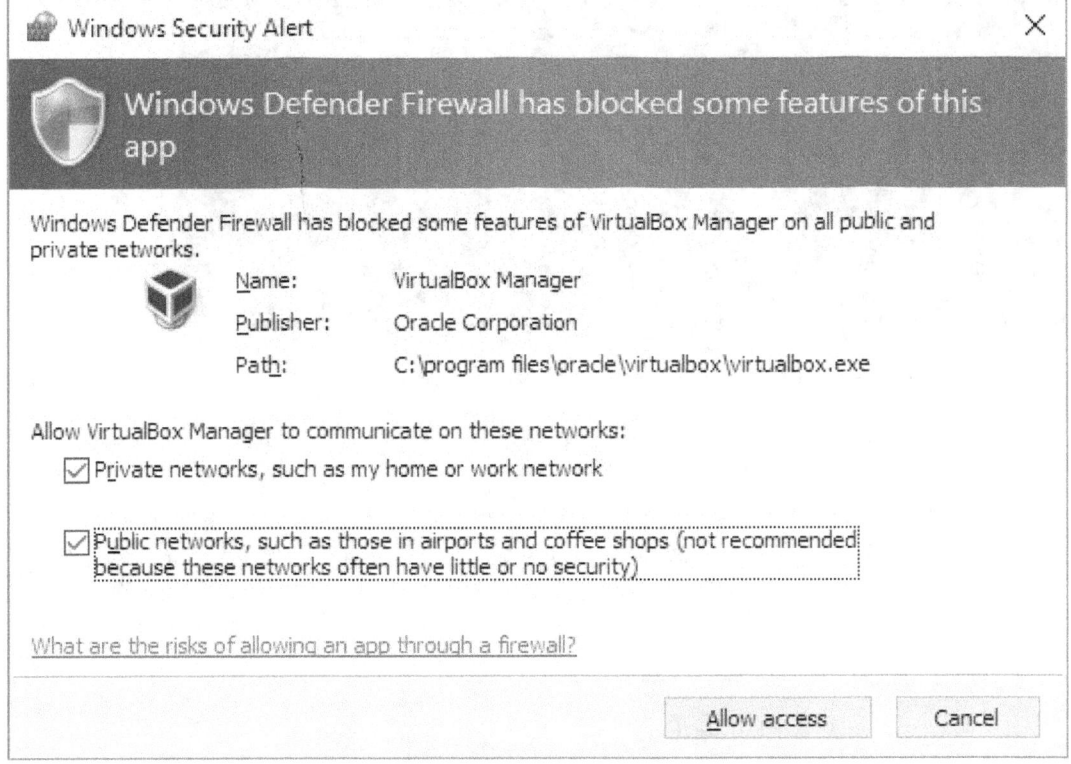

Figure 16.2: Windows Security Alert

If the starting of the YUM Server is successful, the link status of the devices would change to green circular bullets and also the screen of the CentOS-Yum-Srv (YUM Server) would be available for login. Then you can login to the system as the root and then continue to configure the details.

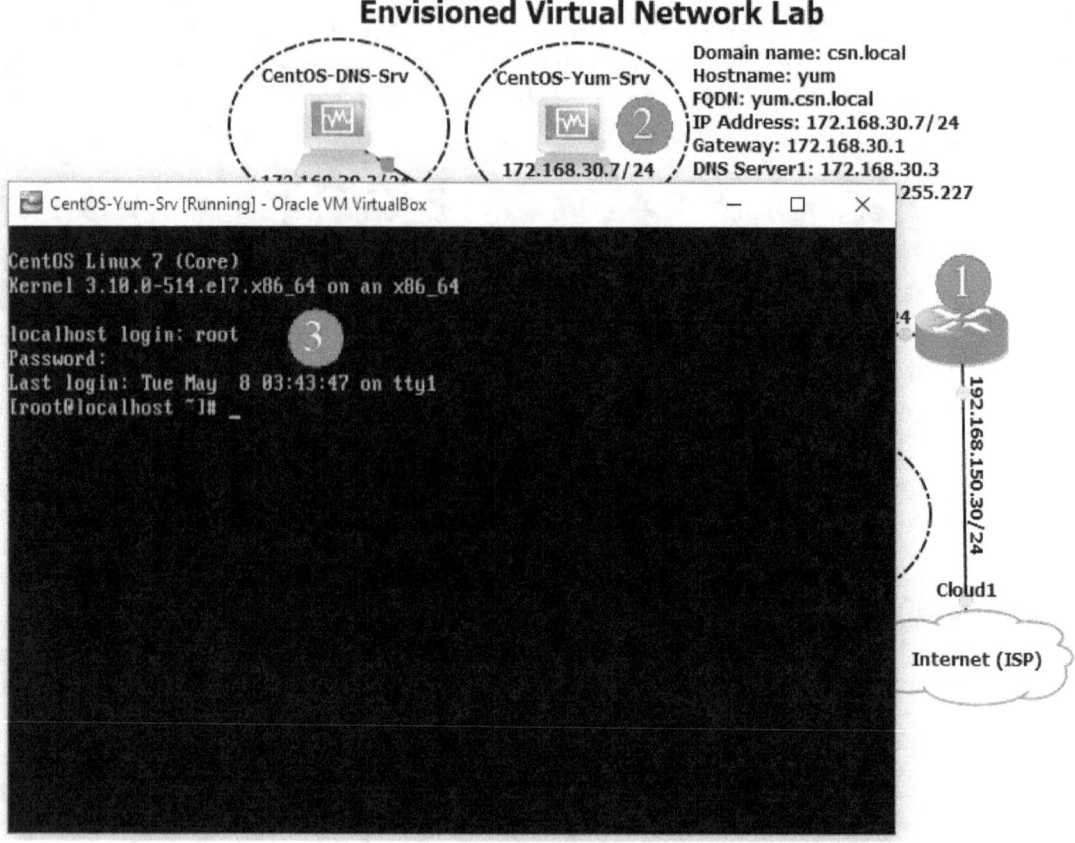

Figure 16.3: Virtual Network Lab with started YUM Server and router

> As we are working in a virtual network, running multiples virtual machines would drastically slow down the system. Since the configuration of the DHCP server is completed, you can shut it down from the GNS3 workspace to release system resources for faster processing. At this point, there is no need for DHCP to be running.

After successfully logging in to the server, configure the hostname by using the nmtui utility as shown in the figure below:

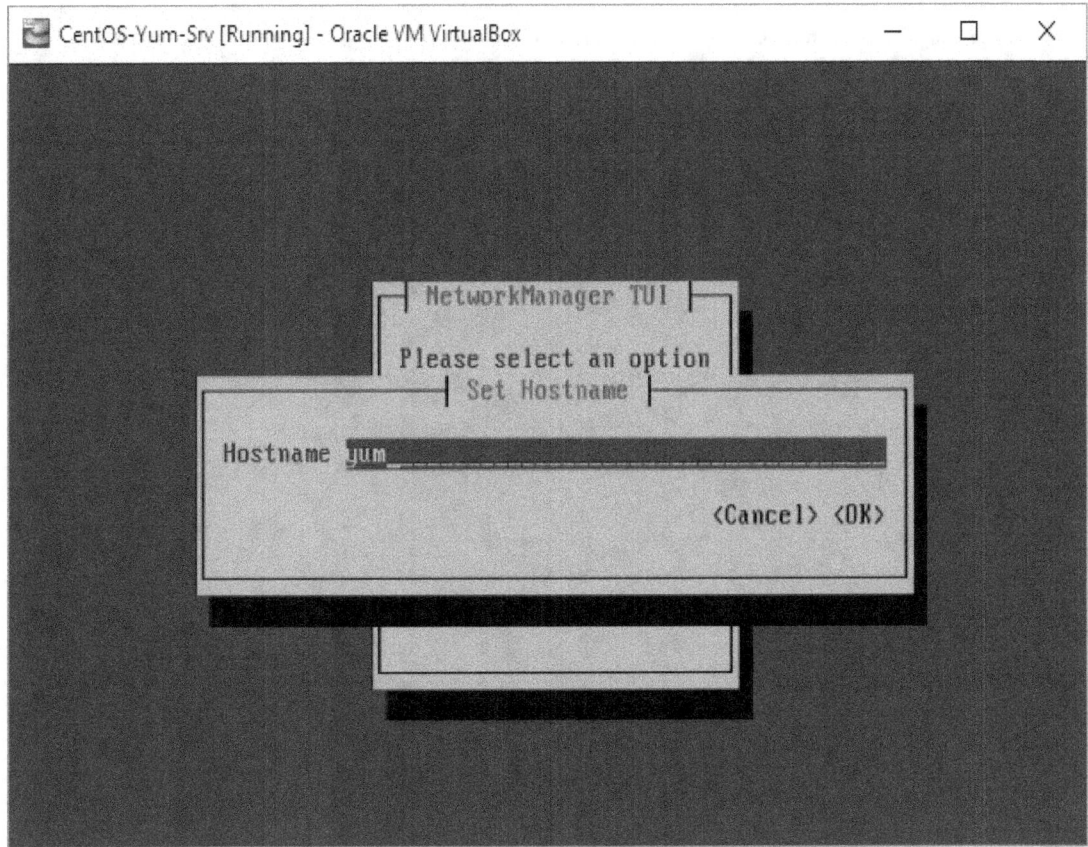

Figure 16.4: Setting the hostname

In the next, configure the IP address details using the nmtui as indicated in the figure 16.5 and figure 16.6.

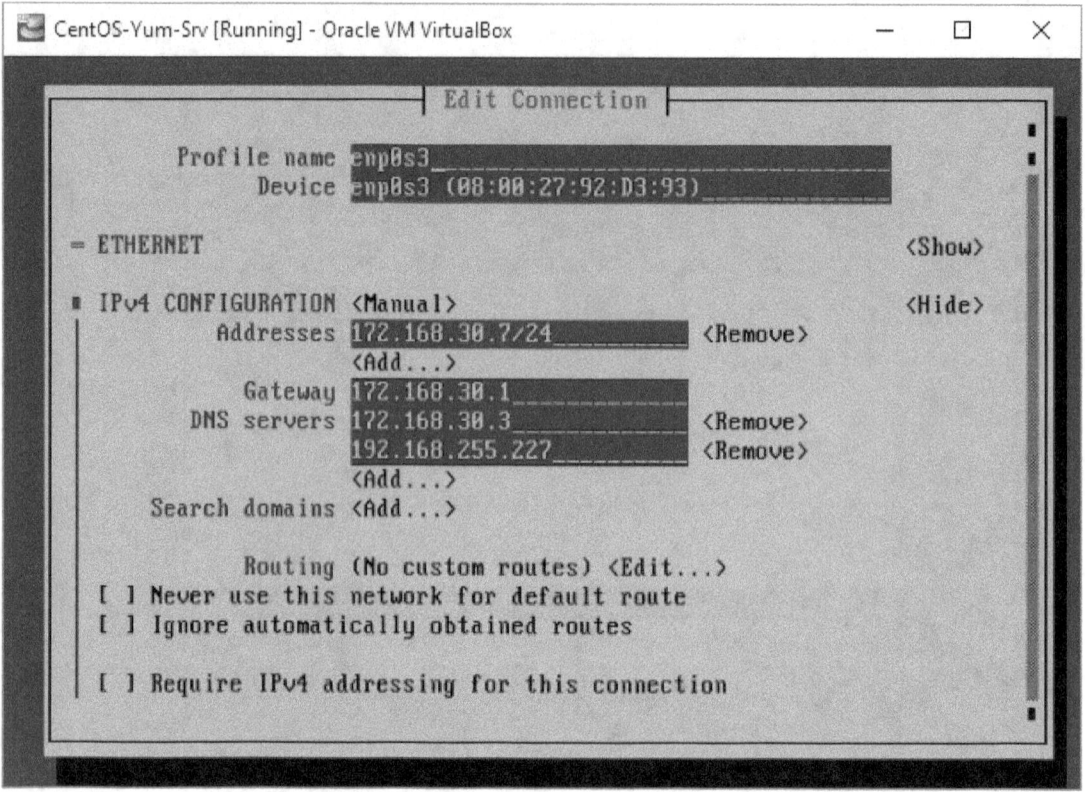

Figure 16.5: Ethernet IPv4 Setting for YUM Server

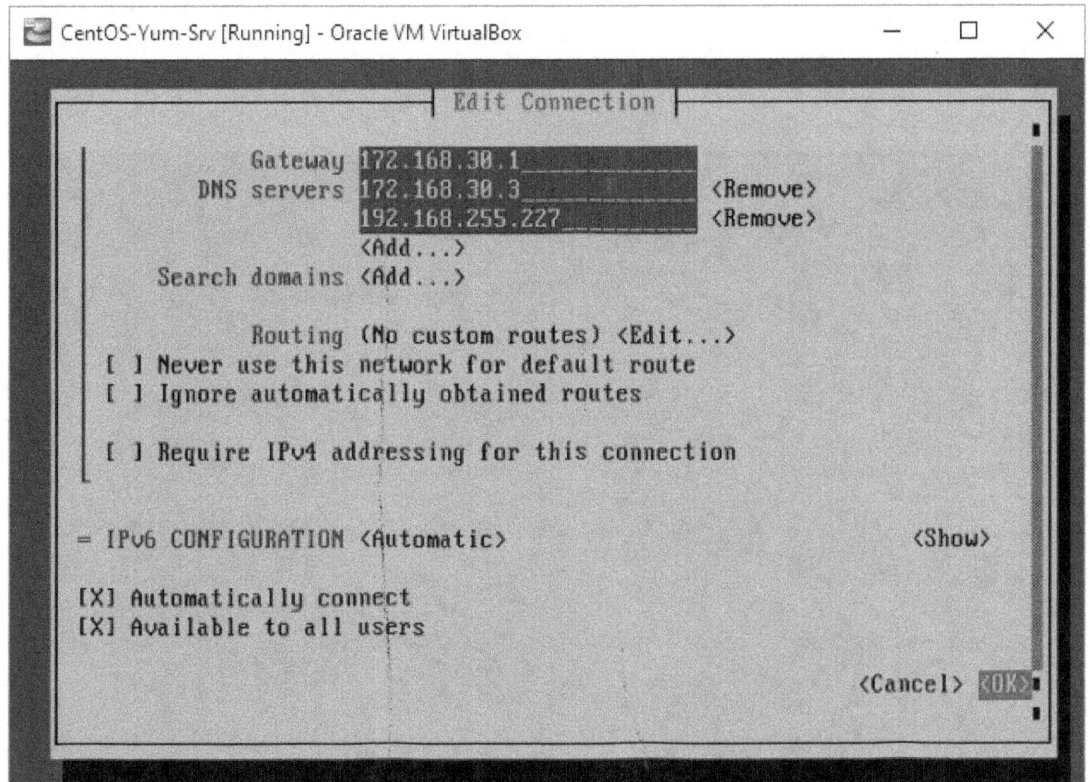

Figure 16.6: Allowing to automatically connect

Once the required manual settings are completed, you must be able to ping the router's IP address (172.168.30.1) as shown below:

CentOS-Yum-Srv [Running] - Oracle VM VirtualBox

```
[root@yum ~]# ping 172.168.30.1
PING 172.168.30.1 (172.168.30.1) 56(84) bytes of data.
64 bytes from 172.168.30.1: icmp_seq=1 ttl=255 time=16.4 ms
64 bytes from 172.168.30.1: icmp_seq=2 ttl=255 time=7.46 ms
64 bytes from 172.168.30.1: icmp_seq=3 ttl=255 time=4.42 ms
64 bytes from 172.168.30.1: icmp_seq=4 ttl=255 time=8.31 ms
64 bytes from 172.168.30.1: icmp_seq=5 ttl=255 time=11.5 ms
64 bytes from 172.168.30.1: icmp_seq=6 ttl=255 time=7.47 ms
^C
--- 172.168.30.1 ping statistics ---
6 packets transmitted, 6 received, 0% packet loss, time 5014ms
rtt min/avg/max/mdev = 4.428/9.290/16.472/3.832 ms
[root@yum ~]#
```

Figure 16.7: Verifying the connection

Before starting to install the packages, it is important to verify whether our router can connect to the internet or not by pinging the 8.8.8.8 after opening the console.

```
R1#ping 8.8.8.8

Type escape sequence to abort.
Sending 5, 100-byte ICMP Echos to 8.8.8.8, timeout is 2 seconds:
!!!!!
Success rate is 100 percent (5/5), round-trip min/avg/max = 212/219/228 ms
R1#
```

Figure 16.8: Verifying the connection to the Internet

> *If the pinging is not successful, try to check the configuration on the router and if the configurations are correctly done, try to reload or restart the router. Since we are using the dynamic IP address on the router's first interface f0/0, the lease might have expired.*

Apache Installation

The packages can be served to the yum clients by the yum server in two major ways; through ftp and http. We will be using the later one, which is http. In order to serve the packages via http, we have to install the Apache HTTP Web server on the to-be YUM Server. Run the following command to install the httpd package on your to-be YUM Server, start and enable the Apache:

    # yum install –y httpd
    # systemctl start httpd
    # systemctl enable httpd

Remote Sync (rsync) Installation

The rsync command can be used for copying and synchronizing the files and directories in local or remote systems to maintain up-to-date changes in the files. Use the following command to install the rsync on the to-be YUM Server.

    # yum install –y rsync

Configure the YUM Repo Server

On the to-be, YUM Server, run the following commands on the terminal to first create folders related to YUM Server, install createrepo, and synchronize the files on the YUM Server from a trusted repo.

    # mkdir -p /var/www/html/repos/centos/7

Downloading the CentOS 7 ISO

You can download the CentOS 7 ISO file to a directory on your YUM Server from one of the trusted links available. In order to download, install the wget utility and change the directory to /var/www/html/repos/centos by using the following commands and then download the CentOS 7 ISO file:

    # yum install -y wget
    # cd /var/www/html/repos/centos/
    # wget https://buildlogs.centos.org/rolling/7/isos/x86_64/CentOS-7-x86_64-DVD-1611.iso

After the download is complete, create a mount point in the /mnt directory by using the following command to mount the downloaded ISO file to copy the contents:

    # mkdir /mnt/iso

Then mount the ISO file using the following command. While mounting, the type of file must be specified as iso9660 for the ISO.

    # mount -t iso9660 CentOS-7-x86_64-DVD-1611.iso /mnt/iso

After successfully mounting the ISO file to the /mnt/iso, the contents can be copied to the directory where we wanted to keep the packages.

    # cp -r /mnt/iso/* /var/www/html/repos/centos/7

> *If you have already download the CentOS 7 ISO file, extract it and copy the extracted CentOS 7 files to the /var/www/html/repos/centos/7 directory. If you have extracted the files onto a Windows system, then copying can be done using the Filezilla utility or by using the USB drive as well.*

The following commands can be run to update the yum and install the createrepo utility onto the to-be YUM Server.

    # yum update && yum install createrepo

The following command would create the repodata files from the existing set of rpm packages in the specified directory.

    # createrepo /var/www/html/repos/centos/7
    # createrepo --update /var/www/html/repos/centos/7

In the following, the rsync is used to synchronize the packages from a reliable source to the newly created repository which otherwise would be getting obsolete any moment. To keep updated on the newer packages the following command is executed.

    # rsync -avz rsync://vault.centos.org/centos/7.3.1611/os/x86_64/ /var/www/html/repos/centos/7

Configuring Cron Job

The cron scheduler is used to perform a task automatically at a certain time without the intervention of the system administrator. It is used to automate the majority of the tasks which are required to be performed at odd hours or some tasks which are too tedious and repetitive in nature. The following cron entry can be made by opening the crontab file so that the packages on the local repository will be updated or synchronized with the reliable source exactly at 2:30 AM every day automatically without the system administrators' need to run the command manually.

    # crontab –e

When the crontab file is opened you can make the following entry in the file so that the syncing of the file will take place at 2:30 AM every day using the cron job.

30 2 * * * rsync -avz rsync://vault.centos.org/centos/7.3.1611/os/x86_64/ /var/www/html/repos/centos/7

In the above entry, vault.centos.org/centos/7.3.1611/os/x86_64 is assumed to be a reliable source for getting the packages updated or synchronized.

Configure the Yum Client

Until this point, we have finished configuring the repository to serve the packages to the clients. However, for the clients to be able to access the local repository, some modifications are required to be made. By default, the clients would be looking for the packages in the repositories specified in the repo files stored in the /etc/yum.repos.d/ directory. Instead of this, if the clients are expected to be using the local repository, a new repo file is required to be created in the directory /etc/yum.repos.d/ whose file name ends with .repo extension. In the following figure, All the CentOS-based Servers can use the local repository for installing the required packages.

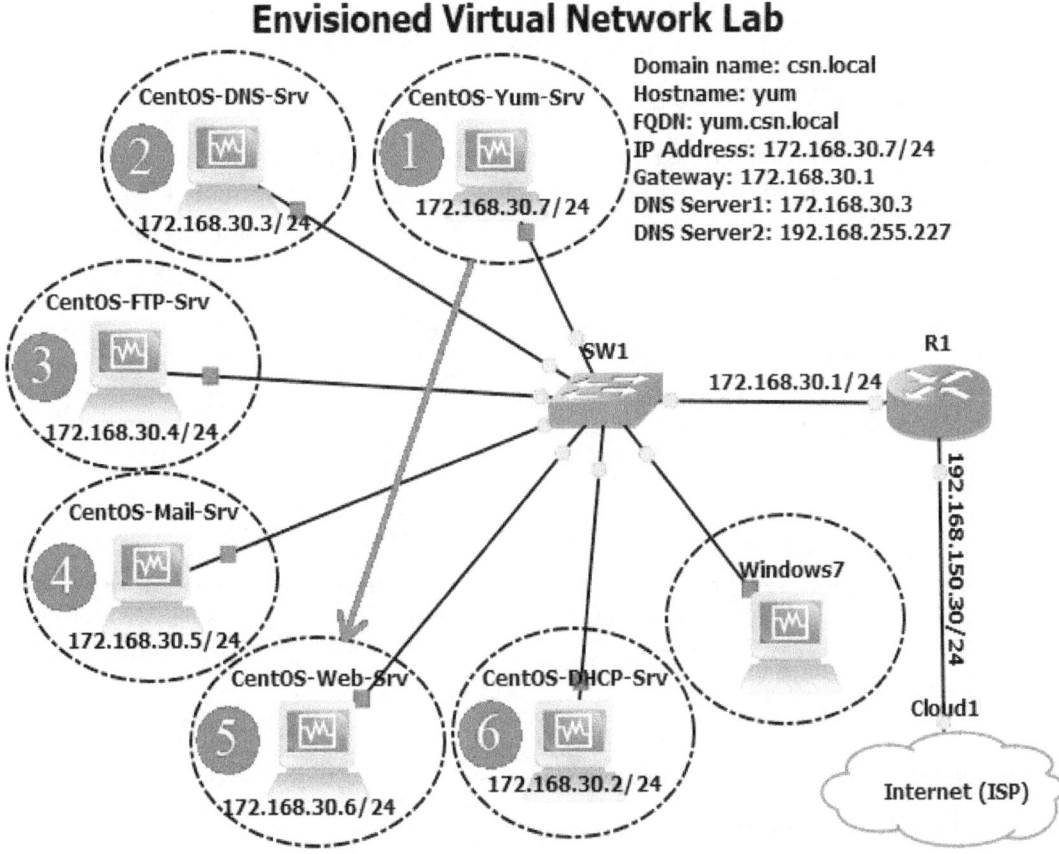

Figure 16.9: YUM Server and the clients

Creating a Repo File

Let us assume that CentOS-Web-Srv (Web Server) requires a package to be installed using the local repository. So, before being able to use the repository, a repo file has to be created in the client system; in this context, CentOS-Web-Srv is going to be the client of the CentOS-Yum-Srv (YUM Server). The following command can be used to create a repo file with the name jnec.repo which in turn must contain the subsequent minimum information so that the client would be able to access the packages successfully.

```
# vi /etc/yum.repos.d/jnec.repo
[jnec]
name=JNEC Repo
baseurl=http://172.168.30.7/repos/centos/7
gpgcheck=1
gpgkey=http://172.168.30.7/repos/centos/7/RPM-GPG-KEY-CentOS-7
```

Once the above information is entered into the jnec.repo file without any errors, the file can be saved and exited. If there are seemingly no errors at all, the client would be able to install the required packages from the repository using the YUM utility.

Testing the YUM Server

After the configuration of the YUM server and the configuration of the client is completed, you can test it by installing a package on the client system (CentOS-Web-Srv). For example, if the client requires net-tools package to be installed, the following command can be used.

```
# yum install -y --disablerepo=* --enablerepo=jnec.repo net-tools
```

The package should be installed successfully if the local repository configuration was correctly done. Else the configurations have to be revisited to check for any possible errors.

Further Reading

Create Local YUM repository on CentOS 7 / RHEL 7 using DVD. (2018, March 13). Retrieved from https://www.itzgeek.com/how-tos/linux/centos-how-tos/create-local-yum-repository-on-centos-7-rhel-7-using-dvd.html

How to configure YUM repository package manager in RHEL 7/CENTOS 7. (2017, February 13). Retrieved from http://www.elinuxbook.com/how-to-configure-yum-repository-package-manager-in-linux/

How to Create Local YUM Repository on CentOS 7 / RHEL 7. (2015, December 25). Retrieved from https://www.techbrown.com/how-to-create-local-yum-repository-on-centos-7-rhel-7.shtml

How to Set Up and Use Yum Repositories on a CentOS 6 VPS | DigitalOcean. (2016, October 13). Retrieved from https://www.digitalocean.com/community/tutorials/how-to-set-up-and-use-yum-repositories-on-a-centos-6-vps

RHEL7: Create a local repository. (n.d.). Retrieved from https://www.certdepot.net/rhel7-create-local-repository/

Setting Up a yum Repository. (n.d.). Retrieved from http://www.informit.com/articles/article.aspx?p=440160&seqNum=3

Setup Local Yum Repository on CentOS 7. (2014, August 27). Retrieved from https://www.unixmen.com/setup-local-yum-repository-centos-7/

Chapter 17
Troubleshooting SELinux

The CentOS 7 versions come with a bunch of security features enabled, which includes SELinux. SELinux is an access control mechanism, that works side by side with the regular access control mechanism in Linux. It stands for Security Enhanced Linux. It is a mandatory access control system, ensuring that users cannot work around the rules already set by the administrators. Most of the system administrators get frustrated and confused when it comes to errors related to the SELinux and they go to the last resort (disable it). It is better to learn SELinux than to just disable it. If we disable it, we really loose a great bunch of security features which the SELinux provides us. Almost all the time, the SELinux is blamed when things aren't working. It is not that the SELinux is not working but it is just us who have not configured it correctly to make it work. In this chapter we will learn the basics of SELinux and the ways of troubleshooting SELinux.

Network Scenario

In order to continue working on the examples and the guided exercises, we will use the CentOS-Web-Srv (Web Server), CentOS-DNS-Srv (DNS Server) and the Windows 7, which we have in the Virtual Network Lab. The DNS will be required for the name resolution of the Web Server while testing from the Windows 7.

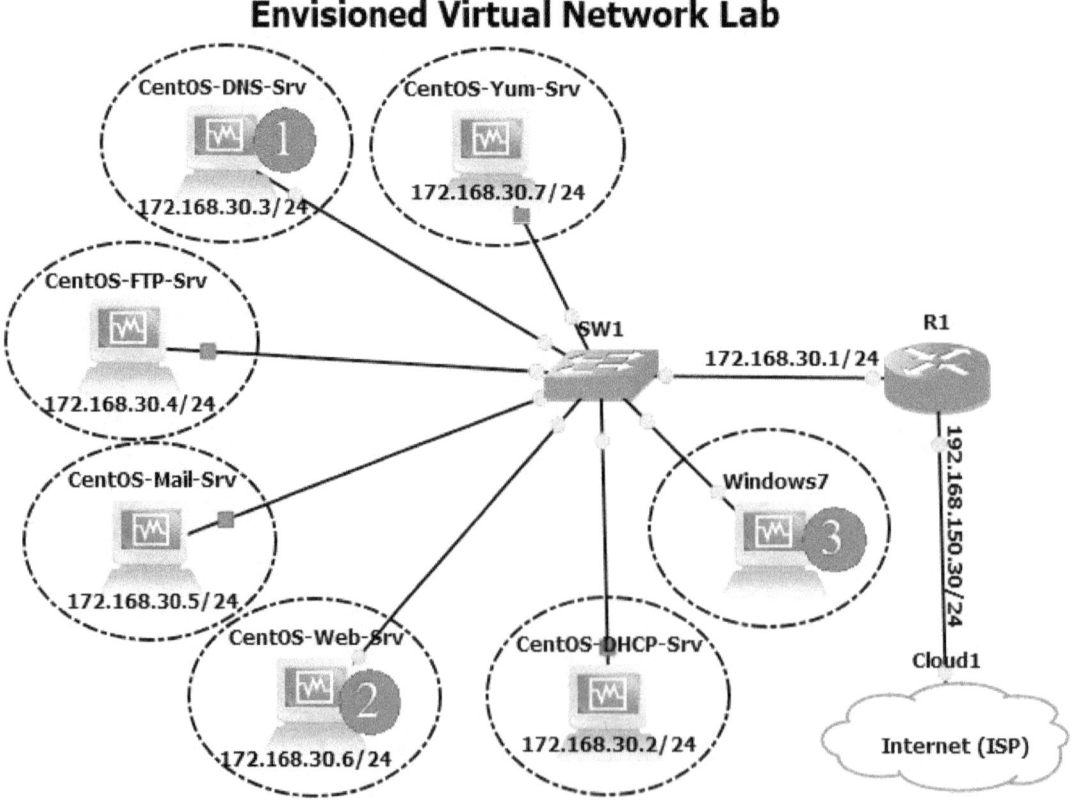

Figure 17.1: Base network with DNS, Web and Windows 7 started

SELinux Configuration File

The SELinux is meant for securing the files on the systems in addition to other security features of the Linux system such as the standard POSIX permissions (good security) and Access Control Lists (better security). SELinux offers us the best level of security for the Linux systems. If you have configured the service correctly and if it doesn't work the way it should be working as per the configuration, then look for SELinux and get it resolved.

The configuration file of SELinux is /etc/selinux/config and it be can be viewed and modified by using vim /etc/selinux/config or by using vi /etc/selinux/config commands.

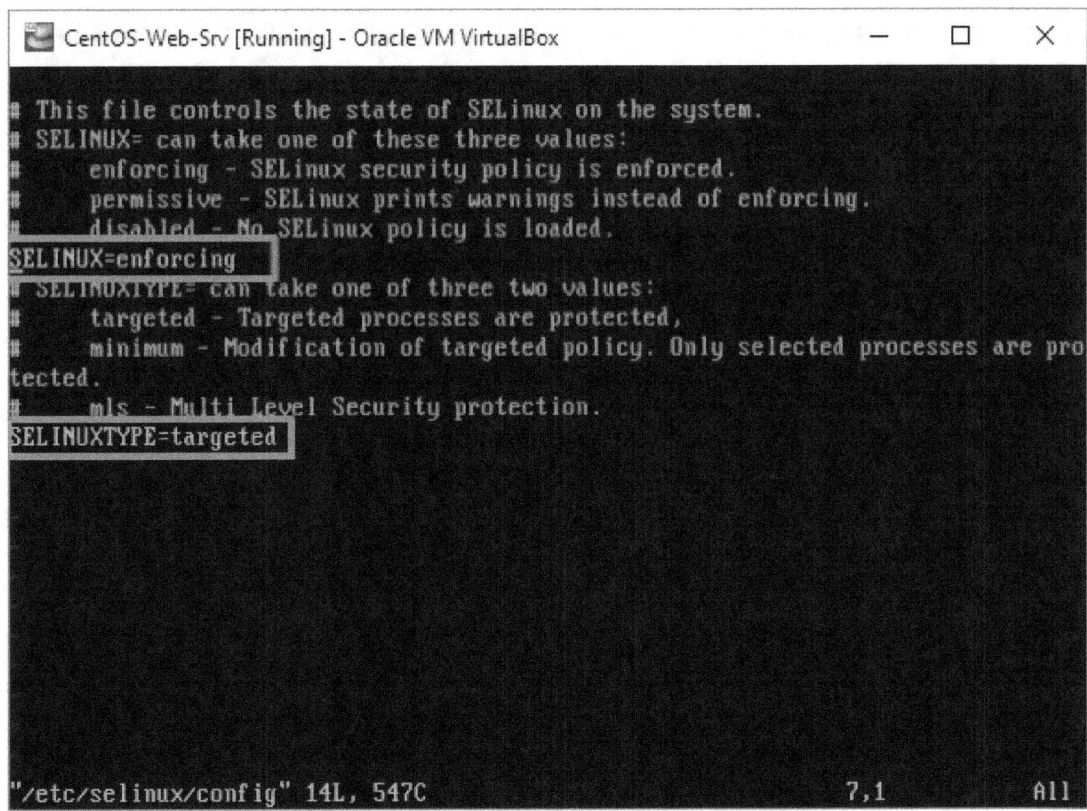

Figure 17.2: Content of the SELinux config file

There are two directives in this file; the SELINUX and SELINUXTYPE. The SELINUX directive dictates the SELinux mode and it can have three possible values as we see above.

The SELINUXTYPE directive determines the policy that will be used. The default value is targeted; with a targeted policy, SELinux allows you to customize and fine tune access control permissions. The other possible value is "MLS" (multilevel security), an advanced mode of protection.

> *In order to continue working on the SELinux, set the SELinux mode to "enforcing" if it is either set to disabled or permissive and restart the system to take the changes into effect.*

Modes of SELinux

The SELinux can be in any of the three modes or states; enforcing, permissive and disabled and by default it is in the enforcing mode. You can change the modes or states.

In the enforcing mode SELinux will enforce or implement its policies on the Linux system and any unauthorized access attempts by users and processes will be denied. Whenever users and processes are denied, access messages are logged to the relevant log files.

In the permissive mode, the SELinux doesn't implement its policy; no access is denied to any user or process even if the unauthorized access (policy violations) are occurring but it logs or keeps the track of the policy violations in the audit log files.

The disabled mode is just what the mode's name suggests. Setting the SELinux to the disabled mode is a blunder we possibly can commit. The experts call it as the last resort or the act of frustration. The SELinux won't be running at all on the system if it is disabled and therefore no security is provided for the Linux system. Remember that there is a huge security risk associated with the permissive and disabled modes and these modes are not recommended at all.

Viewing Context and Labels

Files, folders, processes and ports are labelled according to the permission required to access them. For showing the context of files, folders, processes and ports, the following commands are used with the –Z (upper case) flag respectively:

```
# ls -Z  (files and folders)
# ps -Z  (running applications or processes)
# netstat -Z (ports)
```

Guided Exercises and Examples

For example, you can change to the directory /var/www/ of the CentOS-Web-Srv (Web Server) of our Virtual Network Lab and see the context of the files and folders inside the /var/www/ directory with the following commands:

```
[root@web web]# cd /var/www/
[root@web www]# ls -Z
drwxr-xr-x. root root system_u:object_r:httpd_sys_script_exec_t:s0
drwxr-xr-x. root root system_u:object_r:httpd_sys_content_t:s0
[root@web www]# ls -Za
drwxr-xr-x. root root system_u:object_r:httpd_sys_content_t:s0
drwxr-xr-x. root root system_u:object_r:var_t:s0
drwxr-xr-x. root root system_u:object_r:httpd_sys_script_exec_t:s0
drwxr-xr-x. root root system_u:object_r:httpd_sys_content_t:s0
[root@web www]#
```

Figure 17.3: Context for the files and folders

In the above figure, "ls -Za" shows the context of all the files and folders which are inside the /var/www directory.

The figure 17.4 shows the context of the files and folders which are residing in the /var/www/html/web folder. Just to see how things are getting affected, rename the index.html to index.html.bak inside the /var/www/html/web directory.

```
[root@web ~]# cd /var/www/html/web/
[root@web web]# ls -Z
-rw-r--r--. root root system_u:object_r:httpd_sys_content_t:s0 index.html
[root@web web]# mv index.html index.html.bak
[root@web web]# ls
index.html.bak
[root@web web]# ls -Z
-rw-r--r--. root root system_u:object_r:httpd_sys_content_t:s0 index.html.bak
[root@web web]#
```

Figure 17.4: The context of files in /var/www/html/web directory

For the above index.html file, the context is httpd_sys_content_t and also after renaming, it remained the same.

Next, let's create a file with the name index.html in the /root directory and see what context it inherits. Then you can copy the contents of the file /var/www/html/web/index.html.bak to the file /root/index.html. View the context of the index.html file.

```
[root@web web]# cd /root
[root@web ~]# touch index.html
[root@web ~]# ls -Z
-rw-------. root root system_u:object_r:admin_home_t:s0 anaconda-ks.cfg
-rw-r--r--. root root system_u:object_r:admin_home_t:s0 index.html
[root@web ~]# cp /var/www/html/web/index.html.bak /root/index.html
cp: overwrite '/root/index.html'? y
[root@web ~]# pwd
/root
[root@web ~]# ls -Z
-rw-------. root root system_u:object_r:admin_home_t:s0 anaconda-ks.cfg
-rw-r--r--. root root system_u:object_r:admin_home_t:s0 index.html
[root@web ~]# ls -Z /var/www/html/web/index.html.bak
-rw-r--r--. root root system_u:object_r:httpd_sys_content_t:s0 /var/www/html/web/index.html.bak
[root@web ~]#
```

Figure 17.5: The context of files in /root and /var/www/html/web directories

In the figure 17.5, the context of the index.html file created in the /root directory has admin_home_t even if the contents are copied from the index.html.bak file which is in the different directory.

In the figure 17.6, the index.html is copied from /root directory to /var/www/html/web directory. The index.html file which earlier had the context admin_home_t while it was stored in the /root directory and the index.html.bak file, which was already there in the /var/www/html/web directory is same in every context; same POSIX permission and SELinux context. That is because when we copy, the context of the file gets inherited from the destination directory.

```
[root@web ~]# pwd
/root
[root@web ~]# ls -Z
-rw-------. root root system_u:object_r:admin_home_t:s0 anaconda-ks.cfg
-rw-r--r--. root root system_u:object_r:admin_home_t:s0 index.html
[root@web ~]# cp /root/index.html /var/www/html/web/
[root@web ~]# cd /var/www/html/web/
[root@web web]# ls
index.html  index.html.bak
[root@web web]# ls -l
total 8
-rw-r--r--. 1 root root 251 May  8 17:12 index.html
-rw-r--r--. 1 root root 251 May  8 14:35 index.html.bak
[root@web web]# ls -Z
-rw-r--r--. root root unconfined_u:object_r:httpd_sys_content_t:s0 index.html
-rw-r--r--. root root system_u:object_r:httpd_sys_content_t:s0 index.html.bak
[root@web web]#
```

Figure 17.6: Inheriting the context from the destination directory

If you test your webserver by browsing from the Windows 7 client, you will be able to access sample page created on our Web server. The following figure shows the accessibility of the index.html file after copying from the /root directory as the context was inherited from the destination directory.

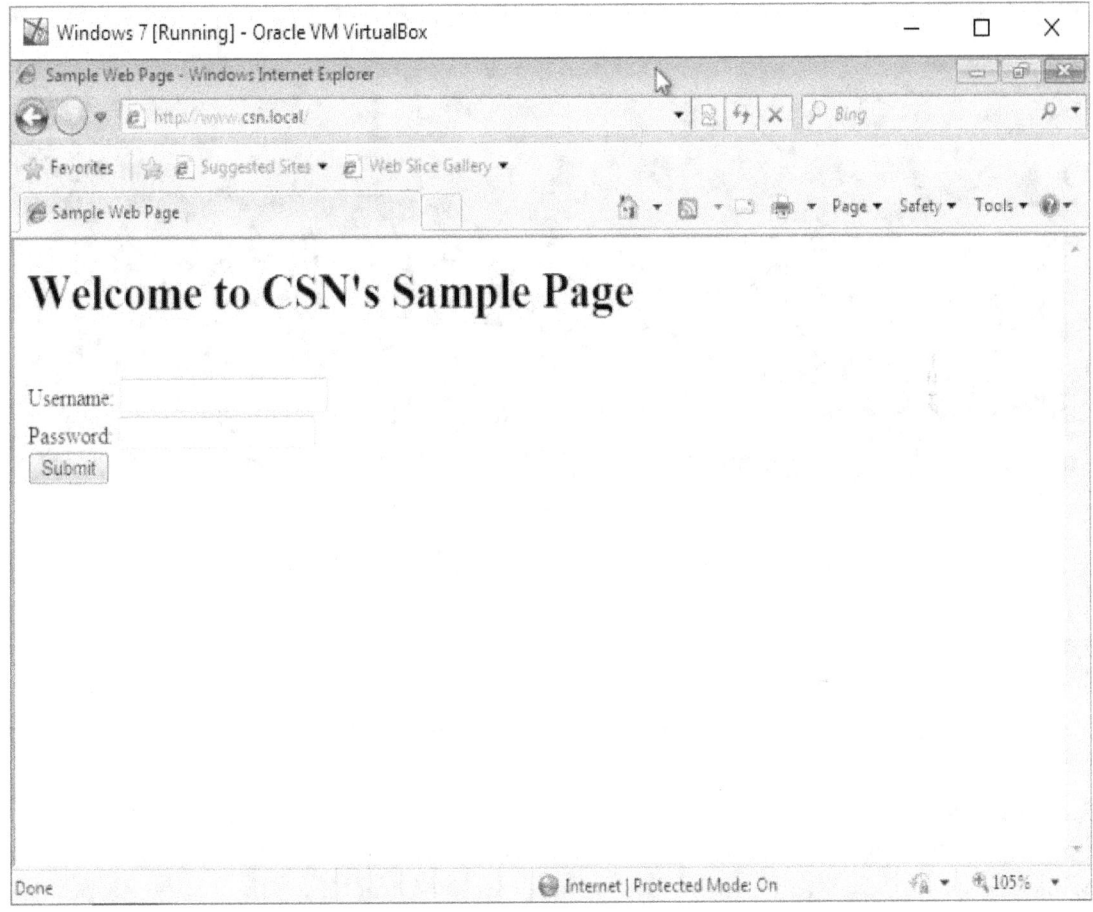

Figure 17.7: Sample page accessible

In the next, we try removing the index.html file from the /var/www/html/web/ directory and then instead of copying, we move the index.html file from the /root directory to the /var/www/html/web directory.

You will notice that when you move the file from /root directory to /var/www/html/web directory, it doesn't inherit the security context from the destination directory, instead it retains the context of the source directory.

```
[root@web web]# rm index.html
rm: remove regular file 'index.html'? y
[root@web web]# mv /root/index.html /var/www/html/web/
[root@web web]# ls
index.html   index.html.bak
[root@web web]# ls -l
total 8
-rw-r--r--. 1 root root 251 May  8 17:02 index.html
-rw-r--r--. 1 root root 251 May  8 14:35 index.html.bak
[root@web web]# ls -Z
-rw-r--r--. root root system_u:object_r:admin_home_t:s0 index.html
-rw-r--r--. root root system_u:object_r:httpd_sys_content_t:s0 index.html.bak
[root@web web]#
```

Figure 17.8: Context not inherited

Now if you try to browse your website from the Windows 7 client, there should be a problem. You would either see the Apache's test page if it was not removed or your page will show an error. This is because, the context did not get inherited while moving the index.html file. The problem is, we moved the index.html file from the /root directory using the mv command and the contexts don't get inherited at all.

Changing the Contexts

So, as per the figure 17.8, the context type for the index.html file is admin_home_t while it was supposed to be httpd_sys_content_t. We can change the context type of a file and folder; the following syntax and example can be used to change the context of the index.html file.

Syntax:

    # chcon   -t   [type]   [file/folder]

Example:

    # chcon -t httpd_sys_content_t index.html

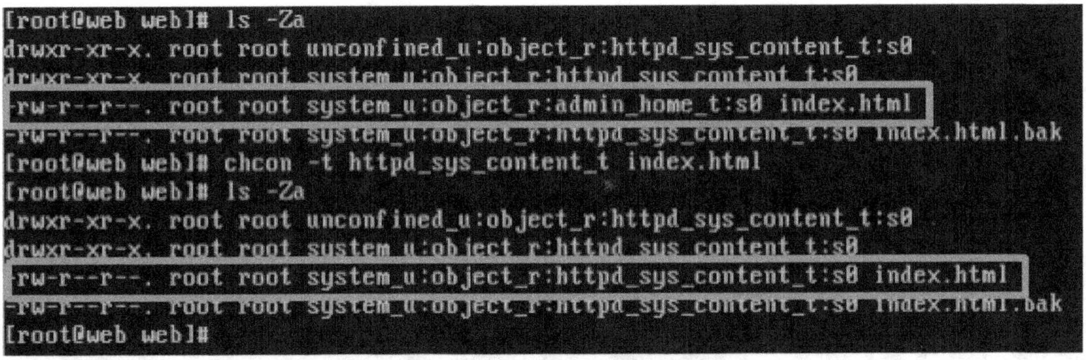

```
[root@web web]# ls -Za
drwxr-xr-x. root root unconfined_u:object_r:httpd_sys_content_t:s0
drwxr-xr-x. root root system_u:object_r:httpd_sys_content_t:s0
-rw-r--r--. root root system_u:object_r:admin_home_t:s0 index.html
-rw-r--r--. root root system_u:object_r:httpd_sys_content_t:s0 index.html.bak
[root@web web]# chcon -t httpd_sys_content_t index.html
[root@web web]# ls -Za
drwxr-xr-x. root root unconfined_u:object_r:httpd_sys_content_t:s0
drwxr-xr-x. root root system_u:object_r:httpd_sys_content_t:s0
-rw-r--r--. root root system_u:object_r:httpd_sys_content_t:s0 index.html
-rw-r--r--. root root system_u:object_r:httpd_sys_content_t:s0 index.html.bak
[root@web web]#
```

Figure 17.9: Changing the security context

Restoring the Contexts

The following syntax and example can be used to restore the context of the files or folders in order to fix the problematic situation.

Syntax:

    # restorecon -vR   [File/Folder]

Example:

    # restorecon -vR   /var/www/html/web

```
[root@web web]#
[root@web web]# ls -Z
-rw-r--r--. root root unconfined_u:object_r:admin_home_t:s0 index.html
-rw-r--r--. root root system_u:object_r:httpd_sys_content_t:s0 index.html.bak
[root@web web]# restorecon -vR /var/www/html/web/
restorecon reset /var/www/html/web/index.html context unconfined_u:object_r:admi
n_home_t:s0->unconfined_u:object_r:httpd_sys_content_t:s0
[root@web web]# ls -Z
-rw-r--r--. root root unconfined_u:object_r:httpd_sys_content_t:s0 index.html
-rw-r--r--. root root system_u:object_r:httpd_sys_content_t:s0 index.html.bak
[root@web web]# _
```

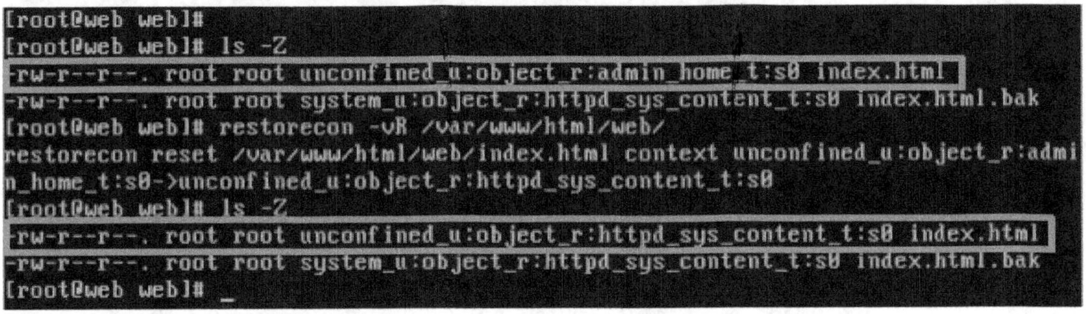

Figure 17.10: Restoring the security context

In the above figure, the context of the index.html file is restored from the /var/www/html/web directory's context.

> *If you wanted to inherit the contexts just like POSIX permissions and ACLs. The cp command is more effective than the mv command while working with files and folders.*

SELinux Log Files

Whenever things go wrong, the SELinux is going to log messages in a file called audit.log which is in the /var/log/audit/ directory. If you open and read this file, we may not understand what it really means. The following figure shows how the content of log file looks like and to a beginner or even to an intermediate SELinux user, it would look alien.

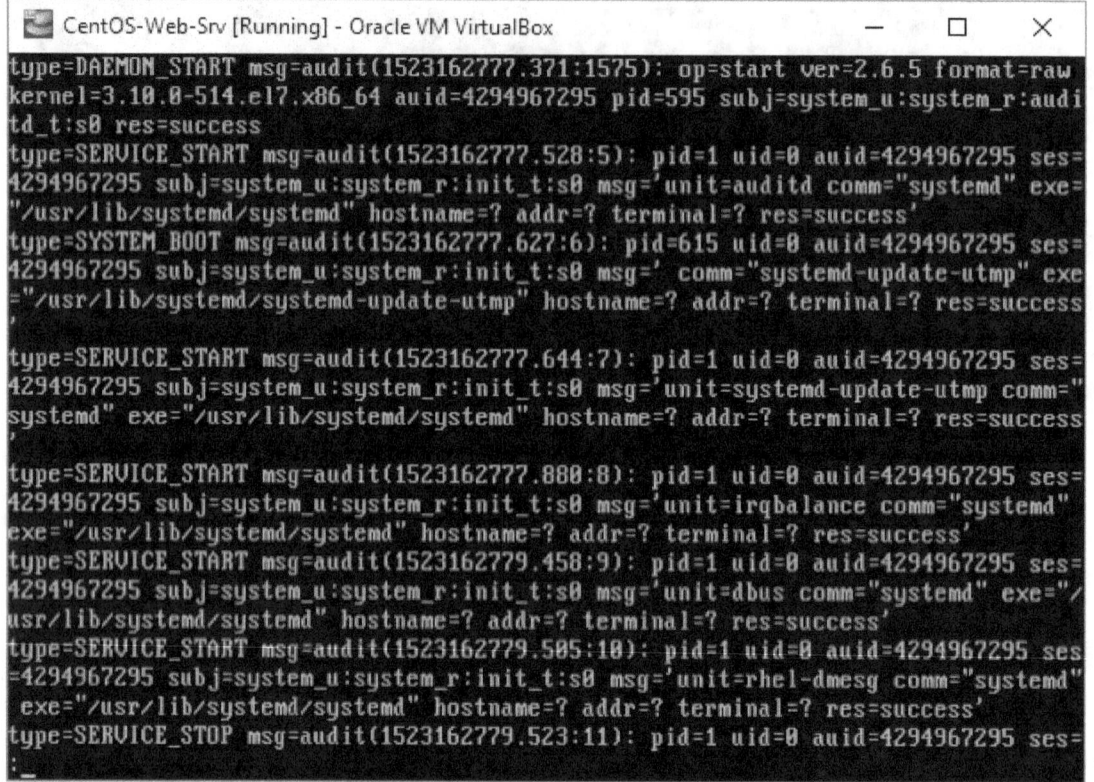

Figure 17.11: Content of audit.log file

To troubleshoot we need some tools, which will make us understand the meanings of the error messages logged in the audit.log file in a very simple and elegant manner. So, we will install setroubleshoot-server package to help us troubleshoot the SELinux settings. To install the package, use the following command:

    # yum install -y setroubleshoot-server

After the installation of the setroubleshoot-server package on the web server, restart the auditd daemon. Actually the systemctl restart auditd.service should work but there is a bug with this version of CentOS and instead we will use the following command:

    # service auditd restart

Now after installing and restarting the auditd daemon, messages will be logged to the /

var/log/messages log file. If you open, you can see the error message written almost in a very clear English language. So, we can easily follow what is mentioned in the error message file and get our problems fixed.

```
Oct 29 20:23:43 web setroubleshoot: SELinux is preventing httpd from getattr acc
ess on the file /var/www/html/web/index.php. For complete SELinux messages. run
sealert -l dae4705c-5202-4f06-b787-e3622c37214d
Oct 29 20:23:43 web python: SELinux is preventing httpd from getattr access on t
he file /var/www/html/web/index.php.#012#012*****  Plugin restorecon (99.5 confi
dence) suggests   ***************************#012#012If you want to fix the label.
#012/var/www/html/web/index.php default label should be httpd_sys_content_t.#012
Then you can run restorecon.#012Do#012# /sbin/restorecon -v /var/www/html/web/in
dex.php#012#012*****  Plugin catchall (1.49 confidence) suggests   *************
**************#012#012If you believe that httpd should be allowed getattr access
on the index.php file by default.#012Then you should report this as a bug.#012Yo
u can generate a local policy module to allow this access.#012Do#012allow this a
ccess for now by executing:#012# ausearch -c 'httpd' --raw | audit2allow -M my-h
ttpd#012# semodule -i my-httpd.pp#012
```

Figure 17.12: Content of the var/log/messages file

Troubleshooting SELinux for the Mail Server

If you remember, we have disabled the SELInux for the mail server in order to make it work. Let us enable the SELinux on the mail server and see if it works for us. Remember to install the "setroubleshoot-server" package on the CentOS-Mail-Srv (Mail Server) and restart the aduitd service. Before enabling the SELinux, we would be able to get access to the mails.

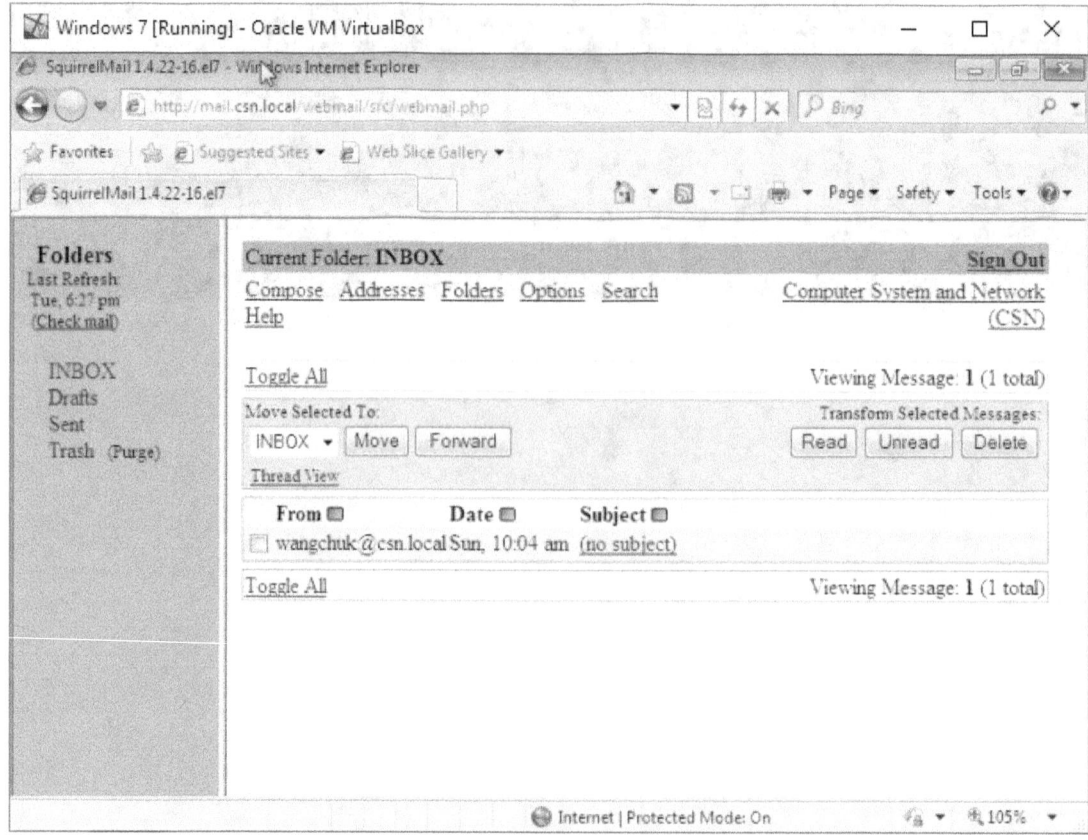

Figure 17.13: Accessing mail with SELinux disabled

In case if you enable the SELinux and restart your Mail Server, you would encounter the following error and would have no access to your mails. Without installing the setroubleshoot-server package on the mail server, just like before, we will be not able to get the SELinux messages in a very clearly.

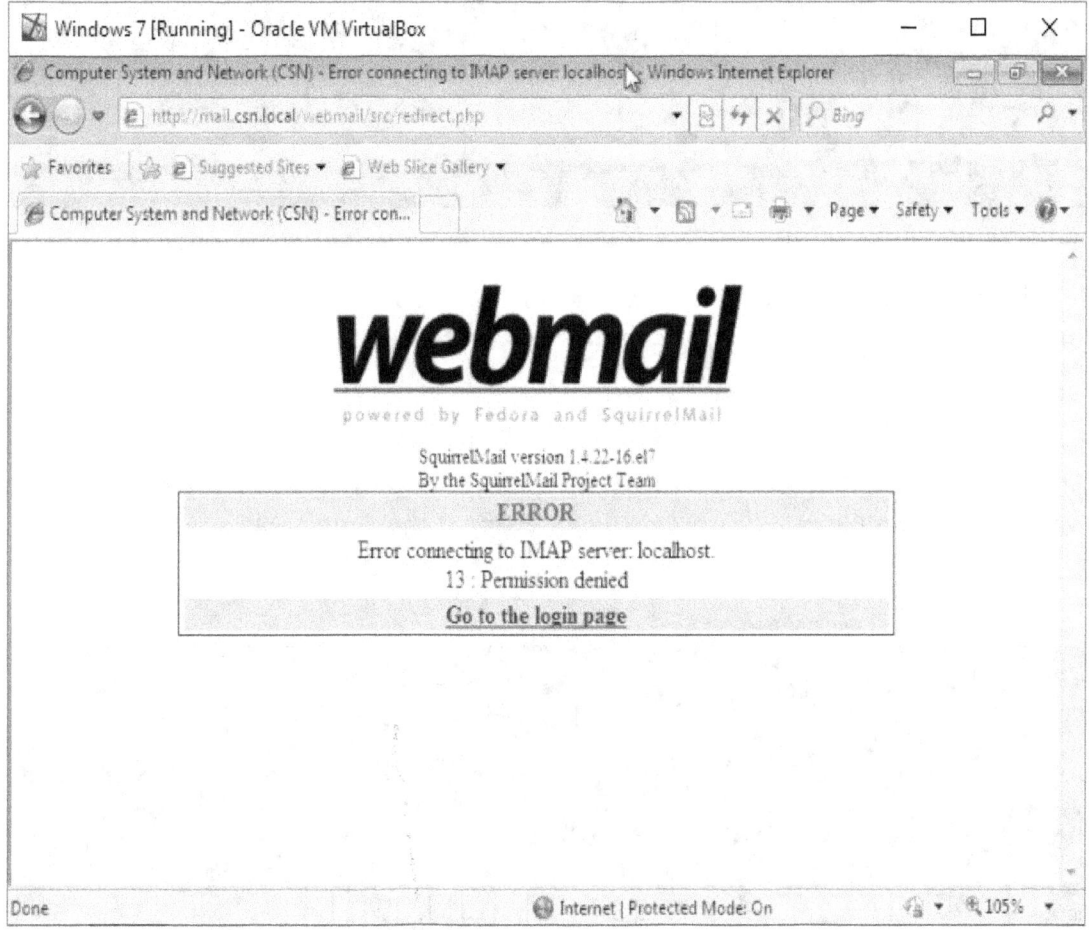

Figure 17.14: Denied access to mails after enabling SELinux

The following is a message logged into the /var/log/audit/audit.log file. It is difficult to get what it is trying to convey. To make it understandable, we have to install the setroubleshoot-server package on the mail server and follow the steps.

```
type=AVC msg=audit(1509323822.825:107): avc:  denied  { name_connect } for  pid=
2133 comm="httpd" dest=143 scontext=system_u:system_r:httpd_t:s0 tcontext=system
_u:object_r:pop_port_t:s0 tclass=tcp_socket
type=SYSCALL msg=audit(1509323822.825:107): arch=c000003e syscall=42 success=no
exit=-13 a0=b a1=7f4a130678d8 a2=10 a3=59f6742e items=0 ppid=956 pid=2133 auid=4
294967295 uid=48 gid=48 euid=48 suid=48 fsuid=48 egid=48 sgid=48 fsgid=48 tty=(n
one) ses=4294967295 comm="httpd" exe="/usr/sbin/httpd" subj=system_u:system_r:ht
tpd_t:s0 key=(null)
```

Figure 17.15: Messages logged in to audit.log file

Install the "setroubleshoot-server" package on the Mail Server and start or restart the auditd.service using the following commands respectively.

```
# yum install –y setroubleshoot-server
# service auditd restart
```

After the setroubleshoot-server package is installed, the messages will be logged into the /var/log/messages file in a clear way. The following is the sample, message logged in the messages file.

```
CentOS-Mail-Srv [Running] - Oracle VM VirtualBox
 access.#012Do#012allow this access for now by executing:#012# ausearch -c 'http
d' --raw | audit2allow -M my-httpd#012# semodule -i my-httpd.pp#012
May  8 19:57:40 mail setroubleshoot: SELinux is preventing /usr/sbin/httpd from
name_connect access on the tcp_socket port 143. For complete SELinux messages ru
n: sealert -l a58822d9-3cc4-494c-8866-93968a7047c7
May  8 19:57:40 mail python: SELinux is preventing /usr/sbin/httpd from name_con
nect access on the tcp_socket port 143.#012#012*****  Plugin catchall_boolean (3
2.5 confidence) suggests   ******************#012#012If you want to allow httpd
to can network connect#012Then you must tell SELinux about this by enabling the
'httpd_can_network_connect' boolean.#012You can read 'None' man page for more de
tails.#012Do#012setsebool -P httpd_can_network_connect 1#012#012*****  Plugin ca
tchall_boolean (32.5 confidence) suggests   ******************#012#012If you wan
t to allow httpd to can sendmail#012Then you must tell SELinux about this by ena
bling the 'httpd_can_sendmail' boolean.#012You can read 'None' man page for more
 details.#012Do#012setsebool -P httpd_can_sendmail 1#012#012*****  Plugin catcha
ll_boolean (32.5 confidence) suggests   ******************#012#012If you want to
 allow nis to enabled#012Then you must tell SELinux about this by enabling the '
nis_enabled' boolean.#012You can read 'None' man page for more details.#012Do#01
2setsebool -P nis_enabled 1#012#012*****  Plugin catchall (4.5 confidence) sugge
sts   **************************#012#012If you believe that httpd should be all
owed name_connect access on the port 143 tcp_socket by default.#012Then you shou
ld report this as a bug.#012You can generate a local policy module to allow this
 access.#012Do#012allow this access for now by executing:#012# ausearch -c 'http
d' --raw | audit2allow -M my-httpd#012# semodule -i my-httpd.pp#012
```

Figure 17.16: Message logged to /var/log/messages file

If you go through the logged messages, the indicated solutions are:

setsebool –P httpd_can_network_connect 1
setsebool –P httpd_can_sendmail 1
setsebool –P nis_enabled 1

Probably, the first solution is more closely related to us because we don't use Sendmail and NIS feature for our mail server. Run the first command and you would be able to use the mail without having to disable the SELinux. So, knowing how to use SELinux and troubleshoot gives us a powerful wing to cross the security issues successfully.

Further Reading

Introduction. (n.d.). Retrieved from https://www.linuxtopia.org/online_books/getting_started_with_SELinux/SELinux_introduction.html

43.2. Introduction to SELinux. (n.d.). Retrieved from http://web.mit.edu/rhel-doc/5/RHEL-5-manual/Deployment_Guide-en-US/ch-selinux.html

An Overview of SELinux - cont. (n.d.). Retrieved from http://globaltechconsultants.org/?q=content/overview-selinux-cont

Chapter 1. SELinux Architectural Overview. (n.d.). Retrieved from https://access.redhat.com/documentation/en-US/Red_Hat_Enterprise_Linux/4/html/SELinux_Guide/selg-chapter-0013.html

Disabling SELinux. (n.d.). Retrieved from https://www.cloudera.com/documentation/enterprise/5-6-x/topics/install_cdh_disable_selinux.html

Exploring SELinux: An Overview. (2016, November 02). Retrieved from https://linuxacademy.com/blog/linux/exploring-selinux-an-overview/

Overview of SELinux changes. (2012, June 24). Retrieved from http://blog.siphos.be/2012/06/overview-of-selinux-changes/

Overview of SELinux in RHEL7. (n.d.). Retrieved from http://en.community.dell.com/techcenter/b/techcenter/archive/2014/11/04/overview-of-selinux-in-rhel7

Overview of SELinux Roles. (2018, March 21). Retrieved from https://knowledge.windriver.com/en-us/000_Products/000/010/000/040/020/000_Wind_River_Linux_Security_Profile_Users_Guide,_7.0/030/010

SELinux - Overview and Configuration. (n.d.). Retrieved from https://www.lazysystemadmin.com/2011/05/selinux-overview-and-configuration.html

SELinux Overview. (n.d.). Retrieved from https://codingbee.net/tutorials/rhcsa/rhcsa-selinux-overview

www.ingramcontent.com/pod-product-compliance
Lightning Source LLC
Chambersburg PA
CBHW062348220526
45472CB00008B/1743